MW01292931

Activist Sentiments

THE NEW BLACK STUDIES SERIES

Edited by Darlene Clark Hine
and Dwight A. McBride

*A list of books in the series appears
at the end of this book.*

Activist Sentiments

Reading Black Women
in the Nineteenth Century

P. GABRIELLE FOREMAN

University of Illinois Press

URBANA AND CHICAGO

© 2009 by P. Gabrielle Foreman
All rights reserved
Manufactured in the United States of America
1 2 3 4 5 C P 5 4 3 2 1
♾ This book is printed on acid-free paper.

Library of Congress Cataloging-in-Publication Data
Foreman, P. Gabrielle (Pier Gabrielle)
Activist sentiments : reading Black women in the nineteenth century /
P. Gabrielle Foreman.
p.   cm. — (The new Black studies series)
Includes bibliographical references and index.
ISBN 978-0-252-03474-9 (cloth : acid-free paper) —
ISBN 978-0-252-07664-0 (pbk. : acid-free paper)
1. American literature—African American authors—History and criticism.
2. American literature—Women authors—History and criticism.
3. Women and literature—United States—History—19th century.
4. African American women—Intellectual life—19th century.
5. African American women authors. I. Title.
PS153.N5F673   2009
810.9'928708996073—dc22   2008055461

Dedicated, in loving memory,
to my grandmother Tommie Jewel (Mazy) Young
and to Barbara Christian, scholar, mentor, activist.

Contents

Acknowledgments

Books that take many years to write incur not only many debts but also many kinds of debts. I'd like to begin by thanking the people who kept me happy and occupied with other important priorities during the time I might have been finishing this book. For the countless Saturdays launching and working on Action for Social Change and Youth Empowerment (AScHAYE) I thank Mia Johnson, Huong Hoang, and Noemi Soto as well as Susan Kim, Kianna Nesbit, and Alma Marquez. Thanks, too, to the many social change organizations, young people, and workshop facilitators who helped lower the average age of boards of directors in California by adding young people to their governing bodies. Without the Kellogg National Leadership Fellowship and its financial support, AScHAYE's work would not have been possible. I should also thank the Kellogg Fellowship for sending me to the National Conference on Black Philanthropy where I met Jeffrey Richardson. During our courtship and marriage, he has provided both steady support of and a welcome diversion from this book while always, without exception, cheering me on. His generosity of spirit, wisdom, and commitment inspire me to keep my eyes on the prize.

Recently, Pete White and Becky Dennison of the Los Angeles Community Action Network (LACAN) and Yusef Omowale of the Southern California Library have been instrumental in helping me launch some side trips from the ivory tower. Thanks to them not only for the work we're doing together to rethink community partners' access to university and college resources, but also for seeing my nineteenth-century research as vitally connected to the justice work they advance. Thanks also to Geri Silva, of Families to Amend California's Three Strikes (FACTS), for working with my students and for her commitment to combating the prison industrial complex. Without these and other relationships that enliven my work and illuminate its relevance, I couldn't continue to do the teaching, writing, and research that I continue to love. For support in this area, it is my pleasure to also acknowledge the Occidental College Dean's Office and Vice President Eric Frank and the Center for Community Based Learning. I also have reason to thank Otto Santa Ana for being an ideal collaborator as we organize workshops and networks to support the further development of senior scholars of color and the communities we serve.

Cherene Sherrard-Johnson provided a more conventional route away from and then back to the task of finishing *Activist Sentiments*. Just as I completed what I thought was the final draft, news broke that Emma Dunham Kelley-Hawkins was not the little-known Black writer we all thought she was. In response, Cherene and I decided to coedit a special issue of *Legacy* examining issues of racial reclassification and indeterminacy. Special thanks to its contributors: Xiomara Santamarina, Eric Gardner, Doveanna Fulton, Katherine Flynn, Reginald Pitts, Daphne Brooks, Frances Smith Foster, and Gene Jarrett. Additionally, beyond the richness of our friendship, Daphne Brooks has offered reading suggestions that made their way into the Wilson chapter and beyond. As with Cherene, Eric Gardner and I have exchanged drafts and ideas that have only improved my work. In addition to pointing me to information on the Latimer and Johnson families that I cite in this book, Reginald Pitts and, more recently, Katherine Flynn, have provided a fabulous diversion that continues to occupy my time and energy. Our collaborations in recovering Harriet Wilson's intriguing life and multiple careers have been enormously rewarding.

At Occidental College, Dean Eric Frank, former Dean David Axeen, and presidents Ted Mitchell and Susan Prager have offered generous support for my scholarship and community initiatives. These deans and presidents have shared a vision of educational excellence, community outreach, and committed teaching that has made Occidental my ideal academic home. Likewise, my department has been good to me from the start and in more ways than I can enumerate here. Thank you to John Swift, Jean Wyatt, Michael Near, Eric Newhall, Daniel Fineman, Martha Ronk, Warren Montag, and Raul Villa as well as to my newer colleagues Leila Neti and Damian Stocking. So many other colleagues have made Occidental a welcome place to be. Special thanks go out to Ron Buckmire, close friend and teaching partner for many years, to Sharla Fett, my new comrade in nineteenth-century slavery studies, and to Elmer Griffith. I could not do what I do without the college's stellar library staff, especially Marla Peppers, Marsha Kay Schnirring, John Dobbins, and John De La Fontaine. Although he once was a graduate student in mathematics and now is an opera singer, to me, Dean Elzinga is an intellectual colleague and devoted friend whose input improves my thinking and writing. I would sing my appreciation to the rooftops if I had a better voice. Noga Tarnopolsky has been the best friend and sounding board imaginable. More family than friends, Melvin Jones, Alex duBuclet, and Sarah Rubin make me want to go home again.

By reading either the entire book or large portions of it, Alexandra Juhasz, Laura Hyun Yi Kang, Rachel Lee, Eve Oishi, and Cynthia Young, members of the LA Women's Group for the Collaborative Study of Race and Gender in Culture, have made this a much smarter book, as has my writing partner and friend Jacqueline Goldsby. I thank the anonymous reader and especially the indefatigable Rafia Zafar for feedback. Rafia not only helped shape the book but also caught stray errors that would surely have found their way into the final version if not for her. For providing not only a model of scholarship but specific archival citations and sage suggestions, I thank Carla Peterson. Over the years, William Andrews, Daina Ramey Berry, Sharla Fett, Eric Gardner, Susan Harris, Elizabeth McHenry, Genna Rae McNeil, Cherene Sherrard-Johnson, Priscilla Wald, Laura Wexler, Richard Yaborough, and Jean Fagan Yellin have offered welcome feedback and suggestions. Jacquelyn McLendon and Jeannie Pfaelzer have offered this and much more. They continue to be a blessing in my life. I am extraordinarily lucky to have benefited as a student from the guidance and opportunities provided by Richard Yarborough, Laura Wexler, and Earl Lewis. Decades have passed since I first met each of them and I remain thankful for their friendship, counsel, and support. For the early development of my love of literary history and archival work, I have to thank Earl and the late, great, Barbara Christian, who remains my model. Thanks to Earl and to Jayne London for graciously opening their home to me while I was a post-doc at the University of Michigan. For requesting that this book be included in their series, I thank Dwight McBride as well as Darlene Clark Hine. For her patience in seeing it through, I am grateful to my editor Joan Catapano.

Without the marvelous research assistants who have been part-time partners in this project, it would never have been completed. Thanks again to Doveanna Fulton, now chair of African American Studies at the University of Alabama, to Araceli Lerma, Tamara Wilds, Dinah Consuegra, Alma Marquez (and her daughter, my godchild, Miquitzli), Malii Brown, Rachel Johnson, and especially to Huong Hoang, Elena Abbott, and Denise Burgher. Denise, Huong, and Elena have been solid bridges of academic and personal support; they have been just what I needed at just the right time. Ronda Thomas, Suzanne

Schneider and Andrea Williams, my hanging partners as much as committed graduate research assistants, added color to my days at the National Humanities Center and embraced my projects as if they were their own. For helping get the final manuscript off my desk, I appreciate the help of Melissa Daniels. I am honored to count these women, once mentees, now accomplished, fabulous people making this world a better place, among some of my closest friends.

As I was writing portions of this book, I benefited from generous funding and fellowship support. I gratefully acknowledge the National Humanities Center (NHC) and the Rockefeller Foundation, the Huntington Library, the Ford Foundation, the American Council of Learned Societies, the University of Michigan's Center for African American Studies, and the offices of the dean and president at Occidental College. I thank the staff at the NHC for their boundless energy, support, and graciousness. Special thanks to the NHC librarians, particularly Betsey Dain for locating obscure nineteenth-century newspapers, and to Karen Carroll for her copyediting expertise.

I could not have uncovered Amelia Johnson's role in the prodigious activism of Black Baltimore between the 1870s and the 1920s without the help of many people. The leadership of Union Baptist Church opened its arms to me even though they knew nothing about their beloved former pastor Harvey Johnson's forgotten wife Amelia. The late Rev. Frank Drumwright Jr. took me to the Johnsons' gravesite even when it was clear he should be resting at home. It is an honor to be counted among the friends and colleagues of the current Union Baptist Senior Reverend Dr. Alvin Hathaway. His devotion to the social gospel and to organizing in Maryland surely continues Harvey and Amelia Johnson's legacy. My friend Susan Kim not only took pleasure in hearing me talk endlessly about activism in turn-of-the-century Black Baltimore, she repeated it to her Baltimore friend Michelle Burts Feist who connected me with the current leadership of the DuBois Circle, who I rightly suspected counted Amelia Johnson among its earliest members. Lenore Burts put me in touch with the organization's current historian, Patelle Harris, who made time to go through the meticulously kept minutes and papers where we discovered Amelia Johnson's central role. Thanks, too, to the Maryland State Archives and to the special collections librarians at Enoch Pratt Free Library, to Alma Moore of Baltimore, and to my in-laws, Linda and Cordell Richardson, for housing me during research trips. For support on the archival work on Victoria Earle Matthews that is included in chapter 4, I would be remiss if I did not thank the special collections staff at the Schomburg Library.

Portions of chapter 1 appeared as "Manifest in Signs: Reading the Undertell in *Incidents in the Life of a Slave Girl*" in the anthology *Harriet Jacobs and Incidents in the Life of a Slave Girl*. An early and abbreviated version of chapter 3 was published as "'Reading Aright': White Slavery, Black Referents, and the Strategy of Histotextuality in *Iola Leroy*" in the *Yale Journal of Criticism*. Chapter 4 appeared as "Reading/Photography: Emma Dunham Kelley-Hawkins's *Four Girls at Cottage City,* Victoria Earle Matthews, and *The Woman's Era*" in *Legacy, a Journal of American Women Writers* 24, no. 2. I am grateful to Cambridge University Press, the Johns Hopkins University Press, and the University of Nebraska Press for granting me permission to reprint from these works.

For permission to quote or reproduce images from their collections, I thank the Middleton A. "Spike" Harris Papers, the White Rose Mission & Industrial Association Collection, and the John Bruce Papers, all found in the Manuscripts, Archives, and Rare Books Division at the Schomburg Center for Research in Black Culture, The New York Public Library, Astor, Lenox and Tilden Foundations. I likewise am grateful to the Dorcas and Harry S. Cummings Collection at the Maryland State Archives, the Nebraska State Historical Society, the Harper's Ferry Historical Park, the Daniel Murray Collection from the Prints and Photographs Division at the Library of Congress, Documenting the American South at the University of North Carolina Chapel Hill Libraries, and the Hargrett Rare Book and Manuscript Library of the University of Georgia for use of their collections.

My deepest appreciation is reserved for my mother, Lynn Foreman, for her unfailing moral support and intellectual interest. For years, she has joyfully read not only my work but the books on which it is based. She has nurtured not only my interest in literature and history but also an urgent sense that it must be accompanied by a commitment to social justice. From my father, the poet Kent Foreman, I inherited a shared cadence and a love of language, literature, jazz, and good food. Thanks Daddy. My grandma, Tommie Jewel Young, I thank for many things, including the way she laced her committed work ethic with an infectious laugh that spread her joy and zest for life, a combination I could have inherited only from her. Although they're stored in my memory, I'll miss her stories about family and anecdotes about DuBois, Robeson, and others. My uncle Reggie Young kept me grounded while beaming with pride and cautioning me that "there ain't nothing worse than an educated fool." My uncle Coleman Grimmette passed on to me a love of photography (and travel) that often finds its way into my work. I thank my brothers Peer Byron and Damon and my sister Ayana for their love, support and children. My nieces, Alana, Erin, and Kesho have remained amused that anything could possibly take this many years to complete. My godchild Teo and his mother, the late Sheri Norwood, shared me with this book. Thanks, too, to my sister-sister Senam Okudweto, the most brilliant academic and artist in the family.

My advisor, the late Barbara Christian, was a giving mentor/activist/scholar who built and lived her commitments. Her concept of local, diasporic, and international community was evident in her home, in the classes she taught, on the boards on which she served, and in the places where she read and organized. The model she embodied lives on in her students and, I trust, in her students' students. In that spirit, finally, I would like to thank the early African Americanists who balanced scholarship and mentoring while they built the programs and disciplines in which so many of us practice. In my field, in addition to Barbara Christian, William Andrews, Hazel Carby, Frances Smith Foster, Henry Louis Gates Jr., the late Nellie McKay, Carla Peterson, Cheryl Wall, Mary Helen Washington, and Richard Yarborough deserve particular recognition. All of these scholars, and many who remain unnamed and less recognized, have paved the way for subsequent generations. To them and to the ancestors who made a way out of no way, never imagining that a Black woman in America could make a living as a scholar-activist, I am profoundly grateful.

A Note on Language

Throughout this book, I use the terms *African American* and *Black* inter-changeably. I capitalize *Black* when I use the word to refer to people of African descent as a matter of practice and principle. I realize that equitable usage would call for me to capitalize *white*, but I'm willing to acquiesce to common practice in that instance. I take my cue, if not my terms, from the journalist T. Thomas Fortune. In a 1906 speech, "Who Are We," he declared:

> You can take your choice of names, BUT I AM AN "AFRO-AMERICAN." All the white newspapers of this country regard you as "negroes" and write Negro with a little "n." They regard you as a common noun . . . Now I get around that undesirable title by adopting "AFRO-AMERICAN" which calls for the use of two big capital A's (laughter and applause). I AM A PROPER NOUN, NOT A COMMON NOUN.[1]

Activist Sentiments

Introduction

On a "granite winter" Wednesday in January 1843, "anti-slavery friends" braved a "mischievous Nor'Wester" wind and snow to gather for a spirited convention in Milford, New Hampshire. Visitors from all over New Hampshire and Massachusetts joined local reformers to raise money and support for "the down-trodden and oppressed."[1] Leading the crowd in raising their voices against injustice were the sons and daughters of Milford itself, the Hutchinson Family Singers, a group of young performers soon to become internationally renowned for their radically harmonic commitment to women's rights, anti-slavery, and reform causes.[2]

Milford later would memorialize events like this and congratulate itself for being distinguished for the "unselfish and sublime work of these splendid men and women in the grandest movement of the century, for human rights."[3] Frederick Douglass remembered Milford fondly, too, recalling a series of meetings he held there as "so full of life and spirit."[4] Yet neither Douglass's reception nor the welcome audience received by the eloquent fugitives who addressed the 1843 convention crowd, helped a local indentured servant called "our nig," though the Milford teenager could have testified to experiencing treatment as brutal as the fugitives.' It is doubtful that she was invited, or that upon reading the announcements she could have snuck away from her "she-devil" "mistress."[5] Had she escaped and managed to travel the blustery two miles to the town's center, the young woman soon to be known as Harriet E. Wilson would have been one of the very few Black women in attendance.[6]

On an early October evening in 1892 almost fifty years later, more than two hundred Black women gathered at New York's Lyric Hall to hear Ida B. Wells give her first official address. Fellow journalist "Victoria Earle" Matthews and the Wells Testimonial Reception Committee turned out a brilliant array. To honor Wells, the night's program was a facsimile of the *Memphis Free Speech,* the newspaper Wells had co-owned until its office had been razed four months earlier. "Iola," Wells's pen name, lit up the stage, and appeared on the white silk badges the ushers wore proudly pinned to their chests. Some of the most important Black women of Wells's time were literally standing behind her. Boston activist Josephine St. Pierre Ruffin, journalist Gertrude Mossell, education reformer Sarah (Highland) Garnet and her sister Susan McKinney, the first Black woman doctor of New York State, joined Matthews as they took their places behind the young journalist. Nonetheless, Wells felt like a "lonely homesick girl who was in exile," as she later recalled.[7] The death threats hanging over her if she dared return to Memphis carried the heavy memory of her close friends' lynching murders earlier that year. Still, with more than two hundred women gathered to cheer her on both figuratively and financially, she responded by publishing *Southern Horrors,* her first exposé of lynching; she dedicated the pamphlet to them.[8]

Activist Sentiments: Reading Black Women in the Nineteenth Century takes as its subject women who in fewer than fifty years moved from near rhetorical invisibility and isolation to prolific literary productivity and connectedness. The study spans from 1859 through the 1890s, or from the year Harriet E. Wilson brought out *Our Nig; or, Sketches from the Life of a Free Black* and Amelia E. Johnson [née Hall] was born, to the decade often called the "woman's era," when Black women organized themselves and insisted that their voices be heard in the national conversation about race, rights, respect, and reform.

In large part, this book examines reading practices and nineteenth-century cultural, sociopolitical, and representational literacies. As the multiple resonances of its subtitle, "Reading Black Women in the Nineteenth Century" suggest, I am interested in African American women's literary production, reception, and consumption and also in the ways in which varied audiences "read" Black women of that century. The vernacular signifying practice embedded in the active verb/al practice "to read" also resonates throughout this project. Nineteenth-century critics often locate Frederick Douglass's *Narrative of the Life* as the paradigmatic articulation of literacy's link to freedom. Yet I take the declaration *Iola Leroy*'s Aunt Linda delivers—"I can't read . . . but ole Missus's face is newspaper nuff for me"[9]—as another archetypical point of departure. It echoes Harriet Jacobs's earlier proclamation that she had "felt, seen and heard enough to read the characters, and question the motives, of those around me."[10] Frances E. W. Harper's Aunt Linda, like Jacobs's Linda, offers an expanded and equally resonant model, one that asserts that social literacy and the power of interpretation are as necessary as, and perhaps even more important than, formal literacy itself.

An emphasis on vernacular reading is a living legacy in contemporary African American culture. To "get read" or "be read" is to be dressed down, or told about yourself, as in, "girl, you just got read" or "oh, no, she's going to *read* you." In *Activist Sentiments,* I am invested in tracing the ways in which Black women's writing "reads" multiple communities and ideologies: ostensible allies, white abolitionists, and white women and families, for example. Weaving together historical research and literary exegesis, this book underscores the resistant critique expressed through Black women writers' signifying "readings."

Harriet Jacobs, Harriet E. Wilson, and Frances E. W. Harper are the well-known authors whose writings anchor this book's chapters. Discussions of the "raceless" novels of the recently recategorized Blackened author Emma Dunham Kelley-Hawkins and the relatively unread Amelia E. Johnson help pave new inroads in understanding how such writing may actively engage racialized debates.[11] Grounded in primary research and close attention to the historical archive, like Carla L. Peterson's *Doers of the Word: African American Speakers & Writers in the North (1830–1880),* this project offers against-the-grain readings that trace the textual imbrications that emerge when Black women's novel and narrative writing are assumed to be happily married to—rather than painfully divorced from—their journalistic prose, organizational involvement, and reception communities.

Activist Sentiments is part literary criticism, part cultural history. It situates its exegeses in the context of antebellum reform and civil disobedience; the meanings of legal, racial, and property classification and citizenship; petition and antiprostitution campaigns; "home protection," temperance, and anti- and pro-lynching rhetoric; and heated international debates about race, medicine, and science. Offering interpretive models that help ground close readings in newly examined historical contexts and original research, I seek to account for the complex genealogies, tropes, and interventions of Black nineteenth-century sentimental—and simultaneously political— literary production.

This project examines how some of the nation's most injured nineteenth-century subjects make use of one of its most popular cultural forms. In doing so, the book both deepens and challenges prevailing interpretations about the relationship between Black women's domestic and political prose and activism. In *Reconstructing Womanhood, Domestic Allegories of Political Desire* and *The Coupling Convention,* literary critics Hazel Carby, Claudia Tate, and Ann duCille broaden the definition of "political" work to include the gendered reform expressed through domestic rhetoric. As duCille contends, writers such as Harper and Pauline Hopkins "were propelled not by an accomodationist desire to assimilate the Victorian values of white society but by a profoundly political, feminist urge, to rewrite those patriarchal strictures."[12] My work is indebted to and in concert with theirs. Like them, I am intrigued by the ways in which these writers and their readers not only take on and reimbue what duCille (via Nancy Cott) and historian Evelyn Higginbotham might call "passionlessness" and purity or "morals and manners" with radically new racial meaning.[13] Yet my deeper investment is also in the ways in which these writers take pleasure and power in their strident critiques of dominant behaviors, groups, and structures. These authors highlight white sexual depravity and familial, national, and historical dysfunction even as they simultaneously seem to reflect dominant values and the modes of expression most often used to communicate them.

The texts addressed in this book offer highly complex and politicized forms of cultural expression, resistance, and critique that simultaneously appear as narratives that transparently forward the accepted models and messages of racial reform and respectability. Entering a "fray of discourses," as Dwight McBride puts it, these authors gauge the expectations and needs of various audiences.[14] To do so effectively, they measure the hybrid worlds or horizons of their audiences, to mix McBride and Bahktin.[15] These texts exhibit "hybrid discourses," to add Carla Peterson's gloss, while also assuming "the possibility of an 'imagined community' beyond their immediate readership, a community preoccupied with the central task of forging a political and cultural nationality."[16] In examining the expression of what we have come to understand as the rhetoric and agendas of reform and the culturally determined, overtly political sensibilities these texts also lay bare, I identify a practice of simultaneous address through which nineteenth-century Black women authors so often forward multiple imbricated agendas. Highlighting this practice illuminates a formal complexity often denied to prose affiliated with sentimental and domestic thematics and conventions, that is, to almost all of nineteenth-century Black women's narrative and novelistic production.

Activist Sentiments necessarily integrates a discussion of the literary and political genealogies of racial indeterminacy, the generic preoccupation with the figure of the mulatta. The mulatta is largely a figment—or pigment—of the racial imagination, a figure, as Jennifer DeVere Brody asserts, whose "status as an unreal, impossible ideal whose corrupted and corrupting constitution inevitably causes conflicts in narratives that attempt to promote purity."[17] As a symbolic personage who disrupts placid racial, sexual, and national mythologies, the mulatta is both highly ambiguous and extraordinarily ubiquitous in nineteenth-century writing. Almost any study of race and representation in this period necessarily addresses this subject to some degree. Indeed, the raceless and racially indeterminate protagonists who feature prominently in this book share their pale complexions with almost every major protagonist in Black women's fiction until Ann Petry's Lutie Johnson appears in 1946.

All of the principal autobiographical and prose writing addressed in *Activist Sentiments* feature light-skinned, racially indefinite, or raceless characters who are traditionally understood to be employed in a transparent rhetorical appeal to white readers. These figures embody a plea for exceptionalist consanguinity, on the one hand, and an easy bridge for white identification, on the other. Following this logic, precisely because of her proximity to whiteness, the mulatta is often seen as the most *affective* figure through which to move whites to recognize Black sentience and humanity and act to ensure Black inclusion in the body politic. Joining Brody, I instead stress this figure's racial surplus and plentitude, charting the various interpretive cartographies authors offer through that figure's use. Ultimately, the writing I discuss displays how racially indeterminate and raceless heroines can simultaneously perform mimetic functions and also operate as a mirror through which white readers are forced to reincarnate their own racialized assumptions, the racial grotesque many habitually project onto others.

Accordingly, the figure of the mulatta embodies the complex nexus rather than the focus of this project. I seek to disaggregate the representational predominance of the light-skinned figure from its putative Anglophilic associations and entitlements and to flesh out the multiplicity of meanings its use communicates in the nineteenth century. In Harriet Jacobs's *Incidents in the Life of a Slave Girl*, the enslaved woman's status as an "intelligent, bright, mulatto girl," to quote from her master's runaway advertisement, is largely incidental.[18] Light skin in Black women's narratives most often signifies a mother's sexual vulnerability or, as in Jacobs's uncle's case, a son's ability to "for once" use his white face to flee to freedom.

In Black women's work, fugitives and the characters based on them rarely pass *for* white; instead, they pass *through* whiteness, as I have put it elsewhere.[19] They pass provisionally. Ellen Craft used her light skin to don the persona of a Spanish gentleman traveling north. Like the famous fugitive George Latimer, who passed for his pregnant wife's master, Craft put on "white(male)ness" to escape with her "manservant" (actually her darker spouse) so they could live as members of a free and legally recognized *Black* family. Harriet Jacobs describes how as a runaway she *darkened* up, literally charcoaling her face to pass as a Black sailor, rightly assuming that her master would alert the public to her light skin, literacy, and black "inclined to curl" hair that can be "made straight."[20] Indeed, we might usefully envision passing (and the skin, mannerisms, hair, and skill sets that facilitate it) as a flexible strategy, as a process, rather than as an objective or state of cross-racial performance, identification, and desire.[21]

The writings I consider challenge gendered assumptions about interracial power, desire, purity, and alliance often mediated through the politics of naming and through the trope of the mulatta. These texts often use the mulatta as a conventional expression of sexual vulnerability, while they also display how Black men and women are targets of the desires of whites of *both* sexes. Linking an appeal for interracial sisterhood, reform, and reconciliation with a seemingly incongruous condemnation of white female power and sexual predation, this writing places white women under gendered and sexual scrutiny. *Activist Sentiments* proposes that incongruity—the simultaneous encomiums offered to white womanhood under an economy of supposed moral and literary mimesis and a skewering indictment of the political economy of white female desire—as a paradigmatic feature of what we might call Black women's sentimental production.

Taking the racially indeterminate protagonist's capacity to pass in numerous ways and situating racial multiplicity (rather than deficiency) as a point of departure, this project stresses what I call "simultextuality" as an interpretive mode. In reworking the use of the tropes and terms of respectability, purity, and sexual vulnerability, I argue these texts often produce multivalent meanings that, rather than being subtextually buried beneath a principally reformist message of affective and emotional connection, are what I call simultextually available at the primary level of narrative interpretation. These uses of multiple social languages are not buried, some *under* the others, as coded discourse is often understood; they are not subtextual, as I argue, but *simultextual*. Put another way, readers don't have to be literary archeologists or meaning-hunting mycologists, nosing around for textual truffles. Rather, this prose creates discursive layers "shot through" with "dialogized overtones" and "artistically calculated nuances," as Mikhail Bakhtin might put it.[22] The allusions to oppressive and resistant dynamics easily recognizable to culturally and historically literate readers—those acquainted with the complicated sexual politics of slavery or the tangled skeins of Northern racism, or those who challenge post-Reconstruction attacks on Black character and communities—add a calculated charge to texts whose reformist messages are simultaneously expressed in more accommodating prose. These strategies allow readers who do not always enjoy shared fields of cultural and social knowledge to take multiple interpretive paths through narratives. Simultexts exhibit their multivalent meanings *on the surface* for those who can access and then interpret them in accordance with collective political and literary concerns.

Conventional sentimentality stresses the transparent and singular relation between the head and the heart, between reading, feeling, and doing. These works' generic affiliations with sentimental modes of expression camouflage what is often hidden in plain sight. This in part explains their earlier exclusion from a Black literary sisterhood that stresses a complex subjectivity that is not a stand-out feature of sentimental representation. As Mae Henderson proposes in "Speaking in Tongues: Dialogics, Dialectics and the Black Women's Literary Tradition," Black women "speak from a multiple and complex social, historical, and cultural positionality, which, in effect, constitutes Black female subjectivity."[23] Her "speaking in tongues" is a merger of glossolalia, the private, unmediated (pre)language of the psyche, and heteroglossia, "the ability to speak in the multiple languages of public discourse."[24] Upon first examination, this early prose hardly seems compatible with the very dialogized heteroglossia "of the Black women's literary tradition," to recall Henderson's title, because it supposedly depends upon its "artless" moral force as its unitary source.

Nineteenth-century women's writing is rarely identified with the intersectional positionality associated with twentieth- and twenty-first-century subjectivity even as nineteenth-century writers' *reception* communities are evidence of just such intersectionalities. That is, nineteenth-century Black women writers speak to, as well as from, "a multiple and complex social, historical and cultural positionality," to recall Henderson's language.[25] When reading their work without considering the fuller contexts of its production and reception, these authors' generic choices seem to align their writing more closely with glossolalia's "private, non-mediated, non-differentiated univocality."[26] But this describes an expression of subjectivity within a closed and formal representational system. Henderson's speaking in tongues, then, is not my simultextuality.[27] One focuses on contemporary Black women authors' textual expression of multiple subjectivity, while the other invites an examination of the formal and historicized strategies by which earlier writers address multiple audiences simultaneously. Considering nineteenth-century authors' simultextual use helps readers to hear and harmonize the seeming dissonance between early texts' "univocal" sentimental affiliations and the dialogic complexity they engage to articulate messages in various social registers.[28]

Like Jacobs and Wilson, Harper, Dunham-Kelley, and Johnson, writers who imagine or enjoy multiple readerships can't assume a set of references that overlap in their entirety or even, following theorist Hans Jaus, a unified system of historical time. The texts I address display literary strategies that can reach those experiencing what Jaus calls "de facto moments of completely different time curves, determined by the laws of their special history."[29] While he contends that we can analyze "the literary horizon of a certain historical moment as that synchronic system in which simultaneously appearing works can be received diachronically in relation," I examine writing that addresses this tension in a single text.[30] Nineteenth-century women often offer simultextual tropes to audiences who are formed by different moments of the "shaped time" that inflect their literary experiences, exposing these time curves as they arch both toward and away from each other.

Activist Sentiments is organized in two sections. In its two antebellum chapters I chart how simultextual discussions disrupt narrative transparency, the faith in the direct and unitary correspondence between emotion, internal change, and public action, and the ideal of a self-effacing narrative simplicity that Amy Lang calls "the keynote of sentimental fiction."[31] Here I examine how autobiographical writers who borrow from fictional models unsettle direct "truth"-correlation demands projected upon narratives and subsequent writing about servitude and its immediate aftermath.[32] By offering multiple interpretive cartographies that often are opposed to or are incongruent with each other, texts such as Harriet Jacobs's *Incidents in the Life of a Slave Girl* and Harriet Wilson's *Our Nig* remap discursive epistemologies and racialized associations. In doing so, their work scrambles the assumptions about truth, transparency, and easy accessibility with which antebellum Black women's writing has been especially associated.

The seeming promise of emancipation and equal protection called on intellectuals, activists, and others to turn their principal energies to the pressing work of a "brighter coming day,"[33] that is, to building educational, vocational, and political institutions and power. Formerly enslaved women such as Elizabeth Keckley wrote narratives in the two decades following the war; and Frances E. W. Harper added serialized novels to her representational arsenal, publishing three novels in the important Black newspaper, the *Christian Recorder*. But the writers of the following years, the late 1880s and 1890s, "found more outlets for publication open to them in both the white press and in African American journals," as Richard Yarborough affirms, "than had been afforded to Blacks at any time since the height of the abolitionist movement."[34] Facing state-sanctioned violence, lynching, and rape, and finding themselves under political siege, writers revisited the value of "race literature" and included novels along with history, biographies, scientific treatises, sermons, pamphlets, books of travel, essays, and contributions to magazines and newspapers to "influence the reading world," as Victoria Earle Matthews put it in an 1895 address.[35] Matthews's declaration that "we cannot afford any more than any other people to be indifferent to the fact that the surest road to real fame is through literature" found a new and welcome audience with what cultural critic Elizabeth McHenry calls the "literary activists" of the late nineteenth century.[36]

Matthews's rhetorical question—"but for Race Literature, how will future generations know of the pioneers in Literature, our statesmen, soldiers, divines, musicians, artists, lawyers, critics and scholars?"—is the postbellum section of *Activist Sentiments*' tuning note, its symphonic "A."[37] "True culture in Race Literature will enable us to discriminate and not to write hasty thoughts and unjust and ungenerous criticism often of our superiors in knowledge and judgment," Matthews contends.[38] The readings in these chapters take up Matthews's call for discriminating the "true culture in Race Literature" by grounding simultextual analysis in a historicized discussion of growing socioculturally literate classes. These readers followed the leading figures, successes, threats, and issues that were outlined in the growing print and public culture concerned with reform, race, and advancement. Rarely is the sustained and sustaining activism of the postbellum authors I address critically linked to the rhetorical strategies they often employ in their fiction, however. Only a handful of critics examine how the unreservedly strident tone found in some writers' nonfiction prose might inform the objectives and discursive strategies in "sentimental" novels by the same authors. Rather than examining how authors intertextually ground their literary strategies in other literary texts, *Activist Sentiments*' postbellum chapters explore the ways in which broader *historical* movements, organizations, and tropes are embedded in, and simultextually complicate, the writings of Frances E. W. Harper, Emma Dunham Kelley-Hawkins, and Amelia E. Johnson.

Novels of the 1890s continue to redefine literacy in relation to the astute extraliterary analysis central to quotidian survival and strategic organizing as well as to the growing formal skills honed in church groups, schools, clubs, and lyceums. As Frances Smith Foster points out, the "commitment to African American literacy and literature was one not simply of individuals but of institutions."[39] Historians including Stephanie Shaw, Deborah Gray White, Elsa Barkley Brown, Tera Hunter, Kevin Gaines, and Evelyn Brooks Higginbotham explicate how Black women workers, clubwomen, and religious denominations were involved in the overlapping activities, organizations, and conventions out of which a shared set of historical referents sprang. Foster's recovery of Frances Harper's postbellum novels and Elizabeth McHenry's *Forgotten Readers* revise many received understandings about Black readership and reception. McHenry examines early Black reading societies and confirms that late nineteenth-century audiences—audiences that writers such as Frances Harper and Amelia Johnson had cultivated through their literary and activist contributions—were knowledgeable about and connected to historical agents and activities.

The novels of this period ground their simultaneous modes of expression "histotextually," a neologism I coin to name how culturally and socially literate audiences share not only epistemologies and literary sensibilities, but also specific historical references upon which one level of interpretation depends; they ground their simultaneous mode of interpretation in these references. Histotextuality overlaps with, but is distinguishable from, other literary terms and categories with which it shares an affinity. It differs from intertextuality, most obviously, in that it is predicated upon the recognizable historicized markers that authors and readers share, rather than on a formal appropriation and recirculation of texts. In his formulation of African American literature, Henry Louis Gates Jr. stresses intertextuality as the mortar that holds "the tradition" together. In one such instance he asserts that "writers read other writers and *ground* their representations . . . in models of language provided largely by other writers to whom they feel akin. It is through this mode of literary revision, amply evident in the *texts* themselves—in formal echoes, recast metaphors, even in parody—that a 'tradition' emerges and defines itself" (emphasis in original).[40] Histotextual prose provides such a mortar not principally from other texts and writers but in the echoes and recast metaphors it borrows from events, debates, and understandings shared with the ever-larger audience that print culture and rising literacy rates engendered. The multiple threads that run through shared but often disremembered historical narratives provide the metaphorical kinship between "race literature" defined more broadly and the narratives and novels I examine here.

As a strategy, histotextuality is akin to, but in ways only slightly resembles, strategies used in the historical novel. While they share many features, one conventional aspect of the classic historical novel, as with sentimental narrative, is transparency. All readers are meant to recognize the types or the historical personages that inhabit the local, but representative, social order of the historical novel. Yet histotextuality is a strategy used to reach the segment of the audience whose prior knowledge and interpretative schemata determine the level of historical and epistemelogical engagement they experience while appealing on a different level to a broader reading public.

The historical novel, says Georg Lukács, brings "the past to life as the prehistory of the present" but does not "consist in alluding to contemporary events."[41] This would be a "simplistic" strategy that Alexander Pushkin, for example, "cruelly ridiculed."[42] The historical novel illustrates great crises, as Lukács comments, "struggles between classes or codes no longer tolerant of each other or even between ways of life," as Philip Fisher affirms. Yet these struggles are linked to an already known clear outcome.[43] Histotextuality, on the other hand, brings into play a contemporaneous set of referents in addition to past ones; it bastardizes the form, Lukács and Pushkin might say, but not illegitimately.[44] That is, while the classic historical novel incorporates the past as a prehistory to explain present contending forces, work employing histotextual strategies goes beyond this, merging past and present referents to effect change in an as yet not determined future. Well in line with other nineteenth-century Black literary interventions, histotextuality directs social empathy and models social or political intervention.

Pauline Hopkins's *Contending Forces* (1900) provides one of the most explicit examples of novelistic correlations between fictional and historical figures. Revisiting her text and the archive she draws upon helps to establish a range of histotextual use and to differentiate her historicized strategies from the more multivalent hermeneutics I will later address at greater length. Throughout the novel, Hopkins's narrator refers directly to legendary people and institutions such as the Reverend Thomas Paul, founder of the African Meeting House (later called "St. Paul's Church"), where "such men as Garrison and Phillips defied the vengeance of howling mobs that thirsted for the lives of Negro champions."[45] By grafting socio-architectural memorials such as Archibald Grimké's 1890 "Anti-Slavery Boston" with the strategies of popular fiction, Hopkins's readers learn about abolitionist landmarks as the novel's villain trolls the streets of Beacon Hill;[46] the narrator points out that the Twelfth Baptist Church was an offshoot of St. Paul's and sat just across the way from Black Boston activists Lewis and Harriet Hayden's well-known boarding house, where countless fugitives (such as Ellen and William Craft) found refuge. These references create neighboring narratives. The backstories that reside in them sit side by side with the fictive realism—stories about lynching and rape, protest and betrayal—that *Contending Forces,* houses. Hopkins's histotextual strategies are authenticating ones. By incorporating highly recognizable historical narratives she lends credibility to the fictional and symbolic stories she unfolds.[47]

Hopkins also presents characters whose fictional names provide only the sheerest fictional veneer. The race woman and suffrage advocate Mrs. Willis, the "brilliant widow of a bright Negro Politician," is an obvious if ambivalent rendition of Josephine St. Pierre Ruffin.[48] In *Contending Forces,* Willis's husband had enjoyed a "seat in the Legislature . . . urged by the loving woman behind him. Other offices of trust were quickly offered him when his worth became known," while his wife later became "the pivot about which all social and intellectual life of the colored people of her section revolved."[49] Likewise, George Lewis Ruffin, who married Josephine as a teenager, was elected to the Massachusetts Legislature before becoming the first African American to secure a judgeship in the North. After his death in 1884, Josephine became a powerful clubwoman and founded the *Woman's Era,* the newspaper of national reach and importance that served as the official organ of the Black clubwomen's movement. She shared her position as editor with her daughter, as *Contending Forces'* narrator archly puts it, "like a title of nobility [she] bade fair to descend to her children."[50] Another of *Contending Forces'* characters, Madame Frances, the "spiritualistic soothsayer and marvelous mind-reader" whose fatidic services at a fund-raising fair contribute to its success, may be loosely based on a fabulously popular Boston medium of the era, the "earnest and eloquent colored medium" Hattie E. Wilson, author of *Our Nig.*[51]

Hopkins sometimes outlines composite sketches of well-known figures or groups that serve as narrative archetypes. Other times she incorporates telling details about a leading figure that her contemporary audience would know—or should learn—in accordance with the text's heuristic mission. Indeed, Hopkins "created fictional histories," or histotextual fictions, "which could explain the present and which had a pedagogical function for both her characters and her audience," as Hazel Carby puts it.[52] The debates described in *Contending Forces* anticipate what would soon solidify into a "battle between W. E. B. DuBois and Booker T. Washington over educational policy and the advisability of black political activism," as critic Richard Yarborough has suggested.[53] Described as the head of a large industrial institution "in the South devoted to the welfare of the Negroes," the novel's Dr. Arthur Lewis promotes accommodation, pronouncing at a community gathering that "politics is the bane of the Negro's existence."[54] Like Washington, Lewis visits the North regularly to collect "large sums of money from the best class of philanthropic citizens."[55] His eventual brother-in-law, the handsome Will Smith, is the novel's radical Boston intellectual. He studies at Harvard and then does further coursework in Germany, Hopkins's nod to DuBois's education at both Harvard and the University of Berlin.[56]

Smith is a leading member of the "American Colored League," "made up of leading colored men all over New England."[57] The fictional league provides yet another layer of historical and narrative connection, for, as the *Christian Recorder* reported in 1889, in that era "the air [was] full of Negro Leagues. It [was] taking like wild fire."[58] Just as Hopkins's romantic plot makes respected family out of political foes, her naming practices suggestively marry institutional goals and leadership. Hopkins's American Colored League captures this mood and series of movements. It recalls the American Negro Academy (ANA), whose second president was DuBois.[59] A reference to the fictional league's longer name—the National League of American Colored Men—also calls to mind T. Thomas Fortune's National Afro-American League (1890–93) and its later rendition, the National Afro-American Council (1898).[60] Boston's Colored National League, whose officers included leading local activists such as Edwin Walker (David Walker's son), Archibald Grimké and others, provides a closer source for Hopkins's amalgamation; the mass meeting it held in October 1899, as Hopkins was finishing her novel, may have inspired the central gathering narrated in *Contending Forces*.[61] The historicity of Hopkins's league is paradoxically both definite and imprecise. It highlights the existence of these organizations even though it is difficult to identify a single organization that serves as her prototype. She so invites readers to recall the immediate past as a prehistory of her fictional moment, and merges past and present referents suggestively as a model for further present textual—and extratextual—action.[62]

For culturally literate readers, *Contending Forces*'s historical heuristics reinforce and authenticate the meanings communicated to its entire audience, working in harmony with the book's narrative plot and mission. In other works, histotextual references create alternative, sometimes dissonant, interpretative possibilities. Histotextuality can be used in a range of ways, to enhance and deepen a text's hermeneutics or to disrupt an assumed and univocal narrative transparency. In *Activist Sentiments,* my focus is on these narrative strategies and reading practices as they characterize much of Black women's nineteenth-century literature. Yet they surely emerge in other discourses, writing, and periods that share conditions and economies of production and reception that resemble those I examine.

Leaving harmonic historicizing to one side, in the chapters that follow I record the oppositional simultextual polyphonics in texts known—and often dismissed—for their putatively conforming and prosaic embrace of sentimental forms and themes. Tracing specific histotextual strategies in putatively "nonpolitical" turn-of-the-century Black women's writings reveals both the potency and the multivalent character of their historical engagement. It is true that the novels that first emerge in the 1890s employ what seems to many contemporary readers to be conventional generic shells. Their valorization of motherhood, endorsements of marriage and traditional women's concerns like temperance, and novelistic use of racially indeterminate protagonists, all characterize writing of this period. The commitment to these concerns was genuine and political, as scholars from Hazel Carby to Evelyn Brooks Higginbotham have illustrated. Nineteenth-century African American women both embraced these concerns and also critiqued the racial biases found in larger economic and gender-inflected cultural and activist contexts.

It is often difficult for contemporary readers—part of an American populace infamous for its amnesia—to identify historical references. The use of
these histotextual conventions, then, often seems obscure to modern readers
because their referents have been disremembered and rarely incorporated
into the standard histories we inherit. Yet the nineteenth-century audiences
who recognized historicized tropes could connect the references to people,
events, and attacks upon which at least one semantic layer of representation
depended. Histotextuality, then, names a method for interpreting sophisticated historicized tropes in narratives whose meaning has previously been
thought to be produced by relying on the texts' thin and putatively singular
or seemingly impoverished mimetic referents. Revisiting the multiple meanings produced by several simultaneously situated interpretive phraseologies is
one way to better access nineteenth-century Black women's literary, cultural,
and political workings.

∗ ∗ ∗

Activist Sentiments' first chapters feature readings of its most familiar texts
and authors. My consideration of Harriet Jacobs expands a discussion of sex
and slavery beyond its conventional, normalized representations to include
homosexual and incestuous abuse that pose larger issues about readers' identification, complicity, and engagement. I then turn to the politics of naming, and to issues of reproductive and historical agency. I argue that Jacobs
challenges conventional power arrangements by setting up a contestation of
paternity between Mr. Sands, Brent's white lover, and Dr. Flint, her owner.
Finally, examining the historical record and querying the circumstances of
Molly Horniblow—or Aunt Martha's—actual motherhood and sale allows
us to further examine the simultextual discussion of sexual unveilings and
idealized maternity that animates *Incidents in the Life of a Slave Girl.*

My reading of Harriet Wilson's *Our Nig* veers away from the historical
research I have published elsewhere and instead traces the critique of human and property relations that *Our Nig* launches through its meditations
about and manipulations of the politics of naming. *Our Nig* recalls the story
of another servant girl and her master, Mr. B., made famous in the runaway
bestseller, *Pamela* (1740). *Our Nig*'s multiple uses of homonymic overlay also
calls attention to both anti-slavery friends and to "slavery's shadows" being
cast in Northern quarters. Its thematic and lexical mergers trouble characters'
nominally unitary and transparent roles. Indeed, *Our Nig* moves beyond a
racial and regional critique of domesticity to simultextually challenge and
complicate both white and Black maternity, a pattern we will see in *Clarence
and Corrine* as well.

The chapter titled "'Reading Aright': Sexuality and White Slavery in Frances Harper's *Iola Leroy*" explores how the novel employs the simultaneously racialized mulatta and the trope of "white slavery." By examining the medical, legal, and civic debates through which *Iola Leroy's* rhetorics gain meaning, it becomes clearer that the story of the "white slaves" who people the novel also references the white slavery scare, the name given to the growing abduction of young white women into an institutionalized system of sexual exploitation in the Progressive Era. *Iola Leroy* reappropriates language that is "already populated with the social intentions of others," as Bakhtin says of the prose writer, "and compels them to serve [its] own intentions."[63] Used to direct energy back to post-Reconstruction Black concerns, Iola's color allows for a historically specified recirculation of white slavery that had served as the (essential) trope repeated in antebellum texts like *Uncle Tom's Cabin* (1852), *Clotel* (1853, 1860, 1864), and *Running a Thousand Miles to Freedom* (1860).

Iola Leroy's examination of sexuality, power, and interracial desire raises the question of how the rhetoric meant to recast white victims of white slavery as sexual innocents revises our understanding of Iola's testimony about her own sexual vulnerability. Following my reading of *Incidents*, I suggest that *Iola* never assures its readers of its heroine's sexual purity. Nor does *Iola* equate white and Black sexual oppression. Indeed, the novel scrutinizes white women's own sexual power over and desire for enslaved women and men in ways that again recall the multidirectional sexual power that *Incidents in the Life of a Slave Girl* likewise highlights.

Emerging historical and genealogical research provides new contexts for considerations of Emma Dunham Kelley-Hawkins and Amelia Johnson, the two rarely examined authors included in this study. As African Americanists well know, we are still in the midst of recovering nineteenth-century writings and the buried biographical, historical, and political contexts of their production. Such research has augmented, for example, our knowledge about Frances E. W. Harper's literary corpus. Frances Smith Foster's rediscovery of the early novels Harper serialized in the *Christian Recorder* inform the ways we read *Iola Leroy.* Julia Collins's recently republished novel *The Curse of Caste; or, the Slave Bride,* which also first appeared in the *Recorder's* pages, likewise has renewed interest in questions of "firsts," influence, and recovery. Similarly, despite Harriet Jacobs's and Harriet Wilson's near canonical status since the 1990s, we knew relatively little about the efforts and movements to which they devoted their later lives until Jean Fagan Yellin's biography of Jacobs and P. Gabrielle Foreman and Reginald Pitts's edition of *Our Nig* emerged in the twenty-first century.[64] The intriguing discoveries of Hannah Craft's *The Bondswoman's Narrative* and *The Complete Fortune Teller and*

Dream Book by "Chloe Russell, a Woman of Colour in the State of Massachusetts," are additional examples of recently reintroduced texts. In some cases, biographical information is so scant that these authors' consanguineous connections to African American community or identity are based on rather anemic information.[65]

While historicized readings confirm Amelia Johnson's lost activist biography and displace the assumptions about her life that emerged from previous considerations of her aracial, supposedly apolitical, novels, conversely, even as recent genealogical research conclusively establishes that Kelley-Hawkins was *not* African American (as critics had previously believed), histotextual readings of *Four Girls at Cottage City* provide strong textual linkages to Black activist engagement.[66] Kelley-Hawkins's shifting racial and authorial identity invites wider analysis of the breadth of Black prose writers' political and narrative strategies. In the chapter titled "Reading/Photographs: Emma Dunham Kelley-Hawkins's *Four Girls at Cottage City,* Victoria Earle (Matthews), and the *Woman's Era,*" I examine how, for culturally literate readers, not only her photographic frontispiece but her characters have linked (and continue to link) Kelley-Hawkins and her work to African American writing.[67] Focusing on late-nineteenth-century reading, photography, and reform, as well as on re-forming contemporary interpretative practices that frame visual, racial, and historical "evidence," I address the ways in which reading race and assimilating iconographic representation became increasingly central to late-nineteenth-century reading culture, bringing into view the emphasis on interpretation posed as critical to women's development. Indeed, the novel takes up the mutually constitutive relation between women's development and reform in ways that mirror the arc described in the pages of the *Woman's Era* and that are expressed throughout the Black clubwomen's movement.

Throughout this project, I examine the ways in which the politics of naming open up polyvalent interpretative possibilities. The convergence between Kelley-Hawkins's Vera Earle and Victoria Earle (Matthews), between multiple Harper characters and historical figures, as well as the inviting convergence of Nig, Nab, and Mag, are particular examples. *Iola Leroy* and *Four Girls at Cottage City* reaffirm that cultural literacy is necessary to "read aright" the texts' "legible transcripts" of named and active civic participation and protest, to borrow from *Iola*'s narrator.[68] In a more specific sense, names covalently bond with their homonymic referents. That is, instead of floating freely, they become bound in mutual orbit or "combine with" historical referents, compounding the interlocking sets of amplified meanings that they provide. These novels' allusions to such figures of resistance were well known to their multiple interpretive communities: those readers, whatever their race, who followed reform issues, clubwomen's and temperance work, those, in other words, who were interested in reform work or what Matthews defined broadly as "race literature."

To date, this book also offers the fullest examination of Amelia Johnson's *Clarence and Corrine* and the newly recovered nonfiction introduced in the last chapter. Rarely examined documents chronicle Johnson's involvement in the Black clubwomen's and Niagara movements. Recovering the context of Johnson's literary production reveals her intimate connection to the inner circle of leaders who organized sustained and radical justice campaigns in late nineteenth-century Baltimore. Their efforts brought Maryland its first Black lawyer, challenged multiple statutes and court cases, got Black students—later the city's leading municipal leaders—admitted to the University of Maryland's law school, and launched organizing efforts to institute a Black high school that was unique in the lower and upper South. Nonetheless, to this date Johnson's literary works have been described as flyweight evangelical domestic tracts. Yet Johnson uses characters who could be read as white to simultextually illustrate shared social problems despite the broader culture's insistence that such issues illustrate Black dysfunction and degradation. Examining Johnson's journalistic writing reveals that, as in her novel *Clarence and Corrine,* she emphasizes white historical and literary examples *in order to* aggressively defend Black progress. Yet, her novels have been almost completely abstracted from the sharp challenges to white violence, racism, and paternalism that characterize her hard-knuckled linguistic stance in other publishing venues.

In both *Clarence and Corrine* and in *Four Girls,* racial construction as incarnated in the "raceless" body's transformational ability has a wide range of expressive possibilities that reach beyond conventional texts in which phenotypically white-skinned but juridically Black characters pass. As we know, more complex and challenging racial signification is often at work in these instances. In *Activist Sentiments,* chapters on *Our Nig, Iola Leroy, Four Girls,* and *Clarence and Corrine* in part explore the sometimes radically transgressive ways in which light, bright, and could-they-be-white (?) characters might be used to please, tease, and create unease for the multiple reception communities their authors claim as their audiences. *Activist Sentiments* augments and reframes the assumption that garnering white readers' sympathy is the principal thrust of the cultural work in which nineteenth-century Black women's writing is engaged. While that dynamic exists, as I would put it, simultextually, this book charts the historical and formal complexity of texts that perhaps reinscribe—but also disrupt and challenge—such dynamics. My hope is that *Activist Sentiments* will provide a stronger foundation for our understanding of the racially inflected conundrums of sexuality and power—and the rhetorics we use to express and address them—both in the past and in the century in which we live.

1. The Politics of Sex and Representation in Harriet Jacobs's *Incidents in the Life of a Slave Girl*

"Rise up, ye women that are at ease! Hear my voice, ye careless
daughters! Give ear unto my speech."—Isaiah xxxii, 9
—Title page, first edition, *Incidents in the Life of a Slave Girl*

Untruth becomes truth through belief,
and disbelief untruths the truth.
—Patricia Williams

Tell all the Truth but tell it slant—
success in Circuit lies
—Emily Dickinson

Harriet Jacobs's *Incidents in the Life of a Slave Girl* (1861) was once dismissed
and then resuscitated precisely on the basis of its value as "truth" even though
it is widely accepted today that "the 'unreliability' of autobiography is an
inescapable condition, not a rhetorical option."[1] Although there are explicit
markers of distance between "truth" and its representation in the text, contemporary critics tend to accept the transparency between the life of Harriet
Jacobs and her narrative self-construct "Linda Brent."[2] For Jean Fagan Yellin,
Jacobs's most important critic, treating her book "as if it were gospel truth"
has led to one of the most important works of recovery in American literary
and historical studies.[3] As Yellin puts it, "you can trust [Jacobs]. She's not
ever wrong. She may be wrong on incidentals like the birth order of her mistresses' children—after all she was a woman in her forties trying to remember
what happened to her as a teenager—but she's never wrong in substance."[4]
Through the lens of the biographer, this approach has brought Jacobs's life
into focus. But for the literary critic, choosing this aperture can blur the ways
in which *Incidents* foregrounds and obscures the text's multiple messages.
The coordinates—right/"wrong," "substance"/incidentals, "trust"[worthy]/

liar—are mapped onto *Incidents,* even though modern critics generally accept
literary theorist Sidonie Smith's maxim about autobiography's unreliability.
Today, truthfulness, as Smith affirms, is viewed as a "complex and problematic phenomenon" that does not emphasize "the truth in its factual or moral
dimensions."[5] In this chapter, rather than emphasize the *auto,* the assumed
transparent self, or the *bio,* I grapple with interpreting *graphia,* "'the careful
teasing out of warring forces of signification within the text itself.'"[6] As its
autodiegetic narrator, Jacobs offers her reception communities explicit directions to look for multiple modes of interpretation. These alternatives are
not subversively subtextual, I argue, but rather, they are simultextual; that is,
they are interpretive paths that offer equally substantive, often competing,
simultaneously rendered reading modalities.

When we pay attention to Black simultextuality, we limn the challenges
to the truth-telling imperatives associated with slave narratives and with the
narrative transparency—the correlation between text and a readily apparent singular meaning—that is considered a keynote of sentimental fiction.
Though the challenges Black male narrators launch against such generic
expectations are generally celebrated, the figure of the nineteenth-century
Black woman is more readily expected to tell just one truth and to embody
the truth.

Truth was highly valued in abolitionist rhetoric. Black authors and speakers
were valued precisely because their bodies stood in its rhetorical stead and
displaced Southern apologist versions of "slavery as it is." Nineteenth-century
truth, for the once-enslaved narrator's audiences, was most threatened by exaggeration of the social evils of slavery, in other words, by overindulgence and
rhetorical excess.[7] "Delicacy" and "modesty," virtues extolled in women's and
even in African American men's narratives, allowed for and even demanded
that narrators systematically come short of the truth.[8] Tracing simultextual
signs of "truthfulness" complicates the ways in which *Incidents* is traditionally read and affirms an alternative interpretation: that Dr. Norcom did rape
Jacobs, which stands alongside the script that Linda triumphed over Dr. Flint,
not only in her fugitive escape, but in her sexual one. The analysis I offer here
is not meant to reassert "truth-telling" and "lying" as evaluative axes, or to
substitute one reading for another. Rather this commentary calls into question the politics of transparency that often frame both our consideration of
Incidents and an approach to Black sentimental writing that discourages the
recovery of the multivalent nuances that I argue characterize the genre.

This chapter traces the simultaneous modes of address that are manifest
in *Incidents in the Life of a Slave Girl's* loud "silences" and their relation to the
truth. Widening traditional categories of exploited and exploiter, I offer an

extended reading of homosexual abuse and interrogate how masters link an imperative toward sexualized silence to security from sale. When, for women, bodily expression (that is, pregnancies and pale children) is constructed as punishable speech, the promise of safety that owners offer in exchange for silence is impossible for enslaved women to carry out, much less collect upon. Jacobs turns the politics of ownership, reproductive agency, and naming under slavery on its head as she complicates her children's paternity and so neutralizes her owner's power to sell her by positioning her lover as her probable buyer. Finally, I examine the sexual politics that swirl around the seemingly saintly figure of Aunt Martha, Brent's grandmother, the historical Molly Horniblow. Querying the implications of Horniblow's sexual history, motherhood, and sale allows us to further examine *Incidents*' polyvalent explorations.

Eenie, Meenie, Minie, Moe, Abuser, Victim, Ally, Foe?

Incidents both advances and simultextually challenges the script that Linda had an affair with the white bachelor Mr. Sands in order to fend off the sexual threat of her owner Dr. Flint. She constantly reiterates that "the degradation, the wrongs, the vices that grow out of slavery are more than I can describe. They are greater than you would willingly believe."[9] This admonition echoes her preface, where she tells her readers that the events related in *Incidents* are "strictly true. I have not exaggerated the wrongs inflicted by Slavery; on the contrary, my descriptions fall far short of the facts" (*InL*, i). How are readers to interpret the narrative tension between a "strict truth" that nonetheless "falls far short of the facts"? The mistrust Jacobs feels for those who will not "willingly believe" the "facts" informs what Frances Smith Foster discusses as an "implicitly argumentative" mode of address that anticipates such resistance; it is what Robert Stepto might call a culture of distrust.[10] These characterizations point contemporary readers to the politics of nineteenth-century reception and to the ways in which distrust of audiences encouraged authors to gauge the distance between the strict truth that falls short and to undertell their stories to match what we might call delicate expectations, while simultaneously indicating to receptive readers that more is apparent for those who choose to look. Such discursive maneuvering works to "thwart the resisting reader's urge to compete with the author for authority," instead enlisting the reader "as a collaborator," as Foster suggests.[11] These dynamics also spawn rhetorical tactics that respond to multiple expectations, both challenging and simultaneously appealing to readers' racialized assumptions and power.

    Incidents seems to both dismiss and genuflect at the feet of authoritative notions of Northern femininity and transparency. Indeed, the text reflects some of the central cultural tensions of the antebellum era. The cult of sincerity that had dominated the previous two decades faded in importance in the fifties. Karen Halttunen argues that the "sentimental typology of conduct," the valorization of transparency of character, was fast being replaced with the laws of polite social performance.[12] She notes that the "most important law of polite social geography was that no one shatter the magic of the genteel performance by acknowledging back regions that alone made the performance possible."[13] *Incidents* reflects that, in an era of shifting truth expectations, the rules of decorum were as compelling as those of disclosure. Understanding an implicit contract with her readership, Jacobs could expect her white bourgeois female audience to play its part—to perceive (but to be "delicate" enough not to admit that they comprehend) the sexually determined Black "back regions" of her textual performance.[14]

Jacobs anticipates her audience's interpretive bind, one Lydia Maria Child articulates when she takes pains to explain why she, a prominent white abolitionist, might be associated with so "indelicate" a text. In her introduction Child writes that she presents the "veil withdrawn . . . for the sake of my sisters in bondage, who are suffering wrongs so foul that our ears are too delicate to listen to them" (*InL*, 4). As Valerie Smith notes, the editor places herself and her imagined readers in the enslaved victim's stead; she substitutes "our" (presumably white) ears in the grammatical place that should call for Black reactions or bodies.[15] Importantly, "ear" as the orifice penetrated by words acts to degender sexual exploitation and to break down oppositions of male/female abuse.[16] By deemphasizing Jacobs's mediation of truth and the politics of sexual revelation and discursive autonomy, Child's introductory claim that as editor she presents the "veil withdrawn," the back regions exposed, stands as *Incidents'* guiding con/text.

In *Incidents,* enslaved men as well as women are sexually terrorized by white people of either sex. In language that characteristically reveals as it also conceals, *Incidents* exposes the homosexual abuse to which male narrators rarely admit.[17] Luke is the slave of a dissipated and sick young owner who has the enslaved man "bare his back and kneel beside the couch, while he whipped him." And, as Jacobs writes in the very next sentence, Luke is forced to serve his owner bare-bottomed, for "somedays he was not allowed to wear any thing *but* his shirt, in order to be flogged" (*InL,* 192, emphasis mine): "As [the young master] lay there on his bed, a mere degraded wreck of manhood, he took into his head the strangest freaks of despotism; and if Luke hesitated to submit to his orders, the constable was immediately sent for. Some of these freaks were of a nature too filthy to be repeated. I left poor Luke still chained to the bedside of this cruel and disgusting wretch" (*InL,* 192).

The language here taps into a familiar anti-slavery critique that explicitly links sexual defilement and the political "despotism" of slavery. It likewise suggests that the North is not safe from the contagion of Southern dissipation, as the young owner had become "prey to the vices growing out of the 'patriarchal institution,' and when he went to the north, to complete his education, he carried his vices with him" (*InL*, 192). Northern pedagogy is ineffective, the text suggests; it cannot purify the patriarchal institution nor fight off the disease of vice and debauchery that Southerners carry with them. Abuse of power, however weakened or weakening, admits no limits in its access to the body politic as represented by the bodies of its enslaved population; each controls by force without consent. By making homosexual exploitation and political abuse analogous, this passage breaks from conventional imagery to assert that the reach of despotic control, of slavery, cannot be contained.

In *Incidents*, white women are also included in a miscegenous sexual politics that so often is characterized by white male desire for ever-available Black female bodies. Indeed, the text "demarcates a sexuality that is neuter-bound, insomuch as it represents an open vulnerability to a gigantic sexualized repertoire that may be alternately expressed as male/female," to borrow from Hortense Spillers.[18] Early on, Jacobs exposes white women with the veil withdrawn by asserting that "from others than the master persecution also comes in such cases" (*InL*, 13). Critics have pointed out that it is the "whispering" Mrs. Flint who realizes her demand to have Linda sleep in her room, who leans suggestively over her slave's body at night.[19] And young mistresses, too, "hear their parents quarreling about some female slave. Their curiosity is excited . . . and they hear talk as should never meet youthful ears, or any other ears. They know that the women slaves are subject to their father's authority in all things; and in some cases they exercise the same authority over men slaves" (*InL*, 52). In this passage, sexualized language again attracts varied agents. The "they" in the clause: "in some cases they exercise the same authority over men slaves" can refer to both the young mistress of "they know that the women slaves are subject to their father's authority" and to the Ur-agent-abuser himself, the master/model whose restless nature knows no bounds with enslaved women, and in some cases, "men slaves." Grammatically, Jacobs signals both homosexual violation and also abuse not very complimentary to the reputation of white women. This passage thus transforms some readers, the women of the North she hopes to "arouse" to "realizing a sense of the condition of the two million women at the North, still in bondage" (*InL*, preface) from a state of mirrored identification with the youthful ears of the innocent belle hearing too much to a state of active culpability as "careless daughters" rise up and transmogrify into sexual aggressors. Subject to Jacobs's narrative control, both mistress and reader are stripped of their usually protected status and, "curiosity" excited, ears exposed, they are sexualized.[20]

This passage likewise tarnishes planters' reputations through the incestuous inferences it raises. The relation between miscegenous abuse and familial contamination is further confirmed when Dr. Flint insists that his young daughter sleep in his room to justify Linda's presence there. One cannot help but wonder, as critic Sandra Gunning does, "if Flint expects the child to be present while he tries to rape her nurse."[21] These masters contaminate their daughters, introducing young girls to transgressive acts and desires via their fathers' own salacious conduct (*InL*, 52).

Sexual abuse of enslaved women was neither visible to the law nor did it elicit public stigma for its perpetuators. So it left "other ears" systematically open to the symbolic penetration that "words that sting like fire" represent in *Incidents*. By placing these normalized "relations" center stage alongside recognizable, even actionable, taboos of incestuously tainted and homosexual abuse, these passages both highlight Black women's defilement and raise questions about the role of all of the parties involved. Jacobs stages enslaved women's abuse alongside other sexually oppressive scenarios; she thus highlights illicit behavior sure to get the attention of many readers even if they were deadened to the plight of enslaved women themselves.

Confession and Commodities; Silence and Sale

Jacobs's simultextual descriptions of varied types and agents of sexual abuse evoke sympathy from her audience and also expose their complicity. Indeed, if readers attend to the polyvalent interpretive paradigm the text sets out, the ways through which *Incidents* both embraces and also rejects discursive victimization emerge.[22] The delimited arena of interracial sexual "victimization" is characterized by a lack of explicit expression, at least by the "victims." For centuries, white women only pointed at Black men, and the legal apparatus need not even be brought to bear on them before they were sold, shot, or lynched. Conversely, recognition of the sexual abuse of enslaved or freed African American women was as alien in concept as it was in fact.[23] What, then, underwrote speech-rights for the enslaved? Literary critic Houston Baker claims that the male slave "*publicly* sells his voice in order to secure *private* ownership of his voice-person,"[24] and so shifts concepts of desire and privatization from a gendered arena (public/private) where the slave is infantilized and feminized to an economically determined sphere where he could own his own person or manhood as agent rather than victim.

When *Incidents* is published, however, the once-fugitive author is already free, so she cannot justify her publishing venture into the masculinized public realm to secure ownership of her person. Nor can she invoke the accepted model of the era in which women writers legitimize their trade by emphasizing explicit ties to an overriding and valorized motherhood. Louisa Picquet (1861) unveils the details of her sexual past only as a last attempt to purchase her enslaved mother; Harriet Wilson (1859) in effect writes in order to "purchase" her son. The Jacobs children, however, were both technically and legally free (despite the fears the narrator expresses), even though illegitimate and Black children were particularly susceptible to involuntary apprenticeship in North Carolina where they were born.[25] Nor does the conventional trope of a mother figure with whom to reunite exist; Jacobs's free grandmother has recently died. Neither does Jacobs make an explicit claim that she is attempting to buy, through this work, a "home of her own" (*InL*, 201). Nor does she make claim to destitution, another popular justification for women writers' indelicate jaunt into the public sphere. Rather, she asks her abolitionist friend Amy Post to mention that "I lived at service all the while that I was striving to get the Book out. . . . [as] I would [not] like to have people think that I was living an Idle life—and had got this book out merely to make money" (*InL*, 242). If Jacobs refuses to invoke received legitimizing strategies, how does one account for her economy of voice and possession? In some ways, Jacobs's model is most often predicated upon the politics of representing desire and sexual autonomy. She sells her voice to secure and express private ownership, not only of her body, but of its discursive embodiment—her voice and text themselves.

As Michel Foucault reminds us, "from the Christian penance to the present day sex was a privileged theme of confession," as it was in African American literary history and particularly in the most popular of all early slave narratives, the criminal "confession." Yet the criminal genre's titillation is often resolved in outrage and punishment—the subgenre itself is predicated upon the suppression of the connected realms of Black speech rights and criminal justice.[26] Jacobs's potential confession, we can easily imagine, with cowering victim and salacious owner, could collapse for her readers into the arousal of sadistic pornography. Yet, by strategically undertelling "what the world might believe that a Slave Woman was too willing to pour out—that she might gain their sympathies," *Incidents* makes good use of the implicit expectations of victimization that Jacobs simultaneously shuns (*InL*, 242). This is particularly true in the scenes of "confession" with Mrs. Flint, Linda's grandmother, and in the extratextual confession described by Amy Post in *Incidents*' appendix.[27] In none of these passages does the text reveal what the once-enslaved girl actually testifies to or confesses. Instead, *Incidents* teases, toying with the acceptable titillation and resolution of confession and absolution without ever really shedding any raiment.

To anti-slavery whites in the North, "blackness and black women in particular signified victimization."[28] While *Incidents* often gives the impression "that the [sentimental] form only allows Jacobs to talk about her sexual experiences when they are the result of victimization,"[29] it is also true that "only when Brent is silenced can she become the object of charity," that she moves, as Gunning asserts, from embodying a delicate tale that situates her as an object of sympathy to telling an indelicate tale that makes her agent and pariah, a potential pollutant to "purer" sensibilities.[30] Marianne Noble maintains that "histrionic victimization is a particularly effective strategy for self-empowerment in a liberal society where most citizens want to be seen as nonviolent and compassionate."[31] Most Garrisonian abolitionists' self-identity hinged on a self-conceptualization that elevated moral suasion and nonviolence when slavery and its defenders were seen as violent threats to the body politic. But racialized dynamics of speech production preclude "histrionic" positioning for Black victims; again, exaggeration threatens truth-telling. Moreover, the very appellation "sexual victim" exonerates one from guilt, and so from compulsion toward confession, especially when one might offend delicate sensibilities. Thus, perversely, Jacobs must be a sexual *actor* to appropriate speech rights; she does so by expressing agency where male authors most often depict female victimization. This agency exhibits itself in the realm of the illicit: it must produce something to confess.

Confession, then, is the currency with which the text purchases the sanitized (and thus legitimate) attention of its readers. Her much quoted "Pity me and pardon me, O virtuous reader" (*InL*, 55) acts to relieve the titillated audience from its excited state; in a sense, by reminding them of their access to and responsibility for virtue, the passage acts to absolve them as much as it seeks to absolve Linda. Through confession, then, *Incidents* converts a religious invocation of pardon into both sexual and political agency.[32] In doing so the narrative "questions the character of a white nation that establishes its moral ideals on a victimizing construction of Blackness" as Brent transforms from "victim to actor on the very terms of the slave woman's oppression," as Gunning points out.[33] Jacobs's victimization then acts with her sexual agency, challenging readers to face their own mirrored complicity as women with sexual power and abusive agency.

Incidents delineates the multivalent relationships between owners, the enslaved, sex, and criminalized speech. Silence, it asserts again and again, ostensibly stands in fungible relation to security from sale. In the first few weeks after Linda has been willed to young Emily Flint and removed from her former mistress's home, Dr. Flint hands a slave mother and her "husband" over to a trader: "you *promised* to treat me well," the mother says. "To which [Flint] replied, 'you have let your tongue run too far; damn you!' She had forgotten that it was a crime for a slave to tell who was the father of her child" (*InL*, 13). The narrator's use of an indefinite article in the phrase, "a slave," links the mother to a collective of enslaved and abused women. Jacobs similarly switches to the plural when outlining Linda's experience as Flint pursues her. The doctor is uniformly relentless but his approaches and interests are varied: "sometimes he had stormy, terrific ways that made his *victims* tremble" (*InL*, 27, emphasis mine). This harassment, we can deduce, was physical as well as verbal. As Jacobs writes, "The secrets of slavery are concealed like those of the Inquisition. My master was, to my knowledge, the father of eleven slaves. But did the mothers dare to tell who was the father of their children? Did the other slaves dare to allude to it, except in whispers among themselves? No indeed! They knew too well the terrible consequences" (*InL*, 35). Did these women form whispering communities of support analogous to those of white bourgeois women who provided each other with advice, solace, and aid?[34] Or did these enslaved women come to understand—as Jacobs suggests—that such sharing constituted punishable speech?

The formula "silence or sale" renders the subject closed to the inquiries of the supportive and/or enraged husband, family, and green-eyed mistress alike. Like Linda's reticence with her grandmother, the sales *Incidents* depicts strongly suggest that at least some enslaved women quickly learn that they can whisper only if they are not the subject; they are required to mute their violation with silence—to reinforce, perversely, their own violation. The shared whisperings "among themselves," then, exclude the assaulted individual whose confirmation of her abuse might actualize the constant threat of sale and endanger others' security as well; her required silence, though it does not ensure her own safety from rape or sale, makes her responsible for maintaining the fragile "security" of her community.

Yet might not the signs of a "favorite" slave's pregnancy, or the child itself, constitute punishable speech? Can her silence perform what is demanded of it? Can it nullify bodily speech? The slave mother who appears early in *Incidents* flings back Flint's commitment—"you *promised* to treat me well"—and he acknowledges their agreement but accuses her of breaching it, replying, "'you have let your tongue run too far; damn you!'" The following comment— "she had forgotten that it was a crime . . . to tell" (*InL*, 13)—concretizes the language of contract represented in the passage. Jacobs transfers the juridical consequences of breaking contracts to a figure of speech, speech that in this nonactionable situation between enslaved and owner nonetheless carries the punitive force of punishment. What is clear, however, is that silence—the enslaved mother's agreed-upon item of exchange—is neither delimited by speech nor defined by its absence. Rather, it is the *issue* who is at issue, for the mother and husband "were both black and the child was very fair" (*InL*, 13). The evidence is transmitted through her and against her own will, creating a bodily legibility that is compulsory for it is produced by her owner's seminal inscription upon his own property.[35] Her tongue, in other words, did not have to produce the telling text. No one has to *say* anything; the child's color speaks for itself. The text depicts the slave mother as *coerced* into an "agreement" in which even her agreed-upon part was never tenable. Not only are contracts between slave and master always nonbinding and duplicitous, they will also turn a slave's speech *and* silence against her.

One might argue, then, that because Linda is said to know "too well the terrible consequences" that "as soon as a new fancy took him, his victims were sold far off to get rid of them, especially if they had children"—because she had seen this—she began her affair with Sands (*InL*, 35, 55). She explains that "of a man who was not my master I could ask to have my children well supported; and in this case, I felt confident I should obtain the boon and that they would be made free." This sentence directly precedes *Incidents'* most oft-quoted "sentimental" lines: "With all these thoughts revolving in my mind, and seeing no other way of escaping the doom I so much dreaded, I made a headlong plunge. Pity me, and pardon me, O virtuous reader!" (*InL*, 55). What is consistently read as a concession to or internalization of true womanhood also can be read in this context as masked and mocking irony. "Doom's" antecedent is most pointedly not only the threat of sex, the ubiquitous trope of "doom" in a sentimental lexicon, but also the threat of sale.

As a disciplinary device, being sold surpassed almost all punishment, including physical "correction." Owners were advised to get women pregnant and men settled; bonds of affection made unmanageable chattel less likely to run. Following this logic, the pledge not to sell one's slaves was the next best thing to a promise of freedom; in some conservative anti-slavery rhetoric, owners—and the system itself—could be redeemed almost as fully by not selling and separating enslaved families as by freeing them, though abolitionist rhetoricians forcefully displayed how even the best-intentioned owners routinely broke such promises. Jacobs inverts the affective disciplinary dynamics so often manipulated by the planter class to domesticate those they enslaved. "I will never sell you," Flint bellows after Sands offers to buy her (*InL*, 60). Indeed, Dr. Flint refuses to sell Linda even as punishment: "I have no right to sell her," he avers to a slaveholder he rightly suspects has been commissioned by Linda's "friends." "I mistrust that you come from her paramour. If so, you may tell him that he cannot buy her for any money; neither can he buy her children" (*InL*, 80). By turning words most often figured in narratives as broken promises into an unreserved threat, Jacobs tactically outmaneuvers her own owner and victimizer; she nullifies the loss she most fears and preserves perhaps not her virtue—but her family.

Sexual Truth, Testimony, and Tyranny

Although Jacobs would have at least a segment of her reception community believe that her owner never "succeeded" in his ultimate assault, *Incidents* simultextually suggests that Norcom did rape his much-desired slave girl. Take the entire passage describing Linda's "plunge" as a paradigmatic example. The paragraph that introduces Sands concludes with these words: "A master may treat you as rudely as he pleases, and you *dare not speak*; moreover, the wrong does not seem so great with an unmarried man, as with one who has a wife to be made unhappy. There may be sophistry in all this; but the condition of a slave confuses all principles of morality, and, in fact, renders the practice of them impossible" (*InL*, 55, emphasis mine). The imperative to remain silent surfaces yet again. Though the immediate referent for the narrator's "sophistry" is her justification for Linda's relationship with Sands, there is reason to interpret her words in "all this" rudeness more broadly.

Throughout the text the question of Flint's "restraint" remains unresolved. Some important Jacobs critics suggest that the actual enslaved girl couldn't possibly have eluded her master.[36] One suggests that Jacobs's attempt to "authenticate herself" to an audience that valorizes middle-class mores and values rests on a "great factual lie, for it stretches the limits of all credulity that Linda Brent actually eluded her owner's sexual advances."[37] Why, critics ask, if Dr. Flint could treat Linda "as rudely as he please[d]," did he choose not to? Flint's language ranges from affectionate to authoritative, but his tactics do not explicitly shift from discursively sexual foul play to physically sexual force.[38] He whispers foul words, writes obscene notes, and then becomes a personal threat. Linda reflects: "My master, whose restless, craving, vicious nature roved about day and night, seeking whom to devour, had just left me, with stinging, scorching *words; words* that scathed ear and brain like fire. O, how I despised him! I thought how glad I should be, if some day when he walked the earth, it would open and swallow him up and disencumber the world of a plague" (*InL*, 18, emphasis mine). Despite the power of verbalized sexual pollution in the representational economy of both domestic fiction and anti-slavery rhetoric—and even accounting for the damage of such abuse in the life of a teenage girl—this passage displays an imbalance between Flint's actions and Linda's reactions; the passion in her language does not seem to have a direct correlation with what Flint "says." Rather it seems likely that abuse is both mediated through audience expectations and that the text transfers Linda's violated body to the body of the word. By both serving for and providing the trope for physical abuse, words act both to describe her violation and to absorb it.[39]

The narrative supports the supposition that the slave girl could very well have been pregnant with her master's child when she began her relationship with a neighboring bachelor.[40] Jacobs describes what are clearly her own circumstances—a kind mistress, a pious grandmother, a respectable and lov-ing Black suitor—again and again in the third person, insisting that there is no escape from the manifold devices men with power will use to have their way. "The slave girl is reared in an atmosphere of licentiousness and fear," she declares,

> the lash and the foul talk of her master and his sons are her teachers. When she is fourteen or fifteen, her owner, or his sons, or the overseer, or perhaps all of them, begin to bribe her with presents. If these fail to accomplish their purpose she is whipped or starved into submission to their will. She may have had religious principles inculcated by some pious mother or grandmother, or some good mistress; she may have a lover, whose good opinion and peace of mind are dear to her heart; or the profligate men who have power over her may be exceedingly odious to her. But resistance is hopeless. (*InL*, 51)

Incidents exposes the pedagogy of submission that the school of slavery teaches its daughters even in the face of pious mothers and good mistresses, teaching its audience the art of interpretation under these circumstances.

Unable to dodge the explicitly illicit message Jacobs narrates in the third person, her receptive audience is instructed to recognize the complex and conflicting signs of the same story when it is narrated in the first person. Ostensibly referring to the threat of an isolated cottage that Dr. Flint is build-ing for Linda's future concubinage, the narrator notes that

> the crisis of my fate now came so near that I was desperate. I shuddered to think of being the mother of children that should be owned by my old tyrant. I knew that as soon as a new fancy took him, his victims were sold far off to get rid of them; especially if they had children. I had seen several women sold with his babies at the breast. He never allowed his offspring by slaves to remain long in sight of himself and his wife. Of a man who was not my master I could ask to have my children well supported; and in this case, I felt confident I should obtain the boon and that they would be made free. (*InL*, 55)

As we have seen, some readers will interpret this to mean that Linda takes "the plunge" with Sands because of Flint's immanent sexual threat. Yet others may recall that Linda has eluded her owner shrewdly on every preceding occasion. The narrative offers several simultextual possibilities at this critical juncture. One is that the analogy of other victims may fully obtain, and that Linda's crisis could well be read as an impending pregnancy. The statement—"I shuddered to think of being the mother of children that should be owned by my old tyrant," a concern she expresses earlier when she wants to be with her free Black suitor—differs importantly from what follows: "I knew that as soon as a new fancy took him his victims were sold" (*InL*, 55). The first is solely a legal issue that emphasizes Flint's property rights; the second, with its inclusive victimization, implies paternity and sexual possession as well. It is this latter scenario that Jacobs's grandmother and Mrs. Flint are all too ready to believe.

To diffuse "the crisis of [her] fate" as best she can, the narrator complicates paternity and names Sands as her children's father. Hazel Carby suggests that "from [Linda's] experience she knew that Dr. Flint sold his offspring from slave women and hoped that if her children were fathered by Sands he could buy them and secure their future."[41] Carby's language reflects the multiple possibilities embedded in Jacobs's own; if Flint sold "*his* offspring from slave women" and Linda's "children were fathered by Sands," then Jacobs presents no reason for Flint to sell them.[42] Indeed, both the narrator's and her latter-day critic's language imply what neither of them say explicitly: for this mother's strategy to work, Sands's role as father must be contested. Understanding this, Jacobs counters the sexual and familial instability and powerlessness that characterizes paternity (and representations of such issues) under slavery; in *Incidents*, an enslaved woman names the father of her children and makes that naming important indeed.

Incidents articulates the multiple codes of silence and self-preservation demanded of Black women both North and South. In the first few moments after her arrival, she confides in her first host, a Black minister she "would not deceive" (*InL*, 160); he responds by warning: "Don't answer everybody so openly. It might give some heartless people a pretext for treating you with contempt" (*InL*, 160). His words "made an indelible impression upon me" (*InL*, 161), an impression arguably transferred indelibly onto *Incidents*. Jacobs's own letters to Amy Post express her perception that Southern *de facto* laws of silence rule Northern dictums of disclosure. She writes, "I had determined to let others think as they pleased but my lips should be sealed and no one had a right to question me for this reason when I first came North I avoided the Antislavery people as much as possible because I felt that I could not be honest and tell the whole truth."[43] Those the minister calls "some heartless people," as Jacobs applies his admonition, are an expansive group. As Linda had learned in the South, those who can be trusted aren't easily emotionally and politically classifiable. Linda had been initiated into a slave's understanding of power's relation to trust upon the death of what Lydia Maria Child calls Linda's "kind, considerate friend." This friend, the mistress who teaches her to read and write, then willed Linda to her niece and so, effectively, to Dr. Flint.

Resisting the simple (sentimental) dichotomies of good and bad, Jacobs separates bodily threat, the fear of actual repossession, from the politics of trust and speech. She relocates the relationship of truth to silence to the realm of Northern power relations invoked by the stinging word "contempt." William Andrews's commentary on James Pennington transfers easily: "As a black autobiographer among suspicious whites, [Jacobs] was not morally obliged to deal truthfully with [her] audience if that meant putting [herself] in jeopardy. On such autobiographical occasions self-interest takes priority over truth by claiming it, appropriating it, to its own needs. In an ultimate sense . . . one could lie and still be true—to oneself. Under such conditions willed autobiographical concealments and/or deceptions might be the truest form of self-expression."[44] Jacobs replots received relations between slave truth and freedom. While in the South an enslaved woman's lips and tongue were muzzled; now North, she seals her lips, the double entendre only too evident, by her own accord.[45] However, this is no imitative adaptation of Northern Victorian mores, discursive or sexual.

By denying others free rein to question her, Jacobs empowers herself on her own terms. She envisions discursive property rights—the license and comfort that make it possible "to be free to *say* so" (*InL*, 174)—as Pennington does, by appropriating them into her own protective economy. Thus she dismisses the legal (and extralegal) economies that bind her and her children to interpretations that grant their bodies to the Master and the master text: "I could not possibly regard myself as a piece of property," she writes. "I knew the law would decide that I was his property, and would probably give his daughter a claim to my children; but I regarded such laws as the regulations of robbers, who had no rights that I was bound to respect" (*InL*, 187). If, as legal theorist Patricia Williams argues, slavery is a structure that denies Black generative independence, then what Jacobs affirms, in her ironic rhetorical overturning of *Dred Scott* and in her strong claims to nondisclosure, is the generative independence in a discursive realm that is denied her by slavery in a biological one.[46]

Jacobs's symbolic relation to her narrator's trajectory of multivalent address stands in opposition to the seemingly transparent regained candor of most male narrators. As Andrews argues, confessing to morally compromising behavior in slavery "is a traditional rhetorical strategy of antebellum Black autobiography." He suggests that "each [author] takes steps to preserve his bond with the reader by repudiating that behavior and requesting the reader's sympathy for the slave in his tragic moral dilemma. Still, he seems to savor the sufficiency of his invention, performance and manipulation."[47] Although Jacobs disavows the sexual past of slavery, she "clearly delights" in the letter-writing maneuvers enacted from her grandmother's garret, and she does so without ever disowning these activities.[48] Though Andrews's analysis does apply to Jacobs, male authors distance themselves from their trickster past by insisting that it is the circumstances of slavery that engendered their behavior; their geographical and behavioral change is often symbolized by a change in name itself.[49] That the audience knows their new names—William Wells Brown, Frederick Douglass—signifies that they can gauge Black narrators' "interior subjectivity unmediated by the distance of manipulative representation": "My character, yes, was forced to be duplicitous; but me, your narrator, transformed by freedom, you can trust," they seem to say; "now that I own myself, my name, I share them freely with you."[50] Whereas the men transform from trickster to true-name-trusted author, the narrator of *Incidents* rejects the implied transformation and textual transparency promised in the narrative resolution by the slave narrative paradigm: she becomes the fictive character, Linda Brent.[51]

Flint, Sands, and Willis: South to North, Daddies to Dandies

By collapsing the rhetorical opposition between North and South, Jacobs further complicates her narrator's status as "truthsayer."[52] She envisions her Northern situation as analogous to her life in the South, a geographical co-ordinate on a racist vector that denies any radical rupture. Indeed, *Incidents* rarely indulges—or lets readers be indulged—in a vision of the North without exposing Northern hypocrisy. Her icy description of her first sunrise "on free soil, for such I *then* believed it to be" (*InL*, 158), crystallizes her sustained condemnation. Nor is this a critique of the North as a geographical concept, as if it were not peopled with actors who are actively complicit in doing the dirty work of slavery's interests. Yankees, she writes, "consent to do the violent work for [Southern 'gentlemen'] such as ferocious bloodhounds and the despised negro-hunters are employed to do at home" (*InL*, 44). Comparing Yankees to dogs and poor white trash, her stinging rebukes are hard to ignore.

The Northern space where Jacobs composes the manuscript that will become *Incidents* recalls her Southern confinement in her grandmother's garret.

She writes in both places secretly and does not allow her new mistress, Cornelia Willis, the "beloved" second Mrs. Bruce, entry to her private—soon to be public—world. "Mrs. Willis don't even know from my lips that I am writing a book . . . Let no one see it" (*InL*, 237–38), she comments as she sends a transcript to her friend Amy Post, whose name, in biting contrast to the Willises', appears unchanged in the narrative. Indeed, the description of her physical space at the Willises' echoes her Southern "loophole of retreat": "I must stop for I am in the only spot where I can have a light—and the mosquitoes have taken possession of me" (*InL*, 243), she writes to Post as if she were in Edenton near her gimlet-made garret light "tormented by hundreds of little red insects, fine as needle's point that pierced through my skin" (*InL*, 115).

Jacobs finds herself working in the eighteen-room manor of Nathaniel Parker Willis, a famous newspaper editor less concerned with social welfare than with social status. Willis's biographer describes the manner in which the family lived: "From early spring till after Christmas the family at Idlewild kept open house, almost always having company staying with them. . . . The place had become celebrated through Willis's descriptions of it in 'Home Journal.'" The editor's habit, his biographer notes, was "to breakfast in his own room and write till noon. Sometimes he would take a stroll . . . before dinner. After dinner he would write letters or do scissors work before the afternoon ride. The evening was spent with his guests, or, if the family were alone, he would write again and come down to a nine o'clock dinner."[53] Contrast this with Jacobs's 1854 description of Idlewild. "My friends . . . were here . . . and saw from my daily duties that it was hard for me to find much time to write as yet I have not written a single page by daylight" (*InL*, 237–38).[54] When Jacobs asks Post to mention in her letter to accompany *Incidents* that "I lived at service all the while that I was striving to get the Book out. . . . [as] I would [not] like to have people think that I was living an *Idle* life—and had got this book out merely to make money" (*InL*, 242, emphasis mine), her characteristic irony communicates her analysis of who, actually, is out to merely make money while laying bare who is most likely to be suspected of trying to profit from their literary production. Capitalizing "Idle" and so linking her life "at service" to Nathaniel Parker Willis's idle and indulgent time at Idlewild, Jacobs underscores the racial, class and gender privileges at work as she labors to write and publish her own book.

By writing secretly, Jacobs matches her cunning against a new but familiar type: in Willis, the licentious Southern plantation owner is replaced by the Northern confidence man, a "modern industrial version of the trickster."[55] As historian Karen Halttunen explains it, the mid-century confidence man was a person of few values, conscious of his less-than-qualifying social beginnings, who dupes society by his attire, charm, and newly made money to marry into status and leisure. In his day, Willis was often criticized for his dandyism in dress; he attempted to "exemplify himself as the epitome of the fashionable gentleman."[56] While he wrote in the best of style and situations, other authors in his life—his sister Sara Payson Willis Parton (or "Fanny Fern") and nurse Harriet Jacobs—published under pseudonyms and didn't share his fortuitous circumstances. Indeed, in *Ruth Hall* (1854), his sister suggests that he marries Cornelia Grinnell, niece and adopted daughter of the wealthy Honorable Joseph Grinnell, for money. Indeed, it was with her inheritance that they built Idlewild on the Hudson.[57] His first wife, Mary Stace Willis of England, was also well off; her father provided his daughter and son-in-law with £300 per annum—about half of their yearly income.

Willis supported a select group of women journalists, but could not be trusted by those too close to home. Like his sister, Jacobs received no encouragement from Willis. He "is too proslavery," she confides to Amy Post; "he would tell me that it was very wrong [to write a book] and that I was trying to do harm or perhaps he was sorry for me to undertake it while I was in his family" (*InL*, 232). Jacobs keeps her job by playing her own trickster—the faithful servant—and plays her role well enough to convince Willis's most thorough biographer that her "attachment to the interests of the family during the whole period of her service was a beautiful instance of the fidelity and affection which sometimes, but not often, distinguish the relation of master and servant."[58] Jacobs had little confidence in the man; though her "master" and Mrs. Willis, unsolicited, secured her official freedom, she composed her narrative and published articles in numerous journals without their knowledge or help.

Incidents' closing passage disrupts the Northern economy of genteel servitude invoked by both Willis's biographer's and Jacobs's own sentimental language: "I still long for a hearthstone of my own, however humble. I wish it for my children's sake far more than for my own. But God so orders circumstances as to keep me with my friend Mrs. Bruce. Love, duty, gratitude, also bind me to her side. It is a privilege to serve her who pities my oppressed people, and who has bestowed the inestimable boon of freedom on me and my children" (*InL*, 201). This passage cloaks domestic desire with the justification of motherhood that is then quickly reduced to the "privileges" of service. Yet the language almost seethes, as the careful usage of "bind me to her side" recalls Luke's being "chained to the bedside" of his abusive owner. Linda's barely checked anger at being "*sold* at last" (*InL*, 200) to the Bruces also serves as a referent that disrupts a closing passage dripping not only with sentimentality but also with an irony that challenges the feminine "fidelity and affection" that characterizes a woman's place within domestic fiction. Jacobs's simultextually appreciative and angry prose both expresses and challenges the costs of a system in which parties suppress the "indelicate" issue, as it were, of division of labor and property exchange.[59]

Aunt Martha's Mask

Valerie Smith contends that from her garret Brent is a voyeur "who sees but remains herself unseen."[60] Just as Linda "remains unseen," so Jacobs shields her grandmother Molly Horniblow, protecting her, in turn, from the sexual unveilings to which her protagonist is discursively subjected. Karen Sánchez-Eppler notes, "The peephole [Brent] bore in the wall of her grandmother's attic does not provide her with a view of the house's interior, (she cannot watch her grandmother care for her children; instead she watches the street)."[61] What the latter observation suggests is Jacobs's glaring emphasis on her grandmother's exteriority. By casting her gaze outside, Jacobs refuses to compromise the integrity of her grandmother's home; consequently, the older woman's privacy—and private life as well—remains intact.

Protecting Aunt Martha's own sexual and private life limits the reach of readers' prurient interests and also acts to counterbalance Linda's own sexualized representation. Pious and domestic, Aunt Martha counsels contentment, submissiveness, and purity; she is, indeed, the only sustained Southern representative of true womanhood in *Incidents*.[62] As Hazel Carby has noted, the grandmother possesses the tenets of true womanhood to an almost formulaic degree. Even if, as Carby contends, in her feistier moments she lacks submissiveness, she consistently counsels it, insisting that her granddaughter should not run away.[63] Early on Linda reflects, "Most earnestly did she strive to make us feel that it was the will of God: that He had seen fit to place us under such circumstances; and though it seemed hard, we ought to pray for contentment. It was a beautiful faith, coming from a mother who could not call her children her own. But I, and Benjamin, her youngest, condemned it" (*InL*, 17). The indicators of the narrator's approval ("most earnestly," "beautiful") only strengthen the passage's tension: its polyvalent pull highlights its parodic bitterness and the ultimate rejection of the grandmother's piety expressed by the passage's end. *Incidents* calls into question the tenets of motherhood—domestic contentment and submission to God's will—by illustrating the limited maternal power true womanhood ostensibly brings to Black women under slavery. By expressing the link between mother and child through the trope of "one's own" in the line "it was a beautiful faith, coming from a mother who could not call her children her own," *Incidents* appeals to bourgeois sentiment. Jacobs shares with her Northern women readers the tenuous legal claim to their offspring; ultimately, neither free nor enslaved antebellum mothers enjoyed rights of "ownership" when it came to their offspring.

This condemnation of passive and submissive motherhood also challenges the grandmother's symbolic status as its defender. When asked to weigh Linda's desire for freedom against maternal obligation, Aunt Martha insists that the latter admits no mitigating circumstances; she denies even temporary abeyance of Linda's responsibilities for her family's later good. When Linda expresses her serious intent to run, her grandmother advises her instead to "stand by your own children, and suffer with them till death. Nobody respects a mother who forsakes her children; and if you leave them, you will never have a happy moment. If you go, you will make me miserable the short time I have to live. . . . Try to bear a little longer."[64] Aunt Martha locates Linda in sole relation to motherhood: as both good mother and good "daughter." According to her, Linda's responsibilities cancel out any personal interest in her own freedom and agency. Aunt Martha's totalizing position anticipates the logic of those who support contemporary concepts of motherhood that insist on its primacy above and beyond the "health of the mother." The very person who nurtures and protects her counsels Linda that the rights to her body again should be subsumed, this time by motherhood's overriding interests.

Aunt Martha is practically reified as Protector of True Womanhood in the climactic passage of revelation. Pregnant, Linda reflects, "I secretly mourned over the sorrow I was bringing on my grandmother, who had so tried to shield me from harm. I knew . . . that it was a source of pride to her that I had not degraded myself, like most of the slaves. I wanted to confess to her that I was no longer worthy of her love; but I could not utter the dreaded words" (*InL*, 56). The tensions between Aunt Martha's acknowledgment of her granddaughter's abuse expressed in "shield from harm," and the projected participation and blame contained in "degraded myself like most of the slaves," echo loudly in this passage, if only because "most of the [harassed female] slaves" are presented as unwilling victims throughout the rest of the narrative. The tension escalates shortly thereafter:

> I went to my grandmother. My lips moved to make confession, but the words stuck in my throat. . . . I think she saw something unusual was the matter with me. The mother of slaves is very watchful. She knows that there is no security for her children. After they have entered their teens she lives in daily expectation of trouble. . . . Presently, in came my mistress, like a mad woman, and accused me concerning her husband. My grandmother, whose suspicions had been previously awakened, believed what she said. She exclaimed, "O Linda!

has it come to this? I had rather see you dead than to see you as you now are. You are a disgrace to your dead mother." She tore from my fingers my mother's wedding ring and her silver thimble. "Go away!" she exclaimed, "and never come to my house, again." Her reproaches fell so hot and heavy, that they left me no chance to answer. (*InL*, 56–57)

These aborted voicings ("the words stuck in my throat" and "they left me no chance to answer") leave intact the narrative possibility that Linda is pregnant with Dr. Flint's child. In another instance of narrative plentitude, her silence also allows to stand Aunt Martha's interpretation of "what she [Mrs. Flint] said," accusations of Linda and Dr. Flint's supposed affair that we can only deduce. Mrs. Flint's words, pointedly, are not reproduced. In this passage, which contains what must be one of the most dismaying *non sequiturs* in the slave narrative genre, Aunt Martha's concern, fear, and protection—all of which presuppose her understanding of abusive sexual and power relations under slavery—transmogrifies into her condemnation and blame. Her new position suppresses that which previously has informed almost all of her actions.

Fully transformed into the defending and deafening trope of true womanhood, Aunt Martha is the relegator of its most recognizable signs. She divests Linda of the loud symbols of domestic feminism's construction, a mother's wedding ring and silver thimble. Aunt Martha's home has previously provided safety in contradistinction to the relative lack of protection and privacy that characterizes homespaces in slavery. Using Mrs. Flint's words, however, Aunt Martha erects walls that turn a zone of safety into an exclusively bourgeois space, "my house," whose inhabitants embrace and protect the purity and domesticity that are, according to *Incidents,* almost impossible to realize under slavery.[65]

In some sense Aunt Martha, her daughter, and Linda are aspects of a gestalt self, with Aunt Martha standing as the covering unit—what Houston Baker might call the "phaneric mask."[66] Carroll Smith-Rosenberg notes that gender roles and the "biological realities of frequent pregnancies, childbirth and nursing" in part accounted for "the roles of daughter and mother [that] shaded imperceptibly and ineluctably into each other."[67] Indeed, the politics of flexible identities that Jacobs offers, symbolized by porous generational parameters between her mother and grandmother, are further blurred in the presentation of *Incidents'* most definitive edition. The large framing portrait found on both the spine and frontispiece of Yellin's widely circulated paperback reveals a white-haired, light-skinned woman seated in an elaborately carved wooden chair. Her body seems to be protected by a dark wrap tied over her shoulders and breasts, by the sturdy chair arm, and by her hands crossed demurely in her ample lap. She looks directly at her readers; she has, her direct gaze tells us, nothing to hide. In the slave narrative this image introduces, the photograph does not only represent "Harriet Jacobs, 1894" as the illustration page declares, it also conjures a more transparent correlation with the comforting and comfortably situated older woman whose presence dominates the narrative, Aunt Martha.

The seeming replacement of Harriet Jacobs by her grandmother supplants the ubiquitous "runaway woman" antebellum woodcut used for the cover of the previous 1973 edition. Indeed, the woodcut "enjoyed a remarkable longevity," remaining standardized "over two continents and two centuries."[68] Iconographically represented by the young Black woman of the engraving—

Figure 1.1.
Harriet Jacobs, 1894.
By permission.

hair shorn, eyes averted, satchel in hand, Linda belongs to a symbolic system where she stands for every runaway "slave girl."[69] There is little tension between the young woman and the Linda of *Incidents*' title page. The
frontispiece in Yellin's meticulously researched edition was the only extant
photo that had been recovered at that time, yet it inadvertently follows Lydia
Maria Child's framing lead by balancing Child's editorial decision to close
with "tender memories of my good old grandmother" (*InL*, 201) instead of
ending with John Brown, as Jacobs wished.[70] Rather than bolstering Jacobs's
collective sensibilities, the photograph places Jacobs in a semiotic system in
which readers see a symbolic Aunt Martha and gentle, genteel womanhood
as the opening image of *Incidents in the Life of a Slave Girl*.

Characteristically, Jacobs's text itself continually disrupts the strategic substitution she offers to resistant readers perhaps concerned at least as much
with their own delicacy as with enslaved women's degradation. Although Aunt
Martha is the embodiment of courageous and respectable motherhood, her
maternity can't be separated from the sexualized moment of her children's
conception. On one level, Aunt Martha's role is angelic nurturer, the mother
forced to wean her daughter (Jacobs's mother) in order to nurse her mistress's
(Mrs. Flint), holding no grudge. Her bodily labor enables the simultextual
labor she performs. Her ability to nurse springs from her own childbearing,
though her children are not the beneficiaries. In a heated volley between Flint
and Aunt Martha, "almost choking with grief," she cries out, "'It was not I
that drove Linda away. My grandchildren are gone; and of my nine children
only one is left. God help me!'" (*InL*, 145). This appeal to the sentiment of
motherhood poses obvious questions. How, after all, were all these children
begotten? What indelicate questions might attentive readers ask here?

Had the grandmother figure in *Incidents* suffered through similar sexual
threats or, like Jacobs, experienced a complicated sexual history, it would
significantly destabilize the climactic passage of revelation and its glaring
signifiers. Molly Horniblow bears children, like most nineteenth-century
women, for more than fifteen years, and so her own mothering overlaps with
her daughter's.[71] Indeed, between Benjamin, Aunt Martha's youngest son, and
Linda "there was so little difference in our ages that he seemed more like my
brother than my uncle." "He was a bright, handsome lad, nearly white" (*InL*,
6), whose "white face [later] did him a kindly service"; slave catchers "had
no suspicion that it belonged to a slave" (*InL*, 24). The narrator suggests that
Benjamin inherited the complexion of his grandmother's white father. Yet
in *Incidents*, the absence of Benjamin's own father, whom Linda, so close to
her uncle's age, might have known, raises nagging questions. Property lists
name Horniblow's children but not their fathers[72]—a sign that whites may

have sired them. Indeed, Jean Fagan Yellin's research unearthed the men who might have fathered the two beloved uncles featured prominently in *Incidents*. Uncle Mark Ramsey, known by a different last name than his mother, siblings, and owners, was probably the son of Alan Ramsay, a white widower and merchant.[73] Yellin suggests that a free Black Edenton native might have claimed Joseph as his child.[74] Yet, if Molly Horniblow had a free Black partner, why weren't they married? If her mistress prevented the union, why not present this in some form in *Incidents*? And, if Joseph's father was a free Black man, whose own *father*, not mother, had been emancipated, then how do we account for the diminished possibility that he inherited his "white face"—one he used to pass both in his escape and, as far as the family knew, permanently into the white race—from his two (mixed-race) Black parents?

Aunt Martha's road to freedom is similarly complex in its narration. Despite the historical mistress's wish that Molly Horniblow be left free, the mistress's brother-in-law, Dr. Norcom/Flint, puts her up for sale. The community was so outraged that "no one bid for her. At last, a feeble voice said, 'Fifty dollars.' It came from a maiden lady, seventy years old, the sister of my grandmother's deceased mistress. . . . She knew how faithfully she had served her owners, and how cruelly she had been defrauded of her rights; and she resolved to protect her. . . . She gave the old servant her freedom" (*InL*, 11–12).

Not included in the narrative is the fact that Hannah Pritchard, the maiden lady who possessed no property of her own and, according to Jacobs, had lived in her sister's household for forty years, also purchased Molly Horniblow's son Mark for $406—not a paltry sum.[75] Nor is the role of Congressman Alfred Moore Gatlin mentioned, though in John Jacobs's narrative "A True Tale of Slavery," published serially in London within a month of *Incidents'* U.S. debut, the author's brother credits him with purchasing both their grandmother and uncle with money Molly Horniblow had entrusted to him.[76] Nor does *Incidents* include that Molly moves into Gatlin's seven-room house after her emancipation. Valued at $364.50 when he bought it, he sold the house to her three years later "for many good Causes and reasons and also in Consideration of one Dollar."[77] It would be conjecture to suggest that Molly Horniblow's relationship with Gatlin was sexual—he was thirty-one years old at the time, nineteen years her junior. Yet, despite meticulous research, their connection has yet to be explained.[78] No matter their relationship, the omission in *Incidents* signals that his presence—like her children's fathers—would significantly undermine her construction as untainted True Woman, a construction Aunt Martha's friend and the *maiden lady*'s role only helps to affirm.

Aunt Martha is a mélange, a complex character construct that simultaneously embodies, reinvents, and condemns aspects of true womanhood. By offering Aunt Martha both in Linda's stead and as an alter ego she rejects, *Incidents* presents violent back regions that only the most dedicated genteel readers would fail to note; she delicately transplants true womanhood—hers, her grandmother's, enslaved women's—in radically different dark soil.

* * *

What marks this text, I would maintain, is not the central question "Is Linda, or until when is Linda, pure?" Rather, it is how ingeniously *Incidents* challenges the supposed transparency of sentimental fiction and also appeals to and critiques its multiple readerships. Ultimately, this text's overlaid voicings illustrate and complicate Sidonie Smith's contention that a woman narrator "may even create several, sometimes competing stories about versions of herself as her subjectivity is displaced by one or multiple representations."[79] Like the other writings I examine in *Activist Sentiments, Incidents* is characterized by a narrative plentitude that reaches various audiences. Thus, although I contend that reconsidering Jacobs's simultextual representation calls for supplementing the conventional understanding of her plot to add that Norcom might well have "succeeded," in no way do I wish to be understood to ascribe to a binary characterization that she is either telling the truth, the whole truth—or that she is lying; this would beg all the questions I mean to raise here. My work does not attempt to substitute one reading (Linda's escape from Flint's sexual intentions) with another (that Flint really raped her); I resist accepting, or offering, any critical exegesis as a definitive one. Instead, I mean to call into question the politics of transparency that often have led critics to accept the narrative's principal script—Linda's sexual "triumph"— and that act to smooth away and quiet down the very tumultuous speech to which her contemporary readers might well give ear.

2. Naming *Our Nig*'s Multivalent Mothers

Liberty is our motto, Liberty is our motto,
Equal liberty is our motto, In the "Old Granite State."
We despise Oppression, We despise Oppression,
We despise Oppression, And we cannot be enslaved.
—"The Old Granite State," The Hutchinson Family Singers

I do not pretend to divulge every transaction of my own life, which
the unprejudiced would declare unfavorable in comparison with
treatment of legal bondsman; I have purposely omitted what would
most provoke shame in our good anti-slavery friends at home.
—Harriet Wilson, Preface, *Our Nig*

There is no one to want me to say me my name.
—Toni Morrison, *Beloved*

In his masterpiece *Hopscotch*, Julio Cortázar offers his readers a "table of instructions" that allows them to choose alternate paths through the novel, paths that will give them completely different narrative experiences; they can either read conventionally from the beginning through chapter 56, or they can follow the author's alternate instructions and hopscotch their way through the text, jumping from chapter 73 back to 1 and from chapter 2 forward to 116. "In its own way," he says, "this book consists of many books, but two books above all."[1]

Our Nig also points readers to the availability of its "many books" by reassembling racialized associations to produce multiple contested racial meanings. In the book's interpretive worlds, power, race, desire, and morality are continuously reassigned meanings and agents of production. As the previous chapter displays, *Incidents*' hyper-moral and sanitized Aunt Martha is additionally the raped or compromised mother of five.[2] Likewise, in *Our Nig*, the seemingly sympathetic white Aunt Abby, for example, figures as an ally; her moniker "Nab" and her physical displacement from the actual and metaphorical parlor make her "Nig's" syllabic and symbolic kin. The economics of family title, however, simultaneously reveal Aunt Abby to be invested in property interests—her own—that underwrite her place as protector of family holdings in which "Nig" still figures as potential and actual fugitive chattel. My readings of the homonymically linked Mag, "Nab," and "Nig" trouble the women's nominally unitary and transparent roles and complicate Mag's characterization as fallen woman/mother, "Nab's" narrative function as good aunt and ally, and "Nig's" role as resurrected mother/author.

Our Nig levels a racial and regional critique of white domesticity while it also challenges and complicates not only white—but also Black—maternity. In the recognizably fictional seduction tale that opens the book, I contend that Black sexual vulnerability is expressed through a simultaneously raced Mag, who is conventionally understood to be Frado's white mother. The first chapter forestalls racial fixity by staging "our Nig's" mother as both "white" and light (and so legally "Black") thereby challenging interpellated racial, class, and familial identifications encoded both in the law and in the foundational narrative strategies of domestic fiction. In conventional mulatta tales and domestic fiction, the narrator is the reader's guide and is often privy to "true" racial classifications before the heroine is. Our Nig overturns these generic conventions and so transfers the trauma of revelation from the protagonist to its dominant readers, disrupting the power and narrative position symbolic of their stable class and racial status. Finally, I attempt to explain why Mag's always already whiteness has been assumed to be fixed and static by limning the importance of the novel's two functional beginnings— the transparently fictionalized opening chapter about Mag, followed by the protagonist-narrator's story as the abandoned child of a white mother and consumptive Black father. Exploring these two beginnings (and emphasizing a proleptic approach rather than a teleological one) further exposes the simultextual disruptions to sentimental resolution that Our Nig provides.

Harriet Wilson joins Harriet Jacobs and Frederick Douglass in subtle but searing reappropriations of power by withholding names and by commenting on the politics of such withholding. Our Nig's "she-devil," Mrs. Bellmont, is directly based on Rebecca S. Hutchinson Hayward of Milford, New Hampshire, where the novel is set and where Wilson grew up. Rebecca Hutchinson's grandparents were town founders; she "hailed from one of the most distinguished families in Milford" and was a second cousin of the famous abolitionist Hutchinson Family Singers, who continued to be based in Milford.[3] They lived in a two-story white house and sprawling homestead where anti-slavery friends and reform-minded visitors were always welcome. The Hayward and Hutchinson families were more directly intertwined than their attenuated lineage suggests. David, the eldest son of the Hutchinson family, married the "Bellmont"/Hayward's eldest child Betsy, and Charles, one of the two sons Wilson collapses into the character "Jack," went off to Illinois with Hutchinson brother Zephaniah before he moved to Baltimore.[4] There the families also remained linked through business associations and Milford visitors. Despite members' peregrinations, Milford remained the central hub for both families throughout the height of the singers' national and international success, years that correspond almost exactly with Harriet's adolescence and young adulthood.[5]

During Harriet's teenage years, Milford was "alive with traffic . . . with radical ideas."[6] Only five miles from the Massachusetts border and fifty miles from Boston itself, it was an abolitionist stronghold, one of three cities in early 1840s New Hampshire to have a subscription agent for the *Liberator* and a station on the underground railroad.[7] At the outer edges of a famous reform family, Nehemiah Hayward and Rebecca Hutchinson, the "Bellmonts," could not escape a climate of activist engagement. They were married, for example, by Rev. Humphrey Moore, also a cousin by marriage, who was elected to the New Hampshire House of Representatives and Senate in the early 1840s where he "gave stirring orations against slavery."[8] Indeed, according to Milford's town history, in no place "in New Hampshire were the seeds of opposition to the institution of African slavery earlier planted."[9] Its largest event was a massive abolitionist rally held when Harriet was in her teens. In January 1843, the radical reformer Stephen S. Foster, the famous fugitive George Latimer and his eloquent peer, George Johnson, the venerable Parker Pillsbury, and New Hampshire anti-slavery leader Nathaniel P. Rogers, all heeded local residents' call to gather in Milford to act for "three millions of our kindred [who] lie bleeding at our feet with uplifted and imploring hands entreating for help."[10] Central to the gathering, the Hutchinson Family Singers subsequently became friends or acquaintances with the major figures in the movement, and were especially close with young fugitives such as Latimer and Douglass. Later, Douglass would sing their praises, writing to John Hutchinson, "I especially have reason to feel grateful interest in the whole Hutchinson Family—for you have sung the yokes from the necks and the fetters from the limbs of my race."[11]

Our Nig reworks the Adam and Eve story through its maternal line and, in doing so, appropriates the power of naming first presented in that genesis. Readers are first introduced not to the famous Hutchinson ancestors but to the Hayward or "Bellmont" progenitors, an idealized family who inhabited a "large, old fashioned, two-story white house, environed by fruitful acres, and embellished by shrubbery and shade trees"; this Edenic scene is the physical space in which *Our Nig* unfolds—and it is soon polluted.[12] Though "years ago a youthful couple consecrated it as home," Wilson writes, upon their "last repose" "the old homestead . . . passed into the hands of a son, to whose wife Mag had applied the epithet 'she devil'"(*ON,* 13–14). Katherine Clay Bassard aptly notes that "we are introduced to the present Bellmonts obliquely through patriarchal generation" and that "John the son" is "named only after the narrator recalls the naming of his wife, the 'she-devil.'"[13] While some critics emphasize the centrality of patriarchal ownership in antebellum narrative, I underscore Mrs. B.'s fall from grace and the ways in which the book suggests that her extended family, or "anti-slavery friends at home," slumbered when it came to the woes and wrongs of its own local kindred.[14]

In *Our Nig,* (mis)naming exhibits a sharp irony that unveils the dynamics of servitude, gender, and race in the North; it is also employed to discursively demolish the text's principal antagonist, Mrs. Bellmont. Throughout *Our Nig,* the character based on Rebecca Hutchinson Hayward appears either as the truncated "Mrs. B." or as the "she-devil" over and again. Unlike any other important character, Mrs. Bellmont is given no first name. Recalling the hated epithet Mrs. B. uses in renaming young Frado "our Nig," Wilson assigns the "she-devil" names that limit the expression of the white woman's humanity. In other words, the narrator switches the script by substituting Mrs. Bellmont's name with one of the haughty abuser's own "Nig's" making.

Through the constant use of the names of "Mr. and Mrs. B.," *Our Nig* recalls another servant protagonist, Pamela, who is trapped as a prisoner against her will by the most famous literary Mr. B., who "uses and abuses his power as a man, as an employer, and as a member of the governing class" with the help of his she-devil accomplice, Mrs. Jewkes.[15] Verse by British poets and satirists Percy Shelley, Lord Byron, Thomas Moore, and Martin Tupper serves as framing epigraphs for many of *Our Nig's* chapters. Though Wilson does not quote *Pamela* (1740–1801) directly, its intertextual shadows claim authority for *Our Nig* as Wilson's text also challenges the ways in which *Pamela* contains its own class and gender-based critiques.[16] Yet, unlike other heroines of British and U.S. domestic fiction, no one in *Our Nig* enjoys a prison-to-palace transformation.[17]

Mag and her daughter "Nig's" doubled, if truncated, kinship to Pamela is communicated first through Mag's story of seduction and then through "Nig's" experience as a servant girl trapped in the B.s' home. If young Pamela avoids her employer's sexual snares, she does so because her parents are forcefully fearful for her virtue, warning her to "stand upon your guard" against the temptations of trading "that jewel, her virtue," for the empty promises of an employer who "has so much *power* to oblige, and has a kind of *authority* to command as your master."[18] Though the book is initially structured as an epistolary exchange between a daughter and her parents, it soon becomes clear that the principal item of exchange is Pamela's virtue. Her parents' voices fade after their fortissimo admonitions reverberate through the opening chapters. While Mag merges into womanhood "early deprived of parental guardianship" and "unprotected, uncherished, uncared for," Pamela's parents' clanging alarm crowds out other "whisperings," misleading murmurs of "an elevation before uninspired to: of ease and plenty her simple heart had never dreamed of as hers" or offers of support cloaked in formal, though nonactionable, terms.[19] Mag, like Pamela, "knew that the voice of her charmer, so ravishing, sounded far above her," but without the parental guardianship Pamela's mother and father so loudly articulate, she "surrendered to him a priceless gem" (*ON*, 5). Thematically, then, Mag's story explicitly converges with (and then diverges from) Pamela's, while *Our Nig's* homonymics suggest a linkage between the two servant girls and their struggles against Mr.—and Mrs.—B.

Moving beyond an ironic reversal of romantic plots in which virtue is far from rewarded, *Our Nig's* use of *Pamela* deftly widens traditional gendered categories and repertoires of abuse. Mrs. B. is unsexed by her own violent language and physical violence, but also by *Our Nig's* intertextual links to *Pamela's* Mr. B. and Mrs. Jewkes. *Our Nig's* Mrs. B. recalls *Pamela's* Mr. B.; his attempt to "ruin" his servant girl overlays Mrs. B.'s attempt to ruin her own. Mrs. B. is Frado's undoer. Yet, *Our Nig* challenges the definition of priceless gems and jewels and a class-transcendent, racially determined teleology of marriage. Patriarchal categorizations associated with marital power, the transfer of ownership from servant to wife in *Pamela,* hold no transformative power for Mag or Frado. Instead *Our Nig* values the ability to govern one's own labor, body, and bodily production.

Examining *Pamela's* Ur-textual presence in the context of Wilson's naming practices illuminates how *Our Nig's* homonymics work to desex and unclass Mrs. B. During the bulk of Pamela's imprisonment at Mr. B.'s Lincolnshire estate, Mrs. Jewkes, a servant herself, functions as the agent of a patriarchal upper-class discipline meant to induce Pamela's forced "consent" to her own sexual compromise. Jewkes deprives her young ward of company and church, subjecting her to tirades and beatings. In declaring "I see you have spirit; you must and shall be kept under. . . . I'll lock you up, and you shall have no shoes, nor any kindness from me, I assure you," Mrs. Jewkes directly anticipates Mrs. B.[20] Both are "self-willed, haughty, undisciplined, arbitrary and severe" (*ON*, 15).

Mrs. Jewkes's role in an explicit attempted rape scene emphasizes her contorted sexual regulation and responsibility. Forced to sleep with Jewkes, the "procuress" literally holds the girl down as the disguised cross-dressing Mr. B. climbs into bed. Jewkes urges him to follow through on his plan to rape the unsuspecting teenager. "Don't stand dilly-dallying, sir," she "will be quieter when she knows the worst," Jewkes exclaims. After the girl passes out, Jewkes eggs him on: "Will you, sir, for a fit or two, give up such an opportunity as this? I thought you had known the sex better," she puns. Like Mrs. Flint in *Incidents,* Jewkes represents an equal, though not penetrative, sexual threat. "Take with you this most wicked woman, this vile Mrs. Jewkes," begs Pamela after Mr. B. finally backs down in this attempt.[21] Indeed, Jewkes stands in as the antagonistic menace once Mr. B. is recuperated by the novel's marital recovery project.

In its intertextual use, *Our Nig* both copies and mirrors, replicates and refracts. Its naming strategies and use of characterization are examples of double mimesis. *Pamela's* Jewkes and Mr. B. converge in *Our Nig's* Mrs. B.; and the American Mr. B. cannot escape the sexual significations of his British predecessor. Likewise, not only the seduced Mag but also the indentured Frado echo the servant girl and subject of seduction in *Pamela. Our Nig* is also doubly mimetic as fictive autobiography that "copies" a novel that itself makes claim to the "real" through its first-person epistolary narration and initial anonymous publication. Copying the copy in this way calls attention to the mimetic practice at work. The copy beckons readers to recognize the text's narrative strategies, the constructed nature enacted in its own claims to "truth." Double mimesis, claims cultural critic Shawn Michelle Smith, "reveals mimesis, and even gender," or in this case marriage, "to be fabrications." It "allows a subject to claim her right to copy those constructions, to represent what is already represented. By claiming the right to copy through double mimesis, the subject usurps ownership," a particular coup for Black women in antebellum America.[22]

Wilson's use of naming strategies allows her to usurp the ownership symbolized by Frado's moniker "our Nig"; she does so by denying the person who has the most power over her life proper appellation. Wilson's *Our Nig* thus echoes Douglass's erasure of William Lloyd Garrison in *The Narrative of the Life's* last paragraphs and anticipates the tension over naming and authorial power in *Incidents in the Life of a Slave Girl.* As readers of Douglass's paradigmatic 1845 autobiography will recall, he closes his text by revisiting the exact language that Garrison uses to open the *Narrative* in his often-cited introduction. Both Douglass and Garrison recall the 1841 Nantucket speech that marked the fugitive's official entrance to the (broader) anti-slavery movement. By ending the body of the narrative with the event Garrison chooses to stress while introducing it, the *Narrative* formally challenges the expected teleology of the slave narrative; it substitutes a circular structure that revises the linear form of Douglass's rise from slavery to freedom.

Douglass's *Narrative* challenges Garrison's power and influence in multiple ways, though this oppositional stance is more often associated with his second autobiography, *My Bondage and My Freedom* (1855). In the *Narrative,* Douglass withholds any explicit mention of the famous editor's name and throws this fact into relief by fulsomely praising the *Liberator*'s effect on his own development without associating it with its founder. When Douglass declares "While attending an anti-slavery convention at Nantucket, on the 11th of August, 1841, I felt strongly moved to speak and was at the same time much urged to do so by Mr. William C. Coffin, a gentleman who had heard me speak in the colored people's meeting at New Bedford," he reasserts his own self-creating authority.[23] In his reflections years later, abolitionist Parker Pillsbury echoes Douglass's self-possession, testifying that in Nantucket "before us stood one trophy, [Douglass], *self*-delivered, *self*-redeemed" (emphasis mine).[24] By naming Coffin, Douglass decenters Garrison, displacing the much-discussed introductory importance of the editor's propelling presence.

However powerful, however eloquent, Garrison is no Zeus to a motherless Douglass as Athena, no God to Douglass as Adam.[25] Instead of emerging fully formed out of Garrison's head, Douglass the (anti-slavery) warrior and namer substitutes Coffin's presence for his mentor's and then links Coffin to a previous incident, the "colored people's meeting in New Bedford." This rhetorical move anticipates his novella *The Heroic Slave* (1853), for in naming an antecedent moment as the originary one, he situates Coffin as first a moved listener, *his* moved listener, who will soon appear as the instigator in Douglass's *re*emergence.[26] Indeed, Douglass, who had been licensed to preach at New Bedford's Zion Chapel, had already addressed many meetings and even been noticed in the *Liberator* itself.[27] In their comments, both Garrison and Douglass describe his "baptismal, the consecrating service" into a life as an anti-slavery activist.[28] Yet Douglass points out that he had already heard—and heeded—the call. When reflecting on this moment, it's not Coffin, and certainly not the unnamed Garrison, who delivers the once-enslaved speaker. Instead, Douglass himself underwrites his own authority. In his intricate (first) closing coup, Douglass uses the politics of (un)naming to simultaneously revise each of the openings of the narrative, both Garrison's and his own. In doing so, Douglass reasserts himself as the self-generating subject so familiar to his readers and critics.

Like Douglass and Wilson, Harriet Jacobs uses the politics of naming to reaffirm her independence and to express disdain for those who cloak themselves and protect their reputations while claiming to be true anti-slavery friends. After hearing a lecturer mention New York abolitionists Isaac and Amy Post, she writes to Amy, "I am glad that your name is not too sacred to be held up by a coloured man."[29] And in the closing chapters of *Incidents* itself she makes this same point, asserting that she spent "nearly a year in the family of Isaac and Amy Post, practical believers in the Christian doctrine of human brotherhood."[30] Like Douglass's closing revisions, this reference's irony emerges from the oft-noted framing tension between Jacobs and her editor, Lydia Maria Child, over the power to announce or withhold names throughout *Incidents.* As readers will recall, Jacobs asserts in her preface that "I have concealed the names of places, and given persons fictitious names," averring "I had no motive for secrecy on my own account, but I deemed it kind and considerate towards others to pursue this course."[31] Child likewise assumes the responsibility for this withholding, declaring, "The names of both persons and places are known to me; but for good reasons I suppress them."[32]

Jacobs's irony is biting for, of course, she has many rational motives for not disclosing sexual improprieties that would stigmatize her—and will have others tell her so within the narrative. Moreover, her reference to the Posts, again, "practical believers in the Christian doctrine of human brotherhood," underscores the even sharper critique embedded in the adjective "practical" and in the matter-of-fact citation of only selected abolitionists' unconcealed names; it is a reminder that at least some do not need or want anonymity to do the practical and practiced work not only to end slavery, but also to establish the "equal liberty" the Hutchinson Family Singers propose as their motto. Like Wilson, Jacobs calls on—and calls out—anti-slavery friends, decrying expectations about racialized disclosure that require Black narrators to unveil themselves while allowing others to shield their reputations and perhaps make less than nominal, shall we say, contributions to the anti-slavery cause.

Appropriating the power to name as Wilson, Jacobs, and Douglass do challenged popular biblical arguments relegating Africans to an originally distinct race, as Thomas Jefferson famously speculated.[33] God gives Adam the power to name beasts and in doing so separates God's children *from* the beasts they are given to master. Ancestors of Africans, the polygeneticist apologists of the mid-nineteenth century reasserted, "were not even descendants of Adam and Eve, blacks had no place in the bible."[34] Those who supported slavery linked economic and religious justifications. As the Board of Managers for the Massachusetts Anti-Slavery Society protested in 1849, slaves, "by creation the children of God, are ranked with four-footed beasts and treated as marketable commodities."[35] *Our Nig* highlights the lessons that students of Genesis glean about naming and humanity—before their masters break up their Sabbath schools or their mistresses interfere with their religious educations.

When Frado gets "serious" about her religious education, her "mistress" preaches a segregated sermon on prayer, avowing its usefulness "'for whites, not for blacks. If she minds her mistress, and did what she commanded, it was all that was required of her'" (*ON*, 52). Mrs. B.'s biblical interpretation echoes the familiar slave-holding refrain "Servants, obey thy masters." It further illustrates that the "words, deeds and actions of those bodies, north and south, calling themselves Christian churches, [are] yet in unison with slaveholders,"[36] a point *Our Nig*'s discourse of ownership and the paradoxically third-person but directly quoted narration of its "mistress's" language in the passage above highlights. Despite Frado's religious ambivalence, the text seems to relish the appropriation of the authorial power that God gives Adam when God "brought them to the man to see what he would call them, and whatever the man called each creature, that would be its name."[37] Wilson the namer makes Mrs. B. the Beast; she does so both descriptively and through biblical analogy. Wilson's appropriation of Adamic power bolsters her commentary, one she shares with outspoken abolitionists and "come-outers," on the bastard (that is, illegitimate) religious ideologies practiced in the North. Through naming, *Our Nig* squarely places Blacks as the equal descendants of Adam, mirroring his power. For a Black woman, this is a particularly audacious move, for her racial and gendered genealogy, according to many traditions, recalls Ham's and Eve's—rather than Adam's—as its genesis.

Extended Family: Aunties' Place and Property

Our Nig's use of homonynmic overlay calls attention to both anti-slavery friends and to "slavery's shadows" being cast in Northern quarters. The she-devil calls her two household *bête noirs,* Frado and Aunt Abby, by the monikers "Nig" and "Nab." "Nab's" naming and victimization cast her as a subject of shared suffering and status. Yet, as the text also stresses, her position differs from the servant girl's. *Our Nig* situates Abby, its most sympathetic white woman character, in many generic and positional registers. This accretion of meanings is exposed through the multiple sites she occupies: nominal ally-Auntie and nigger "Nab," spinster aunt and contestor of interstially complicated gendered and racial proper(ty) rights. Through her, the text launches a simultextual exploration and critique of the politics of possibly allied interests that expose the contradictory investments of anti-slavery friends at home over and again.

Abby is Mr. B.'s supposed maiden sister, the aunt of the Bellmont children, whose claim to the family homestead enrages Mrs. B. and causes Aunt Abby to be consigned, not to the kitchen (reserved for most aunties of race fiction in the nineteenth century), but to an isolated wing of the house. Aunt Abby's life history diverges from Sally Hayward Blanchard's, her historical corollary.

Hayward, the woman upon whom Abby is based, married; after her husband died, she joined her brother's household.[38] Wilson transmutes the historical widow into a novelized "maiden sister" (*ON*, 14) just as Jacobs seems to freely fictionalize the sweet and feeble "maiden lady" who supposedly buys "Aunt Marthy," the grandmother in *Incidents*, and "signs with a cross."[39] To create the trope of "virtuous spinsterhood,"[40] each text offers to readers characters supposedly independent of and unpolluted by intimate ties to white men as a model for transracial alliances based on "shared" gender and economic exclusion, rather than on racial difference.

Our Nig's meditation on the economics of family title opens up the possibility that the ironic naming of both "our Nig" and "Aunt Abby" offers an alliance model to its readers. It is clear that Aunt Abby would have no familial claims if Mrs. B. and her daughter Mary had their way, particularly when "family" signals economic title as well as affective ties. As critic Rafia Zafar points out, "The aunt seems almost as disenfranchised as the young black servant through her inability to have" (or I might add, [have] run [of]) " her own home."[41] She is consigned to an unseen wing of the house, while Frado is likewise confined to the dark L chamber, to "quarters" "she'll soon outgrow," though "when she *does*, she'll outgrow the house" (*ON*, 17), as Mrs. B. makes clear. Likewise, Abby is linked to African American "aunties" that all readers of nineteenth-century narratives recognize as she slyly provides the punished Frado with dinners and offers her "cake and pies" that she was "never allowed" at "home" (*ON*, 26). Moreover, like the kitchen that serves as haven in many narratives, her room is one of the few provisionally safe havens available to Frado.

Aunt Abby's delimited spatial freedom also reflects her lack of familial status and power. The most famous (white) aunt of antebellum fiction, *Uncle Tom's Cabin*'s pragmatic, energetic but cold-hearted Aunt Ophelia, has full run of the house, but is only fully reformed once she learns how to *feel* for and connect with Topsy, her explicitly orphaned symbol of "the lowly." Unlike Ophelia, Aunt Abby's feeling lesson is not to master (maternal) sympathy, for empathy is immediately available to her. On one level, the text suggests, she *is* the lowly. When she attempts to influence household affairs, especially affective relations, she is banished: "If *she* dared to interfere in the least," Wilson writes, "she was ordered back to her 'own quarters'" (*ON*, 37, emphasis in the original).

Aunt Abby, or "Nab, as [the] she [devil] called her" (*ON*, 25) is "Nig's" syllabic and symbolic kin and likewise is not allowed into the parlor, the emblem of nineteenth-century domestic, indeed, sacredly domesticating, space. Mrs. Bellmont, for instance, objects to Frado's "getting pious" by saying "who ever

thought of having a nigger go [to church], except to drive others there? Why
. . . we should soon have her in the parlor, as smart as our own girls" (*ON*,
49–50). Similarly, when Mrs. B. is "irritated by Nab's impudence in presenting
herself unasked in the parlor, [she] upbraided [Frado] with indolence, and
bade her apply herself [to her work] more diligently."[42] In this instance, "Nig"
becomes the grammatical and bodily substitute for "Nab," and the Northern
parlor becomes a scene of whipping as a sign of essential (in)difference.
Critic Richard Brodhead contends that in the mid-nineteenth century "whipping *means* slavery. It emblematizes both the actual practice and the whole
structure of relations that identify Southern slavery as a system."[43] Instead
of being incorporated into symbolic family space, Frado takes the rawhide
for her and "Nab's" merged disobedience, accentuating their shared status as
aliens and outsiders.[44] Aunt Abby's situation mirrors "our Nig's," as Frado's
analogous disenfranchisement similarly underscores the vulnerability of
this "aunt" by linking her not to Northern aunts, to Ophelias, but to African
American aunties. The use of these lexically similar monikers hammers home
the point that "Nab"/Aunt Abby, like "Nig"/Frado, is certainly not "just like"
or a "permanent member" of a Northern idealized family.[45]

Yet *Our Nig* simultaneously parodies the politics of interracial auntie-
hood, as it were. Like her brother Mr. Bellmont, and all the other ostensibly
benevolent family members, Aunt Abby is not willing or able to actualize
the affective relations her shared outside status, and the moniker that signals it, symbolize. As feminist critic Elizabeth Ammons points out, *Our Nig*
"jeers at the myth . . . that there exists some powerful, subversive, sisterly
love among women, grounded in maternal values and standing outside the
capitalist system."[46] Indeed, if "Mrs. Bellmont and Mary provided a much
needed service to their household when they beat Frado," as critic Robert
Reid-Pharr argues,[47] then, I would add, Abby, like her nephew Jack, provides
an equal restraining and regulating function. Theirs is the subtle but violent
work of disciplinary intimacy, for it is not the violence of the household, in
the end, that Abby and other "allies" restrain. Instead it is the text's ability
to forward *escape* as a legitimate option in response to the corporeal and
economic abuse Frado suffers in the Bellmont household.

Our Nig's critique of physical violence and punitive "correction" stands side
by side with her simultextual attack on the gentler forms of regulation and
punishment. Northern behavioral regulation in the mid-nineteenth century
shifted from corporeal punishment, increasingly a sign of degraded status, to
affectional authority—disciplinary intimacy as Brodhead calls it—which was
promulgated in books and home management journals. Such inculcation of
domestic ideals was meant, he writes, for the consumption of "a family closed

off from extended relations; a family prosperous but not luxuriously wealthy; a family where home life is relieved from the heavy labor of primary economic production . . . in which the mother, now the chief presence in the home, is able to devote her whole attention to the raising of her children." Lydia Sigourney advised that women could find time to perform maternal duties by securing "competent assistance, in the sphere of manual labor, that she may be enabled to become the constant directress of her children, and have leisure to be happy in their company."[48] Significantly, Frado and Mary, her young tormentor, are the only real children in the Bellmont household; all of the eldest children are adults. The book thus mocks any justification of a need for maternal relief. *Our Nig* levels a significant critique against a Northern domestic economy that uses physical abuse as the guarantor of white middle-class domestic intimacy, displaying how it is always already polluted in ways that also threaten the white family proper, as Mrs. B's abuse of her invalid daughter Jane makes plain. *Our Nig* goes further still by revealing how the politics of persuasion quite competently assist middle-class families in their bid to secure their own imbricated class- and race-based investments.

There are several instances in which "friends," family, and traditional narrative allies serve as protectors for property interests in which "Nig" figures as fugitive property. Frado's first escape, occasioned by her overhearing that she would be "given away" (*ON,* 12) when she is six, serves as a referent for her later runaway attempts from the Bellmonts. After her first attempt, Mag's new lover Seth goes "in pursuit," and rallies a group to search for Frado and, significantly, "another little colored girl" (*ON,* 12–13).[49] The girls had "climbed fences and walls, passed through thickets and marshes, and when night approached selected a thick cluster of shrubbery as a covert [*sic*] for the night" (*ON,* 13). Mag's maternal "concerns" further indicate that there is a "covert" message to be excavated throughout this passage. After Frado runs, Mag "felt sure her fears were realized, and that she might never see her again" (*ON,* 13). Yet the following sentence states that Mag was comforted "to know that her child was not driven to desperation by their intentions to relieve themselves of her, and that she was inclined to think severe restraint would be healthful" (*ON,* 13). Such a paradox disrupts the very maternal conventions it invokes. Mag claims a naturalized relationship of concern about "her child" while simultaneously wedding it to her plan to abandon her—an unnatural act within the accepted paradigms of nineteenth-century domesticity.

While "binding out" destitute children was quite normal for impoverished parents of any race into the1830s, even the economy of indenture does not overlap with the discourse of punishment employed in this passage. In Philadelphia in that decade, destitute and delinquent Black youngsters were grouped together at a segregated orphanage and indentured out to "masters in the country" by the time they were eight.[50] New York bound out its children later, around the age of twelve.[51] Female societies in 1830s Massachusetts and New Hampshire sponsored relief for helpless girls "in home placements as legally bound domestic servants." Service was "supposed to reciprocally link sponsor and charge in a personal bond of benevolence and gratitude."[52] Just six years old if Frado's and Harriet's lives directly correspond, her work began around 1831, at the height of indenture's practice in Salem, New Hampshire.[53] Yet Frado's age and the language and physical nature of "severe restraint" that anticipates and characterizes her labor do not square with the class-based exploitation veneered with the promise of "healthful" labor and "training" that indenture ostensibly secured for (only) destitute girls.[54] Without a benevolence society or "indenturing committee"—or anyone else—to oversee Frado's "placement," hers was the worst of possible relations between employer and employee.[55] *Our Nig's* economic- and race-based critique points not only South but also toward the labor practices of benevolent friends at home, where, as William Wells Brown puts it in *Miralda* (1861), "that revolting prejudice against the negro . . . has long characterized the people of the nominally free States."[56] One simultextual suggestion is that, rather than revolting against Northern racism, all of Frado's "natural" allies and potential protectors—her mother, the "aunt" who sneaks her food and religion, Jack and James—individually and collectively advance their own economic interests over any affectional or familial ties, "natural" or metaphorical.

"A Friend for Nig" is a central chapter that highlights beatings and betrayals and emphasizes the useful work the whole family does in the service of Frado's continued servitude. Frado is literally kicked outdoors after a session of sadistic torture at Mrs. B.'s hands and the family cannot find her. Aunt Abby avers, "I have hunted everywhere; she has left her first hiding place" (*ON*, 27). Meanwhile, the "good" sister Jane and benevolent Mr. B. are active in their collaborative passivity. When Jack returns home and asks excitedly, "What's the fuss?" his father and invalid sister advise him to "Eat your supper" and "Go home Jack" (*ON*, 27). Jack ignores their advice and with his visiting brother immediately searches for Frado so he can show James "the little creature mother treats so" (*ON*, 27). Unsuccessful, they resort to familiar techniques of hunting human property, tricking Fido, nine-year-old Frado's dog, her "entire confident" and "constant attendant" (*ON*, 24), into acting the part of a hound. The dog leads them "far far into the fields, over walls through fences, into a piece of swampy land. Jack followed close, and soon appeared to James, who was quite in the rear, coaxing and forcing Frado along with him" (*ON*, 28).

Our Nig replicates the geography and tropes of fugitive escapes circulated over and again in speeches, newspapers, annual anti-slavery gift books, and narratives of slavery. The narrator has already outlined how six-year-old Frado "selected a thick cluster of shrubbery as a covert [*sic*] for the night" (*ON*, 13) like Jacobs who will "conceal [herself] in a thicket of bushes" in the Great Dismal Swamp.[57] Likewise, James's "coaxing and forcing" recalls the "healthful restraint" Frado encountered after her first runaway attempt. Here he figures not as the friend promised sardonically in the chapter title, "A New Friend For Nig," but as an antagonistic figure in a slave-catching tableau. Nor is the dog Fido the girl's "double," an "only" true friend and the possible shadow referent of the chapter title that would in itself underscore Frado's isolated status outside of the family.[58] Transmogrifying into metaphorical slave catchers in this scene, her allies return her to what they might call "safety," but to what the text, as does Mrs. Bellmont, might call her "rightful place."[59]

One's "rightful place" is the topic of discussion between Mr. B. and Abby when, alerted by Mrs. B.'s kicks and Frado's cries during this central beating, they rush in "just in time to see the last of the performance" (*ON*, 25). Frado uses their entrance to make her exit, while Mr. Bellmont mutters that he hopes she'll never return.

> "What would become of her? You cannot mean *that*," continued his sister.
> "I do mean it. The child does as much work as a woman ought to; and just see how she is kicked about!"
> "Why do you have it so, John?" asked his sister.
> "How am I to help it? Women rule the earth, and all in it."
> "I think I should rule my own house, John,"—
> "And live in hell meantime," added Mr. Bellmont. (*ON*, 25)

Critics sometimes point out that Bellmont's protestations about his inability to stop Frado's abuse are overtly disingenuous, as his behavior in the preceding rescue/fugitive scene makes plain. In this passage he is clear about (only) one thing: he's quite willing to leave Frado in hell if putting out the fire places him even in the vicinity of heat. His abdication doesn't simply reflect his relation to power but also to familial comfort and convenience. After all, as one critic contends, "the family lives in a house and farm that is completely owned by him."[60] One explanation for the transparent illogic of this exchange then, I would argue, is that the passage does not principally reference Frado's race and place, though it simultextually performs that function.

The discussion between the Bellmont siblings also reveals as a central concern the proper(ty) relations between white men and women. As the narrator points out in the next paragraph, Mrs. B. abhors Aunt Abby because "she did not give her right in the homestead to John, and leave it forever" (*ON,* 25). Mrs. B.'s relation to Aunt Abby, then, likewise might provide a family service her husband cedes to his wife. In almost one breath Mr. B. situates a woman's place quite differently saying both "the child does as much work as a woman ought" and "women rule the earth and all in it." Abby challenges her brother's obviously dysfunctional equation of women's work and women's place. Yet readers are left to reconcile his contradictions, which can be explained easily if they fill in unnamed racial and class markers: "the child does as much work as a [Black] woman ought" and "[white] women rule the earth and all in it." While this passage highlights Mr. B.'s simultaneously mobile, confused, and collapsed construction of women, Abby's challenge does not provide the clarity necessary if race—and Frado—are the passage's only referents.

Abby, we will remember, most pointedly does not rule the earth and all in it. Her response, "I think I should rule my own house, John" need not be read as projection—if I were *you* I would rule my own house. This interpretation calls upon Abby to split from herself in an act of dizzying self-alienation, both to bracket her brother's pronouncements and her own subject position, identifying with him as ruler of "my own house" as she thus simultaneously identifies with Frado, who, like her, ostensibly would benefit from his proper patriarchal reassertion. The text offers up other possibilities. Readers might also take Abby's statement quite literally: she thinks she should rule her own house, the property that she refuses to cede to John as his right.

Aunt Abby's multivalent priorities again are laid bare in the last instance in which Frado, now in her teens, decides to run away. She resolves to speak to Aunt Abby because she has never been far enough away to "decide what course to take." Abby, the text emphasizes, does not provide good cartographical advice, helping to chart a route to the most promising town and offering letters of introduction, as a "good anti-slavery friend from home" would. Instead, "*she* mapped the dangers of [Frado's] course, her liability to fail in finding so good friends as John and herself" (*ON,* 60; emphasis in original).[61] Abby becomes the regulator of Frado's independent will in an instance of domestic intimacy used to solidify white property interests.

Ma' Nig and Maternal Abandonment

Like "Nab," Frado's moniker produces a convenient lexical parallel with Mag's name. The phonological and syllabic equivalency of Mag/"Nig" facilitates the easiest of homonymic substitutions and slippages between mother and daughter. *Our Nig*'s ironic naming practices critique cultural assumptions about gender, safety, and sympathy and align with its sophisticated structure;

the two converge to create a complex shadow protagonist, Mag as "Nig." Indeed, one of the few commentators to take note of the first edition mistakenly referred to the book as *Our Meg*, perhaps to avoid repeating Wilson's actual title, as Barbara White suggests, and perhaps because the homonymic slippages the narrative offers are so inviting.[62]

Our Nig's story of unwanted mother and child advances the text's attempt to challenge the racialized role of bad, "naturally unfeeling" Black mother by substituting bad white mothers, and so households, in its stead. *Our Nig* also destabilizes any unitary (de)romanticized notions of motherhood and offers economic determination as a principal definer of narrative and personal development.[63] In this way, it moves beyond the conventional generic mandates of both sentimental and slave narrative conventions. Frado's development is not a linear progression from one side of the binary opposition (abandoned, oppressed orphan) to the other (redeemed, treasured wife and mother). Nor does it follow the teleological structure of the once-enslaved autobiographer—I once was bound but now I'm free. Rather, Frado's life and feelings overlap with her mother's; as many readers note, as George waits for his mother to return just as Frado had, the text metaphorically and materially attempts to revise Frado's own story both as mother and as child.

The thematics and narrative structure of *Our Nig*'s overlapping antiromance plots produce moments of merger between Wilson's, Frado's, and Mag's stories.[64] By the time *Our Nig* reaches the chapter in which Frado is seduced by someone who is not who he says he is, the story has come full circle, linking Mag's first illicit encounter and each woman's marriage and also signaling the familiar trope of sexually determined fallenness or death that is the illegitimate daughter's traditional fate in antebellum mulatta tales. Mag's opening and Frado's closing chapters not only come full circle, but overlap, creating a temporal and textual palimpsest. When a "still newer companionship" forces itself upon Frado and the narrator asserts "no one wanted her with such prospects" (*ON*, 71), the text moves beyond the creation of a circular structure. Like twentieth-century transparencies used as heuristic tools—skeleton, then organs, then muscles—to display a fully recognizable body, the initial chapter placed on top of the "final" one fleshes out this text, creating an accretion of overlaid meanings. The "her" in the contention "no one wanted her," then, is anything but fixed. Who is the "her" no one would want? Frado the adult or Frado the unborn child? Frado the mother or Frado's yet-to-be-born baby, the presumed daughter who is a trope in seduction tales?

If Frado replaces rather than displaces her own mother, then *Our Nig* interrogates the resurrectionary category of Black maternity. Claudia Tate contends that Wilson "displaces the motherless child (who was herself) with another child who possesses a loving mother (who is the adult Wilson)."[65] Yet if the text positions Mag and her daughter as symbolic equivalents, "Nig" as Mag, the mother who snarls at the "forced" extra labor that childbearing brings, then *Our Nig* does not stop at advancing the strongest critique of white redemptive motherhood we have in antebellum women's literature.[66] Rather, *Our Nig* also unsettles the cultural mythology that Black motherhood protects with a love so supreme that it has the power to transcend social death, to resurrect, while it is also insurrectionary in its battle against the age-old assumptions about Black maternal lack (or surplus) as the key to putative familial and societal dysfunction that have dogged African Americans from studies of slavery to the Moynihan report and beyond. *Our Nig's* complex and plural sensibilities move beyond racial critique and appropriation of domesticity to challenge and complicate one of the most sacred and foundational tenets of antebellum and African American culture.

Both in sentiment and structure, the politics of abandonment and violence, guilt and dark resurrection in *Our Nig* resemble less slave narrative or sentimental conventions than the jumble of desire Toni Morrison creates in the "Sethe," "Denver," and "Beloved" chapters, the only ones in *Beloved* in which the narrative perspective shifts, in *Beloved's* case from the third to the first person.[67] These chapters of longing, claiming, and immediacy signal the merged and temporally free consciousness of a fugitive mother, the daughter she kills to keep from reenslavement, and a sole remaining child, that is, until her embodied "ghost" sister returns. Their musings functionally resemble the first-person use in *Our Nig's* chapter headings in the palimpsested opening and closing chapters and could be interpreted as breaking through temporal and textual constraints. *Our Nig's* first chapter tag, "Mag Smith, my mother" anticipates Frado's insertion into an opening story that does not feature her at all. Mag is not yet "my mother" in the chapter that outlines the seduction, birth, and infant death that precedes Frado's own conception. Wilson's "slippages" may be symbolic of more than her inability to manage form or "difficulties in maintaining narrative distances" that "become evident in the remaining traces of the first person at the beginning and end of the text," to graft together assessments by critics Henry Louis Gates, Jr. and Carla Peterson. These slippages and collapsed distance signal that children's spirits in *Our Nig*—as in *Beloved*—are "looking for the join" of maternal healing.[68]

Our Nig's simultextual contemplations on maternity highlight the book's affinity with contemporary texts.[69] This allows us to complicate the sometimes static ways in which nineteenth-century women's literature has been too often defined as uncomplicated, imitative, and un-Black—that is, disconnected from and defined against ostensibly more complex contemporary reworkings of enslavement, woman- and motherhood, desire and empowerment.[70] Mag's and Nig's stories merge and in doing so represent the character Beloved's assertion that "all of it is now it is always now." When, in that same Morrison chapter about mother and daughter we encounter the words: "I am not separate from her there is no place where I stop,"[71] the commentary recalls *Our Nig's* Bahktinian treatment of Mag and "Nig's" overlapping parental relations, "a living contact with unfinished, still-evolving contemporary reality (the open-ended present)."[72]

Critics often resist acknowledging *Our Nig's* sophisticated spatial and temporal conceptualization. Yet, the shift from Denver's, Sethe's, and Beloved's voices speaking simultaneously, to a merger of those voices in simultaneous expression—"I am you. Why did you leave me who am you?"[73]—can be read as a reflection of the similar emotional and textual morass that *Our Nig* presents for Mag as mother, Frado as mother/daughter, and the ghost, George, as abandoned child, who haunts this text. In doing so, *Our Nig* extends the "I am you. Why did you leave me who am you?" lament Beloved poses, and appropriates and regenders the foundational story of Adam. Weaving together the question made famous by Adam's son Cain, "Am I my brother's keeper?"[74] with the ubiquitous anti-slavery mottos: "Am I not a man and a brother?" and "Am I not a woman and a sister?" *Our Nig* is a powerful tale of naming, abdicated national responsibility, and parental abandonment.

Multivalent Mulattas and Legal Racing

Though race is only one of the axes on which *Our Nig* plots its multiple points, and Blackness, as one critic contends, "is a long time in making itself apparent,"[75] the transparency and predominance of whiteness in the text is hardly stable and secure. Indeed, simultaneity and indeterminancy are two of the book's most salient characteristics. Critics routinely refer to Frado's mother Mag as a "white woman,"[76] without noting that the text, as it *begins,* is hardly definitive. Indeed, Wilson delays any definitive declaration of Mag's racial classification, leaving open for interpretation whether Mag is legally, rather than just phenotypically, "white" until the very last paragraph of the important opening chapter.

Though racially indeterminate characters are "generally translated as white,"[77] in *Our Nig's* first chapter signs of Mag's "whiteness" find colored referents. When Mag hears above her "the voice of her charmer, so ravishing" (*ON*, 1), readers may recall the seduction trope popularized by *Pamela* and extended by the first U.S. bestseller, the late eighteenth-century *Charlotte Temple* (1794). This passage also precisely mirrors the "eloquence" and "kind words"

Mr. Sands uses to seduce Linda Brent; and the purported shame at confessing the "fall" to her grandmother in *Incidents* echoes the very severance "of the great bond of union" that Mag enjoyed with her former companions. Black free and enslaved communities, writers such as Harriet Jacobs and Frank Webb (in *The Garies and Their Friends* [1857]) assert, embrace traditional sexual mores even when individuals (were forced to) compromise them. These texts, like Wilson's, counter and complicate assumed notions about Black sexuality, impurity, and impropriety.

If *Our Nig* provisionally forwards a narrative of the familiar seduction of a legally though not phenotypically "Black" woman, then we can trace how the discussion of African American sexuality and vulnerability that *Our Nig* seems to bracket is expressed through Mag. Jacobs protects Black women from the broad tar brush of Black immorality, as I argue in the previous chapter, by offering the simultaneously sanitized and sexualized Aunt Martha as a visible counter and complement to Linda's "fall." *Our Nig* likewise undertells the scope of the Bellmonts' possessive qualities implied in "our Nig" by expressing sexual fall through the simultaneously raced Mag in the opening, recognizably novelistic, pages. Carla Peterson asserts that the seduction novel continued to be read into the antebellum period and that "cultural anxieties about women's sexuality and blackness became conflated."[78] *Our Nig* both unmoors and engages racialized presumption. It simultaneously exposes white male predation through a rare glimpse of Black female victimization in the form of a seduction novel *and* through a paradigmatic reading of white "fallenness" with a racial twist.

Our Nig forces its audience to puzzle over generic clues to provide for themselves the racial classification that the text itself brackets. Few conventional seduction stories take African American women as their subjects. Thus readers may assume that Mag is "white" precisely because in societal terms, as in most literary ones, Black women have no "priceless gems" to surrender; their jewels have little if any sustainable purchase. Moreover, these narratives point out that Black sexual consideration in the open market was (over)determined by racial values wholly imbued by white Southern principles. While virginity might raise interest on the auction block, its economic complement (though "moral" opposite) was fecundity—both could elevate a purchase price.[79] As in William Wells Brown's *Clotel* (1853) or Frank Webb's *The Garies,* a white buyer who takes home his pretty procurement might be the "envy of all the young bucks in the neighborhood who had competed . . . at the sale,"[80] the paradoxically "happy" middle of such (ultimately) tragic mulattas' stories. Yet, as these and other novels and narratives make clear, a Black woman's (momentary, monetary) worth does not belie the fungible nature of the enslaved woman's status or the full range of violent possession for which young and old buyers of human flesh compete.

Knowing that *Our Nig's* geography is literally miles from this auction block and also important shades away from the terrain of conventional seduction tales both destabilizes and opens up the generic chain of associations that the book's first chapter seems to assert. In addition to the polyvalent referents of Jim's racial commentary that we will soon examine, the structure of *Our Nig* supports its multiple possibilities, the "strategic provisionality" of identity that it poses.[81] Confronted with the classic narrative opening of a traditional seduction tale that describes the early years, the *Black* narrator "*Nig*" tells readers of "*my mother*" (emphases mine), as the chapter 1 heading proclaims; the audience does not yet know in what symbolic and racial territory they will find themselves.

While contemporary readers associate the received frame of traditional seduction narratives with the racial classification of its (white) protagonist, I would suggest that nineteenth-century readers might not so easily dismiss the Black body, Wilson as daughter, that hovers over the first chapter. Since the production of "our Nig's" body via Mag's own (white) flesh and blood was highly transgressive and largely unthinkable, the probability of Mag's *Blackness* is a logical first assumption for contemporaneous readers of whatever ethnicity. This possibility aligns well with other assumptions *Our Nig* might prompt its readers to challenge as the first chapter cleaves away from its sentimental markings and incorporates darker elements: Mag's animalistic lack of "womanly feeling" and her maternal abandonment and cruelty.[82] "It was a literary commonplace to describe black women as so brutalized that they had lost all intrinsic social and maternal sensibilities," affirms Frances Smith Foster, but "almost without precedent in Anglo-American woman's literature to speak of a white woman, especially a mother, in this manner."[83] Even though Foster, like other critics, nonetheless posits Mag as always already white, I argue that these qualities might serve as the indelible characteristic signifiers of Blackness to some readers that Mag's "fair face," even in contrast to Frado's father Jim's "dark" skin, would not.

Again, throughout the first chapter Mag is described in ways that postpone declaring her racial classification. When Jim thinks "of the pleasing contrast between her fair face and his own dark; the smooth, straight hair . . ." (*ON,* 8) for example, the text only offers descriptors of physical appearance and so toys with the language of other narratives and novels in which light-skinned slaves look just as "fair" as the white sisters for whom they are often mistaken. In the fictional anti-slavery work *Autobiography of a Female Slave* (1856), the enslaved protagonist has skin "no perceptible shade darker than my young mistresses. My eyes were large and dark, while a profusion of nut-brown hair, straight and soft as the whitest lady's in the land, fell in showery redundance over my neck and shoulders."[84] In *Curse of Caste* (1865), Claire Neville's "rich tropical loveliness" and midnight black eyes strikingly resemble her white father's young (and presumably white) sister's Belle's dark beauty, which is set off by almond-shaped black eyes, black brows, and black hair that "rippled in curling waves to her slender waist."[85] Likewise, Louisa Picquet, the subject of *The Octoroon* (1861), is described as "easy and graceful in her manners, of fair complexion and rosy cheeks, with dark eyes, a flowing head of hair with no perceptible inclination to curl, and every appearance, at first view, of an accomplished white lady."[86] Antebellum readers were familiar with the disaggregation of racial phenotype and racial taxonomy. Thus when Jim muses that Mag would be "as much as a prize to me as she'd fall short of coming up to the mark with white folks," the language—Mag measured as precisely between Jim, "the African," and the "white folks" with whom Mag has "had trial" (*ON*, 8–9)—can be seen to reinforce an *intra*racial continuum upon which mulattas as type and trope are figured in nineteenth-century culture. Nor does the linguistic contrast between Mag and Jim mark racial difference. Other loose couplings, Eliza and Tom in Harriet Beecher Stowe's *Uncle Tom's Cabin* and Tom and Iola in Frances Harper's *Iola Leroy,* for example, characteristically stress the difference in diction—not legal status—that color and access can make.[87]

Indeed, racial categorization in the antebellum period, when race in law, literature, and culture was seen as increasingly unstable and often unmoored from color, was not to be assumed. In the South, cases that dealt with sexual violation could be dismissed if the race of white women was not explicitly declared. Mary M'Causland's rapist was acquitted because her race was not specified in the suit against him. Neither her Irish-sounding name nor her presumably fair skin was equated with an unequivocal racial declaration.[88] In the 1850s, asserts legal critic Ariela Gross, Americans experienced an upsurge in racial determinacy cases. These trials "not only garnered local attention because of the often salacious subject matter, but they also became the objects of national political discourse."[89] In law as in broader society, status, social acceptance, reputation, ancestry and blood, behavior, and innumerable physical markers—hair, skin, nails, eyes, heels, etc.—all functioned in concert and were sometimes discordant indicators of racial classification.

With the exception of phenotype, then, lonely Mag Smith has no claim to authenticable whiteness. That "she had a loving trusting heart" before she was "early deprived of parental guardianship, far removed from relatives" left to "guide her tiny boat over life's surges alone and inexperienced" (*ON*, 5), of course resonates as an abbreviated trope of sentimental abandonment. Yet, in another register, lack of family also signals the absence of documented pedigree and "the validation as ancestors of racially secure white descendants" that acts as a guarantor countering the possibility of racial admixture.[90] In a genre and era when, once questioned or compromised, any body's "whiteness" needed to be emphatically verified and constantly patrolled, this text does not do so for nearly the duration of its foundational opening chapter.[91]

Degraded status as well as "dark skin and ancestry" were considered racial indicators in antebellum culture. As one lawyer declared, race is not known only by hair and color "but by reputation" and "reception into society."[92] After unidentified "old acquaintances" call, Mag "returned to her hut morose and revengeful, refusing all offers of a better home than she possessed . . . hugging her wrongs, but making no effort to escape" (ON, 6–7). In the lexicon of dominant racist taxonomies, Mag's comfort with, indeed her dogged insistence on, a degraded life affirms an ascriptive identity associated with Blackness. Likewise, Mag's access to white society of any class as an equal is never established. We know "she is above no drudgery" (ON, 6) and that she is recognized by the Bellmonts only as a subordinate worker.

In contrast, the text emphasizes Jim's social as well as phenotypical race and racial affiliations. In his exchange with Pete Greene, who has been "unobserved in a corner of the rude shop," Jim identifies both himself and his workmate as equally linked to a racial community, exclaiming "Where you come from you sly nigger?"(ON, 7). After Pete hazards a guess that it is Mag about whom Jim has been muttering ("Mag Smith you want to marry"), Jim admonishes him, "Git out, Pete! And when you come in dis shop again, let a nigger know it. Don't steal in like a thief" (ON, 7). The fraternal banter— "sly nigger" and "let a nigger know it"—indicates that neither of the men in this shop are white; the passage thus emphasizes a dialogue between *working* independent Black men. The discourse of racial identification that opens and closes this exchange sandwiches marital identification, which is ostensibly its central concern. The implications of criminality that adhere to interracial marriage make no appearance here. They are instead displaced by a politics of racial visibility and working-class pride in contrast to the illegitimate (unemployed) seeing and being implied in Jim's admonition "and when you come in dis shop again, let a nigger know it. Don't steal in like a thief." That ethnic legitimacy extends to Jim's desire for marriage; Pete *guesses* that Jim wants to marry Mag. Though we have no sense of a specified white community with which Mag has any contact, she is in Pete and Jim's social and shared imaginative—and clearly Black—circle of exchange.

These social facts demonstrate Mag's distance from, not proximity to, certifiable whiteness. In the law such social facts were considered "reputation evidence" that established a person's "level of acceptance in a community, including association with blacks or whites." Being degraded in the antebellum era, *ipso facto*, signified polluted blood. So argued the lawyer who attempted to enslave Salome Müller, a German "redemptioner" who was stolen and sold as a child. Certain kinds of associations "almost certainly meant blackness."[93] "The sign of blackness is contracted," maintains Judith Butler, "through proximity, where 'race' itself is figured as a contagion."[94] *Our Nig's* simultextual possibilities delineate the conceptual correspondences that the text uses to invite its readers to "install a (racialized) body at the center of a text that deliberately withholds" totalizing indicators of racial classification.[95] Confronting race as a signifier exposes readers' own assumptions, cultural locations, and racial (il)logic.

(Un)Trustworthy Narrators and Multiple Starts

Only after *Our Nig* makes available its multivalent possibilities does the narrative definitively identify its protagonist's mother's racial classification. In the closing paragraph of the first chapter Jim proposes: "He prevailed; they married. You can philosophize, gentle reader, upon the impropriety of such unions, and preach dozens of sermons on the evils of amalgamation. Want is a more powerful philosopher and preacher. Poor Mag. She has sundered another bond which held her to her fellows. She has descended another step down the ladder of infamy" (*ON*, 9).

In this passage, direct second-person address invokes the conventions of domestic fiction as it also parodies and confronts readers who believe in the "evils of amalgamation," the telling term that finally confirms Mag's racial status. After doggedly deferring any definitive certification of Mag's race, this passage finally reveals the economies of meaning production that undergird Mag's status in multiple registers. This is one of *Our Nig's* "gestic" crossroads, to borrow a term from Brechtian theory, a place and "moment of theoretical insight into [racial] complexities," as theater critic Elin Diamond explains the gestus, that unfolds "not only in the [text's] fable, but in the culture which the [text] at the moment of reception, is dialogically reflecting and shaping." Directly addressing its readers underscores both the gestic revelation and the invitation *Our Nig* extends "to move through and beyond imaginary identifications, to rethink their own differences and contradictions," to apply Diamond to this instance.[96]

If the prototypical narrator of domestic fiction is or approximates a trustworthy guide who either belongs to or seems to identify with the class and racial position of her assumed white bourgeois audience, even the always-already white interpretation of Mag in *Our Nig's* first chapter challenges the paradigm. Our narrator *de*familiarizes words and ideas "so as to enable the spectator to see or hear it afresh" and so challenges the direct and empathetic relation between reader, character, and author so central to domestic fiction.[97] The "amalgamation" announcement distends the usually comfortable and comforting distance between protagonist and reader that the conventional narrator mediates and maintains. This narrator does not familiarize all-comprehending readers with the lives of the lowly for their moral benefit and for "the social benefit of the oppressed" with the "tacit understanding that the narrator's 'lifelike' picture of how the other half lives, a picture both true and immediately apprehensible, will inspire [readers'] compassion as it did hers," as Amy Lang suggests of the conventional narrator of sentimental novels.[98] In this way *Our Nig* is wide wide worlds away from the teleological and transparency expectations of Maria S. Cummins's *The Lamplighter* (1854), Stowe's *Uncle Tom's Cabin* (1852), and other best-selling antebellum domestic fiction with which it is often compared.

Simultextual racial construction, as embodied in the phenotypically "fair" body's ability to transform according to the socio-legal and shifting narrative contexts and relations in which it is called upon to perform, is a central issue here. *Our Nig*'s process of revelation places it closer to a Brechtian model than a "sentimental" one, for "by alienating (not simply rejecting) iconicity, by foregrounding the expectations of resemblance, the ideology of [race] is exposed and thrown back to the spectator" or reader. To apply Diamond's language further, "When [race] is 'alienated' or foregrounded, the spectator is able to see what s/he can't see: a sign system *as* a sign system."[99] By announcing "You can philosophize, gentle reader, upon the impropriety of such unions, and preach dozens of sermons on the evils of amalgamation. Want is a more powerful philosopher and preacher" (*ON*, 9), this narrator mocks the "sincere and highly impressionable reader" that the "optimistic sentimental narrative ordinarily projects."[100]

Readers who imagined that Mag was white before the chapter's close are faced with the deterministic dismantling of the modes of domestic recuperation and redemption. Mag marries as a (last) economic resort, but her narrative is marked by racially based connubial declension rather than deliverance. Jim and Mag's *mésalliance* thus disrupts the very domestic protocols their story's marital teleology invokes. The text exposes this racial, marital, and generic calculus, and parodies dominant cultural presumptions as both naive and as constructed—necessarily bound, and buoyed, as this passage puts it—by economics, philosophy, and religion; in need, in other words, of an entire ideological apparatus to support them.

No matter the narrative path one chooses for *Our Nig*, no trusted narrative guide exists. If readers had understood Mag to be light but "Black," the amalgamation proclamation would then finalize a conventional mulatta story offered, I argue, in the first chapter, by enacting the classic racial transformation but in reverse. By revealing that the character who had been considered "Black" is in fact "white," like its generic model in which the "white" heroine is revealed to be "Black," this chapter overturns the ostensible naturalness of deficient Black motherhood. The growling, abusive, presumably Black mother isn't, it turns out, Black at all. In this way the text sustains racial and affective equivalencies—white mothers can be as brutal and "unnatural" as any mythological or actual Black mother.

While *Our Nig* invokes a racially inverted mulatta tale, the narrative situates its readers both similarly and with a critical difference. In traditional "she thought she was white but she's 'really' not" fiction, readers are often included in what critic Amy Robinson calls the theatrics of the scene of "the pass"—they have access to the b(l)ackstory that remains occluded for the protagonist. Because the "visibility of the apparatus of passing—literally the machinery that enables the performance"[101]—is available to readers, is in this way narratively transparent, it both facilitates their empathy and invites open, chosen identification with the protagonist's most often unwilled, "unfair," racial quagmire—a body legally and socially (re)classified as Black whose internal qualities do not differ from those with which a white middle-class reader presumably identifies. Jim's declaration to Mag that "I's black outside, I know, but I's got a white heart inside" (*ON*, 9), poses this (ostensibly) central point of early passing fiction.[102] Yet even Jim's utterance once again stresses the mobile nature of bodies as ciphers and so disrupts stock generic configurations. "African" Jim (who will soon die of consumption) is in phenotypical, gender, and vernacular drag, standing in for the white-skin, white-soul, Black-status trope of the mulatta who usually articulates—and embodies—the dilemma that Jim poses.

If readers have interpreted *Our Nig* within an inverted tragic mulatto paradigm, however, they are *excluded* and act as "the dupe" in the conventional "passer/dupe" dyad, rather than being aligned with and textually prepared for the moment of exposure by a gentle narrator, the "gentle reader's" mirror. Robinson argues that the cultural performance of passing includes a third category, an "in-group clairvoyant," a representative of the in-group in whose presence the "successful pass" is performed. In the structure of nineteenth-century mulatta narratives, the terms of the performance are turned on their head. As the passing narrative conventionally unfolds, the protagonist— Zoe, for example, in Boucicault's *The Octoroon,* Claire in *Curse of Caste*, or Clarence in *The Garies*—is performing "whiteness," the suitor/beloved is the potential dupe, and readers, held by the hand by a trustworthy narrator, act as extratextual in-group clairvoyants. Sometimes the passing party is both the passer and the dupe while the reader remains the in-group clairvoyant. Even after the moment of revelation when the protagonist's racial and narrative position changes, readers' function and place in this now-triangulated relation remain stable. Analyzing mulatta stories from this vantage point, we see how *Our Nig* transfers the trauma of revelation from the protagonist to self-selected readers who must now face *themselves* the full range of a newly racialized self that includes the racial grotesque—their construction—lodged in the recesses of their own racial (un)conscious.

Mulatta narratives, at least on one level, turn on the discernment of likeness and similarity, offering dominant readers elevated protagonists who are "like them" due to a moral contiguity, the genre's underlying racial logic goes, symbolized by discernible consanguinity. When Mag's whiteness is confirmed, however, *Our Nig's* racial and narrative switch requires a reincorporation of the *dissimilar* generally projected outward and away from the "authentic" "white" body. It reenvisions the semiotics rather than epidermis of mulattadom as not simply racially "similar" (light/"white") but as racially the same ("white"/"white"). Traditionally, the text offers its readers the opportunity to identify with or project onto the "light" heroine. Yet in *Our Nig*, readers discover that "light" is actually white.

Our Nig thus anticipates and actualizes Ralph Ellison's analysis of Black face minstrelsy in regendered form. Empathy and identification, suggest Ellison, are mediated through an imagined masquerade that is circumscribed "by the fear that [the reader/viewer] is not simply miming a personification of his disorder and chaos, but that he will become in fact that which he intends only to symbolize."[103] *Our Nig* heightens that fear by jettisoning a comfortable and colorist mimetic framework that suggests simply a "discernment of likenesses" (as opposed to sameness) that allows for the miming to which Ellison refers. If dominant readers first associate Mag with "Blackness," the racial revelation that she is white would curdle the pleasure of interpretive discovery; they would face a symbolic recorporealizaton of a "polluted" "Blackness" into their own putatively pure and carefully policed "white" bodies. Readers who chose the identification strategy upon which the mulatta tale is contingent—but then are confronted with a Mag whom they thought had Black blood but actually does not—face a narrative of identification as tragic (to them) as the tropes of enslavement that the mulatta of this genre enacts: violation, loss of family and rights, and (social) death.

Our Nig's narrative operations dissolve the fixed boundaries of sanitized whiteness as the narrator mocks the constant legal and cultural patrolling of the contours and confines of racial purity and containment. Readers cannot climb into Wilson's garden without being defiled by Douglassian tar, or in this case rather, by a whiteness that is racially contaminated on its own, an Optic white, to recall Ellison's *Invisible Man,* blindingly whiter, in this case, without adding the drops of black at all.[104] *Our Nig* troubles any neoclassical mimetic paradigm in which the light body stands in for the originary model, genuflecting at the throne of whiteness/sameness and promising cultural assimilation. In both simultextual interpretations—Mag as a "white" woman who embodies putative "Black" behavior, and Mag as an inverted tragic mulatta, a Black woman we soon find out is white—*Our Nig* reveals all bodies to be versatile and constructed circulating counterfeit.

Without granting its dominant readers the protective barrier imagined in traditional tragic mulatta tales by the knowledge that, though the heroine "looks," "acts," and "sounds" "white," she is not legally, they are denied even the possibility of the racial disassociation that the genre's conventions hope to overcome; they are stymied in the option to *choose* cross-racial identification over racially supremacist disavowal. Challenging the reductive simplicity of that implied binary (identification or disavowal) and catching its readers unaware, the strategy of simultextual racial classification further distances *Our Nig* from the transparency of domestic fiction, a transparency that offers a/version of identification that is "immediately accessible" to and for its dominant audience. Yet by removing the process of racial mediation in the quest for racial empathy that characterizes mulatta stories, *Our Nig* paradoxically reasserts the very transparency that, both in sentimental novels and slave narratives, ostensibly comforts readers and establishes a trustworthy narrator. It does so while it also leads them into experiencing the internalization, rather than the projection, of "the unconscious baggage that 'black' bore" for them when they began to read *Our Nig.*[105]

Despite its complex renderings, it is commonplace to envision *Our Nig* through textual hindsight, to analyze it in *a posteriori* retrospect rather than in a process in which readers encounter an indeterminate opening that disrupts some of the fundamental tenets of domestic literature. As theorist Bhabha puts it, quoting Said, "beginning has two faces";[106] and like Genesis, *Our Nig* also starts twice. While its first beginning continuously forestalls its protagonist's racial status, its second opens by definitively announcing her classification. The first sentence of chapter 2 proclaims that Jim was "proud of his treasure,—a white wife" (*ON,* 10), providing resolution and a recognizable "origin" tale for its new protagonist Frado. This definitive declaration follows on the heels of an initial opening marked by racial, narrative, and taxonomical suspension. By destroying Mag as an object of audience sympathy and then by functionally starting the narrative again and introducing the characters, thematics, and geographies central to the body of the text, this second beginning serves as a complex bridge between its introductory protagonist Mag and its narrative "heroine" Frado.

Our Nig's opening passage calls attention to its heightened use of the conventions of domestic fiction. It is, to borrow from theorist Edward Said's depiction of "two obvious wide-ranging categories of literary starting points," "hysterically deliberate."[107] Rehearsing the most recognizable tropes of seduction narratives from *Pamela* to *Charlotte Temple*, "lonely Mag Smith," bereft of solid parental counsel, trades in her "downcast eyes and heavy heart" (*ON*, 5) for the "music of love." She soon surrenders the "priceless gem" he "garners as a trophy" before he leaves "her to her fate" (*ON*, 5). This use of shared vocabulary and thematic conventions associated with the fallen woman cleaves from the rest of the text. Characteristically novelistic, it makes few autobiographically correlative claims in its narration of Mag's initial fall and the pregnancy that results in the birth of a daughter who is not "Nig," either racially or narratively.

Wilson's first chapter's use of fictionalization is hardly passive or simply imitative; its fictionalizing is "hyper-assertive rather than non-assertive," to use theorist Gerald Graff's terminology.[108] William Andrews, Carla Peterson, and Richard Yarborough note the rise of "novelization" in African American literary production in the 1850s and how "early African American novels intermingled fact and fiction so that they came to occupy a special, and potentially empowering 'marginal position between authenticatable history on the one hand and unverifiable fiction on the other.'"[109] Elaborate uses of modes of expected narration die off just as Mag's (first illegitimate) daughter does. Lulled by the predictable flow of the story of fallen womanhood, the text soon highlights how Mag's character cuts against the conventional grain. Instead of tears and regrets at her infant's "passing from earth" and ascension "to a purer better life," Mag "ejaculates" "God be thanked . . . no one can taunt *her* with my ruin" (*ON*, 5). Not to be confused with the humble and feminine Christ-centered faith the narration expresses, Mag's ejaculations and her illegitimate relation to maternity continues with the births of her longer-lived children. By then, the text ceases to even perform the endorsement of sympathetic advocacy for fallen heroines that it shares with its earliest American models and instead looks forward to the conventions of naturalism as Mag "shouts," "snarls," and "growls" (*ON*, 11–12) whenever the topic is her children.[110] Indeed, Mag's role as subject/protagonist formally ends after she abandons Frado at the Bellmonts'. Though the first chapter's opening narration initiates the story as if Mag is *Our Nig*'s heroine, the second destabilizes the generic markers that allow readers to easily locate Mag's role, actions, and treatment as a fallen woman nonetheless worthy of readers' sympathy.

The first chapter performs the full range of the seduction genre: the threat, temptation, possible fall, and resurrection/resolution all occur in one chapter. This calls for a new beginning, one that can unfold in fuller novelistic space and time.

"The choice of a beginning is important to any enterprise," asserts Said. And his argument that there are two kinds of beginnings that characterize narrative openings obtains in *Our Nig*. One "foresees a continuity that flows from it" and "allows us to initiate, to direct, to measure time and construct work, to discover, to produce knowledge." The other is "very much a creature of the mind, very much a bristling paradox, yet also very much a figure of thought that draws special attention to itself" challenging "continuities that go cheerfully forward with their beginnings obediently affixed."[111] The text's first opening challenges racial and narrative "continuities that move along confident of their fixed beginnings." It substitutes the narrative contract it seems to offer its readers via a familiar narrative voice and the trope of fallen womanhood, I argue, with simultextual racial indeterminacy, a bristling paradox that disrupts traditional productions of racial and gendered meaning.

The flowing continuity of *Our Nig*'s second opening, however, offers no stable origin model even though it offers racial identities that seem fixed and knowable. It also overturns racial referents and genealogies acceptable to conventional meaning makers. The very enunciation "his white wife" resolves the dilemma of character origin in the broader narrative frame while it also unsettles the central mythologies of American gender and racial identity. More than resolution, this new beginning achieves "discontinuity and transfer," for, while a beginning is a clear break from the past, to borrow again from Said, "It must also connect the new direction not so much with a wholly unique venture but with the established authority of a parallel venture." Mag's and Frado's thematic/symbolic narratives run parallel, as we have seen. They also bend toward each other and overlap. Cultural anxieties about class-based, familial, and sexual vulnerability transfer from the seduction genre to the narratives of Black women. *Our Nig* simultaneously plays on the racial assumptions that enable these transfers and also challenges them, so as these "two kinds of beginnings" narratively (e)merge, they are revealed to have "aspects that animate one another" to be, really, "two sides of the same coin."[112]

One could say that this chapter, too, has two faces; it enacts the very tensions it seeks to explicate. The naming sections are presented with a confidence in the continuity that flows from them, that is, with a confidence in their historical and intertextual continuities and moorings. Following a different methodological arc, another beginning if you will, the second half argues that Mag's racial indeterminancy highlights the text's ambivalences and ambiguities. What, it asks, are the theoretical implications and bristling paradoxes of Mag's disruptive and polyvalent racial associations? *Our Nig*'s simultextual address and the imbricated racial, sexual, taxonomical, and domestic referents it challenges ultimately call upon contemporary and contemporaneous readers to reflect on their own assumptions, identifications, and alliances. In this way, *Our Nig* unsettles not only traditional representational paradigms but also its readers' own interpretive comfort.

3. Reading White Slavery, Sexuality, and Embedded History in Frances E. W. Harper's *Iola Leroy*

I hold that between the white people and the colored there is a
community of interests and the sooner they find it out the better.
—Frances Harper to William Still, 1872

Some of their methods appear to us as more subtle acts of
resistance and redirection than they actually were at that time.
—Frances Smith Foster

Frances E. W. Harper's *Iola Leroy* (1892) projects the volatile and violent unfolding of the 1890s—institutionalized lynchings and sexual abuse, sexual
and political intimidation, and disenfranchisement—onto a story of racial
recognition, commitment, and family reunion.[1] While much of the United
States envisioned the 1890s as a decade of technological discovery and growing
military and geographical expansion, for Americans of African descent it was
also a period in which the promises of the postwar amendments continued to
sour, an age in which racial and economic violence and physical displacement
reached its peak while the state promoted "private" segregation and received
the U.S. Supreme Court's sanction. *Iola Leroy* recognizes readers' distinct
epistemological foundations as they are guided by their own sociocultural
situatedness and ideological propensities. The novel speaks to the different
socio-ideological contexts of an age celebrated as the Black Woman's and Progressive eras and simultaneously called the "nadir" for Black Americans.

Few nineteenth-century speakers and writers were as committed to—or
as successful at—reaching the broadest possible audience as Harper was.
Early in her career, she had been one of the first Black women hired as a paid
lecturer on the (interracial) anti-slavery circuit. By 1892 when *Iola Leroy* was
first published, in addition to being a prolific and beloved writer, she had
been a leader in the Woman's Christian Temperance Union (WCTU) and

had been the national superintendent of its African American division for nine years. She had worked closely—and clashed loudly—with Elizabeth Cady Stanton and Susan B. Anthony on the American Equal Rights Association (AERA) and been associated with the American Woman Suffrage Association and the National Council of Negro Women. In her lifetime, she was elected vice president of the Universal Peace Union and the National Association of Colored Women. She had served on the editorial board of the *Anglo-African Magazine* and the national boards of the WCTU and the AERA. Along with Victoria Earle Matthews, she was one of the "very few African Americans who published regularly in both the religious press and the secular press, in venues read largely by blacks and in venues read primarily by whites."[2] In short, Harper had her finger on the pulse of the activist movements of her era.

Harper uses multivalent histotextual and homonymic strategies to reach the overlapping communities and readers that comprised her audience through a singular textual platform. On different points of what theorist Hans Jaus calls "de facto moments of completely different time curves, determined by the laws of their special history," her audience brought various needs, desires, and interpretive capacities to the same text.[3] While Jaus contends that we can analyze "the literary horizon of a certain historical moment as that synchronic system in which simultaneously appearing works can be received diachronically in relation," like other authors I examine, Harper takes as her challenge the ability to address this tension in a single text. She offers simultextual tropes to audiences who are formed by different moments of the "shaped time" that inflect their literary experiences, bending these time curves toward each other so that readers "perceive them as works of their present" temporal frame and priorities. *Iola Leroy* allows audiences coming from different directions, as it were, to meet at an intersection of "literary expectations, memories and anticipations," situating them so they can see a "common horizon" of social action that will redeem, in Harper's lexicon, the United States's constitutional and Christian covenant with all of its citizens.[4] *Iola Leroy* is paradigmatic of African American expressivity, then, not in its employment of homogenized literary images, its supposed simplistic and sincere mimicry of domestic literary conventions, or in its putative distance from the concerns of "real" Black women, but rather in its use of various social registers to reach multiple audiences simultaneously.[5]

This chapter begins by examining how *Iola Leroy* both argues for and illustrates the need to expand the use of literacy and interpretive skills by broadening an understanding of the freight of history. The novel encourages non-Black readers to extend their own literary and activist horizons by resisting (pseudo)scientific and (extra)legal encroachments against nonwhites, encroachments that the broader American populace and Anglo progressive community were finding increasingly easy to either support or ignore. Without learning these lessons, such readers are ill-equipped to engage the novel's radically multivalent discussion of cross-racial sexual (im)purity and interracial sexual interaction.

Iola's color allows for a historically specified recirculation of white slavery to direct energy back to post-Reconstruction Black concerns. As with much of nineteenth-century literature, the simultaneously racialized mulatta stands as a multigendered symbol who links African American rights to contemporaneous white reformist rhetoric and organizing efforts.[6] Following Bahktin, we can trace how *Iola Leroy* reappropriates phrases and icons "already populated with the social intentions of others" "and compels them to serve [its] own intentions."[7] In the 1890s, the story of the phenotypical white slaves who people the novel corresponds to the contemporaneous "white slavery" scare, that is, with the furor over the growing abduction of young white women into an institutionalized system of sexual exploitation.

Iola Leroy incorporates and refigures the explosive and imbricated topics of interracial sexual innocence and danger in a decade in which lynching saw its peak. Recontextualizing the rhetoric meant to recast victims of white slavery as sexual innocents recasts an understanding of Iola's own testimony about the abuse she suffers under slavery. As in *Incidents in the Life, Iola Leroy* never assures its readers of its heroine's sexual inviolability. Indeed, *Iola* rewrites the meaning of "virtue" and, like Pauline Hopkins's *Contending Forces* (1900), disaggregates sexual "innocence" and the heroine's subsequent desirability. Like Harriet Jacobs, Harper both strategically borrows from the lexicon of white women's sexual exploitation while simultaneously scrutinizing white women's own sexual power and desire.

Iola Leroy confronts the increasingly accepted meanings projected upon white womanhood, a symbol with explosive symbolic force in the post-Reconstruction era. Miss Nancy's relation with her slave (and Iola's uncle) Robert illustrates the complicated interplay between sexual and familial loyalty under and after slavery. Robert's position in the nexus of ante- and postbellum ownership provides a dark mirror through which to reexamine mythologies of white female purity. The bonds between the two challenge the mythology of innocent white womanhood and complicate Robert's otherwise asexual characterization. His narrative arc ends not with marriage but with land ownership. This enables him to send the now impoverished Miss Nancy "timely aid." Through this relationship—one that spans from the first page of the novel to its last—*Iola Leroy* both illustrates how whites might benefit from interracial reconciliation and histotextually expresses white women's complicity, rather than innocence, in the sexual politics of the 1890s.

In the second half of this chapter, I examine the ways in which *Iola Leroy* resonates with homonymic connections to historical personages that her acculturated audiences would recognize. When "Iola," "Dr. Latimer," and "Vera Earle" appear as principal characters in 1890s novels such as *Iola Leroy* and *Four Girls at Cottage City*, these names carry augmented meanings. They function as allusions to similarly named public figures who were well known in some interpretive communities: those who followed the Black press and the clubwomen's movement; those, in other words, who were interested in reform narratives or what Matthews would broadly define as "race literature." In a literary sense, these names open polyvalent interpretive paths throughout these novels. Borrowing from scientific parlance, characters covalently bond with their homonymic and historical analogues: Ida B. Wells, Martin and Lucy Delan(e)y, George and Lewis Latimer, and "Victoria Earle" Matthews. That is, instead of floating freely, Harper's "Iola," "Lucille Delany," and "Dr. Latimer," and, as we'll see in a later chapter, Emma Dunham-Kelley's "Vera Earle" become bound in mutual orbits or "combine with" their histotextual referents, compounding the interlocking sets of amplified meanings that these names provide. In other words, Harper incorporates extranarrative allusions to reform movements and to contemporaneous and past Black history. In this way, her use of histotextuality names a method for interpreting historicized tropes in narratives whose multiple meanings previously had been thought to be produced by relying on the texts' putatively singularly sentimental, transparent, and seemingly impoverished referents.

Cultural Literacy, Legible Transcripts, and Reading "Aright" in the 1890s

In its interrogation of systems of power and knowledge, as John Ernest contends, *Iola Leroy* is as much "a study of discursive systems" as it is an inverted passing tale and story of racial uplift.[8] Extending Harper's assertion that "under [slaves'] apparently careless exterior there was an undercurrent of thought which escaped the cognizance of their masters" to the reading of the novel itself underscores how she challenges then popular assumptions about racial epistemology and transparency.[9] As Hazel Carby comments, Harper's "'folk' are manipulators of skills that become weapons, not [the] least of which is literacy. Literacy, the power of the word, becomes a lesson for Harper's readership to learn" (*IL*, xix).[10] *Iola Leroy* locates much of its subversive praxis in the "aunts" and "uncles" that remain consistent characters throughout the novel. Aunt Linda's comment, "I can't read . . . but ole Missus's face is newspaper nuff for me" (*IL*, 9), suggests an expanded definition of literacy, one that emphasizes the power of interpretation. Indeed, the close of the first chapter brings home the point that conventional reading does not ensure literacy, declaring that "slavery had cast such a glamour over the Nation, and so warped the consciences of men, that they failed to read aright the legible transcript of Divine retribution which was written upon the shuddering earth" (*IL*, 14). Careless readers, *Iola Leroy* points out, by extension blind to historical scars and wounds, see only exteriors, missing the multivalent meanings embedded in resistant speech and in textual meditations and manipulations that make up a "legible transcript" (*IL*, 14).

Iola Leroy's explanatory narrative posture and the countless examples of Black subversive expression that characterize its beginning not only challenge assumptions about Black expressive intelligibility but also reposition readers by leading them away from the attitudes and assumptions of the master class. Unlike the unreliable narrator of Harriet Wilson's *Our Nig*, for example, *Iola*'s narrator is a trustworthy guide whose challenges are heuristic rather than hostile. Sympathetic readers are offered a model that affirms the notion of expansive literacy. Other readers are shown their history of misreading and invited to retool. This instructive paradigm situates only duped owners and those who willfully choose to identify with exclusionary positions and warped reading practices outside of the novel's narrative community. Though the text uses religious language to offer moral appeals to oppositional as well as sympathetic readers, it does not rely upon such pleas. Indeed, *Iola Leroy* displaces those who resist its message, labeling them both anachronistic and functionally illiterate. It offers all others a way to join a collective project of cultural, historical, and intellectual literacy that will teach the new nation to read aright.

Harper both broadens and deepens Frederick Douglass's paradigmatic emphasis on written literacy, insisting that literacy must be yoked to justice and underscoring that education without the goal of promoting the public good is a golden calf unworthy of mass adulation. In her speech "Women's Political Future" (1893) she writes: "In coming into her political estate woman will find a mass of illiteracy to be dispelled. If knowledge is power, ignorance is also power. The power that educates wickedness may manipulate and dash against the pillars of any state when they are undermined and honeycombed by injustice."[11] Harper posits both knowledge and power as literacy's implied referents (for "knowledge is power"). Yet she goes on, "ignorance is also power." Harper insists that knowledge must be informed by justice if the masses are to learn to become truly literate. Her articulation coincides with

African American women's endorsement of a broader sense of literacy, one that places communal ways of knowing on equal footing with formal and individualized literacy.[12]

If one does not read *Iola Leroy* "aright," Harper's opening directive toward multivalent interpretation might be easily lost, leaving the novel's invective against white sexual power obscured. In a much-cited passage, a Union general expresses how much he was impressed by Iola's "modest demeanor, and surprised to see the refinement and beauty she possessed. Could it be possible," he asks, "that this young and beautiful girl had been a chattel, with no power to protect herself from the highest insults that lawless brutality could inflict upon innocent and defenseless womanhood?" (*IL*, 39).[13] Pairing "innocent and defenseless womanhood" against "lawless brutality" (instead of against "brutal manhood" as one might expect), *Iola Leroy's* political grammar situates white manhood under slavery as brutality itself.

Though in this passage the words "black" and "white" are loudly silent, it condemns white men's abuse of enslaved women while it also shifts the terms and temporal scene of exactly the scenario—lawless brutality wreaking havoc upon defenseless womanhood—that white writers and mobs used to justify lynchings. By both invoking and disrupting the rhetoric of and justification for lynching in the era in which (as well as of which) she writes, *Iola Leroy* indicts the continuation of the very violence ostensibly obscured by the novel's demure uplift emphasis. Harper merges past and present referents to effect change in a not-yet-determined future. She thus moves beyond the conventions of the classic historical novel that, according to theorist Georg Lukács, incorporate the past as a prehistory to explain present contending forces, though the outcome is already known.[14] Unlike the historical novel, *Iola Leroy's* literary strategies direct social empathy and model social intervention to affect a not-yet-determined outcome.

Iola Leroy weds the phraseology of law, pseudoscience, religion, and domestic fiction to challenge the language and assumptions that undergird white supremacy. The novel communicates histotextually what Ida B. Wells's "Iola" expresses in her expository writing. "White men who had created a race of mulattoes by raping and consorting with Negro women were still doing so whenever they could," Wells asserts, while "these same white men lynched, burned and tortured Negro men for doing the same thing with white women, even when the white women were willing victims."[15] While "Iola" is declarative, *Iola* relies on its readers to secure the racial referents. When the highly educated Rev. Carmicle asserts "there are savage elements in our civilization which hear the advancing tread of the negro and would retard his coming" (*IL*, 259), his commentary both offers and transposes a well-worn script in which a "savage" (Black) element is to blame for slowing the progress of (white) civilization. In the Black elite version, the unwashed Southern masses come North retarding the advancement of the more "civilized" elements of the race. Yet Carmicle's sentence structure enacts a symbolic reversal often leveled from the Black pulpit and the Black press. White men—not Black— are savages; their civic barbarity, Harper's simultaneously sacred and secular grammar suggests, retards not only the Negro's rise but also "his"/His, or the Lord's, coming (*IL,* 259). In both the Wells and Harper/Carmicle passages, white men are "lawless" and brutal while African American rather than white womanhood is innocent and defenseless. Indeed, each Iola indicts the violence of a decade in which white male savagery is rapidly and systematically being inscribed on Black bodies and in American jurisprudence.

Throughout her life, Frances Harper indicted lynching in both her prose and her public presentations. Harper's serialized first novel, *Minnie's Sacrifice* (1869), for example, is explicit in its denunciation of white terrorism. Like Iola and her siblings, its protagonists are young people who had no reason to think they are African American until later in their lives. Once their history is revealed, they spend their lives organizing in the South, advocating armed self-defense. The cost of such a stance is not romanticized. The Ku Klux Klan responds to this activism by lynching Minnie.

Harper was invested in broadening the reach of the antilynching struggle to fully engage multiple communities, an agenda that she had advanced in *Iola Leroy.* In a 1903 letter she penned to Rev. Francis Grimké, pastor of the influential Fifteenth St. Presbyterian Church in Washington, D.C., she writes:

> Dear Sir:
> I received your sermons on lynching for which accept my thanks for your remembrance of me. And also permit me to emphasize my gratitude to you especially for your manly refusal to accept the verdict of the mob in the cases of lynching. I hold that as long as there are such things as mental imbecility, mistaken identity, as long as Potiphar's wife stands in the world's pillory of shame that no man however guilty should be deprived of life or liberty without due process of law. . . . *Do these sermons have a circulation outside of our people? Could there not be some contrivance planned by which your sermons would reach larger audiences than they do now? Could not the council plan for their circulation, and the women's clubs be induced to scatter them among the white people in different localities?* . . . If at any time there is any movement to circulate these sermons, though my means are limited, count on me as a subscriber.[16] (Emphasis mine.)

By thanking Grimké for his "remembrance of [her]" in the sermon, Harper situates herself as a race leader, a cited participant in public policy and protest. She refers to Grimké's reference to a document protesting the brutal treatment and lack of protection offered Blacks in the South through a day of prayer signed by "representative men and women" of the race: Harper, Douglass, Daniel Payne, Booker T. Washington, and T. Thomas Fortune, among others.[17]

However impressive his "manly" work, and however thankful Harper is for "such men as you, who can handle our cause as you can,"[18] she implies that Grimké's circle is too small, its influence too narrow. She presses her interest in extending the scope and reach of his protest by using [Negro] women's clubs to spread the word to white people. Grimké was a founder of the American Negro Academy (ANA). Founded in 1897—a year in which Harper served as the vice-president of the newly formed National Council of Negro Women at the height of the Black women's club movement—the ANA was meant exclusively for "men of African descent for the promotion of Letters, Science, and Art."[19] Implicitly denying in their charter that "women as a class are quite equal to the men in energy and executive ability,"[20] as Harper declared in a Women's Congress speech in the 1870s, Grimké, his brother Archibald, Alexander Crummell, W. E. B. DuBois and the younger Alain Locke, Carter G. Woodson, and James Weldon Johnson joined other prominent men—lawyers, editors, college presidents, and professors—to make up the academy's ranks. As the foremost Black intellectual society, they published "occasional papers" sporadically. Yet Harper has little faith, it seems, that Grimké and the groups with which he is associated will disseminate the word without the help of organized women. She diplomatically poses her pointed advice as "questions" about the scope of his audience to illuminate her suggestion that he go back to a larger base, "women's clubs," so that they might build a broader audience that includes "the white people in different localities."[21] Her interest not only in content but in strategic gender and race-conscious address is grounded in the same nexus of investment and activism that is the basis for her polyvalent use of both sexual violence and the "white slave" in *Iola Leroy*.

Forced Prostitution, Rape, and White Slavery's Double Meanings

Never interested in "stories about white men marrying beautiful quadroon girls, who, in doing so, are lost to us socially,"[22] to borrow from her own writing, Harper uses white-skinned mulattos not only to appeal to white women but also to illustrate African American commitment to political and social uplift in the face of Anglo violence.[23] The idea of white slavery enacted through the novel's plot creates a histotextual bridge to the campaign against enforced prostitution of young women caught in an increasingly institutionalized business of sexual exploitation also called white slavery. The homonymic link underscores the connection between the sexual vulnerability long experienced by African Americans and the concern for young white women now expressed by Harper's Anglo contemporaries. Her generic choices reflect her commitment to "appeal to her countrywomen," to borrow from the title of her 1895 poem of the same name, and to the multiracial alliances she tried to broker to advance African American rights.²⁴ *Iola Leroy's* invocation of the mulatta heroine may seem to rely upon the received conventions of domestic race fiction meant also to appeal to white women readers. Yet it is simultaneously an *anti*romantic trope of "white slavery"—and so a resonant indictment of white men—one that the very audience of reformers that Harper targets already found compelling.

Invoking the rhetoric of sexual white slavery, *Iola Leroy* retells the story of a nubile heroine who loses her father only to find that the marriage securing her legitimate status is invalid and she instead is chattel. Read transparently, this is a familiar and recirculated tale of antebellum injustice. "At the level of their telling" to borrow from Richard Brodhead, tales such as *Iola Leroy* recast the story, gauging "dominances and resistances in another social situation, the new [sexual] order of the post-bellum" United States.²⁵ Histotextually drawing attention to a "past" figure—the enslaved woman so often symbolized by the sexually vulnerable mulatta—brings into play the resonant phrases of activists of the time. By linking the plight of white women and African Americans under sexual attack, *Iola Leroy* calls up uncannily similar structures of power that led non-Black reformers to label their "white slaves" innocent and redeemable. *Iola Leroy* charts a map of resistance that counters the potent mythology of African American female promiscuity, one that undergirds the sexual canards used to justify lynching, and one that blames the very victim that activists exonerated in white-authored white slavery narratives.²⁶ By placing *Iola Leroy* at the crossroads—a "white" mulatta who is implicitly threatened with the dynamics of the new white slavery—the novel both invokes activist systems of assumptions and extends them to other narratives of sexual slavery, narratives in which the heroine is everything an extended model against white slavery acknowledges—except white.

By the first two decades of the twentieth century, growing antiprostitution sentiment would develop into what more than one critic has characterized as "the white slavery hysteria."²⁷ Census figures of the 1880s and 1890s confirmed that forced prostitution was on the rise. Indeed, as with lynching, it was becoming institutionalized. Prostitutes, like sharecroppers, could find themselves trapped in a cycle of debt, forced to buy clothing and food from employers who might charge up to four times the market price. When they tried to leave they were sometimes arrested and charged with nonpayment of debt and robbery. And as with lynchings, the power of the state, the police, and the courts, were complicit, or even active, in maintaining this increasingly systematized violence. Harper was well acquainted with the campaigns to fight such abuses. The WCTU had joined the fray against white slavery when it was in full force. Just three years before the publication of *Iola Leroy,* for example, their official paper published an in-depth exposé of the white slave trade.[28]

As a term with well-established roots, white slavery was a forceful metaphor in large part because the two words—in the nineteenth-century Anglo imagination—seemed to almost magnetically repulse. Mid-century white reformers in Great Britain and the United States including Mary Wollstonecraft, Maria Edgeworth, Lydia Maria Child, and Angelina Grimké, used the phrase to expose white women's relation to patriarchal oppression. Nor was the image confined to women's concerns. As Dwight McBride points out, even "American revolutionaries used it to hyperbolize their relationship to the English."[29] The paradoxical contradiction of, and so outrage about, white enslavement drew people to it. For example, Hiram Powers's "The Greek Slave," a marble nude that depicted a young woman captured by the Turks, was the most popular American sculpture of the nineteenth century.[30]

The histotextual pull between *Iola's* plot and the extratextual campaign it attracts into its interpretive orbit works because anti-slavery workers and reformers against white slavery often describe the sexual plight of enslaved women in similar terms. Progressive era reformers depicted white slaves as victims and insisted that the prostitutes involved were "sexual innocents, helpless young women who 'fell' into illicit sex." They viewed these women as victims not only of "male dominance in general but of kidnapping, sexual imprisonment, starvation, and/or seduction."[31] Such arguments held men, rather than sexualized women, accountable. Indeed, these reformers argued that "men were always blameworthy, whether they accomplished their purpose by brute force or subtle persuasion."[32] Organizers insisted that white slaves were not guilty of choosing their sexual fate; only a small leap brought reformers (and they in turn brought their audiences) to the conclusion that anyone could be so seduced. This sentiment was explicitly articulated between 1910 and 1920 when posters "appeared in conspicuous places in major urban areas with the warning: 'Danger! Mothers beware! Sixty thousand *innocent* girls wanted to take the place of sixty thousand white slaves who will die this year in the United States!'" (italics mine).[33] Women of the nineteenth century had organized with just this point in mind. The primary goal of the New

England Female Moral Reform Society and its bimonthly journal *Friend of Virtue* (1836–91) was, in their own words, "to guard our daughters, sisters, and female acquaintances from the delusive arts of corrupt and unprincipled men" and "to bring back to the paths of virtue those who have been drawn aside through the wiles of the destroyer."[34] Harper, Wells, and other African American organizers shared the perspective expressed in *Friend of Virtue* that powerful white men acted as "the destroyer." This shared analysis of power politics aligned their rhetoric—and they hoped, their efforts—with that of other women and reformers of their era.[35]

By invoking white slavery as a trope for Black women's abuse, *Iola Leroy* taps into contemporaneous rejection of pseudoscientific postulations about so-called inherent qualities of sexual deviance that attracted women to prostitution. In doing so, the novel's argumentative arc extends to—and contests—the "medical" claims of subhuman classification used to degrade Blacks politically, economically, and socially. Rhetoric directed against white slavery did battle with increasingly popular theories of deviance that purported that prostitutes were "an atavistic subclass of women." As Sander Gilman notes, to prominent medical and philosophical theorists of polygenetics, "the primitive is the Black, and the qualities of Blackness, or at least of the Black female, are those of the prostitute."[36] Supporters of such views explicitly tied essentialized notions of white prostitution to doctrines of so-called deviantly embodied "Hottentot" women and their American descendants.

White slavery was a particularly useful metaphor for African American organizers who tried to attract reformers' energy back to issues of African American concern. While interest in and agitation for Black rights had dramatically declined in the post-Reconstruction era, reform organizations and their constituencies rallied behind efforts to counter white slavery. Many early antiprostitution activists belonged to the Marlborough Church, where William Lloyd Garrison had been a leading member and "former abolitionists . . . joined forces with 'social purity' reformers to battle the new slavery," as historian Ruth Rosen notes. Increasingly, organizers distinguished white slavery as a subset of antebellum slavery or positioned the two as equal evils. Eventually, the chief of investigations in the U.S. Department of Justice requested that Congress use the Thirteenth Amendment—passed at the close of the Civil War specifically to free slaves—to fight the rising white slave trade.[37] Meanwhile, however, the Supreme Court, Southern Democrats, and the executive branch actively eroded postwar amendments as they applied to the formerly enslaved whose rights they were enacted to protect.[38]

The possibility of forging an overlapping community of interest was obvious to those—such as Harper—who were committed to women's and African

Americans' intersecting concerns. The growing state-sanctioned attack on white slaves and Black ex-slaves and their families was evidenced by institutionalized economic and bodily terror: prostitution, continued rape, debt peonage, and lynching. In *Uneasy Virtue: The Politics of Prostitution and the American Reform Tradition,* historian Barbara Hobson cites studies that examine "pimps' breaking-in system": a "combination of affection, threats, brute force and protection," a process that also describes many slave owners' behavior. It effectively names the allusions to just what Iola's owner intended to do to actualize his desire to "break her in" (*IL,* 38). Again, the specific language used to describe forced prostitution characterized relations between white slave owners and desired enslaved women as well as the methods of intimidation that post-Reconstruction white supremacists used on African Americans.

Throughout the novel, circumstances place Iola in situations that vividly embody popularized dynamics of white slavery. Indeed, the only physical description of Iola in the entire book occurs in the context of her struggle to escape "her reckless and selfish master" whose intent was to "drag her down to his own low level of sin and shame" (*IL,* 39). As the enslaved martyr Tom Anderson announces while planning to ferret Iola away, "she's putty. Beautiful long hair comes way down her back; putty blue eyes, an' jis's ez white ez anybody in dis place. . . . I heerd Marse Tom talkin' 'bout her las's night [sayin'] she war mighty airish, but he meant to break her in" (*IL,* 38). Similar to the innocent girls abducted by male interlopers pretending to be agents of legitimate business, Iola had been remanded to slavery by men who purportedly were there to bring her back from her Northern boarding school to see her dangerously ill father (a rich white planter who had actually already died). Raised to think that she was the wealthy white daughter of parents with nothing to hide, Iola had no reason to question the agents sent by a white cousin intent to enslave her and her siblings, just as the girls and young women of white slavery tales trusted their abductors only to be abused by their sexual overtures. Literally lulled to sleep in her innocent acquiescence, dreaming of returning to the domestic "bliss" of paternal protection, Iola "was awakened by a burning kiss pressed on her lips, and a strong arm encircling her" (*IL,* 103). In this initial white slavery/deception scene, Iola, who thinks she is white, is first accosted by a white deceiver.

Iola Leroy's treatment of Iola's experience under slavery and the association with white slavery disrupt binary oppositions that define virtue as virginity and devalue women who have been sexually abused. Indeed the novel leaves open the simultextual possibility that lecherous owners succeed in their quest to possess their slave girls, body and soul, as well as the possibility that, as many critics suggest, Iola escapes the "racist sexual oppression" of slavery "with her virginity presumably intact."[39] Like other characters and once-enslaved narrators, Iola is sold, we can presume, because she resists white men's advances. Witnessing exactly this, a fellow slave reports that Iola declares to her owner "I'll die first" (*IL*, 41), and, as other historical and fictional women who resisted, is to be beaten for it. Black men describe her as both "game to the last" (*IL*, 42) and as "a tender lamb snatched from the jaws of a hungry wolf" (*IL*, 273), rescued, presumably, before she was devoured. This narrative of sexual escape coexists with rather than countermands a narrative of actualized sexual violence and rape.

Iola's owners clearly express their salacious intent; their power to enact their own unreciprocated desire, is never challenged. Iola herself raises the question of whether she escapes plantation life as an enslaved woman without being raped. Sold seven times because, readers are told, she's so pretty (*IL*, 42), Iola continuously recites facing the "highest insults" from men "whose presence would fill you with horror and loathing" and under whose total power she found herself (*IL*, 274). Indeed her suitor, the white Dr. Gresham, acknowledges Iola's ordeal. His admission that coarse, cruel, and brutal men have bought and sold her for the "basest purposes" (*IL*, 39) can be read as an explicit reference to sexual possession through violent rape.

Iola's later testimony about her ordeal redefines degradation and abasement and aligns morality with the redemptive rhetoric and politics of account-ability used to describe the situation of white slaves. "I had outrages heaped on me which might well crimson the cheek of honest womanhood with shame," she shares with Dr. Gresham. "I have heard men talk glibly of the degradation of the Negro, but there is a vast difference between abasement of condition and degradation of character. I was abased," she declares, "but the men who trampled on me were the degraded ones" (*IL*, 115). Iola's ac-knowledgement and analysis mirror and anticipate her talks with her mother about her "fearful siege of suffering"(*IL*, 196) and with the African American Dr. Latimer before accepting his marriage proposal, in which she admits that she is "prematurely old" as opposed to having a heart "as light as a school girl" (*IL*, 272). When faced with the reality of slavery, rather than having her appeals answered, she confesses to her fiancé, she found herself "dazed" and beyond prayer (*IL*, 274)—signs of defeat, not delivery. Flushed and in tears, she confides that having no earthly power or protection against her vile owners, she was "wild with agony" (*IL*, 274). Iola tells her story simply and without commentary when speaking to her mother, Marie, and Dr. Latimer. When she talks to Dr. Gresham (the only white person who needs to know it, and a man who shares the power and desire, though not the illicit inten-tions of her previous owners), she offers clarification and analysis, placing her personal ordeal in a larger framework. Black women were abased because of their position and trampled on as she was. Degradation of character, she insists, comes with the irresponsible power that white men possess.

Iola's declarations confirm literary critic Elizabeth Ammons's suggestion that the novel is "a parable about surviving rape," one that is expressed simultextually, I argue, rather than by "speaking in code."[40] The possibility of Iola's rape(s) links her both to many enslaved women and to characters who resist and are nonetheless violated, characters such as Sappho who in *Contending Forces* is a revision of the sexual victim as fallen woman. Viewed from this angle, each character's beauty, goodness, and desirability does not rest simply upon an exceptionalist model that valorizes phenotypical resemblance to white women. Rather, these abductions and rapes highlight these protagonists' inescapable connection to the race—one that can extend to white victims—even as each novel's reexamination of degradation and recuperation works to reassess the larger cultural meanings projected onto Black and white womanhood.

The novel does not commit to representations of virtuous Black womanhood. Neither is Iola the only character who complicates an opposition of pure and savaged maidenhood. Iola's grandmother, Harriet Johnson, like *Incidents'* "Aunt Martha," does not stand outside of the sexual relations that produce her light-skinned children. Indeed, once freed and reunited with her son, who takes her back to the plantation from which she was sold off years before, the first person she asks about is her former owner. "What," she queries, "hab become ob Miss Nancy's husband? Is he still a libin?" Informed that he's drunk himself to death, her response is a wistful "he used ter be mighty handsome" (*IL,* 188). Reminded of his intemperance and conscious of his marital status, she still desires the father of her two children. As in the previous texts we have examined, the meanings attached to symbolic Black women and motherhood are not ultimately fixed but rather are fluid and open to redefinition and inquiry. Indeed, the novel's sexual politics leave space for complicit Black desire that stands beside, but does not stand in for, its depiction of the various and virtuous shades of African American womanhood.

Black clubwomen and writers from Jacobs to Harper challenged pseudoscientific theories about essentialized putative African American lasciviousness to reveal connections between power, race, and possession that white men—and women—enjoyed, not only as sexual victims but also as sexual agents and abusers. Like *Incidents, Iola Leroy* exposes the old threadbare lie about interracial desire and authority and reposes the question with which Harper once challenged an audience of feminist activists about their role in Black oppression: "Have women nothing to do with this?"[41] As we have seen, Mrs. Flint has young Linda sleep in her own room and whispers to her at night in her husband's stead. And "young mistresses" "know that the women slaves are subject to their father's authority in all things; and in some cases they [the young mistresses? their fathers?] exercise the same authority over men slaves" (*Incidents*, 52). Likewise, Miss Nancy's interest in her pet slave, "spry Robby," when examined closely, might give rise to some speculation that could be damaging to the reputation of white women.

Miss Nancy (Johnson) and Iola's uncle Robert Johnson serve as distorted mirror replacements for absent parties in familial relation. Their relationship is clearly foundational; it spans the entire novel, literally from the first page until the last. As soon as readers are introduced to Robert, we're told that he "had been separated from his mother in his childhood" and was raised by his mistress who had "fondled him as a pet animal and even taught him to read. Notwithstanding their relation as mistress and slave, they had strong personal likings for each other" (*IL*, 7). One could read the "spunky" and "headstrong" (*IL*, 159) young mistress's selling away of her enslaved rival, Robby's mother, as a familiar trope with a twist. She steals—instead of sells—the illicit offspring, as one critic points out, to rear as a favorite slave.[42] The term "favorite" carries multiple meanings: on its face, it signals special treatment and elevated status. Yet in the lexicon of nineteenth-century enslavement, favorite also carries sexual connotations. One fairly typical advertisement announces that a young woman who has "RUNAWAY from the subscriber" was a "great favorite of some people who called themselves gentlemen."[43] Nancy and Robert's relation offers a regendered version of illicit interracial plantation relations.

Iola Leroy directs its commentary on the racist logic of lynching through Miss Nancy's characterization to illustrate the point Ida B. Wells's "Iola" brings home—that white women possess both sexual desire and racial power. White women, as Harper declared publicly at the 1866 National Woman's Rights Convention, are not "dew drops just exhaled from the skies."[44] Young, "lithe and active" (*IL*, 150), "Miss Nancy" is figured as are other young mistresses, we will recall from Jacobs, who know that women slaves are subject to men's "authority in all things" and sometimes "exercise the same authority over men slaves."[45] "Mrs. Johnson," as Miss Nancy is also called, is connected through marriage to the maturer sexual economies of the plantation. Sexually abandoned and perhaps physically abused by an intemperate, philandering, and finally absent husband, Miss Nancy may be victimized but she is still no "dew drop."[46] She is in sole command of the plantation in *Iola Leroy*'s novelistic time and frame. What better solution and revenge than to take on her absent husband's son as a lover? Not simply "mildly ludicrous," as one critic characterizes her, Miss Nancy can be read, like others with racial power, as more than mildly lascivious.[47] Like Potiphar's wife, as Harper puts it in an address, or as a "white Delilah" in search of an "Afro-American Sampson," to borrow from Wells, white women like Miss Nancy pursue Black men, destroying enslaved families while doing so.[48]

Never fully seduced by intimate access to the white planter class as his sister Marie is, Robert retains what *Iola Leroy* figures as strategic cultural literacy, using his inside knowledge and position to further the collective goals of those who are enslaved with him. Both Robert's soul and his masculinized status are left intact. Only before the Union army approaches does he believe he "is eating his white bread" and "letting well enough alone" (*IL*, 35). When, near the end of the novel, Robert returns to Miss Nancy's plantation after fighting for the Union, the once enslaved elders rib him about his abandoning her. Fully cognizant of his special status, they narrate how "Missus" went "almos's wile" when he left: "Own up, Robby, didn't you feel kine of mean to go off widout eben bidden' her good bye" (*IL*, 175) they ask, eyebrows raised. "I ralely think ole Miss war fon' ob you." They go on, "Didn't yer feel a little down in de mouf wen yer lef' her" (*IL*, 176). Engaging in masterful signifying, they revel in a power reversal they can now celebrate in their newly won freedom.

Miss Nancy and Robert's reunion is less playful. In the plaintive and intimately familiar redundancy of her phrases, the novel expresses the recognizable dynamics of a woman who has "strong personal likings" (*IL*, 7) for a man whom in one sense she once considered a lover. Ignoring the cautionary note when other Blacks she owned fled, she tells Robert that she was convinced "I can trust my Bobby; he will stick to me to the last," only to find "You left me without a word." Finding him gone, she says "I thought maybe you were sick and went to see, but you were not in your room. I couldn't believe at first that you were gone. Wasn't I always good to you?" "You were good," he assures her, "but freedom was better" (*IL*, 151). These lines recollect Douglass's desire to live "*upon free land* as well as *with Freeland*"[49] and expose white naïveté and cultural illiteracy, the expectation of gratitude and loyalty from subalterns whom whites believe have been "petted." Challenging prevalent lynching apologia, Robert pronounces that corporeal and political freedom are more desirable than sexual access to white women's bodies.

If readers recover the sexual simultexts of the novel, its focus on Nancy and Robert's relationship resolves Robert's otherwise inexplicable and paradoxical status as a desirable hero who remains unmarried throughout a novel that uses romance and marriage as a trope for racial tensions, naïveté, and, ultimately, commitment. By *Iola's* end, Robert's geographical and familial ruptures and displacements have been resolved. He stops at Miss Nancy's to collect information so he can find his own mother and family. After serving in the army and now reunited with his biological mother, sister, niece, and nephew, he moves them back to North Carolina where the narrative begins. Like Iola and Dr. Latimer, Robert aggressively chooses to "stand by mama." Indeed, "Stand by Mama"—the last request uttered by Iola's young sister Gracie before she dies— is one of the novel's (and nineteenth-century Black writing's) rallying cries.[50] In an era of enslavement defined by laws that have children follow the legal status of their mothers, this pledge functions both within the text and meta-narratively as astute and necessary political analysis that serves the larger interests of the race.

Robert's return to the South—like Clotel's in the 1867 version of the William Wells Brown novel—signals a commitment to collective African American economic uplift that many whites responded to with virulently racist sexualized rhetoric and violence. At the end of the novel, Robert buys a large plantation that he homesteads to thrifty laborers; and he "often remembers Mrs. Johnson and sends her timely aid" (*IL*, 280). As Harper well knew, having to rely upon a Black man for "timely aid" enacted the greatest fears for white women like Rebecca Latimer Felton, the most powerful Southern representative of the WCTU at the time of *Iola Leroy*'s publication. A popular journalist and powerful speaker, Felton aggressively promoted lynching as she berated white men for supposedly abandoning white Southern women. *Iola Leroy*'s vision of post-reconstruction agricultural development runs directly counter to ideas such as the (white) "wife's farm" that Felton proposed to the powerful Georgia Agricultural Society in 1891.[51] In *Iola Leroy*, Robert—or Black men—establish successful agricultural projects that develop Black labor and leave white women such as Miss Nancy open to—and perhaps dependent upon—Black (financial) advances. By having Robert both stand by mama and support Miss Nancy, *Iola Leroy* both provides a beneficent resolution to their relationship and offers a strident critique of white female sexuality, rebuking them for their complicity in the context of interracial sexual violence.

Harper's use of phenotypically light-skinned characters such as Robert and Iola, like her invocation of white slavery, allows her to simultaneously appeal to sets of readers who may not share "time curves" and literary horizons, to recall Hans Jaus's terminology. *Iola Leroy* reappropriates language that is "already populated with the social intentions of others," as Bakhtin says of the prose writer, "and compels them to serve [its] own intentions."[52] On the level of plot, Iola's color allows for the recirculation of the trope of white slavery—the (essential) story repeated in William Wells Brown's *Clotel*, the William and Ellen Craft narrative, and *Uncle Tom's Cabin*—to direct activist energy back to African American concerns. Simultaneously, marking a phenotypically "white" character "Black" encourages readers to reflect upon the multiplicitous political positions indeterminate racial bodies symbolized in a culture obsessed with racial and juridical classification and engaged in the disenfranchisement of its African American citizenry.

Homonymic Associations, Ida B. Wells, Frances Harper, and the Two Iolas

As with the homonymic associations with white slavery, in *Iola Leroy* characters' names link the novel with previous and contemporaneous struggles for Black freedom and full citizenship rights. The novel's politics of naming recall, for example, the ways in which *Our Nig* augments its interpretative possibilities. *Iola Leroy's* meditations on naming also reaffirm that an expanded sense of cultural literacy is necessary to "read aright" the text's "legible transcript" (*IL*, 14) of civic participation and protest. For Harper, cultural literacy calls for both a sense of the central reform movements of the era in which readers live—that is, a working understanding of campaigns against lynching, Black disenfranchisement, and white slavery, for example—and also a familiarity with historical struggles and leaders. Carby contends that in *Iola Leroy* characters "gain their representativeness from an engagement with history." "Each carries an aspect of the history of the Black community in his or her own individual history, while as a group they represent an historical force: an elite that articulates the possibilities of that Black community."[53] Likewise, the novel as a whole gains its complexity and representativeness from its larger engagements with reform and African American histories.

At almost every narrative turn, *Iola Leroy's* narrative strategies encourage readers to make homonymic and histotextual associations. Carby points out that Harper's readers would recognize her own articles and lectures in the addresses on women featured in "Friends in Council."[54] *Iola Leroy* also includes direct references to Black heroes: Ira Aldridge, Alexandre Dumas, Frederick Douglass, and to slave rebel leaders Nat Turner and Denmark Vesey. When intellectual leaders gather to discuss race issues, the characters correspond to contemporary race leaders. Harper's acculturated readers would appreciate the (almost as) transparent references to race leaders who make cameo appearances in that chapter. Readers of the Black press would credit the ideas of "Bishop Tunster" to Bishop (Henry McNeal) Turner, who at the *conversazione* gives a paper on "Negro Emigration" and advises, "in his bluff hearty tones," that African Americans could "go to Africa," a continent that is to "be redeemed to civilization" and on whose soil "the Negro is to be gathered into the family of nations and recognized as a man and a brother" (*IL*, 246). Known for his rough façade and somewhat unrefined manners, that is, for "his bluff hearty" bearing, Bishop Turner's famous and reprinted speeches provide a clear referent for Bishop Tunster's views.[55] "The sons of Africa, too, can unfettered, untrammeled and unhindered, go to the homes of our forefathers and preach a free, religious, civil and political gospel," avers Turner:

> I know some colored men chafe when they hear an expression about going to Africa. I am sorry I find no term in the vocabulary that will represent them milder than fools; for they are fools. . . . Without reviewing [the continent's] inexhaustible treasures, and how God is holding them in custody for the civilization of the Negro, I merely desire to remark that some of our leading men may blur and slur at Africa till their doomsday arrives. But God intends for us to carry and spread enlightenment and civilization over that land. They are ours and we are theirs.[56]

Likewise, "Mr. Forest, of New York" (*IL*, 243), "a tall, distinguished-looking gentleman" is easily recognizable as T. Thomas Fortune, the New York editor; and "Hon. Dugdale" recalls the Honorable Frederick Douglass.[57] The "counsel's" host, Mr. Stillman, corresponds to William Still, a businessman and author who was known for his hospitality, as it were, because hundreds of former fugitives had stayed at his home, the underground railroad stop in Philadelphia. Professor Langhorne, who raises issues of "partial administration of the law in meting out punishment to colored offenders" (*IL*, 255), could be Professor John Mercer Langston, who had been law professor, dean, and vice president of Howard University.[58] Professor Grandnor could easily be based on Professor Richard Greener, the first Black Harvard graduate and later dean of Howard's law school, who, according to *Men of Mark* (1887), "has risen so fast in the minds of the people that his name is linked with the names of Douglass and Langston," who are also represented at the *conversazione*.[59]

When one associates these leaders with Harper's characters, Miss Delany's equal and affirmatively feminist place and expressions in the "Friends in Council" makes historical, rather than simply narratively utopian, sense. Turner, Langston, and Douglass were ahead of their time in terms of their views of the public place of and leadership rights for women. In that sense they are indeed "friends." Turner praised women "because they 'intend to make a fight for their rights.'" He opened the columns of his newspapers to women writers, ordained a woman deacon (the council of bishops immediately rescinded this appointment), and introduced a woman suffrage bill in the Georgia legislature.[60] According to historians William and Aimee Lee Cheek, Langston, too, was "egalitarian regarding sex as well as race," with a particular appeal to women "with some formal education and those in skilled trades."[61] Fortune worked closely with strong leaders such as Ida B. Wells and Victoria Earle. In the summer of 1895, he was one of four male speakers to present papers at the first National Conference of Colored Women.[62] And Douglass's commitment to both women's rights and specific women—such as the young Ida B. Wells—was legendary.[63]

The men that Harper includes in the world of the novel, those whom she narratively affirms, are progressive "race men," to invoke a favorite late nineteenth-century phrase, even in terms of gender. Thoroughly abreast of the times on almost every subject, to borrow Anna Julia Cooper's phrasing, they do not then "strike the woman question" and suddenly "drop into sixteenth-century logic."[64] Placed near the end of the novel and directly preceding the marital pairings that in Iola Leroy signal egalitarian nation-building as well as romantic resolution, Harper's inclusion of the "council" and its figures again affirms the faith in—as it also builds—a larger cultural literacy on the part of a readership that it envisions as coworkers in community development that is equally devoted to both men and women of the race.

Many of the younger characters, the generation representing the "present" for Iola's readers, are associated with important figures, texts, or movements and so engage what the novel figures as a dynamic history in the making. As critics Carla Peterson and DoVeanna Fulton point out, this strategy is not new to Harper; two characters who are introduced late in Sowing and Reaping (1876–77) share their names with temperance figures and so demonstrate Harper's "awareness of the national dimensions" of her interventions.[65] Likewise, Iola's homonymic resonances, like those of Lucille Delany, who becomes Iola's sister-in-law, and Dr. Frank Latimer, who becomes Iola's husband, carry strong traces of individual and collective uplift. Each character symbolizes the meeting of what Harper might call "upright manhood" and "enlightened womanhood" fully engaged in social protest and community and political organizing.

By 1892 when Iola Leroy was published, Ida B. Wells's "Iola" was a household name in Black communities across the country. As Harriet Jacobs became "Linda" to abolitionists, in the world of print Wells was known simply as "Iola," and, like Jacobs, she even signed her correspondence with her adopted name.[66] Readers were thrilled by her editorials. Maintaining that Blacks were sent to prison for stealing five cents while whites were honored for stealing thousands of dollars, for example, she retorted, "let Blacks steal big."[67] She was the only woman at the 1887 Colored Press Association Convention. Scores of African American newspapers countrywide carried her reprints. "Iola" was the name the masses knew: "Iola" was a fiery journalist, "the princess of the press."

After several months of turmoil, organizing, and boycotts that followed the Memphis triple lynching in which her friend Thomas Moss perished, Wells left a terse editorial to be printed in the newspaper *Free Speech*, of which she was one-third owner: "Nobody in this section believes that old thread-bare lie that Negro men assault white women. If Southern white men are not careful they will overreach themselves and a conclusion will be reached which will be very damaging to the moral reputation of their women."[68] Wells had left town by the time the editorial was printed. While she was gone enraged whites razed her office and threatened to kill her if she dared to return. Wells responded forcefully both to white threats and terrorism and to the surge of African American support she received. She followed *Southern Horrors: Lynch Law in All Its Phases* with a flurry of pamphlets that exposed the U.S. practice to national and international audiences.

That *Southern Horrors* and *Iola Leroy* were each published in 1892, and that in the same year Wells stayed with Harper on the trip north during which her office was destroyed and her life threatened, illustrates Carby's point that "African-American women like Frances Harper, Anna Julia Cooper and Ida B. Wells were not isolated figures . . . ; they were shaped by and helped to shape a wider movement of African-American women. What each of them wrote and lectured about influenced and was influenced in turn by a wider constituency."[69] Indeed, Harper had long fought against isolation and had actively stood with her radical friends and allies. In 1859, when Harper was Wells's age, Harper was intimately involved with John Brown's family. She wrote to Harpers Ferry prisoners as they awaited their sentences, and publicly vowed to help the rebels' families. And as they awaited the martyrs' sentencing, Harper stayed with Brown's wife and daughter at the home of William Still—where escaped Harpers Ferry fugitives were also said to be hiding.[70] She did so in an atmosphere of terror that had anti-slavery activists who might be associated with Harpers Ferry fleeing the country. Like Brown before her, the young Wells stood for the continued and vigorous struggle against white domination. Harper was well aware that "Iola" symbolized exposing institutionalized white mythologies and mendacity and advocating organized, even armed, response to systematic encroachments on African American rights.

Though *Iola Leroy* follows a linear structure that relates the story of Iola's ancestry and girlhood and ends with marriage, the novel simultaneously adapts the modified circular narrative frame associated with Douglass's *Narrative* and modified by Wilson in *Our Nig*, as I discussed in an earlier chapter. In doing so, it provides a histotextual bridge to the beginning of Wells's ("Iola's") literary career. Douglass's afterword, which implicitly comments on William Lloyd Garrison's preface, enlarges the scope of his textual frame, subtly mastering the extra-narrative writing that accompanies the text proper, the preface meant to authorize Douglass's venture into writing. Similarly, the end of *Iola Leroy* functions in two ways. The statement "Iola quietly took her place in the Sunday school as a teacher" (*IL*, 278) follows the expected linear and properly feminine teleology of domestic fiction bestsellers such as *Wide, Wide World* (1850) and *The Lamplighter* (1854) and of postbellum bestsellers such as *What Katy Did* (1872). Iola's Sunday school work also provides a nearly seamless segue to the integral connection, to borrow from historian Evelyn Brooks Higginbotham, between Black women's spirituality and social activism, often located in the church and represented in *Iola Leroy*'s discursive world both by Wells and by the eponymous heroine. When Fannie Barrier Williams, a founding member of the National Association of Colored Women (as Wells was) wrote in 1900: "The training which first enabled colored women to organize and successfully carry on club work was originally obtained in church work. These churches have been and still are the great preparatory schools in which the primary lessons of social order, mutual trustfulness and united effort for the common good, the development of social sympathies grew into women's consciousness through the privileges of church work," she made explicit the place of the church that Harper's original readers would have recognized.[71] After all, Wells, or "Iola" herself, had taught Sunday school in Memphis from 1887 while she was juggling her duties as both a paid teacher and then as coeditor of *Free Speech*. For the character Iola and for many Black readers, "church" was not a place of passive retirement; it more often figured as a site of multiple spiritual *and* public dimensions.

Readers then, as now, were fascinated with the details of authors' lives. Harper could count on a segment of her audience to be acquainted with the evolving trajectory of an increasingly documented race history. Those readers would be attentive to the convergences between the character Iola and the journalist Iola, as well as between Harper's and Wells's shared life histories and commitments. Black newspapers included sketches and brief biographies of race writers and journalists. Emerging histories such as I. Garland Penn's 1891 *The Afro-American Press and Its Editors* included long entries describing the writings of nineteen women journalists and writers accompanied by portrait etchings.[72] These readers knew that both Wells and Harper, like Iola, began their careers as teachers. Indeed, Wells would continue to be a teacher—of Sunday school—for much of her life; and Harper worked with ministers to organize Sunday school programs and programs meant to curb delinquency in Philadelphia.[73]

The religious press, with its wide reach and multiple functions, strengthened the link between Harper and Wells. Its readers knew "Iola." Indeed

Wells took up the name when her inaugural article appeared in the Baptist weekly, the *Living Way. Free Speech,* which she later edited, was also published by Black Baptists. Likewise, Harper published three serialized novels in the A.M.E.'s *Christian Recorder.* Higginbotham notes that "the church-sponsored press played an instrumental role in the dissemination of a black oppositional discourse and in the creation of a black collective will," and women expressed their discontent with the status quo through these channels.[74] Many young women journalists began their careers in journals such as *Our Women and Children* (1888) published by Rev. William Simmons, editor of *American Baptist.* Simmons recruited a young Wells, for example, to become the editor of *Our Women's* "Home" department. Wells followed in Harper's footsteps. As one of Wells's biographers suggests, the journalist was not a transitional figure but rather a "visionary pragmatist" who, like Harper, "blends the imperative of faith and politics."[75]

Young women journalists such as Wells, "Victoria Earle" Matthews, Amelia E. Johnson, Mary V. Cook, Mary Britton, Lucretia Newman Coleman, and Kate Chapman envisioned a continuum between their faith, their journalistic prose, and the fiction they hoped to pen or had already written.[76] In her early twenties, Wells committed to her diary both her fervent prayers and her plans for "my novel."[77] When Iola's new husband encourages her to write a "good strong book" (*IL,* 262), and she finds herself working with a "young pastor who found in her a strong and faithful ally," Iola is in the very place—the activist Black church—where she, Wells's "Iola" and a generation of Black women journalists first found publishing avenues (*IL,* 278). Readers had a clear example of what kind of good strong book Iola, who had just moved South, might produce; *Southern Horrors* had just been published and Wells's subsequent pamphlets and newspaper coverage would appear at the same time as *Iola Leroy's* second and third editions. *Iola Leroy* ends by positioning its eponymous heroine to develop into Wells, that is, into her more radical homonymic counterpart.

Frequently characterized in contemporary criticism as being separated by generation, commitments, and aesthetic choices, Harper and Wells are seen as occupying different ends of the spectrum of Black women's activism and representation. In the accounts of "race women" and journalism in the 1890s, however, they are closely linked. In *The Work of the Afro-American Woman* (1894), for example, writer Gertrude Mossell lists countless works in the clubwomen's movement but writes in most depth about Harper and Wells. Never are the two polarized in such renditions. Rather Mossell, like others, highlights the personally and professionally inflected intersections between their lives and their work.[78]

Iola may take her place as a teacher and helpmate to a preacher in the South, but in the 1890s this functions simultaneously as appropriately gendered action while it also signifies the possibility of oppositional engagement. After all, Lucille Delany, Iola's histotextual model and novelistic guide, is a forceful leader. Aggressive struggle against institutionalized racism wasn't always considered transgressive (that is, unfeminine) precisely because the protection ostensibly proffered to women because of gender—not sitting in smoking cars, for example—was so often unavailable to women who were Black. While a young teacher in the South, for example, Wells boarded a train and was unceremoniously ordered from the ladies' car. Unsuccessful in his attempt to remove her, the conductor called for help and dragged her off the train, wiping his blood from the hand she had bitten. Wells sued, won damages, and set a precedent—soon overturned—that the 1875 Civil Rights Act must be enforced. Likewise, as literary critic Frances Foster avers, "There was nothing demure or passive about [Harper's] politics and her insistence upon her rights." She previously had displayed a similar resistance to segregation. When accosted by a conductor who demanded that she leave a restricted train car, she steadily held her ground: "When I was about to leave," she writes, "he refused my money, and I threw it down on the car floor, and got out, after I had ridden as far as I wished."[79] Rehearsing these biographical and historical narratives illustrates what would not have escaped *Iola Leroy*'s original reading communities, involved, as many were, in broadly defined literary communities. "Iola" was a name African American audiences recognized to stand for contemporary action that stemmed from a long tradition of protest and resistance, a tradition of which Harper, they also knew, was a significant part.

Embedded Genealogies: Martin Delany, Lucy A. Delaney, and *Iola*'s Lucille Delany

Like *Iola Leroy*'s ending, which positions its title character to engage in activism that spans sacred and secular realms, the marriage plots enacted by the Leroy siblings also work in multiple ways. The pairings of Iola Leroy and Dr. Frank Latimer and Iola's brother Harry Leroy and Lucille Delany echo conventional romantic tropes of narrative closure while also extending the novel's politics of naming and its redefinition of interpretive prowess to include cultural and historical literacy as well as formal education. Lucille Delany is the only significant character in *Iola Leroy* whose lineage isn't explained. Her name, then, provides an important clue to her past, a past the audience is implicitly asked to provide by tapping into their own historical and literary landscape. Lucy A. Delaney's *From the Darkness Cometh the Light* provides a symbolic maternal legacy. This slave narrative published in the early 1890s offers a meditation about Black motherhood; and educating Black mothers is the life work of the character Lucille Delany, Iola's "ideal woman." Martin Delany provides the paternal reference that helps to explain Lucille's exalted position in the novel. She functions as his metaphorical daughter in appearance, passion, and commitment. The meanings of Lucille Delany's novelistic presence become both more plentiful and stable when readers recognize the ways in which extra-narrative referents amplify her metastory.

Like Ida B. Wells-Barnett, who refused to give up her lecturing and activism once she was a married woman and mother, *Iola Leroy*'s most political character, Lucille Delany, refuses to resign her position as a teacher, administrator, and educational leader when she marries Harry Leroy. Teaching as the preserve of single women of any race was standard fare well past the turn of the century; when women married, they often summarily lost their jobs.[80] Just three years before *Iola*'s publication, the Black newspaper the *Washington Bee* reported on "Married Women in the Schools." The editors opined in support of the Rev. Francis Grimké that "the action of the School Trustee Grimkie [*sic*] . . . dismissing certain married ladies from school, because they refused to resign, meets the hearty approval of the citizens. It was not only Rev. Grimkie's duty, but it is an unwritten law that has been in vogue in the schools from the time of memory of man runneth not to the contrary, that married women shall not teach."

The *Washington Bee* also contended that, when female school teachers married and so "assumed another name, by act of law their contract previously made, under their maiden names ceases. They do not exist in law."[81] "*Miss* Delany," as she is called through the very penultimate page of the novel, is an assertive, "religious," "wise" woman who will only accept a husband who supports her self-defined vision of personal duty (*IL*, 198). She is in no hurry, as Cooper expressed it in *A Voice From the South* (1892), "to cramp, stunt, simplify and nullify" herself "as to make [her] eligible for the privilege of being swallowed up into some little man." The problem, instead, Cooper goes on, "now rests on the man as to how he can so develop his God-given powers as to reach the ideal of [this] generation of women."[82]

Like Cooper, who reverses the sexual connotations of consummation so that women rather than men are "swallowed up into" the other sex, Miss Delany reverses gendered roles, for it is her passion and commitment that will determine the shape of the couple's professional lives. When Harry proposes, she expresses her reservations, countering that "school-teachers are uncomfortable people, and Harry, I would not like to make you uncomfortable by marrying you" (*IL*, 278). Finding her unwilling to cede her identity to marriage, he joins her in *her* work; the end of the novel finds Harry and Lucille "at the head of a large and flourishing school" (*IL*, 280). Her insistence on creating a marriage contract that supercedes both "the memory of man" and the custom that "married women do not exist in law" provides the last word on Dr. Frank Latimer's earlier comment that a woman as "grand, brave, intellectual and religious" as Miss Delany would "make some man an excellent wife" (*IL*, 242). Harry's earnest commitment to marry Lucille answers the question that Cooper posed in 1892: "Is the intellectual woman *desirable* in the matrimonial market?"[83] Responding with a resounding "Yes," *Iola Leroy* offers this exemplar of an equitable union. Lucille Delany's character and marriage challenge the stance of the disembodied D.C. "citizens" of Rev. Grimké whose "manly" antilynching comments, as we have seen, Harper will later laud, and of others who might object to women's independence and independent identities.

Lucille Delany is introduced as "the most remarkable woman [Harry] has ever met" (*IL*, 198); however, little back story is provided to explain how she developed into his and Iola's "ideal woman" (*IL*, 242). She is presented on two separate occasions, first in the South where she has founded a school "to train future wives and mothers" (in other words, presently single women) and then later on a visit north, when Iola makes the emphatic point that Lucille, like any single woman of "much ability," should not be seen simply as a future wife, "flotsam all adrift until some man [has] appropriated her" (*IL*, 242). Delany increases her teaching force and enlarges her enterprise's quarters until she has erected a large schoolhouse through "her own exertions and the help of others" (*IL*, 200). Harry fleshes out her physical description. She is "of medium height, somewhat slender and well-formed, with dark, expressive eyes full of thought and feeling. Neither hair nor complexion show the least hint of blood admixture" (*IL*, 199). "I am glad of it" responds Iola. "Every person of unmixed blood who succeeds in any department of literature, art or science is a living argument for the capability which is in the race" (*IL*, 199). Yet besides her education at "University of A———" and her achievements as an educator, Delany is a *tabula rasa*.[84] Unlike Dr. Latimer, she has no background in freedom or in slavery nor any familial connections past or present. Her name provides the only key to her associations, linking her to metaphorical parents who share it and whose own achievements and physical attributes might produce such a "lovely," "wise," and "excellent" woman (*IL*, 198).

Delaney's autobiography, *From the Darkness Cometh the Light, or Struggles for Freedom*, asserts an explicit articulation of female agency linked to maternal inspiration that is paradigmatic of Black nineteenth-century narrative. The story of maternal courageousness and dedication to freeing her daughter "with the help of God and a good lawyer" mirrors the merger of intellectual and religious qualities attributed to *Iola*'s Lucille.[85] Throughout Delaney's nonfiction narrative, Lucy's mother Polly is motherhood exalted. Once her husband is sold off, the narrative's focal point is the family's quest for freedom, one dependent upon the matrifocal logic that "no free woman can give birth to a slave as it is in direct violation of the laws of God and man," as her lawyer puts it. Despite their differences, the grandmother in *Incidents* and Delaney's mother Polly are each free women, stolen as children and held captive in slavery. Their descendants' descriptions of these women's feisty, single, skilled, and economically viable maternal role models echo each other. "Dear, dear mother!" writes Delaney, "How solemnly I invoke your spirit as I review these trying scenes of my girlhood so long agone! Your patient face and neatly-dressed figure stands ever in the foreground of that checkered time; a figure showing naught to the on-looker but the common place virtues of an honest woman."[86] Jacobs closes her narrative affirming that "it has been painful to me to recall the dreary years I passed in bondage. . . . Yet the retrospection is not altogether without solace; for with those gloomy recollections come tender memories of my good old grandmother, like light, fleecy clouds floating over a dark and troubled sea."[87] Jacobs's maternal rhetoric precisely invokes Delaney's title *From the Darkness Cometh the Light* as it also mirrors *Iola Leroy*'s subtitle, *Shadows Uplifted,* and her oft-repeated theme of "a brighter coming day."[88]

By the 1890s, when *Iola Leroy* and *From the Darkness* were published, more precise, less imagistic images of Black motherhood were needed to counter attacks against Black women that insisted that the neat dress and patient demeanor of a Black woman with virtue covered not a virtuous woman but something else entirely. In this decade, Black women increasingly were depicted as "prostitutes," "natural liars and thieves," as journalist John W. Jacks would put it in 1895;[89] they spurred on the supposedly bestial nature of the men of their race. Delaney's *From the Darkness* provides a metaphorical maternal lineage and legacy for *Iola*'s Lucille Delany. Her narrative echoes the centrality of Black maternity in *Iola Leroy,* a connection that is missing in Lucille's own personal story even as she strives to provide educational and moral support for other young women.

In *Iola Leroy,* Lucille Delany's most obvious possible paternal antecedent is Martin Delany, who, in William Andrews's words, was "perhaps *the* black renaissance man of the mid-nineteenth century."[90] During his life Delany was a lecturer, newspaper editor, and author of a novel and two political treatises. He also went to medical school, arranged a major expedition to West Africa, and served as a major and recruiting agent in the Civil War. Delany was recuperated in the 1960s, as historian Nell Painter asserts, as the father of Black nationalism. He would be proud to be involved in naming practices that kept historical memory alive and that associated his literary and genealogical progeny with those who contributed to Black progress and fought for Black education. Indeed, he named his own children in just that spirit, for those who advanced literature, arts, and science in the African Diaspora.[91]

Full of "energy and enterprise," as William Lloyd Garrison characterized Martin Delany,[92] Lucille's achievements likewise surpass those of *Iola Leroy's* major characters. She thus reenacts the racial challenge Delany's abilities, vision, and physical presence embody. Martin Delany was a "fine looking" man, who, in Douglass's words, appeared as if he were carved out of "polished black Italian marble." Delany might have preferred that Douglass had chosen a less European metaphor, for he was well aware that his abilities paired with his dark skin provided Black communities with indisputable evidence of the capabilities of the race, to borrow from Iola's description of Lucille (*IL,* 199). As Martin Delany once commented, "Our good co-laborer Henry Bibb," a fugitive turned anti-slavery lecturer and writer, was "much admired," but whites "say that his talents emanate from the preponderance of *white* blood in him. This it will puzzle them to say of me!"[93] Lucille of course answers this same conundrum in relation to the otherwise insistent privileging of light-skinned characters in *Iola Leroy.*

Martin Delany's association with Lucille as a metaphorical ancestor was more than skin deep; they shared a dedication to female education. As publisher and editor of one of the earliest Black newspapers, *Mystery,* and later in conventions and in the pages of the effort he edited with Frederick Douglass, the *North Star,* Delany urged Black women to shun domestic work and to set for themselves higher goals while he urged communities to recognize that "the true guardians of the rising generation" were women who needed and deserved an adequate education. This advocacy in *Mystery* inspired a wealthy minister to start a school for Black youth that later became Avery College.[94] Indeed, at times Delany was more proactive on issues of gender than Douglass, who remains famous for his feminist commitments. Delany introduced resolutions that declared the equality of the sexes and invited women's participation in political deliberations.[95] In Delany's Emigration Convention, Mary Bibb, widow of Henry Bibb, served as a vice president, and other women were elected to positions of power and leadership. He helped to actualize the goal of a class of young women, articulated by several of Harper's heroines and many of the emerging female journalists of the late 1880s to pen good strong books. If Iola mirrors Wells/Iola in her desire to publish fiction,

Frances Anne Rollin, who was about Iola's age when she headed south to teach in freedmen's schools, had similar aspirations. Her hopes to become an author were realized when she connected with Delany in South Carolina and soon published *The Life and Public Services of Martin R. Delany* (1868), the first full-length biography of a free African American.[96]

Martin Delany's disdain for domestic work, his warnings that "men never attain a higher grade of civilization than the women of their race," and his admonition that Blacks would "never become whites' equal until you educate your children and honor and respect your women" enlarge the context of Lucille Delany's work in *Iola Leroy.*[97] Reading newspaper reports that "Blacks were becoming unfit to be servants for white people" Lucille concludes that, if this were the case, they "were unfit to be mothers to their own children" (*IL*, 199). Read through the lens of accommodationist respectability, this response offers a transfer of Black women's energy from a white supremacist domestic sphere to a conservative gender-based one in which women do not escape the ruling assumptions that they are generally "unfit"—both for service, the work that most exploits their labor and degrades their person, and for motherhood. Yet if one is attentive to Lucille Delany's histotextual genealogy she does not transparently act on an internalized notion of a Black woman's proper place as incompetent mother or maid. Her goal is not to transform these "unfit" servants into paragons of true domestic service for the benefit of whites. Taking Blacks out of service ("which is degrading to us as a class," as Martin Delany once publicly resolved)[98] and educating them was one projected outcome of Lucille Delany's educational mission. However, her school's genesis suggests that it is intertwined with the reality of Southern women in service, their principal opportunity, as it were, for employment. Lucille Delany proposes an enlarged domestic sphere that stresses the centrality of Black female education and invests "domestic service" in the economy of self, home, and community maintenance. The logical trajectory of her work also leaves room for its alignment with Nannie Burroughs's National Training School for Girls that would emerge some fifteen years after Harper imagined Lucille Delany's school. Seeking to redefine perceptions of women as "incompetent menials" and to professionalize and make respectable "first-class" service meant that Black working mothers would be physically and economically fit to better care for their own children.[99]

Tracing Martin Delany's presence in *Iola Leroy* may strain the credulity of those who understand Delany and Harper as writers and activists with widely divergent political persuasions and aesthetic beliefs. Until recently, most historians have situated early nationalism and nineteenth-century religious uplift at different poles of the struggle for Black equality, but in more instances than are obvious Harper and Delany share overlapping literary histories and political commitments. Nineteenth-century readers might recall that the two were both regarded as stellar lecturers who, in their early careers, shared podiums, audiences, and the pages of Black periodicals.[100] Though *Iola Leroy*'s readership would not remember, as Harper's antebellum audience would, that she and Delany both published significant literary pieces in the 1859 inaugural volume of the *Anglo-African Magazine*, as we have seen, postbellum chroniclers of the Black press reported on early journalism and race work in detail. For instance, Harper's "Two Offers," the first African American short story, and Delany's *Blake*, one of the earliest Black-authored novels, both appeared serially in the *Anglo-African*'s first volumes.[101] And Delany, like Harper, was a supporter of John Brown. After an unannounced visit, Brown convinced Delany to drop his work for weeks to recruit delegates and convene a convention that would pass a provisional constitution that would govern territory wrested from the U.S. government by force. Brown's emphasis on integrity, sobriety, intelligence, "and above all first-rate moral and religious characters" resonated with both Delany and Harper.[102] Indeed, as Nell Painter points out, Delany's identification of these traits with a "better" and educated class of Blacks who would lead rather than join the masses made his nationalism elitist rather than democratic.[103] This sentiment also finds expression in the leadership model that emerges from *Iola Leroy*.

Petitioning Science, or Martin Delany and Dr. Frank, George and Lewis Latimer

Although Dr. Frank Latimer is introduced relatively late in *Iola Leroy*, his many histotextual facets magnify his narrative importance—that is, the multivalent heuristic work that his character reflected. Like Delany, Lewis Howard Latimer and his famous father George Latimer serve as Dr. Latimer's homonymic referents; their stories provide an augmented interpretative route through the closing section of *Iola Leroy*. Delany's attendance at Harvard Medical School and the widespread front-page coverage of his presence at the International Statistical Congress augment the historical and political frames of reference and association into which Iola's eventual spouse fits. Examining Dr. Latimer's histotextual connections helps to illuminate how *Iola Leroy* comments on the nineteenth-century battleground of race, science, and statistics.

In *Iola Leroy*, the liberal humanist Dr. Gresham, the very light-skinned Dr. Latimer, and a Southern racist named Dr. Latrobe converge at a convention where papers are presented and medical issues are debated alongside science's inevitable connections to race. [104] Latimer's (undetected racial) presence and his acceptance on his own merits are meant to represent a signal achievement in an arena and era in which social Darwinism and eugenics married reactionary politics and racist literature. Latimer builds on Delany's legacy; his narrative presence, to recall Douglass's characterization of Delany's participation at the International Statistical Congress in London, "was an answer to a thousand humiliating inquiries respecting the character and qualifications of the colored race." [105]

Iola's decision to marry light Latimer rather than white Gresham does more than enact a simple (and slight) racial substitution; likewise, his status as a doctor and graduate of the University of Pennsylvania are more than signifiers of bourgeois Black achievement and extraordinary academic pedigree. Prompted by a well-received paper that Latimer has just presented, [106] Latrobe waxes poetic about the benefits of white "heredity and environment." The novel soon reveals "Dr. Latrobe's mistake," as the chapter is entitled, for Dr. Latimer "belongs to [the] negro race both by blood and by choice" (*IL*, 238). Latimer has rejected his owner's mother's postemancipation offer to "overlook 'the missing link of matrimony,' and adopt him as her heir, if he would ignore his identity with the colored race" (*IL*, 239). This hypocritical invocation of matrimony is barbed, of course, for slave mistresses, fictional or historical, rarely sanctioned binding unions between their sons and the enslaved women who bore their descendents. Mrs. Latimer's offer, in tandem with the novel's illustration of the problems of transforming interracial sexual arrangements into legal marriages, heightens the force of the novel's critique of white hypocrisy about interracial sex and law during slavery and beyond.

One of the few white women featured in *Iola Leroy*, Mrs. Latimer might be grouped with Iola's white father's neighbors, the women who never "entered his doors when it became known that Marie . . . presided at his table" as his *wife* (*IL*, 76). It is not a racially neutral "missing link of matrimony" but a racially specific link of maternity that Latimer's biological grandmother is willing to "overlook" or negate. Moreover, Mrs. Latimer's homonymic associations include Rebecca Latimer Felton, the most popular and powerful southern WCTU advocate, whose politics, as we have seen, were rabidly anti-Black. Harper and Latimer Felton's positions put them on warring sides of the WCTU's dealings with race. Indeed Latimer Felton's preoccupation with the "threat" of interracial sex—never consensual in her mind—overrode the historical reality of white access to Black women's bodies with the hysterical pro-lynching rhetoric of putatively predatory Black "beasts" ravaging innocent white women and children. As Iola rejects Dr. Gresham, her second suitor refuses to become an heir to the Latimer (Felton) legacy of white aristocratic entitlements and the structures of cross-class white supremacy springing up to "defend" them. Marrying Latimer and (Wells's) Iola at the level of historicized heuristic symbolism highlights how white hypocrisy in the arena of interracial marriage and inheritance functions as the linchpin of sexualized violence that peaked in the years in which readers first encountered *Iola Leroy*.

The similar decisions that Iola and Frank Latimer make to choose their mothers and so affirm their classification as African American function to reinflect pseudoscientific classifications of race that were obsessively looked over but rarely overlooked in the 1890s. Always, it seems, on the lookout, Latrobe believes that he can recognize the polluting "presence of Negro blood when all physical signs had disappeared" (*IL*, 239). As legal critic Eva Saks argues, in the post-Reconstruction South, "To the law, a black person was not represented by a perceptible physical phenomenon like black skin, but instead consisted in black blood" (Saks, 49), the sign of an overdetermining maternal genealogy. One's mother, in other words, not one's color, continued to determine one's racial status. Character after character proudly affirms this legacy, declaring implicitly what Iola avers when she states, "The best blood in my veins is African blood, and I am not ashamed of it" (*IL*, 208). The novel reappropriates one of the central tenets of slave law and custom to cast aside Latrobe's exclusionary and faulty racial epistemology and Mrs. Latimer's racial condescension. Instead, *Iola* reaffirms Black maternity as a central *positive* conduit of environment and heredity.

Latimer's postponed racial declaration—readers and Latrobe find out together that he is not "white"—brings home both the national irony and the social impossibility of trying "to substantiate blood, to substantiate what is neither a mimetic description [the grandmother's reaction to phenotype] nor a tangible entity [the "presence" that Latrobe insists he recognizes] but instead a semiotic figure."[107] Unlike Iola and Harry's passing, where the narrator and readers know the characters' racial genealogy before the characters do, in this case readers are grouped with Latrobe in the process of discovery. As the audience finds out later, Latimer has already confided to Gresham that he, Latimer, has rejected "all the possibilities which only birth and blood can give a white man in our Democratic country" (*IL*, 240). Latrobe's consequent racial misrecognition, then, challenges the increasing clout of scientific discourse being used to advance racist eugenics in the 1890s, "an entire social science literature of hereditary deviance—a deviance of the blood—[that] upheld the discipline and punishment of the dangerous miscegenous body in the interest of racial purity."[108] Like *Our Nig*'s treatment of Mag, this scenario also confronts readers' own perceptions about racial knowability, testing them to see if they have mastered the lessons of *Iola Leroy's* implied pedagogy and so successfully resisted identifying with Latrobe's mistaken racial epistemologies.

Choosing to write over rather than override her racist assumptions, Latimer's "grandmother" is willing to honor her nostalgic desire to substitute Latimer's white face, which forcefully reminds her of her "dear departed son," in place of her former chattel's mixed "blood." It is just this kind of exchange, what is often called passing, that white supremacists fear, even though many, like Latrobe, insist that their racial perception is infallible, that they can detect such a substitution of the "counterfeit" for the "real." Gresham's proposal to admit Iola into his family (through marriage) mirrors Mrs. Latimer's offer to her progeny. He too had previously suggested that Iola substitute her white face for her commitment to "her race" to sow and reap the benefits of legitimate (read white) family, and of the larger body politic. Gresham's subsequent interactions with Latrobe and Latimer display, even as he is being romantically displaced, that he is finally learning to read aright. Providing white readers with a model of dynamic racial understanding, *Iola Leroy* squarely places the concepts of race and classification, family and legitimacy, citizenship and belonging in the context of the legal, scientific, and representational discourses that imbued them with meaning.

Iola Leroy's original readers may very well have placed its discussion of race and medicine in the context of public discussions about Black ability and access that were foundational in racist pseudoscience. Latimer is presented with impeccable professional credentials, even though many in Harper's audience were well aware of the fact that Black doctors had hardly enjoyed long-standing and unproblematized access to the medical field. For example, Martin Delany's journey to become a physician began in the years immediately preceding *Iola Leroy's* postwar setting. In the antebellum North, letters that attested to "good moral standing," a placement that included "reading" under a medical doctor for three years, and tuition fees were what one needed to be admitted to medical school—if one were white. Delany convinced reputable white doctors to allow him to study with them; along with other Pittsburgh leaders, they wrote the recommendations that five medical schools declined before Dean Oliver Wendell Holmes Sr. admitted Delany to Harvard in 1850. He joined two other students, bound for Liberia, as the earliest Blacks at the medical school. As one of the very first Blacks permitted a formal medical education who intended to practice *within* the United States, Delany's presence was exceptionally rare. Yet the Black students' stint at Harvard was not long-lived. Faced with a white woman who was to be admitted later that year, Harvard's white male students revolted; they signed petitions and succeeded in purging (they might have said purifying) their ranks. When, in *Iola,* Latrobe complains that he will face social and professional degradation if he is forced to fraternize with those who were once enslaved, he echoes Delany's medical student colleagues' remonstrance that Blacks are "highly detrimental to the interests and welfare" of Harvard, whose reputation Blacks ostensibly lower and the value of its diploma they supposedly lessen. Dr. Latimer's success as a doctor emphatically counters such assumptions.[109]

Like Martin Delany and others, novelists such as Harper and Charles Chesnutt recognized that scientific fields as well as literature were battlegrounds in the struggle to discredit the race (or prove it creditable) and incorporated related themes into their works. To challenge theories that supported Black degradation, the *Anglo-African Magazine* (1859, in which both Harper and Delany published) was devoted to "Literature, Science, Statistics and the Advancement of the Cause of Human Freedom," as its masthead proclaimed. It anticipated organizations such as Baltimore's Monumental Literary and Scientific Association (1891) that wed these concerns in their names. Because racial superiority was based on the canard that people of African descent were neither intellectually competent nor competitive, Delany's presence at the 1860 International Statistical Congress in London caused an international uproar that was felt in the highest British and U.S. government circles. Invited to present a paper on his recent African expedition, Delany was introduced along with other overseas participants. Lord Brougham, president of the Congress, former chancellor, and pioneer of anti-slavery reform in the British West Indies, goaded the American minister and former U.S. Vice President George Dallas and the delegation's leader, Augustus Longstreet, by pointedly expressing his hope that the presence of a Negro wouldn't offend their scruples. Delany's gracious acknowledgment and assurance to the body that "*I am a man*" was greeted with cheers throughout the auditorium and was featured in the headlines of the U.S. and international press. The U.S. delegation leader stormed out early and returned home, fuming that he could not be "received as an equal while the Negro was received with open arms." President Buchanan and his cabinet met to consider the secretary of state's stance that the United States should demand British disavowal of Brougham's actions. He had, Dallas insisted, insulted not only slaveholders but "a still larger portion of the American people . . . who consider the Negro race as an inferior one and who repudiate all political equality and social connection with its descendants."[110] Invited by Lord Brougham to join the National Association for the Promotion of Social Science in Scotland, Delany continued to be active in challenging racist social and pseudoscience. Determined as he was to "capture the sciences, and appropriate them to the endowment of his own will," almost twenty years later Delany's book *Principia of Ethnology: The Origin of Races and Color* (1879) was the first to refute increasingly influential social Darwinist theories that placed Blacks at a lower stage of evolutionary development.[111]

Beyond Delany's homonymic associations with Lucille Delany as a significant presence in medicine and in the broader "sciences," he also serves as a symbolic ancestor for Black inventors like Lewis Latimer, whom I argue serves as one of Dr. Latimer's analogues. Lewis Latimer was heir to a hard-fought Black parental legacy that provides a counter-story to the classic slave tale of white paternal denial upon which the novel's Dr. Latimer's modified story relies. The youngest child of George Latimer, he was born in 1848, six years after his father posed as his pregnant wife's master to escape the fast-approaching birth of their first child into slavery. Threatened with being returned to the South, his case promptly became a cause célèbre. As a youngster, Lewis Latimer sold the *Liberator* and later fought for the Union as had his two older brothers. He became a self-taught Renaissance man who played the flute and violin, painted portraits, and spoke French and German. He presented his poetry regularly at Bethel Lyceum meetings and also published it in the *New York Age*.[112] Moreover, like *Iola's* Dr. Latimer, Lewis Latimer was a man of science. In 1876, as Union troops pulled out of the South, he composed Alexander Graham Bell's drawings for the first telephone. By the 1880s he had worked for electricity mogul Hiram Maxim (of what would become Westinghouse) and for Thomas Edison's General Electric, supervising the installation of some of the earliest electric lighting plants in New York City, Philadelphia, Montreal, and London.

By the 1890s, Latimer was a well-established inventor in his own right. He devised the first low-cost electric light filament and authored the "bible" of electric lighting (1890), the first work of its kind, which Victoria Earle Matthews would call "one of the most valuable contributions to Race Literature."[113] Each patent that Latimer recorded announced African American progress and presence in a scientific field that was often used to prove Black intellectual deficiency. Beginning with the statement "Be it known, that I, Lewis H. Latimer, a citizen of the U.S. and resident of" New York have "invented a new and useful improvement," these patents made symbolic restitution to antebellum inventors such as Martin Delany who had been denied national patent protection when, not long before, Blacks were not considered U.S. citizens.[114] Latimer's success laid claim to all the possibilities secured by white "birth and blood in our Democratic country" (*IL,* 240). In 1890, at a time when Blacks were increasingly being denied the judicial assurances of due process, equal protection, and voting rights, Latimer became Edison's legal department's chief draftsman and expert witness. While the courts rolled back Black claims to citizenship, million-dollar questions of intellectual property were settled, usually in his favor, on the basis of Latimer's testimony.[115]

Like his son Lewis, George Latimer's name was linked to questions of property and judicial process. Soon after he and his fugitive wife made it to Boston in 1842, George was identified by the slave owner who had come north to claim and arrest him. When Massachusetts Chief Justice Lemuel Shaw denied Latimer a trial, "Boston went wild with excitement. Placards were distributed and handbills posted throughout the city denouncing the outrage and summoning citizens to a meeting in Faneuil Hall."[116] A broad-based abolitionist community organized a statewide campaign that included grassroots protests and judicial challenges. Galvanized, participants produced large-scale petitions and a triweekly newspaper, the *Latimer and North Star Journal,* with a circulation of twenty thousand.

Latimer's name was deeply associated with what in *Iola Leroy* is described as "high heroic manhood" (*IL,* 265), that is, both personal courage and resistance and effective grassroots action. The latter paid off; Latimer's owner, cognizant that he could neither confront large numbers of protestors (nearly three hundred Black men assembled at the courthouse to protect Latimer from being abducted) nor elude the vigilance committees to escape Boston with his "property," sold the fugitive at a sharply reduced price.[117] When Latimer was "freed," there were citywide celebrations. The groundswell of organization continued as the ex-fugitive traveled with movement leaders— Garrison, Douglass, the Hutchinson Family Singers, and Parker Pillsbury— gathering signatures for the "Latimer and Great Massachusetts Petition." It presented the demands of fully 65,000 "citizens of the State of Massachusetts" who, it declared, "earnestly [desired] to free the commonwealth and themselves from all connection with domestic slavery and to secure the citizens of this state from the danger of enslavement."[118] The second "monster Latimer petition," "nearly a mile in length, was wound on a roller, having a crank at each end, and was, in bulk, as big as a large washtub."[119] Southerners were enraged to discover that the first signatory, who signed with an X, was the fugitive George Latimer himself. This appeal, which included almost as many signatures as the Latimer and Great Massachusetts Petition, was presented in the U.S. House of Representatives by John Quincy Adams before it was blocked. But the Massachusetts version advanced by Adams's son Charles resulted in the passage of the Personal Liberty Act in 1843; it defied the power of the federal government to impel Massachusetts to comply with fugitive slave returns.

Frances Watkins [Harper] was seventeen when the Latimer fugitive-slave case exploded. She lived in Baltimore with her uncle William Watkins, an abolitionist of national repute who contributed regularly to the *Liberator* and had subscribed to Garrison's journal since its inception. Indeed, William Watkins corresponded personally with Garrison and served as "the conduit linking Baltimore blacks with the broader antislavery movement."[120] By 1854, Harper herself was on the abolitionist lecture circuit; serving as the first woman lecturer for the Maine Anti-Slavery Society, she no doubt visited places where Latimer too had spoken when he joined anti-slavery speakers throughout New England.

Latimer was legendary throughout the nineteenth century to the readership from which Harper in large part drew. His case succeeded in "linking the cause of the fugitives with the right of petition" and "stimulated the most thorough professional, ministerial, and popular debate over the duty of resistance [yet] heard in America."[121] Latimer himself became a celebrity. At one event, according to the *Liberator* and the *Salem Observer*, "George Latimer, the lion himself, was present. His appearance caused a sensation among the audience." At the meeting's close, "Latimer stood in front of the rostrum [so that] those who wished might pass along and shake hands with him as is the custom when the president and other distinguished men receive the attention and civilities of the sovereign people."[122] Almost ten years after Latimer's owner left Boston nearly empty-handed, another fugitive, Shadrach, was captured; Blacks "engineered a daring courtroom rescue" in which Latimer was a central player; he kept watch over Shadrach's owner and secured the carriage they used in the escape.[123]

Latimer's celebrity status was followed by the cold economic and social realities that Black people faced in the racist North. Yet memories of the successful mass movement with which his name was almost metonymically associated lingered, assuring future activists that such campaigns could, in fact, help to change history.[124] Decades after Latimer became free, at a meeting at the People's Church in Boston, an aging John Hutchinson (one of the famous Hutchinson Family Singers of Harriet Wilson's Milford, New Hampshire) introduced Frederick Douglass and retold "the thrilling story of George W. Latimer." After Douglass spoke, Latimer, too, was invited to the stage.[125] Correspondence between Douglass and Lewis Latimer about the meeting at the People's Church again illustrates the nexus of association and the historical reflection that *Iola Leroy* both expresses and anticipates. Young Douglass's very first published writing had addressed the Latimer case. Years later, heeding Victoria Earle Matthews's suggestion, he wrote Lewis Latimer to describe that time: it "is fifty-two years since I first saw your father and mother in Boston.

You can hardly imagine the excitement the attempts to recapture them caused in Boston. It was a new experience for the Abolitionists and they improved it to the full extent to which it was capable. I sincerely thank dear Mrs. Matthews for bringing me to your attention."[126] Indeed, Victoria Earle, Lewis Latimer, and others, including T. Thomas Fortune, founded the "Brooklyn Literary Union," "quite a tally-ho," as the newspaper the *Woman's Era* reported, in 1894.[127] Latimer and Matthews continued to be in touch. And the letterhead of the National Association of Colored Women (NACW) that Matthews used to write him includes the name of Frances Harper, who was serving as NACW vice president. As president, Matthews thanked Latimer for his mention of the NACW in an 1897 edition of the *New York Age*. Soon after, Lewis, known as an inventor and poet, would follow his father's activist example and organize a petition drive to protest Black disenfranchisement in New York.[128]

Iola Leroy's use of the Latimer name histotextually challenges racist use of the law and affirms the appeal to constitutional respect expressed within the novel when Dr. Latimer argues that "obedience to law is the gauge by which a nation's strength or weakness is tried" (*IL*, 250). The novel's homonymic engagement with the law was aligned with the many newspaper articles, pamphlets, and at least one full-length book, *Justice and Jurisprudence* (1889), penned and sponsored by Black activists and allies of the period.[129] Years before, abolitionists had been appalled when, ordering that George Latimer be returned to the South, Justice Shaw advanced the argument that despite one's—and his own—personal anti-slavery sentiments, the federal law was supreme. *Iola's* homonymic associations with the case reaffirm for its readers that consistency demanded that white supremacist intellectuals and their sympathizers acknowledge both legal precedents and their own antebellum reliance on formalist interpretations of the law. The link to the Latimer case further reminds *Iola's* readers that if one could argue that the pre-Civil War Constitution ensured the right of property in slaves despite individual citizens' personal convictions or reservations, then the postwar amendments likewise ensured due process, equal protection, and voting rights to African Americans. These novelistic resonances echoed contemporary social action that looked back, as *Iola* does, to antebellum protest for inspiration. In 1889, when three thousand people assembled at Faneuil Hall to condemn lynching, they invoked the "uncompromising spirit of Garrison, of Phillips, of Sumner."[130] In the very site of Latimer mass meetings, their demand that "the bloodthirsty disregard of the law must cease" linked common antilynching rhetoric, symbolized in *Iola Leroy* by the eponymous heroine, to the judicial and legislative strategies used in the Latimer case, represented in *Iola* by her eventual husband.

Readers of the Black press, part of Harper's long-time constituency, would be familiar with the overlapping publishing and activist histories of various

"Iolas," Delan(e)ys, and Latimers. Indeed, Martin Delany's name and presence continued to have currency in the late 1800s. A second edition of his biography was issued in 1883; and in *A Voice from the South* (1892), Cooper quotes Delany, "an unadulterated black man" who "used to say that when honors of state fell upon him . . . the whole race entered with him," before staking her claim that "only the BLACK WOMAN can say 'when and where I enter . . . there the whole *Negro race enters with me.*'"[131] Lewis Latimer also remained in the public eye. He was a regular contributor to the *New York Age*, one of the most widely distributed and respected Black weeklies. Indeed, in the early 1890s, readers of the *Age* might come across Latimer's name more frequently than that of Harper or "Iola." His public appearances as the featured speaker at popular public gatherings were regularly announced. Additionally, in the years that lead up to *Iola Leroy*'s publication, between October 1891 and February 1892, Latimer's poetry, under the byline "written for the *New York Age*," appeared an average of once a month.[132] Indeed, one 1891 poem appears on the same page as Fortune's (gender-bending) "Men Worth Talking About" column announcing that "Mrs. Frances Ellen Watkins Harper of Philadelphia stopped at THE AGE office recently on her way to Boston, and showed me the manuscript of a novel she has written and hopes to have printed in a while. In such parts of it as I was able to scan hastily I discovered an engaging style many interesting situations and a wealth of dialogue. I should like to see the work in print. Mrs. Harper is one of the foremost literary women of the race."[133]

Harper's stop at the *Age* and Fortune's prepublication announcement of *Iola Leroy* illustrate that she and Latimer shared an audience. In an uncanny convergence, Lewis Latimer's "Ebon Venus," which appeared in the *Age* on September 27, 1890, could have been written as a paen to what the novel's characters celebrate about what Lucille Delany's dark beauty represents:

> Let others boast of maidens fair
> Of eyes of blue and golden hair
> My heart like needles ever true
> Turns to the maid of ebon hue
>
> I love her form of matchless grace
> The dark brown beauty of her face
> Her lips that speak of love's delight,
> Her eyes that gleam as stars at night
>
> O'er marble Venus let them rage,
> Who set the fashions of the age,
> Each to his taste, but as for me,
> My Venus shall be ebony

Latimer, like Wells and Harper, had a substantial history with Fortune's papers. These overlapping publishing histories were no anomaly. Subscribers to the popular *A.M.E. Church Review* would likewise link Wells's "Iola" with Harper's. The two women had contributed to a temperance symposium together in 1891; they continued to publish in the paper almost side by side in the following year when an announcement of Harper's soon-to-be published novel titled simply *Iola* also appeared.[134]

The overlapping publishing histories of the very historical agents that provide *Iola Leroy* with some of its histotextual depth illustrate how adept authors were at identifying their audience's frames of reference. Readers of the Black press knew that Wells's and Harper's Iola simultaneously promoted the very values, in Wells's own words, of "earnest, thoughtful, pure, noble womanhood" and political action that the text endorses.[135] These names enact an oppositional sensibility while they confirm the Christian and domestic respectability with which these novels are often associated. Likewise, references to the Delany and Latimer legacies remind readers of histories of Black courage, genius, and protest against sustained institutionalized oppression and discrimination that still plagued the collective. Indeed, as Carla Peterson points out, Harper's (and other Black/ened women writers') "reconstruction publication choices nicely illustrate the critical role of the newspaper or periodical as a vehicle through which members of a nation, or a subordinated group within it, come, in the words of Benedict Anderson, to 'imagine community.'"[136] These histories are available to a culturally and historically literate community that authors were both assured of having and were also committed to cultivating. Reading clubs and reports on reading were part of a movement to deepen literary skills and historical memory and to widen the scope of Black interest, investment, and place as citizens of the United States and the world. Expressing a collective goal of "creating a nation within a nation of readers" (to merge E. Franklin Frazier's characterization of the Black church with Benedict Anderson's metaphor for the work of newspaper reading), *Iola Leroy* redefines and amplifies literacy, affirming a rich, long-standing oppositional, spiritual, and cultural practice of African American communication and interpretation while also reminding readers that formal literacy does not ensure the ability to comprehend all of God's children's transcripts. In this way, by sustained and subtle histotextual maneuvering, *Iola Leroy* draws attention to reading national power aright.

4. Reading/Photographs

Emma Dunham Kelley-Hawkins's
Four Girls at Cottage City,
Victoria Earle Matthews,
and the *Woman's Era*

> Once exposed as a fraud . . . you can never regain your legitimacy.
> For the violated criterion of legitimacy implicitly presumes an
> absolute incompatibility between the person you appeared to be
> and the person you are now revealed to be.
> —Adrian Piper, "Passing for White, Passing for Black"

> What, in fact, does it mean to rely on "evidence" when
> discussing "blackness"?
> —Daphne A. Brooks, *Bodies in Dissent*

Emma Dunham Kelley-Hawkins's *Four Girls at Cottage City* (1895) does not refer explicitly to the racial violence, tangled skeins of interracial marriage, (dis)inheritance, or labor discrimination that are central themes in *Iola Leroy.* Indeed, recent research has established that Kelley-Hawkins does not have any established genealogical claims to African American identity; neither did she, her known ancestors, nor her descendents ever consider themselves to be anything but white Americans. Nonetheless, I include this Black(ened) woman, to borrow a term from Daphne Brooks,[1] because *Four Girls* shares many of its narrative strategies and histotextual gestures with books such as *Iola Leroy* and because in other ways it resembles the focus of writers such as Amelia E. Johnson. Kelley-Hawkins's racial death leaves in its wake a new body of questions about parallel—or perhaps intersecting—transracial themes, means of expression, and textual commitments to women's development in relation to the treatment of religion, reform, and critical reading. Her shifting racial and authorial identities simultaneously invite wider analysis of the breadth of Black prose writers' political and narrative strategies.

I begin by considering the twists and turns in Kelley-Hawkins's taxonomic history and by examining the politics of her recent reclassification as a white woman writer after decades of being categorized as Black. Through my critical lens, the recent discovery does not illustrate historical and interpretative mistakes African American(ist) archivists and critics have made; rather, it illuminates how Kelley-Hawkins is embedded in a cultural and iconographic archive that speaks to the multiple and conflicting investments in reading individual bodies and texts in relation to sociocultural bodies of racial knowledge.

This chapter's focus is on late-nineteenth-century reading, photography, and reform, as well as on re-forming contemporary interpretative practices that frame visual, racial, and historical "evidence." Here I address the ways in which reading race and assimilating iconographic representation became increasingly central to late-nineteenth-century reading culture, bringing into view the emphasis on interpretation that is posed as critical to women's development. In her 1864 essay, "Originality of Ideas," Julia C. Collins counsels female readers of the African American newspaper the *Christian Recorder* to sharpen their analytical skills, averring, "It is good to read, but better to think." "It is best to spend only half that time in reading," she exhorts, and advises her readers to use the remaining time in interpretative practice.[2] Collins anticipates the advice of subsequent Black thinkers, such as Anna Julia Cooper and Victoria Earle Matthews, and reflects the counsel expressed in the columns of the *Woman's Era,* the official news organ of the Black women's club movement. As I will explore here, these principles are in nearly perfect alignment with those undergirding female development in Emma Dunham Kelley-Hawkins's novel *Four Girls at Cottage City.* The novel takes up the mutually constitutive relation between women's development and reform in ways that mirror the arc described in the pages of the *Woman's Era* and that are expressed throughout the Black clubwomen's movement.

I close by examining *Four Girls* and its lead heroine, Vera Earle, in the context of the contemporaneous prominence of journalist and activist Victoria Earle (Matthews) and what I call the "photographic bylines" in the *Woman's Era.* Frances E. W. Harper's choice of her heroine's name in *Iola Leroy* recalls Ida B. Wells's pen name, an echo that supports Frances Smith Foster's assertion that Harper was careful to select "figures who were familiar to and instructive for the greatest number of readers."[3] Kelley-Hawkins's Vera Earle and Victoria Earle share closely coupled homonymic *and* phenotypic features. Additionally, in relation to many of the values *Four Girls* espouses, Vera Earle serves as a double of Victoria Earle, the journalistic name Matthews used. The connections between Vera Earle and Victoria Earle likewise augment the emphasis in *Four Girls* on reading, education, and club work and further connect the novel to a broader overlapping circle of Black literary and political exchange. In this—and in its new—context, Vera Earle familiarly repeats the ways Iola functions as a narratively budding character planted in ground tended by an accomplished and actual writer, thinker, and activist. This histotextual link simultaneously re- and defamiliarizes readers' social understanding of cross-racial tropes, conjoinings, and cultural exchanges.

In the broad publicity about Kelley-Hawkins's shifting racial identity, her case has often been covered much as one might handle a nineteenth-century topsy-turvy doll: flip her upside down, and the Black doll becomes white.[4] Yet this doll itself embodies a much more complex politics of racial revelation, obscuring, and connectedness. Conjoined at the torso—fused together like vertically positioned Siamese twins—the two sides of the figure are inextricably linked. We might modify the formula to create topsy-turvy dolls with a twist: Vera Earle and Victoria Earle, Kelley-Hawkins before and Kelley-

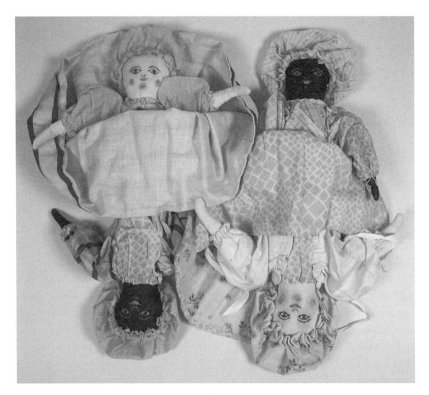

Figure 4.1. Homemade Topsy-Turvy Dolls, ca. 1905. Permission granted by Nebraska State Historical Society.

Hawkins after. Instead of being recognizably "Black" when you turn the dolls right side up and visibly "white" when you turn them upside down, they look the same no matter how you flip them, disrupting the either/or politics of reigning iconographic epistemology. These figures' racial demarcation is based on cultural, social, and historical—rather than optic—cues and markers.

My investment is in placing the iconographic, cultural, and textual politics of Kelley-Hawkins's writing and reception within a Black feminist theoretical and historical context. If one were to lean away from the mutually constitutive model of race I trace above in favor of a more extricable classification based on new genealogical "evidence" that Kelley-Hawkins and her ancestors are, indeed, Anglo-American, one might productively follow different interpretative paths. It makes sense, for example, to situate her and her writing in relation to the important and substantive body of work on white women's reform.[5] Yet I suggest that the discussion sparked by such a fused (cross-) racial consideration of narrative and authorial identity allows us to newly examine how Black and white reformers are mutually informed by each others' work, commitments, and tropes of expression. As Daphne Brooks reminds us, such racial controversies "force us to scrutinize critical methods for defining race and the tools that we use to measure and evaluate its social and political worth and cultural authenticity." This consideration seeks to show how and why race—and specifically blackness—continue to matter in cases of "black(ened) women" who unsettle familiar methods of reading corporeal and cultural race-based identity.[6]

Reading/Photographs

Since its inception, the New York Public Library's digital collection of the Schomburg series of African American Women Writers, has greeted those who visit with the photograph of young Emma Dunham Kelley.[7] The image serves as the iconographic frontispiece of the path-breaking compilation that bears the imprimatur of one of the most prestigious Black archives. This sole photograph accompanies an image of an elegant oversized black fountain pen; both are superimposed over a picture of a sheaf of handwritten prose. Neither the editors who chose Kelley, nor the readers or viewers who visited the collection to find the work of Harriet Jacobs, Amelia E. Johnson, Ida B. Wells, Frances E. W. Harper, Pauline E. Hopkins, and others found this image discordant with their ideas of nineteenth-century Black female authorship. Indeed, Kelley's dark eyes, softly curved nose, crisped curls, and ample lips, "the visible signs of the photographed figure," as Carla L. Peterson has put it, "announce[d] the author as black and the text as black-authored."[8]

Henry Louis Gates Jr. is reputed to have put it another way: "You put that picture up in my barbershop . . . and I guarantee the vote would be to make her a sister."[9] The democratic sentiment embedded in Gates's rhetoric of (a once-denied, once-disenfranchised) citizenry points toward the larger social politics in play in this instance. By acting to "make her" one of their own and by voting her into a historical collective, the imagined community in a barbershop—and let's add, a beauty shop—does not confirm individual identity as much as it affirms the power of collective identification, agency, and enfranchisement.[10]

But in 2005 Holly Jackson asserted, and Katherine Flynn's meticulous research confirmed, that however Emma Dunham Kelley inherited her features, and whatever the vote, vital, church, and census records—state as well as federal—show that throughout her life Kelley-Hawkins and her immediate family were classified as white, and there is no evidence that the society she moved in viewed her otherwise.[11] Without exception and as far back as the early 1700s, her ancestors also identified themselves as white; indeed, they hailed from towns where nonwhite residents made up only about 1 percent of the population. Likewise, her daughters and others in her family considered themselves to be descendants of Cape Cod Anglo-American stock.[12]

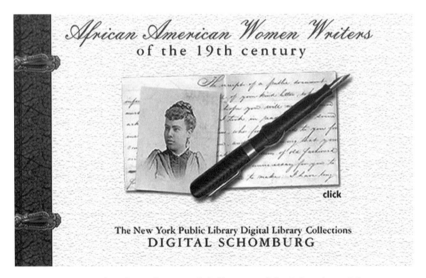

Figure 4.2. Screenshot from the Digital Collection of the Schomburg Library of Nineteenth-Century Black Women Writers. Schomburg Center for Research in Black Culture, The New York Public Library, Astor, Lenox and Tilden Foundations.

Kelley's photograph nonetheless found its way into the (counter-)archive of African American representation because its visual signs mirror those of other artifacts in the larger archive. The photograph was originally included in Kelley's first novel, *Megda*. Formally, it evokes the tradition of middle-class portraiture in the last decades of the century. The sitter is positioned at a slight angle to the camera, which allows her to gaze into the distance, rather than directly at the viewer, in a pose of reflective engagement that affirms, as photographic historians of the period suggest, a sense of middle-class interiority and subjectivity.[13] The frame's sole focus is the face of the young woman. With its plain though slightly mottled light gray backdrop, the portrait lacks the common props—books, curtains, furniture—that conventionally place the sitter within a middle-class, domestic, or familial context. The photograph's rectangular shape, its dimensions, the borders that show the photograph was mounted, and the signature that is inscribed—"Yours very truly Emma Dunham Kelley"—on the expanded bottom border are suggestive of the cabinet cards that were widely popular in the 1880s and 1890s.

The photograph itself could very well have been featured in W. E. B. DuBois's *Types of American Negroes,* the collection of photographs for which he won a gold medal at the 1900 Paris Exposition.[14] DuBois's inclusions of a blond light-eyed African American child and several women, who in age and phenotype resemble Kelley in ways that might unsettle white viewers, were meant to do just that—to illustrate the contingency of race. However inadvertently, Kelley's photograph has done the same thing—in spades. In addition to her full lips and mouth and remarkably curly hair, the lighting that illuminates the fuller side view of Kelley's face while casting her soft profile in slight shadows highlights that her face is darker than the light background. The stark white lace trim of her bodice's collar likewise accentuates the contrast with her darker skin. As the viewer's eye moves away from the sitter's face and central focus, the bust-like image loses the precision that underwrote the era's faith in photography's truth-telling capacities and evidentiary promise. The detail that illuminates the curls of and pins in her hair seems to dissolve into an out-of-focus blur at her shoulders and sleeves, which themselves dissolve into the color of the light gray backdrop itself, almost as if the photograph merges with an etching or painting. If DuBois's photographs are meant to illustrate the contingency of race, this image also accentuates the contingency of the photograph; the image itself seems to comment upon the visual politics of interpretation that it would subsequently engender and that are, in part, the subject of this chapter.

Kelley-Hawkins passed into African American literary archives based on an exchange between a Philadelphia bibliophile, Maxwell Whiteman, and a

Figure 4.3. "Yours very truly Emma Dunham Kelley." Frontispiece, from *Medga* (1891). Reproduced from Manuscripts, Archives, and Rare Books Division, Schomburg Center for Research in Black Culture. The New York Public Library, Astor, Lenox and Tilden Foundations.

prominent Schomburg curator, Jean Blackwell, that resulted in Whiteman's keeping the novelist in his *A Century of Fiction by American Negroes, 1853–1952: A Descriptive Bibliography*.[15] Extant records haven't revealed whether Whiteman's decision that Kelley was Black was based on her photo, that is, on the indexical reliance on the properties of photographic portraiture that dominated the earlier decades of the century, or whether nonvisual information corroborated his classification.

Once included, though Kelley remained a cipher, she was accepted as one of the growing number of early Black writers that history had disremembered and that scholars sought to recover. When, by the 1980s, Gates rediscovered *Four Girls at Cottage City*, "another 'lost' novel by an Afro-American woman,"

Figure 4.4. From
DuBois, *Types
of American
Negros, Georgia,
U. S. A.* (1900).
Reproduced from
the Daniel Murray
Collection. Library
of Congress, Prints
and Photographs
Division; LC-USZ62-
1234.

as he wrote, he decided to "edit a collection of reprints of these works and to publish them as a 'library' of black women's writings."[16]

The little that was once known about Kelley-Hawkins had been mostly gleaned from her novels' front matter. The title page announcement that *Megda* is composed by "FORGET-ME-NOT," under which appears the clarifying parenthetical "(Emma Dunham Kelley)," declares her authorial intention and projects an imagined audience that would recognize her by the pen name under which, presumably, she had previously published. The longevity FORGET-ME-NOT craved may have seemed within her reach in those early years. Published in 1891 by James H. Earle, her first novel was reprinted the next year. Earle also brought out *Four Girls'* second edition.[17] *Iola Leroy,* it turns out, had likewise enjoyed a second printing in the mid-1890s under the aegis of James H. Earle.

The hyphenated name Kelley-Hawkins used when she published *Four Girls* suggests a modern perspective, a feminist sensibility, and an author who did not want her authorial identity to be forgotten. The connection between claiming one's labor and one's name were intertwined (as we saw in the last chapter). For example, in 1889, the *Washington Bee* reminded its readers that when female school teachers married and so "assumed another name, by act of law their contract previously made, under their maiden names ceases. They do not exist in law."[18] After her second marriage, Hattie E. Wilson had continued to use the last name under which she had published *Our Nig,* established a hair product line advertised in at least eight states, and then become a well-known spiritualist speaker.[19] Likewise, as *Iola Leroy's* Lucille Delaney chooses to make her husband "uncomfortable" rather than stunting and nullifying herself to make herself eligible for the privilege of marriage, Dunham-Kelley does not cede her identity—or the recognition and community connected to it through her intellectual work—by giving up her maiden name.

After Kelley-Hawkins passed into the growing canon of Black women writers, little else had been recovered. Following Carla Peterson's general advice that scholars adopt "an approach that encourages speculation and resists closure" to recover a writer whose narrative gestures signaled her desire for authorial recognition, feminist critics doing work on Kelley-Hawkins, Harriet Jacobs, Harriet Wilson, and many others engaged in the "partial recovery and responsible speculation that are the necessary genesis of our work." Now found, after some fifty years, Kelley-Hawkins and her novels are in the process of being reclassified, of passing back, once again.[20]

The few scholars working on Kelley-Hawkins who also engaged the many variegated nuances of nineteenth-century and turn-of-the-century African American literature never stretched to include her writing into an expansive tradition that includes "raceless" prose as well as "'white' novels" penned by such authors as Harper, Frank Webb, Amelia E. Johnson, Paul Laurence Dunbar, and William Stanley Braithwaite.[21] Moreover, many examples of Black-penned prose showcase racially indeterminate *plots* as well as characters. One of the critical interventions I make here is to argue that *Four Girls* fits comfortably alongside contemporaneous texts penned by African Americans. Critics familiar with only feminist "classics" of the nineteenth century, texts such as *Iola Leroy,* insist that "we have stretched our understanding of how black women have written in America to incorporate texts [by Kelley-Hawkins] that do not fit."[22] But these comments are not informed by a familiarity with even Harper's entire corpus. "Two Offers" (1859), which is still thought to be the first short story published by an African American woman, and *Sowing and Reaping* (serialized in 1876–77) have as much in common with Kelley-Hawkins's novels as they do with *Iola Leroy.*

Four Girls at Cottage City is a story about women's moral development, that is, about religious instruction, educational capacity, and commitment to social reform. The book's title aptly suggests its plot and setting: a group of young women who range in age from seventeen to twenty-two (the Dare sisters, Garnet and Jessie, and their friends, Vera Earle and Allie Hunt) leave their families behind and head off to Cottage City, Martha's Vineyard, for a three-week vacation. There they spend their time consuming culture, new goods, and technologies; they go to concerts, make hot cocoa, eat canned salmon, and enjoy the town's newly installed electric lights.[23] They do much of this with the Dares's cousin Fred and his friend Erfort, whom they happen upon as they arrive. Once they find a room, the girls are pictured—at first reluctantly, and then more graciously—singing hymns to gratify their hosts and helping Charlotte Hood, a washerwoman, whose son Robin is crippled and in constant pain. Charlotte Hood shares both her burden and her story and, in doing so, fulfills one of the teleological functions of the novel: she brings all of the young people to Christ and to His social gospel, or rather, to Christian service that was, for many nineteenth-century activists, the heart of reform.

Forwarding what Ann duCille terms "literary evangelism," the feminotheo-centric mission of *Four Girls* refigures Christ and Christianity.[24] Indeed, its second printing complements Elizabeth Cady Stanton's *Woman's Bible,* which also appeared in 1898. Embodying clubwomen's belief that their publications and organizations formed a "woman's movement . . . that . . . is led and directed by women for the good of women and men, for the benefit of all humanity," this novel is insistent upon and consistent about the primacy of women's development.[25] Claudia Tate's *Domestic Allegories of Political Desire* and duCille's *The Coupling Convention* have demonstrated how nineteenth-century Christian values, spiritual feminism, and a narrative commitment to the institution of marriage are political expressions for those whose links to divine recognition, the power of the pulpit, and civil and familial rights had been tenuous at best. The "mission of spiritual uplift," as Deborah E. McDowell affirms, "was as urgent" for Kelley-Hawkins's African American contemporaries as was "organizing against lynching, rape, Jim Crow, and black disenfranchisement."[26] *Four Girls* plots its points on the axis of spiritual feminism while, I argue, its homonymic vectors simultextually point readers toward concerns often seen as inconsistent with women writers' literary evangelism. Its links to Victoria Earle underscore issues of class, labor, and sexuality; through the novel's naming practices, the women's club movement and a national discourse of increasing alienation from citizen rights find a place in the novel's expressive terrain.

In *Four Girls at Cottage City*, nuanced descriptions of eye color and skin tone—an attention to the paler hues that rivals Black poets' paeans to brown skin's marvelous variety—again recall the attention to the range of skin colors that marks Black-authored texts of the period.[27] Though Kelley-Hawkins's heroines have "white hands" (*FG*, 59, 61, 92, 143, 328) and "rosy mouths" (*FG*, 15, 17), Garnet and Jessie Dare have "big black eyes" (*FG*, 17) and "richly colored skin" (*FG*, 150). Jessie's head is crowned with a "mass of dark hair," "coils" that wrap and twist themselves around her small fingers (*FG*, 323) and are "so thick it seems impossible for a pin to go through" them (*FG*, 50). However their literary audience reads their dark hair, dark eyes, and rich complexions, when the girls go to the theater to see performers such as the famous tragedian Margaret Mather, they sit in segregated balcony seats; they manage to enjoy the performance anyway, announces Jessie, as her sister listens, mortified, even "if we do have to get seats in 'nigger heaven'" (*FG*, 81).[28]

Erfort Richards, one of the girls' two male companions, also embodies an interestingly descriptive study of contrasts that invites racial scrutiny. The text emphasizes his "dark face" and "dark cheek" (*FG*, 22, 96, 206, 207, 375) that are set off by "a handsome pair of dark eyes, a small mouth with thin sensitive lips, and a straight, handsome nose. His forehead was broad and very white, and he wore his thick, dark hair brushed carelessly back. His hands were brown and slender, but the fingers looked firm and strong" (*FG*, 22). Even Richards's traditionally phenotypical markers of whiteness are colored by a narrative tone that reflects the ways racial indeterminacy is often expressed in nineteenth-century race novels. It is almost prototypical (rather than paradoxical) for early Black authors to stress a dark-haired, dark-eyed, handsome protagonist's "thin lips" and "straight, handsome" nose, although protagonists in novels by Frances E. W. Harper or William Wells Brown, for example, often have even lighter features.[29] Indeed, Kelley-Hawkins's racial identity does not affect how flagrantly she stages racially ambiguous characters and themes.

The anatomically detailed description of Richards, an effort to relate the multiple signs of the body to a textual shorthand, mirrors the attention paid to photographic portraits such as Kelley's. They both fit within a "hermeneutic paradigm" of viewing the body that had "gained widespread prestige" by the mid-nineteenth century, as Allan Sekula points out. "This paradigm had two tightly entwined branches, physiognomy and phrenology," as he puts it, both of which were "comparative, taxonomic disciplines"[30] and both of which make their appearance within *Four Girls* as the group discusses physiognomy and gets phrenological readings by Professor Wild, an expert who happens to be boarding at the cottage where they are staying (*FG,* 252–53, 257–58, 336–38).[31] Indeed, the minute, almost photographic, attention evinced in Erfort's description recalls the ways in which "physiognomy analytically isolated the . . . various anatomic features of the head and face, assigning a characterological significance to each element: forehead, eyes, ears, nose, chin, etc."[32] Kelley-Hawkins's descriptive prose, like her photograph, invites an interpretative process that requires individual features to be read according to type. Her racialized descriptions link her text to a visual archive engaged by African American (and other) thinkers and writers of her time.

Narrative as well as visual features in the novel further overlap with African American plots and discursive practices. When, upon their arrival at Cottage City, the rain-soaked girls begin to look for a room to let at private cottages, one can read their initial housing misadventures as a representative instance of racialized rejection. Stopping at a household with "Rooms to Let," Vera taps at the door and is greeted by an eager "pleasant-faced, middle-aged" proprietress who inexplicably turns "[stiff]" after she lets in all four girls, causing grey-eyed, straight-haired Vera Earle to wonder if she has "offended her." Instead of offering them the modest but adequate space they request, the woman disappears after escorting them up to a small "dyspeptic looking" attic room (*FG,* 26, 27).

In a nineteenth-century novel featuring variously hued protagonists, the girls could easily be read as encountering prejudicial rather than status-neutral bad manners; their responses could then be read not as melodramatic—but rather as resistant—banter that ranges from caustic to comic to classy. When, faced with all four girls, the less enthusiastic proprietress says she must "go see" if she can accommodate them, Jessie loudly whispers "Anybody'd think she ran a hotel" (*FG,* 26). Left to consider the tiny attic room they are offered, an astonished Vera asks that the "saints forgive" her for commenting that the now-absent proprietress's proper place "in the after-life" might "be in the lower regions," or, to translate the sentiment to less polite prose, she suggests that the rude woman go to hell. Vera then inquires if the woman "really meant to give us to understand that this room is at our command? *Is* she as mad as that?" Garnet affirms, "This is the room she evidently means for us to take . . . No clothes-press, but—can you complain?" she adds, as she "point[s] to the hooks and nails that were driven into the beams and walls" (*FG,* 28).

Even on the level of close reading, Kelley-Hawkins's text resembles race plots that do not necessarily map their commentary in the explicit ways through which audiences often recognize racial protest. In such instances, those with ears attuned to arch racial undertones might hear an unstated, but none-too-oblique, "It's good enough for a Negro" playing a loudly silent call to Garnet's response, "Can you complain?" and likewise register the offense that Jessie notes with her "stage whisper" irony when the woman excuses herself to go see about availability despite the placard in her window announcing "Rooms to Let" (*FG*, 26). When, left alone with the other girls in the attic room they've been offered, Vera adds, "If I were to open my eyes in the morning onto one of my dresses hanging on one of those hooks . . . I would imagine it was myself suspended by the neck," the reference to a trajectory of violence that features inconvenient and insulting prejudice at one end and explicit violence on the other suggests a far more complicated meaning to the reader. Vera's full line—"I would imagine it was myself suspended by the neck and would wonder when I could have done the deed" (*FG*, 28)— makes available the more innocuous expressive possibility that Vera would rather hang herself than stay in such a place. The two interpretations play in forte counterpoint as arch and innocuous interpretations do in so many nineteenth-century texts. Do the girls accept this room and treatment? "No. Let those of us who like the surroundings, stay. I go," announces their leader, Vera Earle, with the assent of all of the girls (*FG*, 28). To avoid confronting such a problem again, they find the house where (dark) Jessie and her mother had taken rooms when visiting several years ago.

Likewise, geographic, photographic, and other evidence emphasizes the convergence of Kelley-Hawkins's and African American experience and imagination. Cottage City, the name of an actual town on Martha's Vineyard, was renamed Oak Bluffs in 1910; since the 1920s it has been a resort where many African Americans summer. Newer scholarship corrects the anachronistic assertions of Henry Louis Gates Jr. that, in the 1890s, audiences would have automatically read the very location of Kelley-Hawkins's novels as evidence of their Black authorship.[33] Yet the correctives go too far, discounting the historical evidence that establishes an earlier Black presence in Cottage City. Though it was hardly a Black resort in the 1890s, Blacks certainly vacationed there, renting rooms in private homes and facing just the prejudicial conditions that, to borrow from the author, "our girls" do (*FG*, 7, 323). As early as 1885, coverage of social happenings in Cottage City appears in the leading race paper, the *New York Freeman*.[34] Ten years later, "Splendid Premium Offers" promise instruction in art, literature, elocution, or oratory (in line with Jessie Dare's aspirations) at the Martha's Vineyard Summer Institute in Cottage City for those who sell the second highest number of subscriptions to the *Woman's Era*.[35] And scholars such as Adelaide M. Cromwell and Carla Peterson have located photographic evidence of African Americans' early presence in Cottage City; a group portrait they each include in their work shows unmistakably nineteenth-century Black vacationers, that is, notably dark-skinned visitors, posing in front of a cottage with a room-for-rent sign in the window.[36] Again, in this switchback-laced path to fuller recovery of nineteenth-century texts and contexts, *Four Girls* jointly inhabits some of the imaginative, textual, visual, and semantic terrain with African American writings of a shared historical place and time.

Acquire the Habit of Reading: Women's Clubs and Literary Critique

The valorization of reading in *Four Girls at Cottage City* mirrors the emphasis on literacy and literature in clubs and the newspapers that supported Black women's organizations, activities, and interests. "Our girls" follow almost exactly the advice that journalist Sarah E. Tanner gave to readers of the *Woman's Era*. She counsels that women should "acquire the habit of reading" and "also the habit of selecting carefully what we read. . . . This . . . will greatly develop our intellectual tendency" and our ability "to appreciate the good and the beautiful." While Tanner is invested in the collective development implied in her second-person address, that is, in "*our* intellectual tendency," her focus on the "masters" displays a rather narrow literary sample. "Read the best novels and romances, authors like Sir Walter Scott, George Eliot, Thackeray, Dickens and Hawthorne," she advises; "with great care *study* the masters . . . like Milton, Dante, Shakespeare, Bacon, Goëthe, Cervantes, Schiller, and others."[37] Vera Earle adopts this approach early in the novel. Like the eponymous heroine of Black journalist Katherine Davis Chapman Tillman's *Beryl Weston's Ambition,* she devours classics, then considered to be the work of "the best modern poets."[38] All of these heroines are absorbed with Tennyson and Longfellow. In fact, *Four Girls* features a chapter called "An Afternoon with Tennyson" (*FG,* 57–77), and, in Tillman's novella, Beryl "sigh[s] over" the same verses and characters, pondering "the hapless Elaine and her hopeless passion for Sir Launcelot."[39] Vera Earle's approach, however, is neither celebratory nor romantic. Rather, she tends to find Tennyson's women wanting; they are "weak—too weak." Her pleasure, again, lies not in rote study (she's read "The Lady of Shallot" eight times [*FG,* 60]), nor mere appreciation, but in rigorous and assertive critique.

In a novel that devotes as much narrative energy to discussions of literature as it does to its protagonists' journey toward religious conversions, Vera Earle and Garnet Dare are the text's most avid readers, and so, I argue, its leaders. Even before they reach their destination, they take out their books, transporting themselves into other literary worlds as they travel. They devour Dickens, Longfellow, and Shakespeare, as well as magazines that include sermons and tracts on denominational debates about dancing and theater. Young Jessie complains that literature takes her sister and Vera far away from group activities; too many books, she pouts, create a "dull set." "You two girls would be perfectly happy on an island, all by yourselves," she moans, "if you only had a book of sentimental poetry." "Don't speak lightly of Tennyson," Vera Earle retorts, as she makes clear that taking him seriously signifies a sustained critique that she shares with others (*FG*, 60). No passive consumers of reading material, they spend page after page offering critical assessments of these authors' treatments of gender and characterization. The novel's audience is included in these literary exchanges both in the mimetic act of their own reading and in their implicit inclusion in the discussions in which the girls and their companions engage. In *Four Girls*, reading is figured as both an individual and a collective act.

In *The Work of the Afro-American Woman* (1894), Gertrude Mossell advises "women starting in literary work" to "read and study continuously. Study the style of articles, of journals. Discuss methods with those who are able to give advice."[40] Readers of the *Woman's Era* were given practical advice on how to develop their analytical faculties through sets of questions that stressed the "importance of careful reading, of individual interpretation, and of being able to form and hold one's own opinion" when reading Scott's *Ivanhoe.*[41] *Four Girls* stresses just this independence of thought and critical ability; in their self-referential discussion of Kelley-Hawkins's first book, *Medga*, for example, each character supports her own point of view, and as a result the narrative validates their differing opinions (*FG*, 113–14). Through repeated examples, *Four Girls* encourages the necessity and pleasure of critique on gendered terms.

The evolution from acquiring the habit of perusing classics to actively critiquing gender roles in part mirrors the shift from social and literary (parlor) interaction to social and political outreach work, a progression that, in its broadest strokes, characterized club work's developmental trajectory. Again, in alignment with African American parallels, *Four Girls* delineates that shift. The girls belong to a literary society that resembles the many women's associations that were the backbone of the club movement whose journalistic organ was the *Woman's Era*. Though never mentioned when the girls are immersed in their conversations about books, the club is central to their decision to raise money for Robin, the crippled child of the washer-woman, Charlotte Hood. "Let us bring [the case] up . . . at our first meeting when we get home," Vera affirms, after Garnet suggests that they could raise the issue with their friends and acquaintances. "Instead of buying our new piano, let us give it towards making Robin a well boy" (*FG*, 342–43).

The girls' excited plans mirror the report of Pittsburgh's "Belle Phoebe" Club to the Federation of Club Women. Dissatisfied with their first year, in which they had been "purely literary" and "accomplished nothing except a great deal of appreciation for each other," the members of that club renamed themselves the Frances E. W. Harper League. "We have grown larger," writes its delegate, "and no longer meet in our parlors" but in A.M.E. churches with "free use of the pianos in each place." "Our platform is broader," the report continues, "seeking no longer to improve ourselves and our own homes, but others." They move from the parlor to the church, where the church is characterized by its public dimensions, its collective nature, and its role as a "deliberative arena."[42] Rechristening themselves to assert both their literary and community-building sensibilities, the women of the Harper League undergo a development that is shared by the protagonists of *Four Girls at Cottage City*.

Indeed, Kelley-Hawkins's emphasis on school girls could very well be read in concert with Anna Julia Cooper's *A Voice from the South,* a book directed to those with shared aspirations to join the educated class.[43] In this regard, both resemble Gertrude Mossell who offered *The Work of the Afro-American Woman* as an inspiration to and an expression of the "budding womanhood of the race."[44] (5). For those attentive to female development, budding womanhood—and especially the accomplishments of newly educated young women—was seen as the promise of the future. Mossell herself was still a "school girl" when she published her first essay, on "Influence," in the *Christian Recorder.* Pauline Hopkins's early literary sally, "The Evils of Intemperance and Their Remedy," won the Boston school girl a prize. Nearby, Miss Lillian A. Lewis, the Boston correspondent for the Black journal *Our Women and Children,* first published essays and delivered her tongue-in-cheek lectures, such as "The Mantle of the Church Covereth a Multitude of Humbugs," while "attending the girls' high school." I. Garland Penn's history of African American journalism reports that, in addition to pursuing her interest in elocution, Lewis was preparing a novel.[45] In the Black press, at least, an emphasis on youth was connected to a reading culture grounded in literacy rates that were higher for the younger generation. Indeed, as Eric Gardner points out, so many "school girl essays" were submitted to the important *Christian Recorder,* for example, that they could not all be published.[46] Likewise, "our girls" share the attraction to phrenology and metaphysics expressed by Mary Britton, who wrote for the first journal for Black youth, Amelia Johnson's *The Ivy;* Britton herself launched a career in journalism when her valedictory address was published.[47] In their interests, the protagonists of *Four Girls* are narrative mirrors of their historical African American peers. Offering a "broader platform" of service and spiritual commitment, like the Belle Phoebe Club–turned–Frances E. W. Harper League and like Iola at the end of Harper's novel, they are poised to contribute to a brighter coming day.

Archiving the Body: The *Woman's Era* Photographic Bylines

As a journalistic icon, Victoria Earle (Matthews) was known for her words and her work and, increasingly as the decade progressed, by her image. In a decade in which roughly 2 percent of Americans of African descent could properly be called educated, and by the end of which only 40 percent of those in the South could read fluently,[48] the appeal of immediate legibility conveyed by visual images, alongside the culture of newspaper reading fostered in Black communities, converged to ensure that "Victoria Earle" was one of the most well-known race women. Though Matthews's work took her throughout the North and South and she published in more than twenty newspapers, her image may have had an even broader reach.[49] A large photograph of "Mrs. Wm. Matthews (Victoria Earle)" serves as the front-page focal point of the second issue of the first volume of the *Woman's Era* (May 1894); another graces the front page a year and a half later, in February 1896. Between those two editions, the newspaper made an editorial shift and began more fully to integrate photographic and newsprint texts. What might be called "photographic bylines," small portrait images of each editor, including the newly recruited, such as Victoria Earle, appeared alongside their reports. As Robin D. G. Kelley puts it in his introduction to Deborah Willis's important history of Black photographers, from early portraiture through the creation of the New Negro ideal to its use in journalistic work, African Americans used photography to "shape collective memory" and to affirm their sense of being subjects worthy of citizenship and protected citizenship rights.[50]

The broader inclusion of photographs in the *Woman's Era* marked the paper—and the women who produced and consumed it—as distinctly modern. Photomechanical advancements enabled the shift. The ability to reproduce images through halftone technology drastically reduced the cost of illustrations in the 1890s. Aspiring or "elite" African Americans and working-class readers alike could afford illustrated volumes and newspapers.[51] While the sketch, as William Simmons used it in his prodigious 1887 biographical compendium *Men of Mark,* was a popular visual form that was used to present dignified and capable Afro-Americans to the public,[52] the photographic portrait squares (in the mathematical sense) the imagistic recuperation of Black subjectivities under attack at the turn of the century. Visual representa-

Figure 4.5. Victoria Earle
Matthews. From Hallie Q.
Brown's *Homespun Heroines*
(1926). Used with permission
of Documenting the American
South, the University of
North Carolina at Chapel Hill
Libraries.

tions of dignified Blacks served as counter-narratives to the overwhelming
quantity of disparaging images found in advertisements, trade cards, sheet
music illustrations, newspapers, playbills, and postcards, that is, "the image
in the popular American imagination of the black as devoid of all the characteristics that separate the lower forms of human life from the supposedly
higher forms," as Henry Louis Gates Jr. puts it.[53] Yet, as the industry of racist
iconography displays, these images were easily manipulated and, though the
sheer volume of stereotyped images naturalized their visual constructedness,
dignified sketches always faced the accusation that they were not "real" or
representative.

The photograph was a helpful weapon, then, as it was associated with
progress, advancement, and reliability. As cultural critic Laura Wexler asserts, "More thoroughly than any hand-drawn illustration or written text
news photography in the daily newspapers represented 'the real.'"[54] The
photographic bylines of Victoria Earle and other *Woman's Era* editors position them as subjects capable, and indeed representative, of being modern.
In a decade in which photographs of lynchings circulated in the U.S. mail
as souvenir cards, the readers and viewers of the *Woman's Era* witnessed a

challenge to the images of the premodern, the retrogressive, the primitive, the abject—all projected onto the Black subject during the decade of literary production and print capitalism in which Victoria Earle Matthews and Emma Dunham Kelley-Hawkins published.[55] As critic Carla Peterson has so well argued, though Kelley-Hawkins's "Christian regeneration seems to align [her novels] with traditions of nineteenth-century sentimentality," they also take as their subject the question of modernity.[56] Indeed, similar novels pose their protagonists as consumers of both material objects and high culture as modern, countering the threat of devolution and contagion ostensibly linked to what in my consideration of Amelia Johnson I call (troping on the phrenophotographer Francis Galton) the "negra delinquens."

Yet within the commodity economy of the newspaper, even dignified images could be smudged and sullied. Again, the newspaper man John Jacks's accusation that all Black women were thieves and prostitutes[57]—a charge that rallied the club movement—displays how easily public images of Black women might slip into the register of the improper. As early as 1862, the writer Fanny Fern fretted that photographic portraits were becoming commodities that circulated women's images in unbecoming ways. "There *was* a time when the presentations of one's 'likeness' meant something," she complained. "It was a sacred thing, exchanged only between lovers or married people, kept carefully from unsympathizing eyes, gazed at in private as a treasure apart."[58] Indeed, the visual access that merged with an unchecked sensuality when actuated through the male gaze is one way to describe the introduction of Alice Dunbar-Nelson (then Alice Moore) to Paul Laurence Dunbar. He had written to her after encountering her photograph and poetry in the *Woman's Era*, to which she was then the New Orleans contributor. When she moved to New York and was teaching at Victoria Earle's settlement house, a courtship developed that was initiated by that photograph. By the 1890s, when Alice and Paul met, the age of mechanical reproduction and the subsequent marriage of newsprint and photography were in full swing.

As *Woman's Era* articles articulated women's interests and actions to counter such issues as convict labor, employment discrimination, lynching, and the public maligning of Black women's characters, their forum, writing, and circulatory spheres were decidedly public. Indeed, they position themselves as the sign of a new racial self, what Gates calls "the Public Negro Self,"[59] gendered inclusively female rather than exclusively male. The photographic bylines featured in the paper approximate in their size and style the intimacy associated with the earlier hand-held daguerreotype "gazed at in private." Yet, in the *Woman's Era*, posed portraits were being placed in the explicit commodity that was the newspaper.

This trained sorosocial gaze and a homosocial economy of pleasure are at work in the viewing politics of the *Woman's Era* as well as in *Four Girls*. Men and white reformers who were also allies perused the paper, but the *Woman's Era* was the official organ of a "woman's movement . . . that . . . is led and directed by women;"[60] its coverage was primarily about women and it is clearly addressed to women and girls. The pleasure of recognition in *Four Girls*, likewise, is sororcentric. When the girls dress or pose—that is, in almost all instances in which they are positioned to be the object of the gaze—they are also the visual subject. Men are shooed away; women are spectators. In addition to providing visual bourgeois models of respectable uplift, in *Four Girls*—as in the *Woman's Era*—women are invited to view other women with pleasure and pride.

Victoria Earle and Vera Earle's Homonymic and Phenotypical Connections

Repeated textual and visual traces, linkages, and imbrications reflect Victoria and Vera Earle's uncanny resemblance. Beyond the near homonymic link— "Victoria Earle" is the journalistic name that Matthews used and the girls use "Vera Earle" as their leader's moniker with some frequency (*FG*, 11, 80, 130, 267, 273)—many of the interpretative paths available in *Four Girls* seem to double back, bringing the reader again and again to Vera's suggestive intersection with Victoria Earle. As with her double, Vera Earle's relationships point to the power of trans-hued sorocentric intimacy. When she makes her first narrative appearance, as the other girls wait for her in the train station to begin their journey, dark Jessie runs "across the wide room, [and,] regardless of the many eyes watching her, [she holds] out both hands to a tall, gray-eyed girl who was just coming from the side entrance" (*FG*, 12). And, in one of the numerous moments of girlhood affection that verge on homoerotism, the narrative again calls attention to the girls' contrasting phenotypes as Vera "laid her fair face lightly against Jessie's rosy one. The big black eyes opened lazily, then smiled up into the gray ones" (*FG*, 17). When read in relation to the novel's homonymics, then, the accented *contrast* between Vera's fairness and Jessie's and Garnet's dark features establishes a cross-hued *connection*, that is, a charcoal to chalk—or perhaps creamed coffee to chalk—continuum of family, affiliation, and affection.

For readers familiar with African American texts, multiple references to "white hands" and light eyes often signify the consanguinity with and between whites *and* African Americans. Blue-eyed Fred's familial relation to the "richly colored" Dare sisters is but one example of a phenotypical continuum that disrupts notions of racial purity and superiority. Vera, who has "white hands" and waist-length smooth hair, spends time parting, braiding, and cajoling Jessie's robust curls into elegant plaits (*FG*, 49–50). This scene repeats a trope of nineteenth-century hairdressing—with a difference; it perhaps unconsciously challenges the racialized power dynamics in hairdressing, that is, the responsibility for physically affirming white beauty standards expressed in the rhetoric and reality of service and slavery.

If one follows the text's homonymic associations, then Vera Earle's clearly Anglo-associated description serves paradoxically not as a sign of *dis*association from Blackness, but rather as an iconographic convergence with white-skinned Victoria Earle's actual features and with her character and gendered commitments. Vera Earle's long smooth tresses and the narrative's insistent emphasis on her height, for example, directly mirror Hallie Quinn Brown's description of the young Victoria Earle as "a tall, lank, straight haired girl" who was wise beyond her years.[61] Vera Earle's personality likewise reflects Brown's later description of Victoria Earle. In *Four Girls*, the "danger of people misjudging" Vera because they "might think her proud, and even heartless; not willing to acknowledge herself in the wrong when she knew herself to be," led to "many—very many—who found it impossible to love her, simply because they did not understand her" (*FG*, 94). Characters' reactions to Vera Earle's defensive haughtiness (*FG*, 93) match Brown's explanation that "perhaps because in [Victoria Earle's] ideas she was far in advance of the times . . . possibly no woman was more greatly misunderstood"; Brown goes on to say that Victoria Earle's "enthusiasm and quick grasp of any situation . . . gave her a forceful, decided manner . . . that was not always understood." Brown's repetition and the combination of her simultaneously emphatic and euphemistic language reveal that many, perhaps very many, found it impossible to love Victoria Earle as well.[62]

Vera Earle's dedicated reading habits also reflect Victoria Earle's devotion to learning. Jessie calls Vera a "great reader and a great thinker" (*FG*, 177); the few references to the twenty-two-year-old's occupation suggest that she makes her living by "writing" (*FG*, 162, 336) and teaching (*FG*, 262). For her, "mental power predominates" (*FG*, 336). She "could tell the author of almost any book that anyone might mention, and be able to give a fair synopsis of the book itself. Her opinions on this or that subject—slavery, dress reform, woman's rights, prohibition, etc., her criticisms on art, ancient as well as modern literature, public speakers, and even her really enviable knowledge of the manner and custom of foreign countries and the government of her own—in all these she had gained for herself recognition" (*FG*, 178). Yet as this novel also makes clear, knowledge without a moral awakening linked to service leaves even the most learned and the strongest—even Vera—mute and unknowing, "dumb" and "ignorant" and isolated (*FG*, 175). Without the power of the social gospel, even the best education is inadequate and wanting. Despite its clarity about Vera's place as the group's leader, *Four Girls* is explicit in its endorsement of communal development and moral action.

Matthews thought broadly and strategically about how to reproduce— that is, to make collective—her quest for knowledge. The clubs that she led placed reading in the context of cultural, moral, and political affirmation and activism. Every account stresses that she was "a great reader" who devoured "whatever she could lay hands on," as Brown puts it.[63] She developed into more than a passive consumer of knowledge. According to the *New York Evening Post*, at the White Rose Mission, Matthews "gathered one of the most unique special libraries in New York," "a collection of books written for and about the Negro in America, not only the well known [sic] authors, such as Washington, Charles Chesnutt and Paul Laurence Dunbar are represented." Included in the library's collection is Harriet A. Jacobs's *Incidents in the Life of a Slave Girl*.[64] In her time, Matthews was lauded for her prodigious journalistic accomplishments. She was one of the few Black journalists published in the white as well African American press.[65] Her 1895 address "The Value of Race Literature" has been characterized as the "manifesto of the women's club movement itself."[66] Contemporaries called her "the 'star' of the [club movement's inaugural] convention" and appreciated for her "splendid and tireless work."[67] Read in histotextual relation to Victoria Earle, then, fair, gray-eyed Vera Earle, as much as the thickly coiffed, black-eyed Dare sisters, sustains the novel's ties to Blackness. Her burgeoning sense of purpose as leader in the girls' "first effort to do good" (*FG*, 361) also recalls *Iola Leroy's* teleology of character development and definition of knowledge and literacy. This emphasis in *Four Girls,* as Sieglinde Lemke puts it, communicated a "pragmatic and communitarian project" of woman's empowerment.[68]

As literary women who did not mimic but rather critically analyzed accepted conventions, Vera and Victoria Earle again converge. Journalist John Bruce, also called "Bruce Grit," testifies to Victoria Earle's rare qualities in two closely overlapping entries documenting a "Woman's Day" speech he gave in Cambridge, Massachusetts. In it, he recalls an 1882 visit with the young Matthews that transformed into a planning session for a literary group called the "Enquiry Club."[69] In the first entry he notes, "our people at that period were not so keen about Negro history as some are now." They imbibed "Shakespeare's immortal tragedies, and dramas," Emerson's philosophy and, he goes on in the second handwritten copy of the presentation, "were studying Browning and Longfellow and saturating their systems with all the knowledge about what white people had done and what they were doing and thinking.

Mrs. Matthews was not that type. She clearly saw, despite her large Caucasian reinforcement, that the important thing for the younger generation of her race to do was to study the history of the Negro."[70] Though writers such as Emerson (*FG*, 337, 373), Dickens (*FG*, 101, 211–16), Shakespeare (*FG*, 102, 115, 254), and Longfellow (*FG*, 255) and references to their work frequently appear as topics of conversation in *Four Girls*, Vera Earle, as we have seen, is likewise no mere imbiber.[71] Instead, echoing Victoria Earle Matthews—a clubwoman known as a prominent advocate of the role of reading and critique in the advancement of the disenfranchised—Vera Earle guides her peers in critical analysis that leads not only to feminist critique but also to critical community engagement.

Like Matthews, Vera Earle likewise embraces a religious ethos that spoke simultaneously to Christian liberation and women's empowerment. In the novel, Vera Earle's connection to club life becomes pertinent when it can be used to forward an agenda of sacrifice in partnership with less privileged peers. Likewise, the field of practice with which Victoria Earle would have been associated at the time of the novel's 1898 second printing was her settlement house, founded in 1897 "to establish and maintain a Christian, industrial, nonsectarian home for Afro-American and Negro working women and girls, where they may be educated and trained in the principles of practical self help and right living," as its certificate of incorporation reads.[72] Here, as in the instances that Evelyn Brooks Higginbotham outlines in *Righteous Discontent*, expanding the arena of respectable service affirms "the capacity and worthiness of poor, working-class black [and non-Black] women for respect."[73] The association with Victoria Earle, a historic agent involved in cross-class social service and advocacy, projects a shadow suggestion of the means of actualizing women's commitment expressed as narrative desire in the novel.

Four Girls expresses its lessons about class, status, and sexuality through the laundress Charlotte Hood—who admits to once plunging into "the gay life" as a painted woman (*FG*, 297). Though the girls are tempted to look down at Miss Hood for both her current and implied past professions (*FG*, 93), she becomes the girls' spiritual superior, or leader, as all are equal in Christ. Vera Earle and Garnet bring Jessie and Allie, and then others, to Hood's "very poor, but very neat looking cottage" to help with her invalid son and commune about their coming to God (*FG*, 117). The novel creates an expansive maternal dynamic between economic classes that is clearly meant to extend beyond the confines of the narrative. Charlotte is their spiritual mother; they spiritually mature by learning to mother Robin. And "Aunt Lottie," an endearing moniker stemming from the name Charlotte, is credited in Kelley-Hawkins's dedication as being a "second mother" who has earned the reward of resurrection (*FG*, 3). This feminotheocentric, though inclusive, nexus of shared work, care, and prayer shows the women's reliance on God, sacrifice, and collective labor.

In some ways, Matthews's later search for housing recalls the initial welcome and then the chilly reception that Vera Earle receives when trying to find a room to let when the girls first arrive in Cottage City. In its coverage of Matthews's search for appropriate quarters for her settlement house, the *New York Evening Post* underscores that "Mrs. Matthews's race is not apparent to the casual observer, [so] it was possible for her to lease the house without explanation."[74] Matthews's own description focuses not on race but on God's centrality in realizing her own mission—the White Rose Mission—and again underscores the core belief in faith in action that *Four Girls* also expresses: "I began to hold mothers' meetings at the various homes where I visited; and you may not believe this, but one day at one of these meetings we prayed especially for a permanent home where we might train the boys and girls and make a social center for them where the only influence would be good and true and pure. Almost immediately Mr. Winthrop Phelps who owns an apartment house, offered us one of its flats, rent free for three months."[75]

The women whom the center served were those African American workers coming north looking for jobs who could, and did, easily find themselves in the hands of unscrupulous employment agents who led them to less-than-respectable work. Matthews worked to convince those who were comparatively well off—though perhaps still working class—to contribute their time and resources. After seeing the "derelicts" who lived in the depressed area where the center was located, Booker T. Washington remarked to Matthews, "My friend I wouldn't change fields with you."[76] The mission's funding material told potential donors: "It is the only institution of its kind in New York City for colored girls—and we are coming to you—hoping to interest you to the slightest degree in our efforts. Just read our brief history—read between the lines—you will appreciate just how much our work means—just how necessary and important it is—we need help—just a little from each one to whom this appeal goes."[77] Despite its mission and some of Matthews's less than upstanding methods (including dances and card games—activities about which "our girls" debate), she continued to draw impressive speakers, teachers such as Alice Ruth Moore, and "intelligent young men and women who frequent[ed] the home" to take classes.[78]

Thus, the feminotheocentric, multi-hued, cross-class and -gender spaces that Matthews fosters mirror the community *Four Girls* likewise models. For readers familiar with late nineteenth-century history and *Four Girls'* shifting racial provenance, the link between its lead heroine and Victoria Earle enlarges the novel's imagined narrative scope; using phenotypical and character associations that suggest intersecting spheres, it leads its readers through a body of whiteness to an affirmation of—and overlapping connection to—the race.[79]

Optic History

Despite the twenty-first-century literary obituaries announcing the racial death of this author, racialized cultural and literary interconnections are not so easily severed, turned over, and made to disappear like a topsy-turvy doll flipped from Black to white. It is worth recalling that Kelley-Hawkins's photographic frontispiece served to pass her into the (counter)archive of African American representation because its visual signs mirror those of other artifacts in the archive. Empirical evidence does not significantly recast the visual "proof" that originally directed Black critical attention to her work. This is no less true for the imagined community signified by Gates's barbershop voters—that is, for African American viewers today—than it was before research offered another sort of indexical, racial evidence. When confronted with the ostensibly definitive sources, such as state and federal census records, church documents, and/or marriage and death certificates, shades of critical resistance may still be cast in the direction of this specific, individual case; but, I would argue, racial taxonomies that categorize Kelley-Hawkins as a Black(ened) author reflect a historically rooted epistemology grounded in *collective* experience and expertise. What I'm suggesting is that empirical research, however strong, does not automatically cut off (at the pass) another interpretive path suggested, in this case, by optic and textual histories. Conventional "evidence" establishes an individual genealogy, while what I'm calling optic histories often reflect upon the *social* body; they read the body's signs in relation to a larger body politic that has historically relegated the evidence of consanguineous relations to the realm of Blackness.

Conventional "proof," as Daphne A. Brooks might put it, "hardly forecloses discussions regarding race." We might begin to examine the ways such cases "[matter] . . . by questioning social and cultural epistemologies that prop up specific kinds of identity 'truths.'"[80] When, in criticism or the beauty/barbershop, "we" claim the relation between such an image, such an author, and the larger African American social body, we claim, we "own" in the vernacular sense, what has so often been unclaimed and disowned by families and power structures and canons that insist on protecting their relation to whiteness.[81] Allowing for the possibility that different kinds of evidence illuminate different critical aspects of our reading of the body (politic)—its history, place, and reception—is just one of the many critical things that Emma Dunham Kelley-Hawkins's iconicity and writings continue to offer.

5. Home Protection, Literary Aggression, and Religious Defense in the Life and Writings of Amelia E. Johnson

> We are continually bobbing and slipping out of the way of our would be repressors . . . but times are changing . . . the colored people are taking up the cudgels in our own defense, and we mean to make a genuinely even-handed fight; no mincing; no stepping back two steps when one is taken; but giving just as hard blows as the white man gives when he gives at all.
>
> —Amelia E. Johnson or "A.E.J."

> "You've Got to Move When the Spirit Says Move"
>
> —Negro Spiritual

In its 1894 first edition, the final pages of Mrs. N. F. Mossell's *The Work of the Afro-American Woman* balance its opening salvo by advertising the race's progress both literally and literarily. The opening announces: "It is worthy of note as well as of congratulation that colored women are making great advancement in literary ventures. In the year 1892 three books were given the world by this class of writers, well worthy of high consideration: Mrs. A. J. Cooper, 'A Voice from the South by a Black Woman of the South;' Mrs. F. E. W. Harper, 'Iola; or, Shadows Uplifted;' and Mrs. W. A. Dove, 'The Life and Sermons of Rev. W. A. Dove.'"[1] At the book's end, a full-page advertisement lauds Mrs. A. E. Johnson's *The Hazeley Family; or Hard but Wholesome Lessons* and *Clarence and Corrine; or God's Way,* each for sale for ninety cents.[2] Turning the page, readers find that agents are wanted to sell *Iola Leroy;* interested parties should apply to Mrs. F. E. W. Harper at 1006 Bainbridge Street. Sharing space with *Iola* and other announcements is the advertisement devoted to "Victoria Earle's" "Aunt Lindy." For fifty cents, if readers wrote to 9 Murray Street, New York, they could gather even more evidence of the work of an Afro-American woman. Finally, claiming in bold type a world audience for the interests of Black America, the *A.M.E. Church Review,* billed as "the leading literary publication of the Colored Race," solicits subscriptions. Based in Philadelphia, the journal's reach "extends to all parts of the United States, to Europe, Asia and Africa, to Canada, Nova Scotia, Bermuda, St. Thomas, British Guiana, Hayti, San Domingo and St. Croix."[3]

Closing a volume that addresses Black women's work, this marketing of ideas displays how women and the journals that featured their writings staked claim to the terms of their own intellectual labor in the print culture of the 1890s. More than a century later, however, Amelia Johnson's work is rarely placed in the calculus of production and reception alluded to in the solicitations, announcements, and commendations represented in Mossell's *The Work of the Afro-American Woman.* Instead, because of its racially indeterminate characters, emphasis on temperance, and literary evangelism, it has been characterized as marginal to both the club women's movement that dominates gendered histories of the 1890s and to the political and representational urgencies of Black life characteristic of historians' and literary critics' work on what has come to be known as the "nadir."

In this chapter I reconsider Amelia Johnson's life and writing paying close attention to largely unmined primary sources that link her to radical reform, judicial redress, and rhetorical, religious, and literary activism. Considering "A. E. Johnson's" newspaper articles and her collaborations with her husband, renowned Baptist preacher, Baltimore civic activist, and Black nationalist author, Harvey Johnson—a partnership that has yet to receive more than a glancing consideration—illuminates the ways in which, to borrow from Johnson herself, she bobs and slips "out of the way of our would-be repressors." Both Johnsons give "our white brother a taste of the lash of criticism, which is only fair, seeing that it is ever his delight to lay it upon us," as she puts it. Johnson's language reveals her appreciation for pugilistic prose. Here she uses it to describe her husband's writing; this comes from her introduction to the now forgotten 1903 collection of his sermons, essays, and published pamphlets, *The Nations from a New Point of View,* which she signs, simply, "AEJ."[4] Johnson maps desire and delight, sarcasm and consanguine familiarity onto the body of Harvey Johnson's writing to reveal a personal, familial, and national cartography of racial relations. She calls attention to the corporeal aspects of democratic rhetoric and racial interchange, ones we can taste and feel. She admires, if not advocates, a combination of liberating postures and moves, those that allow the implied "us" to move "out of the way of our would-be repressors," and one that encourages us to snatch the whip out of our white brothers' hands and aggressively lay on the discursive beating Blacks were meant to take.

Johnson both delivers sadistic jabs and offers sentimental salve in her prose. She also stresses what might be called an authorial ethics of public engagement and care that helps readers evaluate writers' reception claims. To better understand her rhetorical choices in the novel *Clarence and Corrine,* I begin by situating Johnson in relation to her literary and cultural contributions and in the context of her role in the sustained movement for Black empowerment launched in post-Reconstruction Baltimore.

The Johnson household was a principle locus of civic, legal, and literary activism from the 1880s through the 1900s. Indeed, many challenges to Jim Crow in Maryland were launched from her home and home church. They were spearheaded, by all accounts, by the collective efforts her husband led. My analysis counters the masculinist and individualist paradigm that has characterized interpretations of Harvey Johnson's legal and civic challenges to white supremacy. Instead, I read the work of the Brotherhood of Liberty, the organization he and others founded, through a gendered lens, highlighting the ways in which women were central to their legal and grassroots campaigns—and the representations of those actions and cases. Amelia Johnson's literary status has been diminished by the scant, almost anorexic, information that has accompanied her recovery. Instead of finding meaning in Johnson's life and writings through concrete social interactions (to borrow from historian Elsa Barkley Brown), readers have a "tendency to attribute inherent meaning to certain activities" in ways that obscure rather than explain "historically specific developments of social relations between black men and black women."[5] Such reductive class- and gender-based assumptions have adhered to Johnson, who is often seen simply as "a preacher's wife" instead of being placed in the context of what Evelyn Higginbotham characterizes as the complex and also "deep horizontal comradeship" possible across genders.[6]

As this chapter progresses, Johnson's *Clarence and Corrine; or God's Way* (1890) serves as its tuning note, its symphonic "A." Building on my analysis of Harriet Wilson's *Our Nig* in chapter 2, I query how each novel's use of racially indeterminate mothers functions to aggressively challenge readers' racialized generic and cultural expectations. Johnson challenges—or, I argue, dethrones—the exalted rhetorical place of pure white womanhood in the 1890s. By situating her writing in terms of the violently anti-Black prohibition rhetoric of Rebecca Latimer Felton, the foremost white temperance activist of the South, I argue that Johnson's writing works to expose what historian Crystal Feimster calls the "rape-lynch" dynamic and its framing of the links between law, terrorist violence against Blacks, and the white protected domestic sphere.[7]

Arguing that *Clarence and Corrine's* temperance thematic offers an egalitarian racial distribution of familial disrepair (or a straightforward indictment of white slovenly behavior) helps to remap our understanding of racial indeterminacy in nineteenth-century Black women's writing. Before the twentieth century few writers focus their attention on dark-skinned female protagonists. Such writing is often characterized as being steeped in a culture of bright, light, and damned-near-white literary entitlement, as if the authors believed that light characters were the only ones worth representing, at least fully; as if readers of nineteenth-century Black women's fiction were happy to see anything in print no matter its content; and as if garnering white readers' sympathy was the most crucial cultural work worth doing. That dynamic exists, as I put it throughout this book, simultextually. Yet, I hope that examining the formal complexity of fully historicized texts that sometimes reinscribe—but as often interrupt and contest—such dynamics will help to illuminate the chiaroscuristic play and critique embodied in such writing.[8]

Public Standing and Civic Action: The Life and Legacy of Amelia E. Johnson

Fleshing out Amelia Johnson's nineteenth-century literary and social standing enlivens an understanding of her readerships and reception history. "One must be informed as to whether [an] author be sufficiently public-spirited or interested in the well-being of his fellow man to give him the right to talk as he does," Johnson writes, using a lexicon of civic interest.[9] Johnson published her first novel in 1890, thirteen years before she penned these words and so affirmed that readers should consider an authorial ethics that takes into account an author's public standing and civic action. By then she was the already established editor of the first journal for African American children, which she founded a full thirty years before Jessie Fauset and the NAACP's important *Brownie's Book*. As a predecessor to the *Woman's Era*, Johnson's journal, along with Rev. William J. Simmons's *Our Women and Children*, provided an early venue for women writers and editors of African descent. Though it is no longer extant, Johnson's eight-page journal, founded in 1887, was well-received and reviewed across regions and races.[10]

Unlike Charles Chesnutt, who published his earliest stories in the *Atlantic Monthly* during these same years, and who at first remained "raceless" as an author although his characters' Blackness was obvious, Amelia Johnson's protagonists were indeterminate while no one doubted her own racial identity.[11] Johnson was connected to a vibrant group of active Black women through her editorial work in the late 1880s and her participation in the National Association of Colored Women (NACW), whose inaugural conferences she attended.[12] The 1896 meeting was held at Washington D.C.'s Nineteenth Street Baptist Church, pastored by Rev. Walter H. Brooks, one of the Johnsons' closest friends.[13] Sharing the platform with Frederick Douglass's daughter, Rosetta Douglass-Sprague, Brooks welcomed the "mighty company" with an address that elicited Douglass-Sprague's response that "our progress depends on the united strength of both men and women—the women alone nor the men alone cannot [sic] do the work."[14] Though Johnson didn't assume leadership positions in the NACW or write for its publications, her contemporaries recognized her as a leading race woman.

By the mid 1890s Amelia Johnson was obviously an author of some importance in the Black community. In 1894, the year of Mossell's first edition of *The Work of the Afro-American Woman*, Katherine Tillman's expansive article "Afro-American Women and Their Work" appeared in the *A.M.E. Church Review*. Tillman groups Amelia Johnson with the giants Frances Harper, Victoria Earle Matthews, and Anna Julia Cooper.[15] Similarly, the Amelia Johnson entry in I. Garland Penn's 1891 volume on Afro-American journalism is almost twice as long as those of many of the women featured; and she is quoted affirming the literary talent of at least one of her peers, signifying her presumably recognizable status as a commentator on, as well as contributor to, race journalism. Indeed, Penn includes excerpts from at least eleven newspapers and journals offering reviews of *Clarence and Corrine*; seven of them are "unexpected tributes" from "members of the white race." Interestingly, though Tillman, Penn, and Lawson Scruggs, who edited *Women of Distinction: Remarkable in Works and Invincible in Character* (1893), praise her contributions to the race, none mention that the characters in her novels are racially indefinite. In the context of her much-noted work as an editor and of the Baltimore campaigns associated with Harvey Johnson reported in the Black press, her racial politics, that is, her "affection for the race, and loyalty to it," as Penn puts it, was, in her times, self-evident.[16]

Indeed, Scruggs characterizes Johnson as a race warrior. Johnson's 1892 *New York Age* article in defense of Afro-American literature,[17] he says, "is sufficient to hush in *eternal silence* the *enemy* of the progress the race has made, who now bobs up and claims that our literature is not original. Mrs. Johnson gives this false doctrine such *original* blows from the gigantic intellect of an Afro-American, and pursues her enemy with such vehement logic, that she not only confuses, but, like a champion of the truth, she refutes and conquers him"[18] (emphasis in the original). Using decidedly masculine, indeed, military language, Johnson is described as shifting from a defensive posture to an aggressive one, using both her "gigantic intellect" and ruthless ability to pursue, conquer, and silence "the enemy." Johnson's stance was shared with other women, notes historian Evelyn Brooks Higginbotham, who "adopted the discourse of strident black nationalism."[19]

Johnson used her intellect and ability in the service of the race in multiple arenas. In an era when military, technological, and racial "advancement" informed rhetorical, cultural, and policy interventions, developing the potential of the "New Negro" through its youth was crucial work.[20] Black leaders considered race literature central to supporting uplift efforts and to fostering historical memory and race pride. As W. E. B. DuBois put it in *The Negro Church,* a volume he edited in 1901, "It is impossible for any race . . . to hold the influence over their offspring, unless they provide themselves with literature" to keep before their children. The Negro Baptists of this country must, he goes on, "provide literature capable of . . . increasing race pride of the rising generation or they must be entirely overshadowed by the dominant race of this country."[21] Earlier, in 1887, Professor Mary V. Cook, who had already delivered papers such as "Woman's Work in the Denomination" at Baptist conventions nationally, gave an address in Louisville, Kentucky, titled "Is Juvenile Literature Demanded on the Part of Colored Children?"[22] That year Amelia Johnson responded to the need, if not to Professor Cook's specific call, with unprecedented action. Her paper *Joy* provided verse and fiction for young Black readers, who, by 1900, ten years after the journal's run, still made up a full 60 percent of African Americans' literate class.[23] Likewise, Johnson's three novels feature young protagonists. Writers like Mossell followed Johnson's literary lead; in addition to *The Work of the Afro-American Woman,* Mossell wrote *Little Dansie's One Day at Sabbath School* (1902), a children's book whose title echoes the themes of Johnson's second novel, *The Hazeley Family* (1894).

The African American youth agenda stood at the crossroads of struggles for education and a seemingly ubiquitous focus on "home training," "home maintenance," and "mothers' meetings." As a "multiple site" of integrated secular and sacred movements that included organizing protests against employment discrimination and inadequate schools, and hosting club meetings, the Black church was almost always the meeting house standing at that intersection. In her work on gender and Black Baptist movements from 1880 to 1920, Higginbotham displaces the notion that the church is the "exclusive product of a male ministry" or male ministerial authority, and instead characterizes it as the "product and process of male and female interaction" and as a social space for public discussion.[24]

According to the few records that exist, Amelia and Harvey Johnson worked together as each spouse's mission and ministry broadened in scope and gained national attention. Their base, Union Baptist Church, was growing remarkably in reach, numbers, and influence. Located in the upper South, Union had grown from a membership of 268 in 1872 (when Johnson became the congregation's leader) to an almost fourfold increase five years later when he married Amelia E. Hall. In 1885 Union could claim 2,000 members. That year the Johnsons hosted Frederick Douglass, who gave the inaugural speech at the three-day convention of the Mutual United Brotherhood of Liberty (which Harvey Johnson had just founded, and which he led with, I argue, what must have been Amelia Johnson's strong support).[25] Union Baptist pursued its mission in harmony with secular organizations whose memberships were drawn from its own church, from the six churches it had founded, from other denominations, and from civic and labor groups. In concert, they advanced an activist agenda and a social gospel mission. According to Amelia Johnson, their church would become the largest in Maryland by the turn of the century.[26]

As First Lady of Baltimore's Union Baptist, Johnson was engaged in the inner and public workings of one of the most radically theological and activist Black Baptist congregations in the nation. Acting as Harvey's "guide in all his business matters," Amelia was reported to have "critically read, typed and edited the numerous" articles and pamphlets that streamed from her husband's pen for over thirty years.[27] Harvey Johnson exhibited his respect for Black women through his solicitation of Amelia's feedback and his support for her own writing. In public as in private, Harvey Johnson was an advocate for his women congregants, Baltimore's female workers, and, within the American National Baptist Convention, for "black feminist theology."[28]

Black literate communities and Baptists across races would be well acquainted with the Johnsons' mutual efforts and productivity as an example of what Rosetta Douglass-Sprague might call "the united strength of both men and women."[29] Reviews of Amelia Johnson's first novel appeared in Baltimore and Kentucky papers in the same year as did reviews of Harvey Johnson's 1890 pamphlet, *The Hamite*.[30] And the next year, when his *The Question of Race* was printed, reviews of it appeared in at least two other common sources, including a paper in Brooklyn. The Johnsons' writing circulated in circles that directly and indirectly overlapped. In addition to the five papers that reviewed her novel and his published sermons and essays in 1890 and 1891, for example, scores of others noted her or his publications.[31] Amelia Johnson's articles would be featured in the *Richmond Planet* and the *New York Age* (two of the leading Black dailies), papers that regularly covered the efforts of Harvey Johnson and the Mutual Brotherhood of Liberty.[32] Indeed, when another long piece titled "Some Parallels of History" came out in 1899, the link between them was made even more explicit. The article was by "Mrs. A. E. Johnson," under which, in smaller print, appeared "Wife of Rev. Dr. H. Johnson, Baltimore, Md."[33] While this byline might be seen as an attempt to legitimate and make respectable a woman's venture into the once-masculinized arena of historical analysis, with ten years of novel and newspaper publishing behind her, and at the end of a decade of Black women's speaking and writing, one can also envision this marital marker as a horizontal link between recognized allies in Black leadership.

The most explicit demonstration of the Johnsons' collaborative partnership is Amelia's introduction to the culmination of her husband's work, *The Nations from a New Point of View* (1903), a collection of his widely circulated and confrontational writings. By this point Harvey Johnson was a nationally known figure with connections to preeminent leaders in ministerial, legal, and academic spheres. Yet, rather than asking his close friend Walter Brooks, the influential pastor of Washington D.C.'s 19th Street Baptist Church or, perhaps, W. E. B. DuBois, whom Johnson knew, to introduce his collection,[34] he chose Amelia E. Johnson, or "AEJ," to acquaint readers with his written legacy.

Ample evidence suggests that the Johnson home was for years at least one site of Baltimore's civic activism. One of the extant photographs of Brotherhood of Liberty members was taken on the stoop of Amelia and Harvey Johnson's Druid Hill Avenue home, not at Union Baptist, the thriving church located just blocks away, straight down Druid Hill, nor at the Brotherhood office downtown on Saratoga Street.[35] The location itself doesn't seem to have been chosen for aesthetic reasons. Considering Harvey Johnson's indignant critique of whites robbing "the historical safe deposit box" of the truth of great African civilizations and history to deposit the false "rubbish and trash" that undergirds white superiority, the photograph unsurprisingly does not feature the props of Western "progress."[36] The Roman columns, for example, that appear in so many Black-produced studio photographs of professionals and "New Negroes" at the time are noticeably absent. Nor is the photograph situated inside the Johnson home where common indicators of "civilization"—Western musical instruments, books, and plush furnishings—could be exhibited. Instead, a multigenerational group of thirteen suited men with hats in hand stand arranged outside on about five narrow steps in rows of three or four.[37] On the top of the stairs, at the focal center of the photograph, stands Harvey Johnson, whose white hair is almost perfectly framed by the dark doorway of his home. Characteristic of his collective style and his individual status, he is positioned both behind the other, photographically larger, Brotherhood members, as he is also positioned dead center and above them. The Johnsons' modest middle-class home sits directly on a narrow sidewalk, no more than three feet, perhaps, from the street itself.[38] The closely cropped image and studied pose suggest that the person who took the shot likely had equipment set up in the street itself. Hardly an easy photograph to arrange, its being taken at the portal of the Johnsons' house—that is, at the threshold between domestic and public spheres—signals both the importance of their home to the Brotherhood's public work and the ways in which the group's activism illustrates how "private" and domestic issues affected the public life of African Americans. Tellingly, however, neither Amelia Johnson nor any of the few women members of the titularly male Brotherhood are pictured.

The private papers of the DuBois Circle affirm that Baltimore's women activists as well as men gathered at the Johnsons' Druid Hill home. Women's influence in late nineteenth-century Black Baltimore's civic and political campaigns is well documented; rarely, however, do individual names appear in the public record. The DuBois Circle, however, includes some of the most recognizable names of Baltimore—although "Mrs." or "Miss" rather than "Rev." or "Mr." precede them. One of them, "Mrs. Harvey Johnson," was an early and important member. She hosted several meetings at 1923 Druid Hill Ave. Indeed, the group's first public meeting was held at Union Baptist Church. Members were "greatly pleased at [its] success" and "gave a vote of thanks to Mrs. Johnson, thru whose efforts the meeting was made possible."[39]

Founded by Black women in 1906 (the year in which women were accepted as full-fledged voting members of the Niagara Movement), the DuBois Circle of the Niagara Movement, as it was called at its founding, met bimonthly in members' homes. At the Johnsons' in November 1907, the gathered women discussed a report for school improvement and a future petition drive. The group clearly placed their civic activism in the context of national struggles. Pledging "stick-to-it-iveness," they wrote Senator Joseph Foraker to thank him for his much-lauded stance (by the Black press) during his Brownsville investigation, planned meetings with the local school board, discussed "public meetings of protest" and court cases such as *Mrs. Reed V. the Pullman Co.*, then pending in the U.S. Circuit Court in Minnesota.[40] They partnered with the leading men of the city, Brotherhood members including Reverends Harvey Johnson and G. R. Waller, and with Ashbie Hawkins, for example, to present at public addresses where members spoke out about education and suffrage.[41]

The DuBois Circle minutes not only clarify questions about the specific identities of "the most prominent colored" lady activists of Baltimore (to paraphrase from an earlier nineteenth-century source), they also provide a glimpse of the city's women activists' relational, geographical, and political contexts by naming their concerns, where they lived, and the association's relation to other groups. The records also provide additional insight into the expansive

Figure 5.1. Group portrait of Brotherhood of Liberty. Courtesy of the Maryland State Archives, Special Collections (The Dorcas and Harry S. Cummings Collection). Unknown photographer. Group portrait of African-American Lawyers and Ministers, c. 1900 MSA 5354–1–1.

definition of "literary work," the "special feature of the circle," as members decided in the organization's second year. This literary circle, like others, as Elizabeth McHenry has proven, both implicitly and explicitly "furthered the evolution of a Black public sphere and a politically conscious society."[42]

The circle was evidently named after DuBois not only because of his Niagara Movement leadership and direct relationship with Baltimore residents but also because of his literary contributions. Early meetings included time to discuss chapters from *The Souls of Black Folk*. Members also read regularly from the *Chronicle*, which seems to be their own publication.[43] Amelia Johnson recited original poems, and with others planned literary and musical programs. These details—the kind often disparaged as too domestically bourgeois, not sufficiently connected to mass or political concerns, or simply supplementary to the real organizing efforts of men—emerge side by side with the overtly and centrally important political work these women take on, often with their male counterparts and with national women's groups.[44]

In *Forgotten Readers* Elizabeth McHenry challenges scholars to "expand our perspective" and look to the "churches, private homes and beauty parlors" that have been sites for literary interaction.[45] The Brotherhood of Liberty and the DuBois Circle similarly affirm that the home, like the church, has been a site of literary and political interaction for Baltimore men and women. Though, citing her ill-health, Amelia Johnson overcame her colleagues' protests and resigned after two years, she remained, as her colleagues called her, "a faithful worker and inspiring helper."[46] Alongside DuBois himself and the Rev. G. R. Waller and the second Mrs. Waller, "Mrs. Harvey Johnson" is one of the seven "honorary members" listed on the DuBois Circle annual programs from 1914 until her death in 1922.[47] Her faithful work and the details about it provided by the DuBois Circle minutes demonstrate the Johnsons' continued and contiguous civic, literary, and domestic collaborations and the ways in which Baltimore's men and women, like the Johnsons, used their homes, churches, and organizations for mutual and collective support.

Mutual Appeals and Cross-Gendered Partnerships: Women, the Law, and Baltimore's Brotherhood of Liberty

While an emphasis on individual sacrifice and achievement often orders historical memory, we can also place the Johnsons' early activist efforts within a post-Civil War ethos of Black collective action. Churches and secret societies as well as public associations that emerged from the antebellum tradition of mutual aid groups that were "based on similar ideas of collective consciousness and collective responsibility, served to extend and reaffirm notions of family throughout the black community. Not only in their houses but also in their meeting halls and places of worship, they were brothers and sisters caring for each other," says Barkley Brown.[48] These spaces, notes historian Jeffrey Kerr-Ritchie, were "vitally shaped by the contributions of freedwomen" whose actions "assumed a communal mantle that challenged the gendered straightjacket of male suffrage."[49] The Johnsons embody this ethos.

As we have seen, Amelia and Harvey Johnson's home as well as their church each served as a site for public discussion and civic organizing efforts. The Mutual United Brotherhood of Liberty, which became the chief civil rights force in Baltimore from 1885 to 1905, must have been the focus of much of the Johnsons' lives and energies. As the Maryland State Archives puts it in the material they produce for the public: "By the early 1880s, Johnson began to lend his reputation, his pulpit, and his finances to a burgeoning 'race' effort among black leaders nationally."[50] Harvey Johnson's biographer, A. Briscoe Koger, reports that "the entire amount" of the earliest litigation that Johnson and other emerging leaders would spearhead, "$145.00, was borne by Dr. Johnson, himself."[51] Yet this investment, just under six weeks' salary, represents a significant expenditure for the Johnson *household;* one that, despite his role as provider and head of the family, he might well have run by Amelia, "his guide in all business matters."[52]

Within both a progressive familial and collective framework, Rev. Johnson's "reputation, pulpit and finances" were not singularly his; they also belonged to his and Amelia's immediate family, to their extended kinship network, the brothers and sisters of Union Baptist, and to the nexus of church and civic activists with whom he pursued his mission. As historian Thomas Holt puts it, for recently freed communities, "autonomy was not simply personal" but "embraced familial and community relationships as well."[53] The activities in Maryland that I examine here extend the cross-gendered "communal solidarity over the collective rights of emancipation" outlined by Kerr-Ritchie and Barkley Brown in their work on Virginia—where, like Rev. Waller and his second wife, Harvey Johnson was born and where he maintained a small farm outside Richmond for much of his adult life, into at least the late 1880s.[54] Building on Black Maryland's long tradition of civic organizing and cross-gendered communal actions, "mutual" and "brotherhood" took on historically specific meanings that connected this new legal organization to a history of collective work for Black support and survival.

Despite its name, from its inception the Brotherhood spearheaded court cases and legislative challenges meant to secure rights and protection for Black women as a legal class, regardless of economic class. Frustrated with the reentrenchment of white structural power in education and employment, furious about and deflated by growing anti-Black violence, and unwilling to accept weak-kneed Republican inaction, Rev. Johnson had decided to organize the Brotherhood and to rely upon "God and a good lawyer," as once-enslaved writer Lucy Delaney put it.[55] Founded at Harvey and Amelia's house on a long June day in 1885, the Brotherhood's inaugural act was to recruit the first Black lawyer to successfully stand before the Maryland bar.[56] After challenging the state's ban on attorneys of African descent, Harvey Johnson traveled to Washington and personally convinced a promising, freshly minted Howard law school graduate, Everett J. Waring, to join the newly organized civil rights effort in Baltimore.[57]

The Brotherhood's next legal efforts were to secure legal protection and employment for Black women. Like the Brotherhood, their new lawyer had faith in the power of marrying organizing and legal strategies. As Waring put it in his 1887 article "The Colored Man before the Law" in the *A.M.E. Church Review:*

> That there is efficacy in an appeal to law for justification and vindication may be exemplified by reference to three cases occurring in Maryland. . . . 1st. Three Baltimore ladies were denied accommodations on a steamer, sued the company, and won. 2d. A young colored girl was terribly beaten by a white man who refused to pay her wages due. . . . the girl sued and recovered heavy damages. 3rd. In Baltimore City, I had the pleasure of winning a suit against a white dry goods merchant for striking a colored lady with a yardstick. Finally, through the efforts of . . . the Brotherhood of Liberty, the obnoxious Bastardy Law has been declared unconstitutional. . . .
>
> I cite these cases to illustrate in a practical way what can be accomplished in the courts. . . . Let similar efforts be made everywhere, and when white men deny us our rights, let us call them into court and compel them to defend the wrong.[58]

Waring's words recall Harriet Jacobs's earlier resolve "to stand up for my rights" so whites would have no choice but to conclude "to treat me well. Let every colored man and woman do this," she encourages her readers, "and eventually we shall cease to be trampled under foot by our oppressors."[59] The Brotherhood understood and encouraged the dynamic relationship between collective action and individual commitment to stand up for one's rights.

The Brotherhood was both sincere and savvy in its integration of women's concerns into their legal and grassroots organizing agenda.[60] In their first cases, women served as primary actors, either as litigants or as the central beneficiaries of the Brotherhood's, and of Black Baltimore's, legal activism. When, in 1884, union member George Johnson, his wife, and three sisters were denied first-class accommodations on the steamer *Sue* despite having paid the first-class rate, they consulted their pastor, Harvey Johnson, who secured counsel, as Waring narrates above. Only the women sued, and the case of the steamer *Sue* was reported as an instance of illegal discrimination against ladies who, denied first-class staterooms, refused to retire to the squalid second-class sleeping car.[61] Soon after, newspaper coverage reported that the Brotherhood would attempt to repeal the Bastardy Act, "which afford[ed] no protection to the virtue of Maryland colored women."[62] In renderings of their activities by members (such as the *A.M.E. Church Review* article that Waring penned), women workers, travelers, and consumers were seen as sympathetic victims and also as agents and legal partners. Waring often suggests that "they sued" or "she sued"—and won—and he uses the more exclusive "I" or "the Brotherhood" as the agent who brought the case forward.[63] As news of these cases circulated, the Brotherhood did battle on multiple fronts: it sought restitution for specific claims and succeeded in forcing major concessions from businesses supporting Jim Crow to protect their overarching segregationist aims. Finally, it challenged the larger ideological apparatus that situated white women as the sole victims of physical and sexual violence and insisted that Black men—and only Black men—were the "brutes" who preyed on the virtue of the "weaker sex."

Though its membership was overwhelmingly male, women participated in Brotherhood actions and planning both formally and informally and in ways that were both internal and external to the Black community, to borrow from Barkley Brown's analysis of gender and postemancipation political participation.[64] The Brotherhood included women, unlike the prestigious American Negro Academy, whose membership (with the exception of Anna Julia Cooper) was open only to "men of African descent." According to a list included in the pamphlet *The Brotherhood of Liberty or, Our Day in Court* (1891), four of seventy-four life members were women.[65] Among them was the first Mrs. G. R. Waller.[66] An additional sixteen of those who appear on the Brotherhood roll, like J. W. Cole or E. M. Winston, used non-gender-specific initials, as A. E. Johnson did in her own publishing.[67] In its last pages, the pamphlet's author, founding member Rev. William Alexander, also lists "contributors"; alongside the names of the Brotherhood's first lead counsel Everett Waring, and H[arry] S[ythe] Cummings, who had just become the first Black elected to the city council, are Matilda Crist, Elizabeth Reeves, and four other women.[68]

Because legal spheres were more fluid and flexible than a political arena defined by the franchise and by municipal, state, and federal political representation, Black women litigants were active collaborators, as we have seen, in more visible ways. As importantly, they were crucial to the internal workings of the grassroots movement that fueled larger actions that attracted national attention. Barkley Brown disaggregates formal, or external, political participation—in her analysis, voting—from other forms of political participation to elucidate the manifold ways in which women's actions undergirded political activity usually coded as male.[69] Similarly, though the face of the Brotherhood and its formal leadership were made up of clergymen and lawyers, women joined in mass meetings, petition drives, write-ins, conventions, and fundraising to support its work.

Black Maryland's challenge to the Bastardy Act is one example of how the Brotherhood's legal appeals and women's grassroots activism converged. Beginning in 1860, after eighty-five years of race neutral protection for free women, the act allowed only unwed *white* women to sue the fathers of their children for support, with the assurance that jail time would ensue if fathers ignored their claims.[70] Blacks interpreted this new legal exception as a broad-based, cross-class assault not only on women but also on the broader community as yet another example of anti-Black social policy to discourage marriage.

White women and families were considered more "chaste," Black leaders argued, because the state was invested in that unit. By "converting" children born illegitimately into socially and legally recognized offspring when their parents entered "the honorable relation of lawful matrimony," "the taint and disabilities of bastardy" from "unoffending children" and women were removed, according to an 1876 decision of the Maryland Court of Appeals.[71] Without the legal equivalent of the shotgun wedding that white women could count on, Black women's mates were held less responsible for out-of-wedlock pregnancies, child support, and, ultimately, for marriage. Black women and children, in other words, were left with the continued "taint and disabilities of bastardy."

This impacted intracommunity relations (the first bastardy case the Brotherhood brought to court was between a Black plaintiff and the defendant, her Black lover) and also left Black women open as targets of white sexual predation, a fact not lost on members of either race. As a speaker at one mass meeting put it, "The white people have mingled with us in the dark, but when we want to bring the clear light of day upon such things . . . they are shocked."[72] This campaign championed the rights of working-class girls and women who were most vulnerable on the job, that is, in the homes and businesses of "villainous," obviously white, "men [who] may by deception destroy the happiness of homes of colored people without fear of being legally punished," as Rev. Alexander put it.[73]

In addition to providing a legal disincentive for men who engaged in interracial sexual coercion and rape, challenges to the post-1860 Bastardy

Code were aligned with legal efforts throughout the South to safeguard interracial families, particularly at the time of a white partner's death. Seeking equal protection under the Fourteenth Amendment, African American women sought to defend inheritance rights that were directly connected to the bastardy cases. As Blacks were seeking to revise the act in Maryland, the Georgia Supreme Court in the 1887 case *Smith v. DuBose* affirmed that "whatever rights and privileges belong to a . . . bastard white woman and her children, under the laws of Georgia, belong to a colored woman and her children, under like circumstances, and the rights of each race are controlled and governed by the same enactments or principles of law."[74]

While the Brotherhood did not advocate "social equality" by challenging antimiscegenation laws or customs, the logical extension of its equal protection arguments and sexual critiques linked the protection of all women under the bastardy laws to full marriage rights regardless of race.[75] In his 1888 *A.M.E. Church Review* article "The Unconstitutionality of the Law against Miscegenation," Aaron Mossell (brother of Rev. C. W. Mossell, a life member of the Brotherhood, and brother-in-law of Mrs. N. F. Mossell) makes that case explicitly.[76] The maintenance of white superiority, he argued, not solid constitutional interpretation, guided laws governing racial marriage, as racial intermingling in itself did not pose a problem to "promiscuous intercourse." If this were not the case, he declared, citing Maryland and Virginia statutes, "they would erase the word white from their bastard laws and thus bring the black woman under their protection."[77] Aaron Mossell's argumentation directly mirrors Maryland's rhetorical campaign to protect the sanctity and virtue of the Black home and family. Both provide a legal and economic challenge to white men's theretofore nonactionable and almost unlimited access to Black women, one often sanctioned by the state, even, on occasion, against the will of the parties involved.

The campaign to include all women in the Bastardy Act faced formidable opposition from white politicians and the legal establishment. The path toward repeal was full of labyrinthine twists and turns. After a loss in court and a dismissal from the intransigent legislative Assembly, the Brotherhood employed broad grassroots strategies to shore up its judicial tactics. When "a subscription was opened in the leading colored paper in Baltimore to defray the expenses" of an appeal to the Supreme Court, it served both to put the Assembly on public notice and to raise much needed funds. Petitions with hundreds of signatures "of colored citizens" from neighboring counties underscored the broad-based support the campaign could still gather after a protracted struggle.[78] By all accounts, the most effective pressure was brought to bear by the mass meetings held by Baltimore's women, who led what a

Brotherhood member later called an "uprising." "After the adjournment of the legislature without changing that law, a meeting of ladies was called at Samaritan Temple, headed by the most prominent colored ladies in the city. At this meeting, a strong protest was made against the law, and the appeal to the good citizens of the state to blot it out. At this meeting, the ladies resolved themselves into a Sisterhood, as an auxiliary to the Brotherhood of Liberty," reported one contemporary commentator.[79] Faced with the prospect of "two hundred or more" organized women in support of the Brotherhood's efforts, "it was at this time," literally days later, that "the new code" was "quietly accepted by the Assembly," suggests a professor at Baltimore's Johns Hopkins University in his 1890 report on the *Progress of the Colored People of Maryland Since the War.*[80]

Though history has only preserved men's names in this civic campaign to overturn anti-Black public policy, men and women clearly collaborated to recodify the Bastardy Act. John Prentiss Poe, who served as dean of the University of Maryland's law school and the Maryland attorney general, faced the fact that the Assembly's hand had been forced. He rewrote the new code by simply omitting the qualifier "white" and so allowed all women to share in the act's protections.[81] Though the later records of Baltimore's Niagara Movement women include Amelia Johnson and other women who were related to the recognized leaders in this struggle, the "most prominent colored ladies of the city" and their uprising sisters, the more than two hundred women who came together across class and denominational lines to fight the bastardy laws, remain unnamed.[82] Yet it is hard to imagine that Amelia Johnson was not among them. She was an active, outspoken, "prominent colored lady" and the respected partner of one of the leading forces, perhaps *the* leading organizing force, behind the campaign. The ethos of social gospel and civic organizing that pervaded the Johnsons' home and their place of worship would logically extend to the meeting halls where Baltimore's women gathered in their own defense and in support of the Brotherhood's efforts, as is the documented case decades later.

Black women's sexual vulnerability intersected with the challenges they confronted in employment. Facing segregationist policies that barred Blacks from professions like teaching, and belonging to families in which men were underemployed and underpaid, girls and women were forced to work as menials in the homes and businesses of white men who faced no consequences for their predation. Indeed, as white men's "special prey" when in service, as one Black mother put it, it was women who absorbed the costs of such abuse, regularly losing either their "virtue" or their job.[83] Years after one incident, another woman related how, as a new bride, she was fired because she refused to let "the Madam's husband kiss me." Looking back at her thirty years in Southern service, she summed it up in these words: "Nearly all white men take undue liberties with their colored female servants—not only the fathers, but in many cases the sons also."[84] The nexus of seeking employment opportunities and protecting families from sexual abuse linked the Brotherhood's challenge of the Bastardy Act to its subsequent efforts to ensure adequate state-sponsored schools for Black children and youth.

Education was one necessary front in the battle against poverty and the limited spheres of domestic employment. In Baltimore, graduating from high school was also directly connected to securing teaching jobs, which were coveted positions for rising Blacks, and particularly for women of the race. At the turn of the century when the term was coined, "the talented tenth" described a utopian goal, not a material reality. Despite their growing visibility and absolute numbers, between 1890 and 1910 only 1 percent of Americans of African descent enjoyed employment in "professional service." As Higginbotham points out, the "harsh realities of job discrimination and the lack of black public schools in the South" kept Blacks educationally disenfranchised and trapped at the lowest level of the labor market. Of the steady 1 percent with access to post-primary-school education, men were increasingly steered toward the ministry, medicine, and the law, all of which increasingly required professional training and academic credentialing as the nineteenth century approached its end. Though the "elite" lauded women like Dr. Susan McKinney, the first Black woman doctor in New York, and Dr. Halle Tanner Johnson, the first woman of any color admitted to practice medicine in Alabama, in 1900 a full 86.67 percent of all Black women in professional employment were teachers. In contrast only 24.4 percent of African American professional men chose teaching as a career. By the turn of the century, "teaching assumed a feminine identity."[85]

The Brotherhood's struggle for public schooling mirrored the fight for "black teachers, equitable salaries and adequate public school facilities" in Southern cities throughout the 1880s and 1890s.[86] Baltimore's decade-long struggle and eventual (if limited) success differentiated it from Virginia, Tennessee, and the Deep South in its entirety. In the late 1880s the Brotherhood, along with its education committee's spin-off, the Maryland Educational Union, and other community partners, succeeded in breaking the color barrier in public school teaching. In a multipronged and long-term campaign, they used the model of grassroots activism that had been so successful in their campaign to change the Bastardy Act while also working to secure political allies within the city council.[87] Waring, who in addition to being the Brotherhood's lawyer was the editor of the local paper, the *Star,* encouraged Blacks across economic strata to "storm the fortress."[88] And they did, holding mass meetings and write-ins, forming women's auxiliaries, passing resolutions and urging supporters to pledge continued agitation. The combination succeeded. In 1887, the day after the mass meeting in which participants reviewed the mayor and city council members' records, the city passed the ordinance to hire Black teachers, though they would only allow this in still-segregated schools and faculties.[89]

Since Black teachers couldn't join white faculties—even in schools in which all the students were African American—the fight for public school appropriations to build much needed *additional* schools met two supplemental goals: providing additional jobs in all-Black faculties and fully integrating teachers into their students' communities.[90] The Brotherhood had pressed to grant young scholars the high school diplomas (a certification that had been denied them until 1889 even if they finished the available track) that were requisite for teaching in Baltimore. But without more facilities, children who wanted to learn were effectively kept out of that pipeline. By 1896 Harvey Johnson could take pleasure in an educational victory. Working with a Black councilman, Dr. J. Marcus Cargill, they passed an ordinance to establish a separate high school, one that did not share its facilities with the grammar school.[91] Though entrenched segregation, terrible conditions, and a pace that was hardly deliberate characterized the process of school improvements, these efforts were critical in increasing the number of Black teachers in more and better schools devoted to African American students.

The two-decade-long struggle to build an educational and employment foundation for Black Baltimore was one way in which Black protest severed Maryland from the general disenfranchisement enacted in the South. Higginbotham affirms that "as late as 1910, no southern black community could claim a single public school offering two years of high school."[92] Yet in Baltimore, the Brotherhood and its partners managed to lay a foundation for a tradition of educational excellence. In 1889, the colored high school shifted to a curriculum "so arranged as to make the school equal in every way to the State Normal School for whites." One contemporaneous commentator avers that between two thousand and three thousand people packed the Ford Opera House for the first graduation ceremony in which nine students were granted certificates long denied Black scholars. None other than Mayor F. C. Latrobe, who in the past had vetoed bills to open such educational opportunities, handed out the diplomas.[93]

Investing human and financial resources in Baltimore's struggle for educational justice paid dividends for generations. Women like Martha Eulalia Reed—mother of Cab Calloway and the daughter of Andrew and Anna Reed, most likely the "A. J. Reed" who served as the Brotherhood's president and on its executive board in 1891—directly benefited from these efforts. She graduated from high school and went on to college before teaching in the Baltimore public schools. Cab Calloway's father, who received his initial education in Baltimore, went away to Lincoln University, and then clerked in Baltimore law offices, also benefited from the Brotherhood's work. Cabell Calloway Sr.—pool hall owner and general "hustler"—had been an early contributor to the civic group.[94] Cab Calloway himself would attend Frederick Douglass High School, which developed from the Colored High and Grammar School that started granting diplomas in 1889 as a result of the city-wide effort.[95] Indeed, by the twenties when Cab Calloway was there, fully one-third of Douglass High's graduates pursued college or normal school education.[96] Among them would be Thurgood Marshall, who would continue the work done by the Brotherhood and Baltimore men and women.

Though the historical record chronicles Baltimore's late nineteenth-century civic efforts in almost exclusively male terms, this belies the complex engagement of its Black citizens across genders. As a former teacher who continued to be committed to youth issues and racial access, as a novelist who wrote about working-class characters,[97] as one of the most "prominent colored ladies" in the city and an important early member of the DuBois Circle of the Niagara Movement, Amelia Johnson was almost surely an active participant in the struggle to empower Black teachers, women, young people, and laborers. Recovering Johnson's visible position as one of the leading women of the race and recuperating the importance of her partnership with one of the most radical church leaders involved in the era's civic and legal affairs sheds new light on her political activities and literary decisions and strategies. Moreover, as I'll argue in the next section, her tactic to place indeterminate racial characters in a temperance plot affirms the possibility that such characterization might function as a politicized representation of *white* familial depredation. To borrow from Ralph Ellison and to paraphrase from the work of literary theorist Hortense Spillers, slipping the yoke, Johnson changes the joke, that is, the assumptions about race and familial/sexual degradation that fed legal and physical violence against Black communities in the forms of lynching and bastardy laws that were so recognizably urgent for the communities that the Johnsons, collectively, were fighting to empower.

Racial Inequalities, or Snatching the Whip and Switching the Script

Clarence and Corrine, the first of three novels published by Amelia Johnson under the name Mrs. A. E. Johnson, preceded *The Hazeley Family* (1894) by four years. The now-unknown *Martina Meriden Or What Is My Motive* (1901) followed seven years later.[98] As author of one of the very earliest works of sustained fiction by an African American woman to appear in book form, Johnson broke through a myriad of racial barriers at once. *Clarence and Corrine* was the first novel by an African American or by a "lady author" published by the powerful American Baptist Publishing Society, as the *Baptist Teacher* reports. It was also the "first Sunday School book published from the pen of a colored writer." Indeed, in I. Garland Penn's compendium of journalists of the race, he excerpts no fewer than ten reviews of *Clarence and Corrine* in Black and non-Black, secular and sacred, journals.[99] Perhaps it was Johnson's success that prompted prominent author and businessman William Still to close his introduction to Harper's new novel, published two years later, with the assertion that "thousands of colored Sunday Schools . . . will not be content to be without *Iola Leroy.*"[100]

Clarence and Corrine tells the story of dark-eyed, racially indeterminate siblings early deprived of parental guidance by way of drinking and death. Practically orphaned, poor, and without reputation, family, or prospects, they are separated and lose touch. Corrine becomes the servant of a mean-spirited mistress. Her health is broken, but she finds God and good friends along the way and is eventually adopted. Clarence encounters setbacks on his journey to economic self-sufficiency, but is never tempted by drink or degradation. As a hard worker he struggles on, eventually ending up on a farm quite close to his sister's adopted home. There, mirrored by another pair of siblings, Charlie and Bebe Reade, they all thrive. In the last chapter, Clarence has become a doctor and the siblings properly marry each other in the form of both a romantic novel and, as Ann duCille points out, a classic comedy.[101]

Clarence and Corrine; or God's Way reads as a temperance tale that delivers on its titular promises of redemption, an "all's well that ends well" story in which a preacher's wife "passionately pursues" palatable messages and "the formula of happy endings," to reformulate into one tongue twister the characterizations of Johnson's writings that Barbara Christian and Hortense Spillers offer in their introductions to Johnson's two reprinted novels. Yet contemporary readers might benefit from slowing down this teleological dash toward the narrative finish line by putting first things first as a reading process and practice, and also by placing *Clarence and Corrine* in the context of both the political culture in which its author was immersed and her larger and widely lauded literary contributions: her newspaper writings and work as the publisher and editor of *Joy*.

Amelia Johnson's novelistic strategies anticipate the tactics used in *The Power-Holding Class Versus the Public* (1900), one of the two book-length treatises that carry the Brotherhood of Liberty's name. Amelia Johnson's emphasis on class and seemingly neutral treatment of race are directly reflected in *The Power-Holding Class,* which (though it seems to never have been mentioned in historical accounts of the Brotherhood) is an important indicator of the rhetorical range the group embraced. *The Power-Holding Class* takes as its subject a fictionalized conversation between President McKinley and Senator Hanna that indicts the ruling class without ever explicitly mentioning race. Indeed, its only racialized indication is fulsome praise and citations of *Justice and Jurisprudence,* references that readers familiar with the Brotherhood's work would have easily recognized though they would likely have gone unnoticed by others.

The Brotherhood's earliest book, *Justice and Jurisprudence* (1889), the first full-length inquiry that argues against legal encroachments on African American rights that was produced by or at the direct behest of Black citizens, is explicit about its racial mission; its inquiry into the postwar amendments is conducted "for the advancement of the African race in America."[102] Though its authorial provenance is still undetermined, *Justice and Jurisprudence* was clearly commissioned and perhaps written by members of the Brotherhood. Its purpose was to serve as a written corollary to the legal challenges the organization launched from the late 1880s through the turn of the century.[103] This direct approach is just one tactic that the Baltimore Brotherhood and its branch in Rhode Island employed.[104] Considering Amelia Johnson's narrative tactics in connection with her situated political culture and the rhetorical range through which the Brotherhood communicated its legal and economic challenges to those in power elucidates how and what we identify (as) political rhetoric.

If, as literary critic Barbara Christian suggests, racial indeterminacy "in this country is generally translated as white,"[105] then *Clarence and Corrine*'s formal simultextual reaffirmation and challenge to that assumption anticipate the rhetorical maneuvers evidenced in *The Power-Holding Class.* It also builds on strategies we see in the novelistic narratives such as *Our Nig,* as I discuss in chapter 2. In other words, Johnson's work links to at least two African American representational traditions: to post-Reconstruction political and economic tracts and to earlier fictionalized prose, each of which is shot through with religious justice and reform rhetoric, references, and ideology.

Emphasizing the plight of poor families and abandoned protagonists, *Our Nig* and *Clarence and Corrine* (sometimes cited as the first two nonserialized novels penned by African American women) feature inadequate, racially indeterminate women—white women, following Barbara Christian's commentary—who, in a departure from the dominant literary trope of valorized white motherhood, are situated as victimizers as well as victims. Indeed, treatment of mothers in these novels—and of anti-maternal domains—are so similar that *Clarence and Corrine* seems to raise the titillating but unlikely intertextual possibility that readers such as the Johnsons were able to track down a copy of *Our Nig* for their well-stocked libraries.[106] Like *Our Nig*'s Mag, who snarls and barks at and then abandons her young daughter Frado, *Clarence and Corrine*'s Mrs. Burton is a lazy, neglectful woman, apathetic about her own condition and indifferent to her children's need for sustenance and their desire for a better life.

Mrs. Burton's presence, like Mag's, orders and dominates the novel's initial unfolding to be abruptly jettisoned from the narrative soon thereafter. In *Our Nig*, Mag never tries to make the best of a bad situation. Rejecting both maternal and "American" values, she has no aspirations. She does not strive or scrape to make things better for her children or her local community, and, by extension, for the nation. Instead, the narrator tells us, faced with difficulties, Mag retreated to her "hut morose and revengeful, refusing all offers of a better home than she possessed . . . hugging her wrongs, but making no effort to escape."[107] *Clarence and Corrine* opens by offering a similar scenario. In contrast to the "neat vine covered homes" in the "pretty town" in which they live, the Burtons's "weather-beaten tumble-down" cottage marred the scene "like a blot upon a beautiful picture."[108] Moreover, Mrs. Burton doesn't build up her children, as it were, or even protect them from their drunken father. Rather she is a source of additional discouragement. When twelve-year-old Clarence shares his "ardent desire to possess an education" (*CC*, 9), for example, she silences him with the command "I tell you it's no use talking" and orders him to get some branches to start a fire (*CC*, 8). With her voice ringing out "sharp and harsh" (*CC*, 8), her response recalls *Our Nig*'s central scenes of abuse. Mrs. Burton's command to get branches instead of schooling aligns her son's prospects with a biblical-based trope of Southern racial subordination. If he took her advice, he would make himself content with being no more than a hewer of wood. Soon after this exchange, Corrine Burton finds her mother dead in the old rocking chair that had served, as Spillers points out, as her sole and permanent location of inaction.[109] Indeed, in *Clarence and Corrine* and *Our Nig*—as in domestic representations generally—the absent mother heightens the phantasmagorical (and in this case dark) shadow that figure narratively casts.

Amelia Johnson's narrative strategies, like Wilson's, invite readers to reflect on the relation of whiteness to the chain of private-to-public-sphere signifiers in play in each novel: mother, home, family, race, nation. Arguing for the centrality of Black women's development in 1892, Anna Julia Cooper articulated an "axiom" that she says is "so evident that it seems gratuitous to remark it": "The atmosphere of homes is no rarer and purer and sweeter than are the mothers in those homes. A race is but a total of families. The nation is an aggregate of its homes."[110] By having Mag and Mrs. Burton—who, again, read simultextually as white women—opt out of home maintenance or nineteenth-century worthy womanhood, these novels turn the table on the centrality of motherhood in the evaluation of racial progress.

Mrs. Burton is situated as poor victim and passive victimizer at best. At worst, she is a bad mother complicit in her children's ruin. Nonetheless, *Clarence and Corrine* provides moral explanations for Mrs. Burton's squalid life and death. Her discouraged son provides the novel's sympathetic framework of understanding. "How could she live, battered and beaten, starved as she was, and by our father too; the one who could have made us all comfortable and happy," Clarence asks. "But instead of that," the boy goes on, "he's made us miserable—no, it wasn't him, either; it was that dreadful, dreadful stuff, whiskey. Yes drink ruined our father, and now it's killed our mother" (*CC*, 19). Clarence's classic anti-drink rhetoric accompanies the seemingly sympathetic stance forwarded by the narration: the "poor broken-spirited, abused woman would wake no more in this world" (*CC*, 18). Yet, the text's half-hearted conviction is hardly persuasive. When the Burtons's landlady, Rachel Primrose, proclaims "Why didn't she work and keep herself from starving; I'm sure I'd a great sight rather do that and keep myself and my children decent, than to give way and just sit down with my hands in my lap and let everything get topsy-turvy" (*CC*, 23), Primrose's position as narrative antagonist doesn't quite undermine the stinging truth of her indictment.

For readers who view Black women as both historically steady workers and as women who have consistently mothered white children as well as their own, Mrs. Burton's character, as much as her racial indeterminacy, presents her as decidedly un-Black. The fact that Mrs. Burton doesn't have the strength of character to protect—or even feed—her children signifies that she is without the good sense that God gave her, as the old folks say. From within a cultural and literary matrix that positions Black women and mothers as survivors rather than criminals, as competent protectors who haven't the luxury to passively rock away despite the range of abuse they experience, it is deprived and depraved white motherhood—not Black—that produces children and families who don't know God's way.

Black women's counter-analysis of race's relation to exalted (and depraved) notions of motherhood did not necessarily follow a racially accommodationist understanding of respectability; that is, Black women rejected, as their rhetoric also indicated that they emulated, white mothers as their models. Black women's domestic work gave them a bird's eye view of white women and their children. Underpaid in the South, even educated professionals were often forced to take on domestic or manual work of some kind. "For some black women teachers," Higginbotham points out, "the end of the school term marked not vacation, but employment as laundresses and seamstresses in order to make ends meet."[111] According to an 1898 report, the "great majority" of Black Baptist ministers, for example, made $200 to $400 a year, "while many never see $100 in money yearly. These eke out their scanty salaries by manual labor"; and their wives most often worked.[112] An aspiring class in economic terms, even "elite" women tended to have access to inside knowledge about white people's homes and home training. In their quest for "morals and manners," for respect and respectability, Black women's personal understanding of white women's intimate lives made maternal mimicry an ambivalent process. Indeed, Black women could be highly critical of white maternal practices and values. Paradoxically, then, the simultextual pleasure of the text for *Clarence and Corrine*'s Black readers might be located in Mrs. Burton's potential *whiteness.*

One of the evening's speakers at the 1896 annual convention of the National Association of Colored Women underscored Black women's critical relation to their white peers. Holding white motherhood accountable for social ills, she announced to her audience that she was "convinced that the foundation of race prejudice, lynching, bloodshed and strife had its origin by the fireside." "If mothers," white mothers, "were more careful to teach their children properly, much of these would disappear." Shifting scenes of violence to the hearth, she brought home the point that white women were no innocents, no dewdrops just exhaled from the skies, to borrow from Frances Harper. Nor was their complicity indirect or passive. Rather, she laid the responsibility for the depraved actions of white communities at the dainty (or dirty) feet of white women themselves.[113]

Despite *Clarence and Corrine*'s "raceless" characters and ostensible associations with whiteness, contemporaneous racial politics simultaneously align the novel with Blackness. Following the racist assumptions reflected in and produced by the dominant ideological apparatus, Mrs. Burton's comfort with and insistence on leading a degraded life affirms her Blackness. *Clarence and Corrine* asserts—and also belittles—these very assumptions. The novel both produces and switches the conventional racial script. Johnson's sly simultextual indictment rests on the fact that, counter to the novel's seeming generic affiliations, in it, neither racial taxonomy, maternal responsibility, nor narrative transparency are stable or secure. In *Clarence and Corrine* as in *Our Nig,* "careless and unkempt" motherhood is at odds with the protocols of conventional domestic representation. As "racelessness" codes each mother as white, her cruelty and lack of "womanly feeling" code her—for those who follow racist hermeneutic protocols—as nonwhite.

Frances Smith Foster's assertion that "it was a literary commonplace to describe Black women as so brutalized that they had lost all intrinsic social and maternal sensibilities" but "almost without precedent in Anglo-American women's literature to speak of a white woman, especially a mother, in this manner" holds as true for Mrs. Burton as it does for *Our Nig*'s Mag, about whom Foster writes.[114] The painstakingly neat homes readers encounter in so many novels after narratively passing through the thresholds of huts whose exteriors are described as drab and rundown are meant to reflect the interior worth of the heroines who transcend their circumstances and transform their surroundings. Yet "dismal as was the outside" of the Burtons's "wretched abode, still more so was the inside" (*CC*, 6). Again, Mrs. Burton makes no effort to improve her humble surroundings. The floor is "unacquainted with soap and water"; dirty "chipped plates" are "piled in confusion on the table," and the stove is "littered with greasy pots and pans." Disorder reigns. Even Mrs. Burton's sense of proper gendered difference is called into question—at one point she is "apparently" and ineffectively attempting to darn a "tattered garment bearing but small semblance to either male or female attire" (*CC*, 6). Mrs. Burton's hardened apathy and inattention to ordered domestic space align her with temperance tropes in which a mother is temporarily victimized into apathy. It simultaneously reflects the racist renderings of Black women forwarded shamelessly by a white supremacist ideological apparatus that was churning out virulent images of a putatively incompetent race incapable of "elevation" or "improvement."

Readers unacquainted with Johnson and her previous work might have assumed that *Clarence and Corrine*'s characters were white, despite the persistent cultural associations of degraded womanhood with nonwhites. The generic expectations of conventional anti-drink stories and Johnson's history of authorship with the American Baptist Publication Society would bolster such an assumption, as would the fact that her characters don't exhibit any of the vehemently racist renderings with which postbellum Black characters were so consistently drawn. Again, Mrs. Burton's decline can certainly be accounted for by using a temperance abacus. In this case, those who discovered Johnson's racial identity through numerous national reviews in predominantly white papers might have felt as if they had been subject to literary counterfeit. Had white readers assumed that Mrs. Burton, for example, was one of their own (as they well might have), the moment of narrative and biographical merger would call for a racial recalibration. In this new formulation, the substitution of *Black* maternal depravity in the place of white maternal victimization shifts the equation. By doing so, *Clarence and Corrine* reveals the artificial values assigned to each racial category and so exposes the fragility of putative white maternal superiority.

Johnson's use of racial indeterminacy, like Wilson's before her, issues a challenge to racially resistant readers. Johnson's characters and their claims to whiteness are compromised with the revelation that they were born, as it were, to a Black woman author. Knowing this, many white readers would perceive Johnson's protagonists, at second glance, to be products of an exogamic marriage between author and characters, and so to be heirs of a bastard and miscegenous literary genealogy. This echoes *Our Nig*'s second-chapter revelation of Mag's undisputed whiteness. Had readers believed that Mag, in all her degradation, was Black as I've discussed in chapter 2, they would be confronted with their own racial assumptions.

Reproducing this strategy, Johnson rearranges the supposed signs of Black maternal depravity and provides a distorted mirror effect not present when white authors situate white heroines as absolute victims of the demon drink. The calculus of sentimental meaning production is characteristically mediated through the relation between author, character, and reader. As Jane Tompkins puts it, sentimental prose is "by women [authors], about women [characters], and for women [readers]."[115] In *Clarence and Corrine*, Johnson's authorial relationship with her reader is more direct than it is in conventional narratives and novels. In the production of meaning crucial to Johnson's audience's racial projection and identification, the lack of an explicit racialized articulation within the novel invites the substitution of her own racial identity for those of her characters. The book's consequent racial simultextuality produces the possibility of a stark recorporealizaton of "polluted" Blackness into racist readers' own putatively pure and carefully policed notion of racial and bodily identity. The shadowed doubled racial possibilities for readerly textual infusion play on racial otherness (and sameness). Again, this makes a critical difference in our assessment of the cultural, political, and literary work that *Clarence and Corrine* does.

Temperance and Bad Parental Temperaments

Temperance, the reform cause that *Clarence and Corrine* first trumpets, was "arguably the largest social movement of the nineteenth century."[116] As one of the most acceptable causes from which to launch social action at the century's end, it was so compelling for women in and before the Progressive Era that members in the Women's Christian Temperance Union (WCTU) far outnumbered those in organizations devoted to women's suffrage, though these issues increasingly overlapped. For Black radicals and reformers, male and female, temperance was as pressing a concern as other issues during and before the nadir. At the National Federation of Afro-American Women's

convention in 1896, for example, Ida B. Wells reported on resolutions that
included motions on home life, temperance, education, Justice Harlan's dissent in *Plessy v. Ferguson,* the lynch law, and the convict lease system. Wells
began the report by announcing that delegates were committed to holding
meetings where "the mothers of our race [will] be taught the necessity of pure
homes and lives." The committee's second resolution, Wells continued, was to
"heartily endorse the noble work of the WCTU as an absolute necessity to the
best physical, mental and spiritual uplifting of all people."[117] Anti-temperance
work had the potential for collective cross-racial action. As Frances Harper
put it in an *A.M.E. Church Review* temperance symposium in which Wells
also participated, "Slavery was the enemy of one section, the oppressor of one
race, but intemperance is the curse of every land and the deadly foe of every
kindred, tribe, and race which falls beneath its influence."[118] Both women
called on temperance activists to abandon white supremacist rhetoric in the
fight against the demon drink.

These were not the gendered sentiments of those simply preoccupied with
morals and manners. Anti-drink adherence may have been associated with
class and status and secular/sacred divides, but race leaders came together
across gender lines to support the cause. Martin Delany had been the record-
ing secretary for the Temperance Society of the People of Color in the City
of Pittsburgh. Frederick Douglass and Henry Highland Garnet were staunch
temperance supporters.[119] T. Thomas Fortune and Harvey Johnson both broke
from the Republicans to support the Prohibition Party for a time. And Wells,
whom Fortune had glowingly suggested was as good at political reporting as
any man, took the demon alcohol as her subject in one of her rare pieces of
published fiction.[120] A serious concern even when isolated from other issues,
Black leaders and lay people also highlighted the interstitial connections
between anti-drink activism and rhetoric, the freighted term "home protection," enfranchisement, and movements against Jim Crow and lynching.

When Amelia Johnson employs the widely recognized temperance thematic, it both converges with reform concerns and provides a means of challenging the race-based and race-baiting policies forwarded by prohibition
advocates such as Rebecca Latimer Felton. The wife of a doctor-turned-
Georgia legislator and later a U.S. congressman, Felton was, like Amelia
Johnson, her husband's secretary and counselor. Felton ran her husband's
campaigns and emerged as one of the most powerful women, if not *the* most
powerful woman, in post-Civil War Georgia. An advocate for many reform
causes, she became the most popular and effective Southern speaker for the
WCTU from the late 1880s into the next century. Felton lectured all over the
South and in cities from Baltimore to Boston and beyond.

In the mouths of Felton and other white Southern champions, the fight against the demon drink was vehemently anti-Black. Like so many turn-of-the-century advocates, Felton linked white economic empowerment to "home protection," suffrage, and prohibition campaigns. "Home protection" was a sounding note that carried the most personal and intensely political resonances. Home signified the state, the South, and the households that Southern white women supposedly despaired to leave unattended for fear of Black men drunk with thoughts of political and sexual equality. White appeals for racially exclusive voting rights were cast in ever more stridently racist and nativist tones and recalled earlier rhetoric meant to empower white women over and against what they considered the unwashed herds, "Patrick and Sambo and Hans and Yung Tung," to borrow earlier invective from Elizabeth Cady Stanton.[121] Felton's focus on the putatively "dangerous" and "ignorant" Black men who supposedly threatened white women's bodies and the body politic after the Fifteenth Amendment offered a resonant justification for extending the franchise to include women—and for disenfranchising Black voters.

Felton's most famous speech makes explicit the ways in which improper bodily intake and association could diminish the power associated with white citizenship. Not only white women but also white men, "the bone and sinew of prosperity and patriotism," as Felton put it, were at risk if they didn't take proper precautions against liquor and lust-filled Black threats to the nation and its putatively legitimate rights bearers. Felton condemned "the corruption of the negro vote, their venality, the use of whiskey and the debasement of the ignorant and the incitement of evil passion in the vicious." White men had to stop Blacks from voting, drinking, and "ravaging" white women, she insisted. They should put an end to equalizing "themselves at the polls with an inferior race," with "lust-filled fiends in human shape." Cheered on "to the echo" by "representative men," from the podium at the gathering of the powerful Georgia State Agricultural Society, Felton thundered: "If it takes lynching to protect woman's dearest possession from the drunken, ravaging human beasts . . . then I say lynch, a thousand a week if it becomes necessary."[122]

Heard from the platform and heralded by the white press, Felton had harped on these themes for years in speeches she gave beginning in the late 1880s. She was invited to give addresses all over Georgia and throughout the nation. She also printed her beliefs in her newspaper contributions to the *Atlantic Constitution*. Felton articulated a link between Black prospects for equality at the polls and in the parlor, that is, between Black suffrage and Blacks serving as suitors to white women. Bolstered by and in accord with tracts published by Harvard professors, reports issued by respected statisticians, and speeches given by Southern senators and their Northern converts, Felton and others asserted that white women proved irresistible to so-called depraved Black men.[123]Though Felton's nationally reported Tybee Island speech took place in 1897, racial invective and the assertion of Black criminality linked to sexual immorality and home protection had spiked dramatically as early as 1889, the year before Johnson's *Clarence and Corrine* was published.

Felton's language reflects the easy slippages between "improper" fraternity, franchise, and transgressive intimacy. In addresses to white men who had, according to Felton, abandoned their responsibility to protect their wives, sisters, and daughters from economic and physical violence, she declared, "As long as politicians take the colored man into your embraces on election day to control his vote," as long as you "make him think that he is a man and a brother . . . so long will lynching prevail because the causes of it grow and increase."[124] White men's affection for Black men, their "embrace," is the "cause" of putative African American political and libidinous excitability. Feminized, seduced, and subordinated by whites who embrace the African American man to "control his vote," Felton positions Black men as rivals as well as threats. Her language suggests that white men's choices leave white women not only politically but also sexually displaced. Her imagery is vividly, if not explicitly, erotic. Supposed Black sexual attraction/predation and its "growing" causes activate mythologies about racial physiognomy. And the "increase" of lynching, as she avers elsewhere, links directly to the "curse of slavery [that] is still following hard upon the footsteps of our nation's progress because of hybrid races of mulatto and mestizo varieties."[125] While she holds accountable the "bad white men" of the antebellum South who caused such "violations of the moral law" to occur, her concern with postbellum threats is with the increase of the "better educated more economically independent, more politically empowered" Black classes who are more likely, according to Felton, to commit the "rape" of white women.[126]

Inverting conventional racial dynamics, Johnson makes morally compromised men who could be read as white rather than Black the threat to women and girls, and so indirectly anticipates and responds to the discursive, political, and physical wave of anti-Black violence that crested during the years of Felton's prominence. Like Felton, Johnson indicts white men for abandoning families in need of protection. Yet for Felton, white men's guilt is linked to their leaving their women vulnerable to the putative danger posed by Black "fiends" plied with the alcohol that white men have provided them in exchange for their vote. When Johnson's "raceless" narrative is read as white, what emerges is a violently dysfunctional male-headed household. Unlike the scenario that Felton paints, white men do not endanger their women indirectly by misusing liquor for its political trade value. Instead their own consumption makes them monsters. Mr. Burton's presence—not his absence as in Felton's rhetoric—causes the insecurity and fear that reigns inside the home. His wife's swollen eye, "ill usage," and lack of desire "to be decent," as she says sharply to the children, when "your father is likely to come home drunk at any time, and knock and beat a body about as he does" (*CC*, 8), stems from *white* dissipation. Significantly, the females in the household suffer most directly. In addition to his beating Mrs. Burton, young Corrine must dodge his blows, when, for instance, he raises himself out of his stupor to greet his daughter's announcement of his wife's death with a "clenched hand" and an "upraised fist" (*CC*, 18).

Read purely within a "raceless" temperance rubric, as a modified version of the very popular drunkard narrative genre, liquor and external factors, rather than the man himself, would be the target of the novel's indictment. With Johnson's authorial role engineering a cross-racial story, however, *Clarence and Corrine* enters the additionally charged arena in which Felton also operates. Elaine Frantz Parsons explains that nineteenth-century "writers chose to tell of drunkards ethnically, socio-economically, and religiously like themselves. As awkward as it made their position, they sympathized, even identified with, the drinker."[127] If readers who knew Johnson's work and race interpreted *Clarence and Corrine* within a rubric of sameness (as a Black story about same-race characters), the sympathetic politics of identification and reform that Parsons outlines would prevail here. Alcoholic binges, not Black men, would be the demon. Temperance, discipline, and a healing God would bring families back together. Told within a same-race rubric, temperance narratives posit drunkards as formerly good men whose drinking is at odds with their essential natures.

In the cross-racial retrogression narratives that rose in popularity as drunkard narratives also did, however, drinking is in concert with—it enhances—the putatively innate bestial nature of Blacks. Switching the script in *Clarence and Corrine*, Johnson offers no backstory to affirm Mr. Burton's essential goodness. Nor does she waste any narrative energy in advancing a recuperative story line.[128] As he scurries away from the death scene, leaving his children to their own devices, the narrative likewise abandons him. This literary evangelical tale suggests that he is not worthy of redemption, and so underwrites the inference that Burton, rather than the demon drink, is the real fiend. *Clarence and Corrine* functions simultextually as an instructional intraracial tale and as a cross-racial tale in which "the liquid demon," compromised manhood, "home protection," and victimization are linked to the rape-lynching threat, public funding for Black education, and disfranchisement. In other words, in moving into the charged arena of drink and the racial daemonic, Johnson gives white men "a taste of the lash of criticism" that is "his delight to lay" upon Blacks.[129]

Felton linked her consistent assertion that Black education had not helped to decrease the number of lawbreakers to her thoughts on race, criminality, and its basis in the home, thereby attacking two causes—education and home reform—that were central to Black civic and club movements. "The negro's education in books has been largely unproductive of good results," Felton announced in a speech to the Georgia Sociological Association, "because it antedated the proper training of the mothers in their lewd homes. . . . These lewd homes continue to be crime-promoters. They pull down faster than book education can build up."[130] Nineteenth-century Black women were often called upon to defend their virtue. The most infamous attack was launched by John W. Jacks, the president of the Missouri Press Association, who, in 1895, specifically targeted Ida B. Wells and characterized Black women as "prostitutes" who were "natural liars and thieves."[131] Felton's speeches and articles delivered a similar punch: "Education has no more effect on them morally and intellectually than it has physically," she proclaimed in "Why I Am a Suffragist." "God made them negroes and we can not make them white folks by education." Appropriating the Hutchinson Family Singers' famous anti-slavery anthem "Get off the Track!" for a radically different purpose, Felton thundered on: "We are on the wrong track. We must turn back."[132] Women such as Johnson who were immersed in political culture and statewide legal and civic campaigns had every reason to take on the rhetoric of popular temperance activists like Felton, just as Wells and others faced off with John Jacks.

Felton uses a double-edged sword when engaged in her battle for home protection and (racial) purity. Her reactionary call to arms sometimes collided with her forward-thinking progressive advocacy. Her long-standing advocacy for Georgia's poor included a campaign for prison reform to protect women and juveniles, be they Caucasian or African American.[133] Yet, her support for individual women convicts didn't assure a sympathetic or sisterly stance on the larger issue of Black female criminality—especially when it came to the propagation of respectability. As historian Leann Whites points out, in addition to promoting lynching, Felton was prepared to demand sterilization for "erring" Black women. "Perhaps you may decide my plan is too radical," Felton declared to one audience, "but I do believe that a criminal woman should be made immune to childbearing as a punishment for her crime." Though Black women were not explicitly Felton's subjects here, Whites claims that she did have them "particularly in mind when she proposed this scheme."[134]

Felton's criminal anthropology, as we might call it, not only focuses on the physical Black body, it also views delinquency through the aperture of Black homes that captures, she asserts, a crystal clear picture of Black motherhood: "We have a problem to work out in this country—as to the best methods for the intelligent education of the colored race. . . . Until we can find clean living, as a rule, and not simply as an exception in the colored homes of this country, we are simply walking over a hidden crater. . . . The plan of prevention of crime, by making criminals immune to the propagation of their own species, would go very far towards shutting off an influx of infanticides and brazen prostitution among the ignorant and shameless."[135]

Replacing the category "homo delinquens," à la Francis Galton, with "negra delinquens," Felton's sterilization plan was a base attempt to actualize white surveillance over racial undesirables in the larger social body.[136] For Felton, Black criminality was proven by its ability to disrupt *white* homes and white clean living—the real, self-reflexive, and generative subject of Felton's concerns—that were sullied by "brazen prostitution," or more clearly, by interracial sex.

This familiar rallying cry was used to vent anger and justify the broad-based anti-Black violence against which the Johnsons organized.[137] Again positioning Blacks not only as criminal but also as romantic threats, Felton's language reveals her primary—and primal—concerns. Her goals in advocating government intervention to "protect white women and children" would "create the kind of motherhood that was critical to the larger economic, social and political well being of the [white] South."[138] Cloaked in the language of protection, Felton's twin concerns center on Black congenital criminals and consanguineous families, that is, on those with claims to white paternal legacies and protections that Felton wanted to claim for white women alone.

Black analysis and activism employed similar language about protection and motherhood to indict white men in radically different ways. African Americans understood the assaults on their persons and characters to be projections of white male predatory behavior. When home protection referred to Black homes, it was whites who needed to be monitored and held accountable for ignorant, shameless, and unclean living in their own households—where Black women were preyed upon while employed in domestic service. As the Brotherhood's legal and organizing efforts had, *Clarence and Corrine's* simultextual use of indeterminate racial characterization—when read as white—challenges the racism of ideologues in an era where the rhetoric of white home protection translated to exclusion from protection at best and violent terrorism and abuse against Black men and women at worst.

In her introduction to the Schomburg reprint edition of *Clarence and Corrine,* Hortense Spillers asserts that even though the novel had little to do with the "urgencies of coeval Black life," for contemporaneous Black readers and reviewers who praised the novel, it "is unimportant exactly *what* and *how* Mrs. Johnson wrote, but altogether significant *that* she did."[139] They found Johnson's signal contribution as "a first" important, Spillers suggests, but otherwise, as she puts it, "its authorship is somewhat beside the point."[140] Ann duCille disagrees in part, pointing out that the issues of reform and redemption that Johnson foregrounds, the "*what*" the novel takes as its subject, were compelling, indeed urgently so, for nineteenth-century readers, whatever their race.[141] We might also reassess the "*how*" in Spillers's assertion (an "inequality" in philosophical and mathematical parlance) that "*what* + *how* Johnson wrote < *that* she wrote."[142] Instead, it is useful to change the relation and offer an equation that suggests that "*what* Johnson wrote = *that* + *how* she wrote." *Clarence and Corrine*'s formal outcomes, I am arguing, may have been viewed by her reception communities through the interplay between her specific and situated literary biography, the political communities to which she belonged + the narrative conventions she employed.

If works of African American literature are dissolved into their referents, then, like other nineteenth-century women's writing, *Clarence and Corrine*'s most "literary" moments—the places that query the connections between historical and representational epistemology—are illuminated by acknowledging the reading cartography embedded in the historically specific nexus of her life and work. Like Harriet Jacobs and Harriet Wilson before her, Johnson engages the seeming dissonance between her text's generic affiliations and its multivalent complexity.

References to Black women's protest and resistance have been obscured, disremembered, and unincorporated into public histories. Without such access, the multivalent layers of the work they produced fade and the texts seem to simplistically adopt the transparency, the "sincerity," to recall DuBois's characterization of Harper's prose, associated with the domestic fiction and popular Christian instructional literature whose generic conventions they appropriate. Attending to the multiple meanings produced by several simultaneously situated interpretative modalities is one way of accessing *Clarence and Corrine*'s more complex discursive strategies and Amelia Johnson's literary and activist sentiments.

"Journeying," © 2008 by Julius Lester. Used by permission of the artist.

Coda

On Burials and Exhumations

Cemeteries
are our only
tended gardens
we tend to die
—Saul Williams

the future is blossoming around
us. yet the fields of our destiny
have been gardens untended
over grown, and malnourished
we have come to cultivate this garden
—Anonymous

I gathered up the historical and psychological threads of the life my
ancestors lived, and in the writing of it, I felt joy and strength and
my own continuity.
—Alice Walker, *In Search of Our Mothers' Gardens*

It seems I've always had a critical affinity for narrative beginnings but it's
untended endings that tend to haunt me. While doing the research for this
book, two authors seemed to call to me, beckon me even, to find them and
pay my respects. Standing at Harriet Wilson's grave, its majestic stone jutting
cleanly from the ground, I was overcome by the prospect that my companion
and I were perhaps the first to visit her there in just over a hundred years.
"Hattie E. Wilson" had been buried well, her name etched deeply in local
Quincy granite. After looking for her for years, Wilson's three-foot tombstone
sitting right off the main cemetery road wiped out my Zora-inspired fears
of a grassy unmarked grave.[1]

I set out to visit Amelia Johnson's grave with as much trepidation. The
late Rev. Frank Drumwright Jr. seemed stalwart and strong when, in 2003,
I first visited Baltimore's Union Baptist Church, which, to me, was still the

Johnsons' congregation. He had written and produced a play about Harvey Johnson in the 1990s, he shared with me after services, but knew nothing of the congregation's then-first lady. No one at Union seemed to realize that their beloved past pastor's wife Amelia was also a published author and activist. When I returned to Baltimore, Rev. Drumwright strained against his wife's concern and his own failing body to drive me to the Johnsons' grave site, rightly convinced that the passed-on, handwritten directions to the unmarked yard would never guide me there.

As beloved as Harvey Johnson remains today, as celebrated as both he and Amelia were when they died in the 1920s, their bones were unceremoniously unearthed just twenty years later. Laurel Cemetery, the premier gravesite in Black Baltimore from its founding in 1852 until the 1940s, was dug up after a land-grab coup by white business and city leaders. In its day, Laurel had been no stranger to august public farewells. Bishop Daniel Payne, the esteemed A.M.E. leader who had led Wilberforce for thirteen years as the first president of any Black-run college in the Western Hemisphere, had been laid to rest there. Frederick Douglass had come to eulogize him. Some thirty years afterwards, in 1823, Harvey Johnson's funeral at Laurel was attended by two thousand mourners and was front-page news in the *Afro-American's* national edition.[2] Yet neither public stature nor civic contribution, recognition nor family, had protected Baltimore's dead from having their remains spread out like fertilizer in a remote field once used to inter farm animals. Now that past had been buried and Laurel Cemetery's once-regal headstones were poorly transplanted in some stranger's overgrown acreage adjacent to sprawling, mowed side and back yards. I cried silently standing at that grave, Black efforts and lives welling up in the face of such stunning disregard.

What has haunted me in the years during which this book and I have grown together and apart is how easily Black women's lives are carelessly unearthed, the evidence of our work scattered and thrown away. Had her own mother's story been lost, Alice Walker wrote in "Saving the Life That is Your Own," it "would have no historical underpinning, none which I could trust, anyway."[3] As I join others to recover the buried archival remnants that seem to have both stubbornly and patiently waited for our coming, what has inspired me is our ancestors' literary activism and the ways in which we, their cultural kin (to borrow from Karla Holloway), build on their struggles for expression and justice.[4] This project is meant to help recover the individual strands and collective strains of their stories. I seek to recuperate for these texts and their authors the various, multiple histories and complexities that have been long and systematically denied them.

Activist Sentiments: Reading Black Women in the Nineteenth Century charts the years directly before the Civil War to those that marked the century's end, examining how writers moved from near rhetorical invisibility and isolation to prolific literary and activist productivity and connectedness. In it, I pay particular attention to social literacy and the power of multivalent interpretation. As the book weaves together historical research and literary exegesis, I realize that my writing sometimes perches on a delicate line; as I land after a certain analytical turn or historical jump, I watch myself poised midway between straightening up triumphantly and tipping over while trying to maintain my own critical coordination. Those balancing moments sometimes bring up methodological questions, particularly for those of us who are attentive to history's multiple timelines and to temporal frames punctuated by measurable markers: the passing or enforcement of a law or statute, the publication dates of a newspaper, the invention or application of a specific technology. Take, for instance, my discussion of the relation, in the calculus of print capitalism and modernism, between *Four Girls at Cottage City*'s character "Vera Earle," the popular writer, clubwoman, and activist "Victoria Earle," and the specific body of photographs of club women editors that emerge in sustained circulation the year after the *Four Girl*'s first printing in 1895. In my account of this instance, as in others, the narratives and histories that serve as my principal subjects anticipate a convergence of dynamics that come together an important beat late. My goal is to account for the ways in which these texts circulate as living words, as it were, alongside reception histories that are not fixed but fluid.

The disciplinary fields that document, engage, and theorize the historical and narrative legacies I and so many colleagues examine mirror that movement from early critical isolation to the plenitude of our present academic moment. Yet as I finish this book, I must acknowledge that I am just a slightly older version of a younger me, a woman who came of age in the heady times when nineteenth-century texts were first being rediscovered and reprinted, while the novels of their literary descendents broke onto—and then seemed to dominate—the *New York Times* Best Seller lists. Then, I had yet to greet a fresh masterpiece with my present fatigue-laced enthusiasm or "maybe this summer" insouciance. The possibility that history might not record the unarguably historic achievements of contemporary Black women felt real to me as I studied writers, many of whom had been popular and widely reviewed before they were forgotten and disremembered. Despite the seeming permanence—even popularity—of gendered and racialized subjects of study, I still catch myself glancing over my shoulder to catch the shadows that mark the absence of Black women's images in the intellectual archive.

The academic recognition and plentitude nineteenth-century studies of race and Blackness presently enjoy coexist with our own new nadir; they are coeval temporal happenings on a completely different time curve, to borrow

language from *Activist Sentiments'* introduction. Despite the achievement
and power of some individuals of African American descent, Black communities bear the brunt of violence as principal targets in today's attacks on
people of color, the poor, and the disenfranchised. In Los Angeles, where
I live, African Americans experience hate crimes at a rate nearly ten times
higher than any other group.[5] In the United States, Black women are the
fastest growing population in the incarceration industry, a campaign that
has over one million African Americans, about half of all inmates, impris-
oned. As Black women, we make up nearly 70 percent of newly diagnosed
HIV cases in the United States.[6] Between 2000 and 2005 nearly 61 percent
of people under age twenty-five with HIV are African American.[7] In cities
such as Chicago, New York, and Detroit, between 66 percent and 75 percent
of Black male high school students do not graduate.[8] Black college students
have a 43 percent graduation rate, 20 percent lower than our white peers.[9]
These are the uncultivated "fields of our destiny," to borrow from the unidentified author whose words serve as one of this chapter's epigraphs. They
are "gardens untended over grown and malnourished."[10]

Over this book's pages hover the ghosts of recovered archives and ancestors. They inform my discussions about texts, their histories, and the critical
apparatuses we bring to interpretation. They make visits to my classrooms,
I sometimes think, and appear on the walls of my home. Above a heavy
dictionary, my symbolic inheritance from my granddaddy Foreman, hangs
a photograph of Niagara Falls taken by the accomplished Black lawyer and
dentist Hamilton Sutton Smith. In it, tiny dark figures (my punctum) appear
like cutout silhouettes against the luxuriant snow, that, shimmering and vast,
dominates the frame even with the falls looming in the background. The
image, so formally rich in composition and texture, sometimes reminds me
of a huge print that I encountered every time I went to visit Momma and
Pop, my other grandparents. Standing on the front porch, waiting eagerly
after ringing the bell, on my tiptoes I could peep through the heavy door's
glass cutouts to see the picture that hung in the entry hall, a somber Black
boy enveloped in an all but monochromatic room, the brown of his skin the
only thing to interrupt the image's flat and unrelenting whiteness. Now, on
my walls, another photograph hangs, one that memorializes a Detroit man
beaten to death by police.[11] White words painted on a black backdrop take
up almost the entire frame; the chalkboard-like image, punctuated by several small red handprints, recalls what we do not learn in school. They also
underscore, as Karla Holloway puts it, that "Black death is a cultural haunt-
ing."[12] This message, one that connects my activist sentiments to those who
came before me—before us—reminds me of what cannot be buried when we
pledge to preserve what's come before so we can continue to persevere:

We remember that when people lose
their lives as a consequence of injustice
their spirit wanders, unable to pass over—seeking resolution.
We remember that our lives are a continuation
of those who have come before, and that many
of those who are our kin have died as a consequence of injustice—
and so are wandering—seeking resolution.
We remember that as long as the souls of our kin
wander then so too do we—
and so we make places for their souls to be.

We are helped to remember our right to be here.
We are helped to remember our responsibilities.
We create our justice daily.
We do.

They did. Harriet Jacobs, the writer, school founder, and housing organizer; Harriet Wilson, once "our Nig," then successful entrepreneur and "eloquent and earnest colored trance medium"; Frances Harper, anti-slavery lecturer, novelist, temperance leader; Victoria Earle Matthews, journalist, NACW leader, founder of the White Rose Mission; Amelia Johnson, critical player in Black activist Baltimore and the DuBois Circle. They help us to remember our right to be here. They help us to remember our responsibilities. They help us feel the joy and strength of our own continuity. They do.

Notes

A Note on Language

1. Thornbrough, *T. Thomas Fortune*, 134.

Introduction

1. Fugitives George Johnson and George Latimer spoke at the convention. Newspapers noted Johnson's eloquence. Through Latimer's case he became a cause célèbre. The organizing against his owner's claims to the fugitive led to one of the most serious acts of civil disobedience in the nineteenth century. *Herald of Freedom*, "Milford Convention," January 13, 1843; *The Liberator*, "Anti-Slavery Melody," January 20, 1843.

2. *Herald of Freedom*, "Milford Convention," January 13, 1843. This convention was one of their early performances covered in the anti-slavery press. "They are not performers—They are Abolitionists," reports the *Herald of Freedom*, "with as much heart and fire as they have music." *The Liberator* titles its coverage of the Milford meeting by referring to the Hutchinson Family Singers' performance. *The Liberator*, "Anti-Slavery Melody," January 20, 1843.

3. Ramsdell, *History of Milford*, 522. *The North Star*, June 9, 1848. The centennial was in 1894.

4. *The North Star*, June 9, 1848.

5. "My Mistress was wholly imbued with Southern principles," writes Harriet Wilson in her Preface (np); also see Harriet Wilson, *Our Nig*, 23, 12.

6. Ramsdell, *History of Milford*, 202; there are no other Black females listed in Milford in the 1840 census. If the age given on Wilson's death certificate is correct, then she would have turned eighteen in March 1843, several months after the convention. She would have reached her "majority" then, but it is not clear when she was released from her service to the Haywards. See Foreman and Pitts, *Our Nig*, viii.

7. Wells-Barnet, *Crusade for Justice*, 79. Also see McMurray, *To Keep the Waters Troubled*, 171.

8. "To the Afro-American women of New York and Brooklyn, whose race love, earnest zeal and unselfish effort at Lyric Hall, in the City of New York, on the night of October 5, 1892—made possible its publication, this pamphlet is gratefully dedicated by the author." Wells, *Southern Horrors*.

9. Harper, *Iola Leroy*, 9.

10. Jacobs, *Incidents* (Painter edition), 21.

11. See Flynn, "A Case of Mistaken Racial Identity" and "Profile, Emma Dunham Kelley-Hawkins." Also see Holly Jackson, "Mistaken Identity," *The Boston Globe,* February 20, 2005.

12. duCille, *Coupling Convention*, 32.

13. Ibid., chap. 2, particularly 31–32; Higginbotham, *Righteous Discontent*, chap. 7, particularly 188.

14. McBride, *Impossible Witness*, 2.

15. Ibid., 152.

16. Peterson, *Doers of the Word*, 14.

17. Brody, *Impossible Purities*, 16.

18. Jacobs, *Incidents*, 97, last page of chap. 17.

19. Foreman, "'White' Mulatta Genealogies," 508.

20. Jacobs, *Incidents*, 97, end of chap. 17.

21. For more on this subject, see Foreman, "Passing and its Prepositions."

22. Bakhtin, *Dialogic Imagination*, 279.

23. Henderson, "Speaking in Tongues," 19.

24. Ibid., 22. See also Mikhail Bakhtin, "Discourse and the Novel" in Bakhtin, *Dialogic Imagination*, 271–75.

25. Henderson, "Speaking in Tongues," 19.

26. Ibid., 22. See also Mikhail Bakhtin, "Discourse and the Novel" in Bakhtin, *Dialogic Imagination*, 271–75.

27. As Frances Harper narrates, "Some of the shrewder slaves, coming in contact with their masters and overhearing their conversations, invented a phraseology to convey in the most unsuspecting manner news to each other." *Iola Leroy*, 9.

28. Lucy A. Delaney's *From the Darkness Cometh the Light, or Struggles for Freedom* (1891) and Annie L. Burton's *Memories of Childhood's Slavery Days* are both featured in *Six Women's Slave Narratives*.

29. Jaus, "Literary History," 28.

30. Ibid., 30

31. Lang, "Class and the Strategies of Sympathy," 135.

32. For more on this subject using different authors as examples see McBride, *Impossible Witness*.

33. Harper, *Iola Leroy*, 282. The "Note" that closes *Iola Leroy* includes this last poem.

> There is light beyond the darkness, Joy beneath the present pain; There is hope in
>   God's great justice
> And the negro's rising brain. Though the morning seems to linger
> O'er the hill-tops far away, Yet the shadows bear the promise
> Of a Brighter coming day.

Frances Smith Foster chose the last line as the title of her Harper anthology.

34. Yarborough, "Introduction," *Contending Forces*, xxviii.

35. Matthews, "The Value of Race Literature," 126, 135; McHenry, *Forgotten Readers*, 192.

36. McHenry, *Forgotten Readers*, 190. Matthews, "The Value of Race Literature," 136.

37. Matthews, "The Value of Race Literature," 145.

38. Ibid.

39. Foster, *Three Rediscovered Novels*, xxv.

40. In contrast to Gates, Hazel Carby groups early African American women writers together but resists formulating either a singular or pluralized Black literary tradition and, indeed, "is critical of traditions of Afro-American intellectual thought that have been constructed as paradigmatic of Afro-American history." More recently, Ann duCille asserts that her work assumes no single tradition of Black women's writing and stresses a pluralized approach. I join with others in modifying Gates's emphasis on formal revision, and affirm duCille's admonition about the dangers of constructing singular and homogeneous models of reading. Categorizing the patterns we sometimes claim constitute tradition, however, gives us insight into the cultural work these writers engaged. See Henry Louis Gates Jr., "Foreword," in Cooper, *A Voice from the South*, xvii; Carby, *Reconstructing Womanhood*, 16; and duCille, *The Coupling Convention*, 9.

41. Lukács, *The Historical Novel*, 53, 71.

42. Ibid., 53.

43. Fisher, *Hard Facts*, 16. Here he builds on Lukács who comments that Scott "presents great crises of historical life in his novels. Accordingly, hostile social forces, bent on one another's destruction, are everywhere colliding." *The Historical Novel*, 36.

44. Pushkin ridiculed simply alluding to contemporary events in historical art and Lukács derided using history as a decorative backdrop for otherwise contemporary stories. It was in "bringing the past to life as prehistory of the present," as Harper does, that produced great writing. See Lukács, *The Historical Novel*, 53, 200.

45. Yarborough, "Introduction," *Contending Forces*, 276. Hopkins refers to Wendell Phillips and William Lloyd Garrison. Garrison founded the New England Anti-Slavery Society in the African Meeting House in 1832. Maria Stewart gave the first speech by an American woman to a "promiscuous" audience of men and women from its pulpit, and Angelina Grimké spoke there, despite resistance from angry mobs. August the First celebrations were held there. The meeting house remained a central location for Black resistance and worship for many years and was remodeled in the 1850s, when it attained the name "St. Paul's Baptist Church."

46. Archibald Grimké, "Anti-Slavery Boston," *New England Magazine* (December 1890), 441–59, as cited in Dickson D. Bruce Jr., *Archibald Grimké*, 66.

47. Also see Stepto's "Narration, Authentication and Authorial Control" in his *From Behind the Veil*, 4–5. I build on his description of the ways in which extratextual documents are integrated or appended to slave narratives.

48. Hopkins, *Contending Forces*, 143.

49. Ibid., 148.

50. Ibid. Hopkins writes that Mr. Willis's "foot on the stairs mounting to the two-room tenement which constituted their home in the early years of married life, had sent a thrill to her very heart as she sat sewing baby clothes for the always expected addition to the

family." Profiles tend to stress the newly wedded couple's trip to England; yet two years after their marriage, the 1860 census shows them residing in a tenement with about thirteen in-laws and others. Josephine is seventeen or eighteen years old; their first child is six months old. For more on Hopkins's ambivalence about the figure of Mrs. Willis, see Lois Lampere Brown, "Defensive Postures in Pauline Hopkins's *Contending Forces.*"

51. Hopkins, *Contending Forces,* 197. While Mrs. Willis is certainly and directly based on Josephine St. Pierre Ruffin, the Wilson reference is a bit looser. Though Wilson was undoubtedly one of the most well-known colored mediums in Boston and her age coincides with Madame Frances's, she was a healing clairvoyant and trance medium. Madame Frances is a trance fortune teller. Of course, Hopkins takes novelistic license as she makes histotextual incorporations. See Foreman and Pitts, "Introduction," *Our Nig,* for more information on Wilson's life as a Boston Spiritualist.

52. Carby, *Reconstructing Womanhood,* 128. In the 1890s, Hopkins gave special lectures on Toussaint L'Ouverture and other topics in Black history. See Yarborough, "Introduction," *Contending Forces,* xxix; McKay, "Introduction," *The Unruly Voice,* 3. Her later audiences were heterogeneous, and according to Hazel Carby (building on DuBois) included "those in professional service . . . [predominantly] teachers and clergy" but also "male and female tobacco factory operatives, male blacksmiths, wheelwrights, book and shoe makers, butchers, carpenters and joiners, cotton and textile mill operatives, machinists" as well as "female dressmakers, milliners, seamstresses and tailoresses" as well as domestic workers. Carby, *Reconstructing Womanhood,* 127.

53. See Yarborough, "Introduction," *Contending Forces,* xxxvii. One might add that Hopkins's clear antagonism to accommodation but sympathetic delineation of her Washingtonian character is aligned with many of her contemporaries' take on Washington in 1899 and 1900. According to some historians, explicit anti-Washington expression did not coalesce until 1901, with the emergence of William Monroe Trotter's *The Guardian.* Publication of *The Souls of Black Folks* in 1903 of course further articulated this opposition. See Bruce, *Archibald Grimké,* 92, 102.

54. Hopkins, *Contending Forces,* 250.

55. Ibid., 242.

56. Ibid., 385.

57. Ibid., 224.

58. *Christian Recorder,* October 31, 1889, as quoted in Williams, *The Christian Recorder,* 115.

59. The academy was committed to fighting assaults against Black individuals and communities—as Hopkins's League also is—but the ANA had an archival and scholarly activist bent.

60. Though Fortune was known to disdain the term "Colored" that Hopkins employs, her local league structure, including visiting speakers from the South and elsewhere, recalls Fortune's organization.

61. Other officers included Edward E. Brown and James Wolff. The meeting was held at Charles Street Church, and received press coverage. Grimké sent the open letter to President McKinley that he read at the meeting, along with newspaper coverage, to Booker T. Washington. See Dickson D. Bruce Jr., *Archibald Grimké,* 90.

62. The league's first national meeting took place in Chicago, January 25, 1890, with 135 delegates from 23 states. In July 1893, Fortune disbanded the league for lack of financial

resources necessary to advance the organization's agenda. Some local leagues, however, continued. The league was reconstituted as the National Afro American Council in 1898 in Rochester, New York. One of the principal objectives was to fight lynching, which precipitates, in *Contending Forces*, the meeting that Hopkins outlines. Neither the league nor the academy was based in New England. The academy, founded in 1897, met in Washington DC. The council's constitution is found on the Library Congress site at http://lcweb2.loc .gov/cgi-bin/query/r?ammem/murray:@field(DOCID+@lit(lcrbmrptl203div0)) (accessed November 21, 2008).

63. Bakhtin, *The Dialogic Imagination*, 300.

64. Yellin, *Harriet Jacobs: A Life*; Foreman and Pitts, "Introduction" and "Chronologies," *Our Nig.*

65. We still have almost no idea who "Hannah Craft" is, and there is little information available on Chloe Russell. See Gardner, "The Complete Fortune." Also see *African American Review* 40, no.4 (Winter, 2006) on Julia Collins.

66. See Flynn, "A Case of Mistaken Racial Identity." Also see Holly Jackson, "Mistaken Identity."

67. Scholars who are not adequately familiar with the range of nineteenth-century prose fiction often point to the ways in which Kelley-Hawkins's ethnically neutral fiction falls outside of the racial uplift writing of Hopkins and Harper. Yet this ignores the range of African American early writing. Harper's "Two Offers," published in the 1859 inaugural edition of the *Anglo African*, was followed by many others. As Barbara Christian points out in her introduction of Amelia Johnson's *The Hazeley Family*, Johnson's three novels featuring nonracial characters mirror Paul Laurence Dunbar's novels published between 1898 and 1901: "Afro-American writers used various tactics to overcome racial stereotypes." Christian, "Introduction," *The Hazeley Family*, xxvii. When Holly Jackson erroneously claimed that ethnically neutral characters fall outside of African American literary traditions, journalists reproduced the mistaken claim. See Scott McLemee's "In Black and White," *Inside Higher Education*.

68. Harper, *Iola Leroy*, 14.

Chapter 1

1. *Incidents in the Life of a Slave Girl* had long been thought to have been composed by Lydia Maria Child, its editor. Until Yellin's 1987 edition, many twentieth-century Black writers, anthologists, and historians denigrated and dismissed the book as well. Among them were Sterling Brown, Arthur Davis, Ulysses Lee, Arna Bontemps, and John Blassingame. See Yellin, "Text and Contexts," 287 n. 2; Yellin, *Harriet Jacobs: A Life*, xvi, xviii, xx; and Blassingame, *Slave Community*, 373. Sidonie Smith affirms the notion of unreliability as she quotes Francis R. Hart in *Poetics of Women's Autobiography*, 46.

2. Jean Fagan Yellin, Mary Helen Washington, Linda Mackethan, and William Andrews, to name a few, all basically accept a one-to-one correlation between Jacobs's life and her representation of it. Yet Andrews argues that slave narrators' "actual life stories frequently dispute, sometimes directly but more often covertly, the positivistic epistemology, dualistic morality, and diachronic framework in which antebellum America liked to evaluate autobiography as either history or falsehood." Andrews, *To Tell A Free Story*, 6.

3. Yellin, *Harriet Jacobs: A Life*, xviii.

4. Washington, *Invented Lives*, 9.

5. Sidonie Smith, as quoted in Olney, *Autobiography*, 5.

6. Sidonie Smith, in Olney, *Autobiography*, 20.

7. Lunsford Lane, for example, writes that he chooses "to come short of giving the full picture" rather than to "overstate." See Preface, *Narrative of Lunsford Lane*, available at http://docsouth.unc.edu/neh/lanelunsford/menu.html (accessed November 17, 2008) and Andrews, *To Tell a Free Story*, 115. Solomon Northrup also states that the point of his narrative is "to repeat the story of my life, without exaggeration." *Solomon Northrup*, 3. William Lloyd Garrison says of Douglass's *Narrative of the Life*, "I am confident that it is essentially true in all of its statements, that nothing has been set down in malice, nothing exaggerated, nothing drawn from the imagination, that it comes short of the reality, rather than overstates a single fact in regard to SLAVERY AS IT IS." Douglass, *Narrative of the Life*, 38.

8. Edmund Quincy, a white Garrisonian, noted of William Wells Brown's narrative, that it was told with greater "propriety and delicacy" than was Douglass's. See Andrews, *To Tell a Free Story*, 108.

9. Harriet Jacobs, *Incidents in the Life*, 28 (hereinafter cited in the text as *InL*).

10. Frances Smith Foster, "Resisting Incidents," 69; Stepto, "Distrust of the Reader in Afro-American Narratives," 301–2.

11. Frances Smith Foster, "Resisting Incidents," 70.

12. See Halttunen, *Confidence Men and Painted Women*, 40, 52; and also Smith-Rosenberg, *Disorderly Conduct*, 26.

13. Halttunen, *Confidence Men and Painted Women*, 107.

14. The parlor, Halttunen asserts, mediated between the public and the private. Her "back regions" refer to the indelicate preparation of bourgeois parlor performances—dinners, parties, and the intricate rules of formal visits. Black back regions is a pregnant metaphor that resonates temporally (back when), geographically (back South). One metaphor for white and Black female difference was medically construed as located in the back regions or buttocks (see Gilman, "Black Bodies, White Bodies," 204–42). Jacobs may well assume a bourgeois reception. Such a contract of delicacy is well illustrated in Jacobs's relationship with Mrs. Willis, who never inquires as to the circumstances of Jacobs's children's conception, yet is assumed to know. Jacobs writes of this to Amy Post: "I had never opened my lips to Mrs. Willis concerning my Children—in the Charitableness of her own heart she sympathized with me and never asked their origin—my suffering she knew." *Incidents*, 235.

15. Valerie Smith, "'Loopholes of Retreat,'" 222.

16. In nineteenth-century iconographics and physiognomy, ears were constructed, as were genitalia, as organs that exposed pathological essence, particularly of prostitutes and sexual women. See Gilman, "Black Bodies, White Bodies," 224. Also see Shawn Michelle Smith, *American Archives*, 68–93, especially 77 and 84.

17. Foster notes parenthetically that "rare indeed is any reference to sexual abuse of slave men by white women, and homosexuality [or homosexual abuse] is never mentioned" in narratives authored by men. "'In Respect to Females . . . ,'" 67. Similarly, Mary Helen Washington maintains that "in the male slave narrative . . . sexuality is nearly always avoided, and when it does surface it is to report the sexual abuse of female slaves. The

male slave narrator was under no compulsion to discuss his own sexuality nor that of other men." *Invented Lives*, xxiii.

18. Spillers, "Mama's Baby, Papa's Maybe," 77.

19. Sánchez-Eppler, *Touching Liberty*, 22; Spillers, "Mama's Baby, Papa's Maybe," 77.

20. Garfield, "Earwitness," 110, makes a similar argument using a different passage. She writes, "The discerning white reader should find herself in her black sister's place, in the humiliated nakedness of confession; and Jacobs, seizing the agency of discourse in which she is supposedly the logical victim, adroitly unwrites Child's protection of her readership. In the epigraph's mute addendum about bared bodies, the code of black sexuality is subtly revised, the categories of vulnerable black teller and decorous white listener undermined."

21. Gunning, "Reading and Redemption," 143.

22. Carby, Washington, and others argue, I think rightly, that male depictions of Black women as victims deny these women agency in other parts of their lives, and limit women's expressive agency. See Carby, *Reconstructing Womanhood*, 35; Washington, *Invented Lives*, xxii–xxiv.

23. See Angela Davis, "Rape, Racism and the Myth of the Black Rapist," and "Legacy of Slavery." In antebellum Missouri, if a white man forced himself on an enslaved person he did not own, he could be charged with "trespassing." The concept of master/slave rape was inconceivable since someone who owned property could not be a trespasser on it. These relations reveal themselves in recent scholarship as well. In Tushnet's *American Law of Slavery*, for example, when rape is mentioned white men are never the culprit. And though the antebellum social system sometimes recognized that Black-on-Black rape could occur, the legal apparatus of the South refused to give such standards judicial consideration. In other words, legally, Black women could not be raped. See McLaurin, *Celia, A Slave*, 93.

24. Baker, *Blues, Ideology, and Afro-American Literature*, 50.

25. The North Carolina Supreme Court codified earlier state practice in 1855 declaring that the "county courts had power to bind out all free base-born children of color without reference to the occupation or condition of the mother." Bardaglio, *Reconstructing the Household*, 104. However, Sawyer draws up the children's bill of sales in Jacobs's grandmother's name; they are no longer, then, legally under his power.

26. See Foucault, *History of Sexuality, Vol. 1*, 61; Sekora, "Black Message," 489.

27. Post's description does not reveal any details when she describes Jacobs's "suffering." She writes, "Even in talking with me, she [Jacobs] wept so much, and seemed to suffer such mental agony, that I felt her story was too sacred to be drawn from her by inquisitive questions." Harriet Jacobs, *Incidents* (Yellin edition), 204.

28. Gunning, "Reading and Redemption," 135.

29. Valerie Smith, *Self-Discovery and Authority*, 222.

30. Gunning, "Reading and Redemption," 136–37.

31. Noble, *Masochistic Pleasure*, 9.

32. In *Reconstructing Womanhood*, Carby argues explicitly what Mary Helen Washington maintains, that Jacobs is "informed not by the cult of domesticity or domestic feminism but by political feminism; *Incidents* is an attempt to move women to political action." Mary Helen Washington, *Invented Lives*, xxxii.

33. Gunning, "Reading and Redemption," 144, 146.

34. See Smith-Rosenberg, *Disorderly Conduct,* chaps. 1 and 2, and esp. Auerbach, *Communities of Women,* chap. 1.

35. See Chinn, "Introduction," in *Technology and the Logic of American Racism,* esp. 7, for a theorization of the politics of bodies used as evidentiary material in systems of subordination.

36. Frances Smith Foster, "Resisting Incidents," 67.

37. Fox-Genovese, *Within the Plantation Household,* 392.

38. Flint's tactics do include the physical. I thank Richard Yarborough for his suggestion that this physical abuse might be a loophole for a shift to physical sexual abuse as well.

39. Jacobs's transference from the sexual to the rhetorical is developed more fully in Foreman's "The Spoken and the Silenced," 317–18.

40. Timing supports this possibility. She begins her relationship when she is fifteen; born in 1813, Jacobs then dates 1828 or 1829 as the year she begins her affair with Sawyer. Joseph Jacobs is born circa 1829. It is also in 1828 and 1829 that Mrs. Norcom's suspicions get particularly heated. See Harriet Jacobs, *Incidents* (Yellin edition), 54, 35, and Yellin's attendant note, 266 n. 5.

41. Carby, *Reconstructing Womanhood,* 58.

42. Jacobs stresses throughout the narrative that Flint sells the children he fathers. She does not mention his sale of other children, and emphasizes, as Douglass does in both his 1845 and 1855 narratives, that masters often sell children that remind them—and their wives—of their own philandering.

43. In the same letter Jacobs writes, "I never would consent to give my past life to any one for I would not do it with out giving the whole truth." The tensions between the two statements, between self-protection and possession and layers of consent between an artful narrator and her "trusted" friend Post, and between Jacobs and an untrustworthy public, aptly demonstrate seemingly irreconcilable "warring forces of signification" and truth. Harriet Jacobs, *Incidents* (Yellin edition), 232.

44. In Andrews, *To Tell a Free Story,* 161 (my substitution); Andrews, here, doesn't apply his brilliant analysis of the male trickster narrator to Jacobs. Instead, his reading, too, suggests a transparent relation between Jacobs and her tale.

45. Jacobs's silence on any personal sexual interest or involvement echoes her construction of her grandmother as a nonsexual being. Though in her twenties when Jacobs escapes to the North, not only does this narrative not end "in the usual way with marriage," never does she even intimate another romantic "lover" after her free suitor moves from Edenton.

46. Patricia Williams, *Alchemy of Race and Rights,* 163. In the infamous 1857 Dred Scott Supreme Court decision, Justice Taney, writing for the majority, declared that African Americans were not sovereign citizens of the United States and had no rights that whites were bound to respect. *Scott v. Sandford.*

47. Andrews, *To Tell a Free Story,* 165–66.

48. Valerie Smith, "'Loopholes of Retreat,'" 215.

49. Andrews develops this fully in *To Tell A Free Story,* 148.

50. For a full discussion, ibid., chap. 4.

51. As Yellin points out in her memoir to Jacobs's publishers and the New England

anti-slavery circle active in helping her publish *Incidents,* Jacobs's identity was never in question. By 1862 she had publicly merged her public persona and her private one, publishing an article in *The Liberator* by "Mrs. Jacobs, the author of 'LINDA.'" Yellin, *Harriet Jacobs: A Life,* 161.

52. The Black or Oriental woman as soothsayer has a vivid iconographic history. Examples include Whoopi Goldberg's Oscar-winning portrayal of a medium in *Ghost.* She was only the second Black woman to earn this honor. Black women are featured as oracles, truthsayers, or soothsayers again in *The Matrix,* where Gloria Foster and Mary Alice are all-wise, all-knowing and, in one instance, comfortably ensconced in a humble kitchen making cookies.

53. Henry Beers, *American Men of Letters,* 330.

54. Jacobs writes that she told Mrs. Willis "in the Autumn that I would give her Louisa's services through the winter if she would allow me my winter evenings to myself but with the care of the little baby and the big Babies and at the household calls I have had but a little time to think or write." Harriet Jacobs, *Incidents* (Yellin edition), 237–38. At this point, the Willises had four children (the last child to survive was born in 1857), to whom Jacobs was nurse.

55. Haltunnen, *Confidence Men and Painted Women,* 24.

56. Auser, *Nathaniel P. Willis,* 24. His treatment of his destitute sister, who later became known as the writer Fanny Fern, reveals this. She fictionalizes her scathing critique of her brother in the novel *Ruth Hall* (1854). Jacobs's belief that Willis was pro-slavery, or at least in no way anti-slavery, is confirmed by the stated policy of his paper, the *Home Journal:* "It is entirely neutral in politics, free from all sectionalism and sectarianism." Not until after the South seceded did he take a public stance. Ibid., 128.

57. Beers, *American Men of Letters,* 337.

58. Ibid., 285.

59. Linda's "benefactress" says to her when she returns home free: "You wrote to me as if you thought you were going to be transferred from one owner to another. But I did not buy you for your services. I should have done just the same, if you had been going to sail for California tomorrow. I should, at least, have the satisfaction of knowing that you left me a free woman." Harriet Jacobs, *Incidents* (Yellin edition), 200. Without impugning Cornelia Willis's motives, their exchange can be read to signal that Willis's sincere effusion works to silence Jacobs's feelings of outrage at the broader issues of commodity exchange and power relations.

60. Valerie Smith, "Loopholes of Retreat," 215. Barbara Christian notes that the word "voyeur" reflects a kind of choice that may not be appropriate in Jacobs's case: the slave woman *must* remain unseen. However, by boring through "the interstices," she chooses to remain sighted, to have a view of the outside world. Christian, private correspondence, December 1996.

61. Sánchez-Eppler, "Harriet Jacobs," 87–88.

62. Jacobs offers her mother, too, posthumously. Aunt Nancy, in contrast, is not submissive. Jacobs writes, "When my friends tried to discourage me from running away, she always encouraged me. When they thought I better return and ask my master's pardon . . . she sent me word never to yield." Harriet Jacobs, *Incidents* (Yellin edition), 144. Mrs. Flint is true womanhood's opposite. The white woman who harbors Linda is much "too" radical:

she hides the runaway, in conspiracy with her cook, without her husband's knowledge, much less his permission. Jacobs's grandmother, without a husband, can be the assertive head of her household without conflicting with dominant notions of true womanhood.

63. Carby, *Reconstructing Womanhood*, 57.

64. Aunt Martha later moves from an ideological embracing of true motherhood to personal considerations of her own burdens of caring for the children, asking "Linda, do you want to kill your old grandmother? Do you mean to leave your little, helpless children? I am old now, and cannot do for your babies as I once did for you." Harriet Jacobs, *Incidents* (Yellin edition), 91.

65. Jacobs invokes the concept of an expandable family throughout *Incidents*, as she consistently refers to Mrs. Flint as Aunt Martha's foster daughter (see ibid., 85, 145–46) in direct opposition to white families, who deny more direct biological ties. Aunt Martha sides with her white "daughter" over her Black grandchild.

66. Baker explains this term, which he borrows from Hugh Cott, this way: "Rather than concealing or disguising in the manner of the cryptic mask (a colorful mastery of codes), the phaneric mask is meant to advertise. It distinguishes rather than conceals." Baker, "Caliban's Triple Play," 390.

67. Smith-Rosenberg, *Disorderly Conduct*, 60.

68. Wood, *Blind Memory*, 80.

69. This particular image was composed circa 1840 by an anonymous engraver who also produced the ubiquitous runaway male engraving. As Marcus Wood puts it, these "images of the runaway were so familiar that they possessed a terrible semiotic inertia." Ibid., 92.

70. After John Brown's 1859 assault on Harper's Ferry and trial, Jacobs composed an additional chapter to add to her already finished manuscript. Child strongly suggested that Jacobs use the original draft—without the Brown chapter—as the basis for her published narrative. Yellin, *Harriet Jacobs: A Life*, 141.

71. Yellin's research confirms this. She notes that her grandmother's eldest, Betty, was probably born in 1794, her youngest, Joe, in 1808 (Jacobs, *Incidents* [Yellin edition], 268). Yet these years include only the five children who survived. Yellin notes that four probably died early or in childbirth. Carroll Smith-Rosenberg notes, "The clean lines that distinguish the generations in twentieth-century families . . . were inconceivable in most eighteenth- and nineteenth-century homes. The ages of biological siblings could span the twenty-odd years of their mother's reproductive life, easily permitting . . . mothers and daughters to be pregnant and give birth together." *Disorderly Conduct*, 22.

72. Yellin, *Harriet Jacobs: A Life*, 6.

73. Yellin, *Harriet Jacobs: A Life*, 25.

74. Alfred Churton deeded a Black son "Joseph," serving Josiah Collins (as Molly's son Joseph did) use of some property. Alfred Churton was one of the founders of Providence, the tract of land bought by Edenton Blacks, for their own church, meeting house and cemetery. Churton's father, Joe, was freed by his master. Yellin, *Harriet Jacobs: A Life*, 25 and 272–273 n. 19.

75. See Harriet Jacobs, *Incidents* (Yellin edition), 262 n. 6.

76. See John Jacobs, "A True Tale of Slavery," 86.

77. Harriet Jacobs, *Incidents* (Yellin edition), 263. She also suggests that the money

Horniblow had saved might not have been sufficient to buy herself, her son, and their home and that she borrowed the balance from Gatlin. See 264 n. 13.

78. See Yellin, *Harriet Jacobs: A Life*, 21–22.

79. Sidonie Smith, *Poetics of Women's Autobiography*, 46.

Chapter 2

1. Cortázar, *Hopscotch*, 2.

2. In *Incidents*, 145, Harriet Jacobs quotes Aunt Martha saying she has nine children. She may have been including the grandchildren and great grandchildren she in large part raised; the number of biological children she had was five. See Yellin, *Harriet Jacobs: A Life*, 6, 25.

3. Rebecca Hutchinson was also a direct descendent of Anne Hutchinson. White, "'Our Nig' and the She-Devil," 29.

4. Elizabeth (Betsey) Hayward marries David Hutchinson in 1829. Evidence suggests that the two may have lived with the Haywards before moving to the Hutchinson homestead. Betsey is the only Hayward sibling who is not represented by a corresponding character in *Our Nig*, though Harriet Wilson combines two brothers into the character Jack. Ibid., 44. Charles married his *second* wife, Sophia Nagle, in 1853—well after the years covered by *Our Nig*. See Foreman and Pitts, eds., Chronology II, xx.

5. The Hutchinsons received their first notable recognition in 1843 when Harriet Wilson was a teenager. They became famous, performing at abolitionist gatherings, giving concerts, and singing for dignitaries throughout the 1840s. For a photo of their family homestead in Milford see Brink, *Harps in the Wind*, photo section.

6. Ibid., 22.

7. Leonard Chase was the Milford agent listed on the *Liberator*'s masthead. There are no Milford agents in the subsequent years (1843–52).

8. White, "'Our Nig' and the She-Devil," 27. Ramsdell, *History of Milford*, 373.

9. Ramsdell, *History of Milford*, 106.

10. Call for the anti-slavery meeting at Milford, quoted in full in ibid., 107–8.

11. Brink, *Harps in the Wind*, 286. Douglass also wrote the introduction to Jonas Hutchinson's *Story of the Hutchinsons*. See White, "'Our Nig' and the She-Devil," 51 n. 35.

12. Foreman and Pitts, eds. *Our Nig*, 13 (hereinafter cited in the text as *ON*).

13. Bassard, *Spiritual Interrogations*, 194.

14. The Milford Rally document closes by pronouncing "Let the thundering eloquence of DOUGLASS and REMOND, and the soul-stirring tale of LATIMER, unite to break the death-like slumbers of the Granite State! Finally we extend the invitation to every friend of humanity—to all who can feel for others' woes and others' wrongs." It is signed by forty-seven local men and women. Ramsdell, *History of Milford*, 108.

15. Doody, "Introduction," in Richardson, *Pamela*, 8–9.

16. Much like *Uncle Tom's Cabin*, *Pamela* images appeared on everything from teacups to fans; it "changed the life of the novel as a literary genre." Ibid., 7.

17. "My prison has become my palace," writes Pamela. Richardson, *Pamela*, 378.

18. Ibid., 46, 52. These are Pamela's father's words; emphasis in text.

19. Ibid., 6. Mr. B. makes a formal proposal complete with articles for her "serious consideration." Pamela rejects it on moral grounds, though the text also makes plain that she has no standing for sympathy or redress in the court of public appeal, much less legal standing. The "contract" depends entirely on Mr. B.'s will and whim, and so is no contract at all; ibid., 227–31. For a reading of how *Incidents* and *Pamela* correspond, see Valerie Smith, *Self-Discovery and Authority*, 37.

20. Richardson, *Pamela*, 163.

21. Ibid., 242.

22. Shawn Michelle Smith, *American Archives*, 105–6.

23. Douglass, *Narrative of the Life*, 151.

24. Pillsbury, *Acts of the Anti-Slavery Apostles*, 328.

25. Recall that Athena, the battle goddess, Zeus's favorite child, was motherless. She emerged, fully-formed and dressed in armor, from Zeus's head.

26. On *Heroic Slave*, see Yarborough's "Race, Violence and Manhood" and Foreman's "Sentimental Abolition in Douglass' Decade."

27. James, "Autobiography of Rev. Thomas James," 8, cited by McFeely in *Frederick Douglass*, 83; and *Liberator*, March 29, 1839. See McFeely, *Frederick Douglass*, 393.

28. Parker Pillsbury writes "that proved none other than the baptismal, the consecrating service of Frederick Douglass into the lifework and ministry which he has since so wondrously fulfilled." *Acts of the Anti-Slavery Apostles*, 328.

29. Harriet Jacobs, *Incidents* (Yellin edition), 230.

30. Letter from Harriet Jacobs to Amy Post, ibid.

31. Ibid., 1. See Smith, *Self-Discovery and Authority*, 39–40.

32. Harriet Jacobs, *Incidents* (Yellin edition), 3.

33. Jefferson, *Notes on the State of Virginia*, 143.

34. See Bay, *White Image in the Black Mind*, 30.

35. William Wells Brown, "Memoirs of the Author," 26–27.

36. This is the familiar language of Douglass's appendix critique on Northern religion; *Narrative of the Life*, 157.

37. Genesis 2:19–20.

38. White, "'Our Nig' and the She-Devil," 43.

39. Harriet Jacobs, *Incidents* (Yellin edition), 11.

40. Wald, *Constituting Americans*, 161.

41. Zafar, *We Wear the Mask*, 146.

42. The full sentence reads, "Her mistress soon followed, irritated by Nab's impudence in presenting herself unasked in the parlor, and upbraided her with indolence, and bade her apply herself more diligently." Harriet Wilson, *Our Nig*, 56.

43. Brodhead, "Sparing the Rod," 142.

44. In no way do I mean to equate the representational work such a proxy, or merged, beating does in *Our Nig*, with the physical abuse that Wilson experienced.

45. While Harriet Wilson writes "it was now certain Frado was to become a permanent member of the family," her irony is biting. This sentence directly follows a passage describing in detail the mental and physical abuse Frado suffers. Wilson follows the sentence about family directly with the sentence, "Her labors had multiplied." *Our Nig*, 18.

46. Ammons, "Stowe's Dream," 182.

47. Reid-Pharr, *Conjugal Union,* 104.

48. Brodhead, "Sparing the Rod," 147.

49. See Foreman and Pitts, "Introduction," *Our Nig,* xlvii n. 19.

50. Frey, "House of Refuge," 12.

51. In his study of two Black orphanages in New York, Carleton Mabee writes, "Both Black orphanages, like American orphanages generally, used the indenture system—an inheritance from English poor law—by which they bound out their more responsible children by contract to families to work or learn a trade, from about the age of twelve until the age of twenty-one," or eighteen for girls, white and black, who were generally indentured to learn "housewifery." See Mabee, "Charity in Travail," 69. On girls and "housewifery," see Frey, "House of Refuge," 21.

52. Lasser, "Pleasingly Oppressive Burden," 158.

53. Foreman and Pitts have established that Harriet Wilson's birthday was March 15, 1825. See "Introduction," *Our Nig,* vii. There's no evidence to confirm when exactly Harriet was placed with the Haywards. If her mother is the Margaret (Mag) Smith whose death was reported in the area newspaper, the Amherst *Cabinet,* Harriet may have been just five years old. See ibid., xxviii.

54. Zafar, *We Wear the Mask,* 128, asserts that the "reader remains unsure whether [Mag is worried] because the mother will miss her or because she fears her plans will go awry. In any event, once located, Frado is forthwith deposited at the Bellmont household."

55. The House of Refuge in Philadelphia had an indenturing committee "whose duty it shall be to decide upon all applications for apprentices, and to indenture them with their consent," Frey, "House of Refuge," 21 n. 63. Lasser, "A Pleasingly Oppressive Burden," 58, points out that the Salem Female Charitable Society placed their last charge in 1838 as benevolent relations dissipated as they saw it, undermined by an erosion of a mercantile economy.

56. *Miralda,* a revised version of *Clotel,* appeared in the *Weekly Anglo African* from December 1860 through March 1861.

57. Harriet Jacobs, *Incidents* (Yellin edition), 98.

58. White, "'Our Nig' and the She-Devil," 22, suggests that the dog motif, "Frado's double," is a brilliant commentary on the quality of the white humans.

59. For similar readings see Foreman, "Sentimental Subversions," and Wald, *Constituting Americans,* 164. Wald also points out the lexical similarity between the names "Fido" and "Frado."

60. Reid-Pharr, *Conjugal Union,* 104.

61. Wald suggests that "the pronominal resonance" in the "she" in this passage suggests "Frado's susceptibility to her benefactors' perspective," *Constituting Americans,* 166. She notes that Abby undermines Frado, while also noting her place as "Frado's strongest female ally," ibid., 164.

62. See White, "'Our Nig' and the She-Devil," 46, nn. 3, 20.

63. For more on class and labor in *Our Nig,* see "The View From Below: Menial Labor and Self-Reliance in Harriet Wilson's *Our Nig,*" in Santamarina's *Belabored Professions,* 64–102.

64. In other early novels, similar narrative structures and overlaps are recognized. For example, Carla Peterson asserts that in *Clotel* and its introductory materials, William Wells

Brown presents himself as a kind of palimpsest, "a record of the multiplicity of African American identity and experience through temporal evolution." Peterson, "Capitalism, Black (under)Development," 564.

65. Tate, *Domestic Allegories*, 38.

66. See Ammons, "Stowe's Dream," 177, and Reid-Pharr, *Conjugal Union*, 90.

67. Morrison, *Beloved*, 200–217.

68. Gates, "Introduction," in Harriet Wilson, *Our Nig*, xxxvii. Peterson, "Capitalism, Black (under)Development," 565; Morrison, *Beloved*, 213.

69. Harryette Mullen makes this point in her introduction to Fran Ross's *Oreo*, xiii, asserting that "from a position at the intersection of black and white, both Wilson's Frado and Ross's Oreo articulate astute critiques of America's hypocrisy about race. . . . Both authors employ innovative narrative strategies, resulting in complexly discursive, generically hybrid texts."

70. I thank the L.A. Women's Group for the Collaborative Study of Race and Gender in Culture for its feedback on an earlier chapter. The group includes Gabrielle Foreman, Alexandra Juhasz, Laura Hyun Yi Kang, Rachel Lee, Eve Oishi, and, until 2005, Cynthia Young. I borrow Cynthia Young's language here.

71. Morrison, *Beloved*, 210.

72. As quoted in William Andrews's "A Poetics of Afro-American Autobiography," 85. From Bakhtin, *Dialogic Imagination*, 7. Edmund Husserl calls this ongoing reality the living present, *lebendige Gegenwart*.

73. Morrison, *Beloved*, 216.

74. Genesis 4:9.

75. Reid-Pharr, *Conjugal Union*, 100.

76. See Bassard, *Spiritual Interrogations*, 195; Gubar, *Race Changes*, 224; Ernest, *Resistance and Reformation*, 57; and Stern, "Excavating Genre in *Our Nig*," 440, 444, for example.

77. Christian, "Introduction," in Amelia E. Johnson, *The Hazeley Family*, xxvii.

78. Peterson, "Capitalism, Black (under)Development," 568.

79. The most explicit rendering of the fractionalized dynamics of sexuality and sale is William Wells Brown's oft-quoted rendition of Clotel's sale where "the bones, muscles, sinews and blood of a young lady of sixteen were sold for five hundred dollars; her moral character for two hundred; her improved intellect for one hundred; her Christianity for three hundred; and her chastity and virtue for four hundred dollars more." *Clotel*, 43.

80. Webb, *The Garies*, 2.

81. Butler, "Discussion," 110.

82. Mag repeatedly snarls and growls. See Harriet Wilson, *Our Nig*, 16, 17 for examples.

83. Frances Smith Foster, *Written By Herself*, 88.

84. Griffith, *Autobiography of a Female Slave*, 10.

85. Andrews and Kachun, *Curse of Caste*, 3, 51.

86. Mattison, *Louisa Piquet, the Octoroon*, 1.

87. Black anti-slavery authors often stress the difference in diction and literacy between their (self-)educated protagonists and whites. See Mr. Peterkin, Ann's owner in Mattie Griffith's *Autobiography*, and the post-Nat Turner scene in Harriet Jacobs's *Incidents* when white patrollers come to search Aunt Martha's and are goaded by the letters they find—and that Martha can read while they cannot.

88. Hartman, *Scenes of Subjection*, 99–100.

89. Gross, "Litigating Whiteness," 18.

90. Harryette Mullen examines the severing ties to kin and community in the context of passing narratives. See "Optic White," 71–89.

91. I thank Laura Kang of the L.A. Women's Group for Collaborative Study for her response to an earlier draft; I have borrowed her language here.

92. Gross, "Litigating Whiteness," 5, 9.

93. Ibid., 16, 17.

94. The subject of this passage is Clare Kendry, who is nicknamed "Nig" in *Passing* (1929). Butler, "Passing, Queering," 269.

95. This is Elizabeth Abel's language, "Black Writing, White Reading," 105, as she explores her own racialized reading practices in Toni Morrison's "Recitatif."

96. Diamond, *Unmaking Mimesis*, 53, xiv.

97. Brooks, "Fraudulent Bodies," 15.

98. Lang, "Class and the Strategies of Sympathy," 134.

99. Diamond, *Unmaking Mimesis*, 46, 47.

100. Lang, "Class and the Strategies of Sympathy," 134.

101. Robinson, "It Takes One To Know One," 721.

102. See Mullen, "Optic White," 85, for other examples.

103. Ellison, "Change the Joke and Slip the Yoke," 67.

104. See Douglass, *Narrative of the Life*, 59; see Ellison, *Invisible Man* where the protagonist is working at Liberty Paints, 195–96.

105. There are many historical and contemporary examples. I refer to Patricia Williams who writes of a classmate who, having "lived her life as a red-haired, gray-eyed white person, was told that she was one-sixteenth black. . . . Before my eyes and despite herself, she began to externalize all the unconscious baggage that 'black' bore for her, the self-hatred that racism is. She did not think of herself as a racist—nor had I—but she literally wanted to jump out of her skin, shed her flesh, start life over again. She confided in me that she felt fouled and betrayed." *Alchemy of Race and Rights*, 61.

106. Bhabha, "Representation and the Colonial Text," 93.

107. Said, *Beginnings*, 43.

108. Graff's "Literature as Assertions," as quoted in Peterson, *Doers of the Word*, 146.

109. Peterson, *Doers of the Word*, 148. She quotes from Andrews, "Novelization," 9. Also see Yarborough, "The First Person in Afro-American Fiction," 105–21.

110. See Cathy Davidson's introductions to *The Coquette* (1797) and *Charlotte Temple* (1794).

111. Said, *Beginnings*, 76, 77.

112. Ibid., 33, 72, 77.

Chapter 3

1. President Harrison's 1889 call for legislation to protect the Black franchise made Southerners particularly worried that Black votes, if guaranteed, could make a difference. See Fredrickson, *Black Image*, 262.

2. Frances Smith Foster, "Introduction," *Minnie's Sacrifice*, xiv–xv.

3. Jaus, "Literary History," 28.

4. Ibid., 30.

5. The novel has been perceived as lacking in "honesty and imagination" and directed toward a readership "outside the black cultural community." For this and comments on the alternative homogenization that stems from the novel's putative use of countermyth see McDowell, "'The Changing Same,'" 93, 95, 99, and Christian, *Black Women Novelists*, 22. Houston Baker has dismissed the novel as describing "no significant orbit." *Workings of the Spirit*, 31. These late twentieth-century assessments echo DuBois's diplomatic dismissal in the 1911 eulogy he penned for the NAACP's *The Crisis*. Harper was "not a great singer," he declared, "but she had some sense of song," "not a great writer, but she wrote much worth reading. She was, above all, sincere," as quoted in Frances Smith Foster, *A Brighter Coming Day*, 25.

6. On how race creates a differently gendered subject, see Spillers, "Mama's Baby, Papa's Maybe."

7. Bakhtin, *Dialogic Imagination*, 300.

8. Ernest, *Resistance and Reformation*, 183.

9. Harper, *Iola Leroy*, 9 (hereinafter cited in the text as *IL*).

10. In the introduction to *Iola Leroy* Carby aptly revises her earlier contention that "Harper placed in the mouths of her folk characters a poorly written dialect that was intended to indicate their illiteracy." Carby, *Reconstructing Womanhood*, 78. Frances Smith Foster notes that Harper depicts "heroic folk characters." *A Brighter Coming Day*, 4.

11. From Harper in Lowenberg and Bogin, "Woman's Political Future," 245. This speech was delivered in 1893 to the World's Congress of Representative Women in Chicago.

12. For more on Black women's orality, sexual resistance, and formal literacy, see Mullen, "Runaway Tongue," 245.

13. See Ammons, *Conflicting Stories*, 30. Also see Foreman, "Looking Back from Zora," 652.

14. See Lukács, *Historical Novel*, 52, 72. The historical novel does not allude to present events, he asserts. Phillip Fisher comments that the struggles between classes and codes in historical fiction are linked to a known outcome. *Hard Facts*, 16.

15. Wells, *Crusade for Justice*, 71.

16. Harper, "Count on Me as a Subscriber," in Frances Smith Foster, *A Brighter Coming Day*, 322–23.

17. See Woodson, *Works of Francis J. Grimké*, 1:281.

18. Frances Smith Foster, *A Brighter Coming Day*, 323.

19. See Washington, *Invented Lives*, xviii.

20. The "Coloured Women of America" speech was delivered in 1877 at the Women's Congress and was later published January 15, 1878. Frances Smith Foster, *A Brighter Coming Day*, 271.

21. Harper, "Count on Me as a Subscriber," 322–23.

22. Frances Smith Foster, *Minnie's Sacrifice*, 91.

23. See Christian, "'Uses of History,'" 168, and Frances Smith Foster's entry on Harper in Hine, *Black Women in America*, 1:356, for example.

24. From "An Appeal to My Countrywomen," Frances Smith Foster, *A Brighter Coming Day*, 385–86.

But hark! From our Southland are floating
Sobs of anguish, murmurs of pain,

And women heart-stricken are weeping
Over their tortured and their slain. . . .
When ye plead for the wrecked and fallen,
The exile from far-distant shores
Remember that men are still wasting
Life's crimson around your own doors.

For more on Harper and multiracial coalitions see Christian, "Uses of History," 168, and Foster's entry on Harper in *Black Women in America*, 1:356, for example.

25. See Brodhead, *Cultures of Letters*, 201.

26. Many critics have argued that Harper and other Black women writers "naively" create counterstereotypes, "saints" and not women, to resist the stereotypes to which I and they refer. See Kimberly A. C. Wilson, "Function of the 'Fair' Mulatto," 104–15; McDowell, "Changing Same," 95; Christian, *Black Women Novelists*, 22–23; Elder, *Hindered Hand*,16; and Blyden Jackson's *History of Afro-American Literature*, 1:393–95. Jackson argues that "very little in [*Iola Leroy*] links it to the 1890s. Very little in it, furthermore, commends it either to us or to its own day." It is characterized, he suggests, by its "saccharinity and its milksop gentility." By not addressing the "raped," "enslaved" servant of the ante- and postbellum period—women who worked with their own hands—Pauline Hopkins, Emma Dunham Kelley, and Frances Harper, Alice Walker tells us, "turned away from their own *selves* in depicting 'black womanhood' and followed a black man's interpretation of white male writer's fantasies." See Walker, "If the Present Looks Like the Past . . .," 296–99.

27. Hobson, *Uneasy Virtue*, 114.

28. Rosen, *Lost Sisterhood*, 117.

29. McBride, *Impossible Witness*, 162. Yellin, *Women and Sisters*, 53.

30. The anti-slavery press commented on "The Greek Slave" as an effective icon of protest. William Wells Brown laid a picture of a Black woman, "The Virginia Slave," in front of Powers's sculpture as "its most fitting companion" while in London. Though Powers denied that his piece was meant as an anti-Black-slavery work, Douglass and others commented upon it in the Black press. See Yellin, *Women and Sisters*, 122.

31. DuBois and Gordon, "Seeking Ecstasy," 33.

32. Hobson, *Uneasy Virtue*, 55.

33. Rosen, *Lost Sisterhood*, 115. Journals and newspapers also emphasize this theme.

34. Hobson, *Uneasy Virtue*, 55.

35. Harper was well aware of WCTU president Frances Willard's racism. Wells, too, became involved in struggles with white feminists who refused to take strong stands against racist exclusion and violence. By no means do I mean to romanticize the relations of female activists of the nineteenth century.

36. Gilman, "Black Bodies, White Bodies," 226, 229.

37. Hobson, *Uneasy Virtue*, 46; Rosen, *Lost Sisterhood*, 117.

38. The Slaughterhouse cases severely restricted the Fourteenth Amendment. The Fourteenth Amendment, Justice Miller declared, had not fundamentally altered traditional federalism; most of the rights of citizens remained under state control, and with those the amendment had "nothing to do." *United States v. Cruikshank* in 1876 arose when a group of freedmen in Louisiana defended the county seat from whites who claimed that democrats had won a contested election. The victors slaughtered some fifty blacks who had laid down their arms under a white flag. The U.S. Supreme Court overturned the

convictions declaring that the federal government was only empowered by the postwar amendments to prohibit violation of Black rights by states themselves and that the punishment of individuals should be acted upon, as always, by state and local authorities. Finally, in 1877 President Hayes retired the last federal troops (in Louisiana and South Carolina) during contested elections and let the democrats take over. Said the *Nation*, "The Negro will [now] disappear from the field of national politics. Henceforth, the nation, as a nation, will have nothing more to do with him." See Eric Foner, *A Short History of Reconstruction*, 582.

39. Tate, *Domestic Allegories*, 148. Tate would find Ammons's conclusions more compelling if she had offered more textual evidence, 262 n. 36. Ammons, *Conflicting Stories*, 31, 32.

40. Ammons, *Conflicting Stories*, 31, 32.

41. Harper, "We Are All Bound Up Together," address to the Eleventh National Women's Rights Convention, 1866. In Frances Smith Foster, *A Brighter Coming Day*, 218.

42. Ammons, *Conflicting Stories*, 33.

43. Foreman, "Who's Your Mama?" 519.

44. Harper, "We Are All Bound Up Together," Eleventh National Woman's Rights Convention, 1866. Frances Smith Foster, *A Brighter Coming Day*, 218.

45. I read Jacobs's imprecise antecedent in this quote as an example of the simultextual expression of sexual abuse that disrupts paradigmatic white male-enslaved female dyads. Instead, both white men and women in this passage are figured as agents of abuse, as both enslaved men and women can be its victims.

46. Harriet Jacobs, *Incidents*, 52. Nancy Johnson is referred to as "Miss Nancy" seventeen times in the novel and as "Mrs. Johnson" twelve times. See Frances Smith Foster, *A Brighter Coming Day*, 218.

47. Ammons notes that she "is no less racist—or dangerous—for being mildly ludicrous." *Conflicting Stories*, 33.

48. In *Southern Horrors*, 5, Wells writes of "Afro-American Sampsons [sic] who suffer themselves to be betrayed by white Delilahs." Logan, *We Are Coming*, 78.

49. Douglass, *Narrative of the Life*, 122.

50. Iola rejects Gresham's invitation to share his Northern home and have "my mother to be your mother," while thinking of Gracie's admonition. Harper, *Iola Leroy*, 116, 118.

51. Whites, "Rebecca Latimer Felton and the 'Wife's Farm,'" 367.

52. Bakhtin, *Dialogic Imagination*, 300.

53. Carby, "Introduction," in Harper, *Iola Leroy*, xxii.

54. Ibid., xvi.

55. See Dittmer, "Education of Henry McNeal Turner." He writes, "A large, powerful man, crude and awkward of manner, Turner evoked the image of the two-fisted frontiersman," 254.

56. Simmons, *Men of Mark*, 575.

57. Douglass is referred to as "Honorable" because of his diplomatic appointments. Coverage in T. Thomas Fortune's *New York Age*, for example, sometimes uses this title. Mrs. N. F. Mossell's references in *The Work of the Afro-American Woman*, 37, offer other examples.

58. In *Iola Leroy*, Harper associates Professor Langstone with Georgia. Yet, Bishop Henry

McNeal Turner, her Tunster as I argue, is the Black leader most strongly associated with Georgia. In his thirties, in the aftermath of the war, Turner was the major figure in Black Georgia, the state with the largest Black population (an honor Turner shared, perhaps, with William A. Pledger); he later became the presiding elder and superintendent of Georgia's A.M.E. missions. Under his leadership, a dozen schools and universities, most notably Morris Brown College, were established. See Dittmer, "Education of Henry Mc-Neal Turner," 253–72.

59. Simmons, *Men of Mark*, 214. In *Iola Leroy*, the character is said to be from North Carolina; Greener is affiliated with South Carolina where he graduated from South Carolina University, was admitted to the bar, and was active in politics. Ibid., 212–13. Gatherings that included the constellation of thinkers represented in *Iola Leroy* were common at conventions and congresses, and were mentioned in reports of these meetings. For example, Harper, Douglass, Still, Fortune, and Turner were among fourteen respondents to the question "The Democratic Return to Power—Its Effect?" in the *A.M.E. Church Review* 1, no.3 (January 1885): 213–51.

60. Dittmer, "Education of Henry McNeal Turner," 262.

61. Cheek and Cheek, "John Mercer Langston,"109.

62. T. Thomas Fortune, Henry B. Blackwell, and William Lloyd Garrison are listed together as presenters of an address entitled "Political Equality." *History of the Club Movement*, 6. Booker T. Washington is also listed on the program.

63. One should be careful about confusing Douglass's feminism with a true egalitarianism, as Mary Helen Washington cautions. As she points out, in 1892, the same year as the publication of both *Iola Leroy* and *A Voice from the South*, Douglass responded to Monroe Majors's query (as Majors put together his important volume *Noted Negro Women: Their Triumphs and Activities* [1893]) that "I have thus far seen no book of importance written by a negro woman and I know of no one among us who can appropriately be called famous." Mary Helen Washington, "Introduction," in Cooper, *A Voice from the South*, xl. She quotes from a Douglass letter to Majors (August 26, 1892) reprinted in Dorothy Sterling, *We Are Your Sisters*, 436.

64. Cooper, *Voice from the South*, 75. The quote is "While our men seem thoroughly abreast of the times on almost every other subject, when they strike the woman question, they drop back into sixteenth-century logic."

65. Peterson, "African American Literary Reconstruction," 48. Fulton, "Sowing Seeds in an Untilled Field," 212–16, especially 212–13.

66. Patricia A. Schechter calls Wells's use of "Iola" a blending of her private and public identities. *Ida B. Wells-Barnett and American Reform*, 17.

67. Thompson, *Ida B. Wells-Barnett*, 22.

68. Wells became an antilynching activist in direct reaction to the hanging of Moss and two other Black business owners. The Memphis media tried to justify mob action by intimating sexual impropriety when, in fact, the Black grocers' economic success had precipitated the violence. *Crusade for Justice*, 66.

69. Carby, *Reconstructing Womanhood*, 115.

70. Frances Smith Foster, *A Brighter Coming Day*, 16. Boyd, *Discarded Legacy*, 50. Still and Harper remained close friends and neighbors. Indeed he writes the introduction to the second edition of *Iola Leroy*.

71. Higginbotham, *Righteous Discontent,* 16, 17.

72. Biographical encyclopedias and compendiums produced in the late 1880s and early 1890s include Gertrude Mossell's *The Work of the Afro-American Woman* (1894), Lawson A. Scrugg's *Women of Distinction: Remarkable in Works and Invincible in Character* (1893), and Monroe Major's *Noted Negro Women: Their Triumphs and Activities* (1893). William Simmons, who had produced *Men of Mark: Eminent, Progressive and Rising* (1887) and was publisher of the journal *Our Women and Children,* was working on a volume on women when he passed away in 1890.

73. In 1851 Harper became the first woman to teach at Union Seminary, the A.M.E.-sponsored school for Black students. Frances Smith Foster, *A Brighter Coming Day,* 9. Wells's "lifelong devotion to Sunday School teaching began in Memphis out of a renewed commitment to God and Christian living in her New Year's resolution in 1887." Wells taught Sunday school in Memphis while she was also teaching, coediting *Free Speech,* and caring for her sister Lily. Later, Wells "launched her community building work" in Chicago from Grace Presbyterian Church where she taught the men's bible class for ten years, "lecturing the teachers and officers of the Sunday School" and addressing the annual business meeting. Schechter, *Ida B. Wells-Barnett and American Reform,* 67, 73, 187. Harper would serve in 1894 as the director of the American Association of Education for Colored Youth.

74. See Higginbotham, *Righteous Discontent,* 11.

75. Schechter, *Ida B. Wells-Barnett and American Reform,* 34.

76. Mary V. Cook, professor of Latin and mathematics at State University in Louisville, Kentucky, edited a column with the *South Carolina Tribune* and the *American Baptist* and was editor of the educational department of *Our Women and Children.* Publishing under the name "Grace Hermine," she was "gifted with the pen, and in the near future will become an author," wrote I. Garland Penn. *Afro-American Press,* 367–74. Lillian Lewis was writing a novel titled *Idalene Van Therse;* her articles appeared in the *Boston Advocate,* the *Boston Herald,* and the *Richmond Planet* (ibid., 382–84). Mrs. Lucretia Newman Coleman was said to have written a novel entitled *Poor Ben.* She published essays and poetry in the *A.M.E. Church Review* and the *American Baptist* (ibid., 385). Miss Kate Chapman, later the author Katherine Chapman Tillman, affirmed that it was her aim "to become an authoress, because, chiefly, having been strengthened by good books myself, I would like to give to my country and people a like pleasure." By age nineteen, she had published in the *Christian Recorder,* the *American Baptist, Our Women and Children,* and the *Indianapolis Freeman;* she would go on to write essays, addresses, and two extant novellas (ibid., 390–92).

77. Wells, *Memphis Diary,* 99.

78. Mrs. N. F. Mossell, *The Work of the Afro-American Woman,* 13, 32. Mossell notes Wells's consternation at the letters pouring in from Memphis warning her not to return south while she is in Philadelphia "on a visit to Mrs. F.E.W. Harper and to take a peep at the doings of the A.M.E. General Conference." Ibid., 33.

79. Frances Smith Foster, *A Brighter Coming Day,* 17, 16.

80. Women sometimes wed clandestinely to maintain their employment. Alice Dunbar secretly married fellow teacher Henry Arthur Callis who was twelve years her junior. See Gaines, *Uplifting the Race,* 210.

81. *Washington Bee*, December 14, 1889.

82. Cooper, *Voice from the South*, 70–71.

83. Ibid., 72.

84. Since Delany is from Georgia, we can assume that University of A is Atlanta University. In 1890, Atlanta University had graduated only one woman; Fisk, twelve; Oberlin, five; Wilberforce, four. See Mary Helen Washington, "Introduction," in Cooper, *Voice from the South*, xlviii. See Harper, *Iola Leroy*, 244.

85. Delaney, *From the Darkness*, 35. Frances Smith Foster also points out that *Iola's* Lucille Delany's "character and achievements resemble in essence" (if not in the particulars) those of her namesake, the once-enslaved narrative writer Lucy Delaney Foster. *Written by Herself*, 185. On this naming also see Eric Gardner, "'Face to Face,'" 52. For his groundbreaking work on Delaney's life, see the entire article, particularly 53–65.

86. Delaney, *From the Darkness*, 42, 50.

87. Harriet Jacobs, *Incidents in the Life*, 201.

88. Frances Harper, "Note," *Iola Leroy*, 282. The closing words in the author-penned note concluding the novel are these:

There is light beyond the darkness,
Joy beyond the present pain;
There is hope in God's great justice
And the negro's rising brain.
Though the morning seems to linger
O'er the hill-tops far away,
Yet the shadows bear the promise
Of a brighter coming day.

89. In 1895, John W. Jacks, president of the Missouri Press Association, specifically targeted Ida B. Wells in an infamous indictment of Black women's morals. See McMurray, *To Keep the Waters Troubled*, 245–47.

90. Andrews, "Introduction," in *Two Biographies*, xxxiii.

91. In her article, "Martin R. Delany: Elitism and Black Nationalism," Nell Irvin Painter highlights Delany's postbellum misguided collusion with Southern democrats in South Carolina and suggests that twentieth-century praise for the resurrected Delany has been contingent upon selective historical memory. See Painter, "Martin R. Delany," esp. 149–50, 170–71. Delany's sons were named after Charles Lenox Remond, the U.S. abolitionist; Alexandre Dumas, the Afro-French writer; and Ramses Placido, the Egyptian ruler and the Afro-Cuban poet and rebel who is a character in *Blake*. Other sons were named in honor of a third-century Black bishop and a Haitian emperor. His only biological daughter was named Ethiopia.

92. In a review of Delany's *Condition, Elevation, Emigration and Destiny of the Colored People*, Garrison writes "Dr. Delany is both 'black and comely'—so black as to make his identity with the African race perfect. . . . He is a vigorous writer, an eloquent speaker and full of energy and enterprise." Sterling, *Making of an Afro-American*, 149.

93. Ibid., 227, 101.

94. Rollin, *Life and Public Services of Martin R. Delany*, 49–50.

95. Douglass brokered a compromise at the National Convention of Colored Freemen

in Cleveland in 1848 in which he substituted a resolution explicitly inviting women to participate with a ruling that all colored persons could be delegates, including women. Sterling, *Making of an Afro-American*, 112.

96. As Carla Peterson points out, other Harper characters (Jenny from "Fancy Etchings" for example) strive to be writers. "African American Literary Reconstruction," 43. See Penn's section on "Our Women in Journalism," *Afro-American Press*, 367–427, for many accounts of young journalists who aspire to write novels as well. Wells published at least one short story, "Two Christmas Days: A Holiday Story," first published in the *A.M.E. Zion Church Quarterly* in 1894. Frances Anne Rollin published under the name Frank A. Rollin. Andrews, "Introduction," in *Two Biographies*, xxxv.

97. Speech in South Carolina, 1876. Sterling, *Making of an Afro-American*, 308.

98. Ibid., 111.

99. On Nannie Burroughs, the Baptist Woman's Convention, and the National Training School for Women and Girls, see Higginbotham, *Righteous Discontent*, 211–21.

100. More than ten years earlier, when, in 1848, Delany moved on from *Mystery*, the paper he had founded and edited, to join Douglass and William Nell in launching the *North Star*, the *Mystery* was purchased by the A.M.E. church. It became the first Black religious paper in the United States. Later, under the name *Christian Recorder*, it would publish Frances Harper's three postbellum serialized novels.

101. The *Anglo-African* declared on its masthead that it was devoted to "Literature, Science, Statistics and the Advancement of the Cause of Human Freedom," the same goals articulated by Victoria Earle Matthews in her "The Value of Race Literature" (1895). Delany contributed scientific pieces and Harper, who was on the editorial board, added other articles to the magazine that year as well.

102. Sterling, *Making of an Afro-American*, 169.

103. Painter, "Martin R. Delany," 170.

104. Latrobe finds his homonymic resonance, suggests John Ernest, in the prominent Latrobe family and particularly in the patriarch Benjamin Henry Latrobe, a "symbolic architect of the exclusionary dominant cultural system." Ernest, *Resistance and Reformation*, 201.

105. Sterling, *Making of an Afro-American*, 214.

106. See Ernest, *Resistance and Reformation*, 201, for references to Latrobe and Gresham.

107. Saks, "Representing Miscegenation Law," 58.

108. Ibid., 45.

109. Nell Painter's and Dorothy Sterling's accounts of the Harvard purging differ slightly. See Painter, "Martin R. Delany," 154; Sterling, *Making of an Afro-American*, 130.

110. Rollin, *Life and Public Service of Martin R. Delany*, 129; Sterling, *Making of an Afro-American*, 214, 215.

111. The full name of Delany's last book is *Principia of Ethnology: Origins of Races and Colors with an Archaeological Compendium of Ethiopian and Egyptian Civilization from Years of Careful Examination and Enquiry*. It is known both as *Principles of Ethnology* and as *Principia of Ethnology*. Though Painter's focus is on Delany's collusion with white Democratic elites and she doesn't spend much time discussing Delany's last book, her argument highlights that the book's refutation of Anglo accounts of Black evolutionary

development runs at a crosscurrent with Delany's local politics. See Painter, "Martin R. Delany," 170.

112. There is evidence that Latimer published poetry in both 1887 and 1888 in *Leisure Hours: The Society Journal* in Philadelphia, where Harper resided. He also continued to write for the *New York Age*. See the Latimer file, Spike Harris Collection, Box 28, SCM 76–30, Schomburg Library.

113. Lewis H. Latimer, *Incandescent Electric Lighting*. Matthews, "Value of Race Literature," 139. Matthews defined race literature broadly including a "general collection of what has been written by the men and women of that Race: History, Biographies, Scientific Treatises, Sermons, Addresses, Novels, Poems, Books of Travel, miscellaneous essays and the contributions to magazines and newspapers." Ibid., 126.

114. Latimer's first patents situate him only as resident of a city, county, and state. Beginning in 1886 the language changes, announcing that he is a "citizen of the United States and a resident." This modification corresponds to increasing nativism and anti-immigrant shifts in law and language. For the full patents and drawings, see http://edison.rutgers.edu/latimer/557076.pdf (accessed December 2, 2008). In 1852, Martin Delany corresponded with the Patent Office in Washington to obtain a patent on drawings that outlined how to get locomotives to cross mountains under their own steam, which would make stationary engines obsolete. Sterling, *Making of an Afro-American*, 139.

115. Klein, *Hidden Contributors*, 102.

116. Philip S. Foner, "Introduction," in *Life and Writings*, 54.

117. Asa Davis, "Two Autobiographical Fragments," 4. Davis's source is the November 11, 1842, issue of the *Boston Atlas*.

118. The petition itself is reprinted on the Web site "The George Latimer Case: A Benchmark in the Struggle for Freedom," available at http://edison.rutgers.edu/latimer/glatcase.htm (accessed December 2, 2008). It is reprinted with permission of the Massachusetts Historical Society.

119. "Washington Correspondence," *Emancipator*, from the Bowditch *Latimer Case* scrapbook at the Massachusetts Historical Society, datelined February 20, 1843, though with a February 25 date as part of the clipping at its end. Thanks to Ellen Garvey for this citation.

120. Ripley, *Black Abolitionist Papers*, 3:97.

121. Filler, *Crusade against Slavery*, 210; Wiecek, "Latimer: Lawyers, Abolitionists," 220.

122. Norman and Patterson, *Lewis Latimer*, 29–30.

123. Horton, "Community Organization and Social Activism," 194.

124. George Latimer left his wife Rebecca and his four children when Lewis was ten. Unable to support the family, Rebecca eventually sent all three boys to Massachusetts State Farm School to be trained as apprentices. The eldest, George, was placed on a farm, while Will and Lewis ran away and returned to Boston. All three joined the Union army. Though the abandonment is barely mentioned in most accounts, Reginald Pitts reports that the elder George Latimer spent time in the Middlesex County jails. By 1870, according to the census, he was back in Lynn, Massachusetts, working as a paperhanger. Latimer Family Papers, Queens Library, and private correspondence, Reg Pitts, May 2003.

125. May 10, 1894. Hutchinson, *The Story of the Hutchinsons*, 2:219. This volume is also

published in 1894 and includes George Latimer's second autobiographical sketch. Like many reformers, both Hutchinson and the senior Latimer lived in Lynn, Massachusetts, where Douglass, too, once lived. Research historian Reginald Pitts shares that Latimer is in Lynn by the 1870 census; he's in Boston after 1879 and is back in Lynn by 1884, according to the directories. Pitts, personal correspondence, April 2003.

126. Russell, *Black Genius*, 301–2. Reginald Pitts notes that this letter was transcribed by Russell from the private collection of Dr. Winifred Norman, Latimer's granddaughter. The Latimer Family Papers Group deposited in the Long Island Division of the Queens Borough Public Library does not mention whether or not this letter is listed, and the one to which it is responding is not listed in the Frederick Douglass Papers at the Library of Congress. Pitts, personal correspondence, March 2003.

127. "Bethel's progressive minds have decided to have a 'Brooklyn Literary Union,'" *Woman's Era* announced. "They will associate Victoria Earle, T. T. Fortune, T. McCantz Stewart, L. H. Latimer, J. C. Carter and many others. Quite a tally-ho." *Woman's Era* 1, no. 8 (November 1894): 11.

128. February 9, 1897. Latimer File, Spike Harris Collection, Box 28, SCM 76–30, folder 3, Schomburg Library. The report of Lewis Latimer's petition drive can also be found in the Spike Harris Collection, Box 28, SCM 76–30, Schomburg Library.

129. *Justice and Jurisprudence;* we now know that it was penned by the Mutual United Brotherhood of Liberty (MUBL), a group led by Dr. Harvey Johnson of Baltimore's Union Baptist Church.

130. Harvey Johnson, "White Man's Failure," 14–16.

131. Cooper, *A Voice From the South*, 31.

132. See the *New York Age*, October 10 and November 14, 1891. In 1892 his poetry appears in the February 13 and 20 editions. This is the last extant edition in microfiche circulation during 1892 and 1893. Latimer's involvement in literary circles and the stream of poetry that he published must have made him an even more attractive homonymic choice for Harper, one of the most beloved poets of her era.

133. *New York Age*, December 12, 1891.

134. The temperance symposium is found in the *A.M.E. Church Review* 7, no. 4 (April 1891): 372–81. The announcement of Harper's "Iola" was published in a poorly replicated microfilm that I can best attribute to the April 1892 publication, 381. Vol. 1 (1892) includes Well's article "Afro-Americans and Africa"; vol. 2 features Harper's poem "The Black Hero."

135. Wells, "Woman's Mission," 181. See also Wells's "Model Woman," 187. Both were first printed in the *New York Freeman,* which eventually became the *New York Age.* It was edited under both names, and earlier as the *New York Globe,* by T. Thomas Fortune. The first article appeared on December 26, 1888, the second on February 18, 1889.

136. Peterson, "African American Literary Reconstruction," 41.

Chapter 4

1. Brooks, *Bodies in Dissent*, 137.

2. Collins, "A Letter from Oswego," 127. See also William L. Andrews and Mitch Kachun, "Editors' Introduction," in Andrews and Kachun, *Curse of Caste,* and Foreman, "*The Christian Recorder.*"

3. Frances Smith Foster, *Written by Herself,* 141.

4. For a different interpretation of the topsy-turvy analogy see Sánchez-Eppler, *Touching Liberty,* 133–41. See, for example, Scott McLemee, "In Black and White," and David Mehegan, "Based on Work of Brandeis Doctoral Student," as well as Farai Chideya's NPR interview with Holly Jackson ("The Truth about Emma Dunham Kelly-Hawkins"). Though it's impossible to recover the full context from the sound-bite quotations that appear in newspaper articles, Mehegan quotes Henry Louis Gates Jr., chairman of Harvard's African and African American studies and the general editor of the Schomburg series, as saying, "I am persuaded she was not black, and I welcome the finding. . . . In the next edition we will delete her works" (par. 2). Mehegan's article offers one of the few nuanced reports that has appeared about Kelley-Hawkins's reclassification, writing, and critical context.

5. Among the many authors who address the nineteenth-century white women's club movement are Karen Blair, Anne Ruggles Gere, Anne Firor Scott, Mary Kelley, and Theodora Penny Martin.

6. Brooks, *Bodies in Dissent,* 135.

7. See http://digital.nypl.org/schomburg/writers_aa19/ (accessed December 4, 2008), although the Schomburg is sure to remove this image. Kelley was not yet married at the time this photograph was taken.

8. Peterson, "New Negro Modernity," 113.

9. This is quoted from Mehegan, "Based on Work of Brandeis Doctoral Student," paragraph 14. Gates is also thus quoted in Chideya's interview with Jackson ("The Truth about Emma Dunham Kelly-Hawkins") and on historian Caleb McDaniel's blog, *Mode for Caleb,* (par. 5).

10. I add the beauty shop to give women a vote and to affirm the collective Black politics this statement points to, as well as to avoid the problematic image evoked by "putting up" (pinning up?) a woman's photo in a predominately male space.

11. Flynn, "Profile," 280. See also Flynn, "A Case of Mistaken Racial Identity," 6.

12. Flynn, "A Case of Mistaken Racial Identity," 10, 13.

13. As Roland Barthes puts it, "Almost all three-quarter face photos are ascensional, the face is lifted towards a supernatural light which draws it up and elevates it to the realm of a higher humanity." *Mythologies,* 93.

14. Shawn Michelle Smith, *Photography on the Color Line,* 4.

15. See Flynn, "Profile." In a Douglassian coincidence, it turns out that Whiteman was indeed, a white man. Jean "Blackwell," later Jean Hutson, did very well. She became chief curator at the Schomburg and was the second Black woman to graduate from Barnard (after Zora Neale Hurston, "Jean Hutson").

16. Gates, "Foreword," in *Schomburg Library,* xx.

17. See Hite, "Introduction," in Kelley, *Medga,* xxvii. *Four Girls in Cottage City* was published first by the Continental Printing Company in Providence, Rhode Island, in 1895. It was a small, evidently short-lived press, not even noted in Providence city directories or in the monthly publication *Providence Magazine,* by the board of trade. Nor was the Brown University research librarian able to track down information on Continental in the several books on Rhode Island publishing that they have (correspondence with Stephen Thompson, April 2003). The research librarians at the Rhode Island Historical Society didn't turn up anything on either Continental or Kelley-Hawkins (correspondence with research librarians Robin Flynn and Meredith Sorozan, April 2003). Continental

did publish several other works including *Republication of the Letters of John Wilbur to George Crosfield; together with some Selections from his Correspondence and other Writings; with an Introductory Essay by the Meeting for Sufferings of New England Yearly Meeting of Friends* (1895); *Stenotype: or Shorthand by the Typewriter* by Denis Quinn (1895); *Outlines of Lectures in Elementary Economics, Brown University* by Henry B. Gardner (1896). None of this furthers our understanding of Emma Dunham Kelley-Hawkins much.

18. *Washington Bee*, December 14, 1889.

19. See Foreman and Pitts, "Chronology" and "Introduction," in *Our Nig*, xi, xl. For more on Wilson's hair products, see Foreman, "Recovered Autobiographies and the Marketplace" and the 150th Anniversary Penguin Classics edition of *Our Nig*.

20. See particularly, Sherrard-Johnson, "Why Emma?" 164–65, and Peterson, "Subject to Speculation," 116, 114, as quoted by Sherrard-Johnson. Foreman and Sherrard-Johnson note that some reporters and critics have suggested that Kelley-Hawkins's work will be— and deserves to be—"reforgotten" (McLemee, "In Black and White," par. 2). They respond that "such reviviscent insinuations recall the politics of disavowal and dismissal that are part of the reception history of nineteenth-century women's literary production." Foreman and Sherrard-Johnson, "Racial Recovery, Racial Death," 157.

21. Tate, *Psychoanalysis and Black Novels*, 23. Two Frank Webb novellas, *The Wolf and Two Lambs* and *Marvin Hayle*, were published in *New Era* in 1870. Dunbar's novels include *The Uncalled* (1898), *The Love of Landry* (1900), and *The Fanatics* (1901); Amelia E. Johnson's novels include *Clarence and Corinne; or, God's Way* (1890), *The Hazeley Family* (1894), and *Martina Meriden; or What is my Motive?* (1901). William Stanley Braithwaite also published *The Canadian* in 1901.

22. Holly Jackson, "Mistaken Identity," par. 24. Some of Jackson's claims and comments seem to indicate that she may not have been very familiar with the breadth of nineteenth-century African American literature. On NPR, she mischaracterized *Iola Leroy* as "the only novel by a black woman before the twentieth century" (Chideya, "The Truth about Emma Dunham Kelly-Hawkins"); critics in the field corrected the perception that *Iola Leroy* was the first African American woman's novel (perhaps the basis for such a claim) in the 1980s.

23. Electric lights replaced gas lights in Cottage City in 1894. The production and popularity of canned salmon boomed in the early 1890s (Stoddard, *A Centennial History*, 100). For more on this topic see Sherrard-Johnson, "Radical Tea," especially 229–32.

24. duCille, *Coupling Convention*, 54.

25. Ruffin, Presidential Address, 19.

26. See Elizabeth Davis, *Lifting as They Climb*, 19. On women's development, see Tate, *Psychoanalysis and Black Novels*, 177; McDowell, "Introduction," in Kelley-Hawkins, *Four Girls*, xxxi, xxxvii; and Tarbox, *The Clubwomen's Daughters*, 85.

27. Kelley-Hawkins, *Four Girls at Cottage City* (hereinafter cited in the text as *FG*).

28. Canadian actress Margaret Mather was on a North American tour in 1883–84 and later in the decade as well. She is noticed in the Black press. See *New York Freeman*, January 23, 1886, for example. I thank Carla Peterson for sharing this reference and others from *New York Age* with me.

29. Here I refer to cultural critic George Lipsitz's comment that Chuck Berry's song, "Brown Eyed Handsome Man," "enjoyed great popularity among blacks who knew that he meant brown *skinned* handsome man." Lipsitz, *Time Passages*, 115.

30. Sekula, "The Body and the Archive," 10–11, 12.

31. Also, discussions of mesmerism and mind-reading occur throughout the novel.

32. Sekula, "The Body and the Archive," 11.

33. Hite, "Introduction," in Kelley, *Medga*, xxx. See also Jennifer Harris, "Black Like?" 409–10.

34. Photos of African Americans in Cottage City date from as early as 1875. A few Blacks, such as Phoebe Ballou and Priscilla Freeman, also owned property during the 1880s and likely rented rooms to summer vacationers. The *New York Freeman* includes a long list of visitors to "this favorite sea side resort" in a column headed "Cottage City (Mass) Resort." Also see the advertisements section, "The Terrell Cottage." Renamed *New York Age*, the paper lists a large number of visitors to Cottage City in its coverage of "New Bedford Gaiety." See Cromwell, "The History of Oak Bluffs," 8–13, and Holland, "The African-American Presence on Martha's Vineyard," 11. Also see the Jones and West family photo in Banks, "The History of Martha's Vineyard."

35. Cromwell, "The History of Oak Bluffs," 13; Peterson, "New Negro Modernity," 116. Beginning in 1894, *Woman's Era* advertised serially for these lessons. See, for example, March 1, 1894, 9, and March 24, 1894, 9. "The Martha's Vineyard Institute" also advertised in *Woman's Era*. See May 1, 1894, 13.

36. Cromwell, "The History of Oak Bluffs," 13, suggests that this is the Thayer Cottage at a "date unknown." Peterson, "New Negro Modernity," 116, dates the photograph as late nineteenth century. A large sign announcing "Rooms to Let" is clearly displayed in one of the cottage's front windows.

37. Tanner, "Reading," 13.

38. Tillman, *Beryl Weston's Ambition*, 232. The novella *Beryl Weston's Ambition* was first published in July and October 1893, in the *A.M.E. Church Review*.

39. Ibid. In reading Anglo and Anglo American literature, these heroines follow the precepts that Medora Gould offers in her *Woman's Era* literature column; Gould takes the recent publication of Longfellow's entire poetic *oeuvre* in one work, for example, as the subject of her very first column.

40. Gertrude Mossell, *The Work of the Afro-American Woman*, 100.

41. McHenry, *Forgotten Readers*, 239.

42. "Report of the Frances E. W. Harper League," 104; Higginbotham, *Righteous Discontent*, 9, 10.

43. Cooper, *A Voice from the South*, 9.

44. Gertrude Mossell, *The Work of the Afro-American Woman*, 5.

45. Penn, *Afro-American Press*, 405, 381, 382. An interest in writing, elocution, and dramatic arts characterized many young Black women of this period. For example, as a young woman, Ida B. Wells had "organized and acted in a dramatic club" and, while in Memphis, had been "scouted by New York talent agents." Schechter, *Ida B. Wells-Barnett and American Reform*, 20. In Kelley-Hawkins, *Four Girls*, 99–111, the characters debate whether or not theater—which they clearly enjoy—can be done so with religious sanction. In Kelley's first novel, her characters flirt with elocution and acting even more than they do in *Four Girls*. See, for example, the chapter in *Megda* titled "The Entertainment," 146–65. Community engagement and these activities were not considered dichotomous. See Schechter, *Ida B. Wells-Barnett and American Reform*, 20.

46. Eric Gardner writes, "*The Recorder,* in both its attention to prize-winning work

from the Institute of Colored Youth and in its hesitancy to take 'school girl essays' from beyond Philadelphia, is especially emblematic." Email Exchange, 2006. Confirmed, July 8, 2008.

47. Penn, *Afro-American Press*, 415, 416.

48. Gaines, *Uplifting the Race*, xiv, 261. The report of the Negro Baptists in 1903 to the Eighth Atlanta Conference states that according to the 1900 census, illiteracy in the South reached over 50 percent; they suggest that this may be overdrawn. "It is perfectly safe to say that 40 percent of the colored people are illiterate and 20 percent of those who can read and write are not fluent readers." DuBois, *The Black Church*, 116.

49. In winter 1895–96 Matthews went to several southern states to make a study of the conditions under which Black women lived. Attending the Atlanta Congress, she vigorously opposed its tendencies toward conservatism, says Wilson Jeremiah Moses. In Atlanta, she joined T. Thomas Fortune to edit the *Southern Age*, a paper he had renamed in reference to the *New York Age*. She concretized her concern for Southern women, issues of labor, and sexual vulnerability when she returned to New York and founded the White Rose Mission. On Fortune and Matthews, see Thornbrough, *T. Thomas Fortune*, 153 and Moses, "Domestic Feminism," 966.

50. Robin D. G. Kelley, "Foreword," in Willis, *Reflections in Black*, ix.

51. Wexler, "Techniques of the Imaginary Nation," 365.

52. William J. Simmons, *Men of Mark*, 9, writes that "the illustrations are many, and have been presented so that the reader may see the characters face to face." He has gone to great lengths to secure these cuts and sketches, as his acknowledgments make clear.

53. Gates, "Trope of the New Negro," 130–31.

54. Wexler, "Techniques of the Imaginary Nation," 367.

55. See Goldsby, *A Spectacular Secret*, chap. 5, on the distinction between photographic and hand-drawn illustrations of lynching in the Black press.

56. Peterson, "New Negro Modernity," 111.

57. McHenry, *Forgotten Readers*, 362 n. 6.

58. Quoted in Shawn Michelle Smith, *American Archives*, 93.

59. Gates, "Trope of the New Negro," 133.

60. E. Davis, *Lifting As They Climb*, 19.

61. Hallie Q. Brown, *Homespun Heroines*, 208.

62. Ibid., 215.

63. Ibid., 208, 209.

64. *New York Evening Post*, n.d., from White Rose Mission Folder, Special Collections, Schomburg Library.

65. According to A. Monroe Majors, *Noted Negro Women*, 212, "Victoria Earle" reported for "*The New York Times, Herald, Mail* and *Express, Sunday Mercury*, the *Earth*, and the *Photographic World*." She was New York's "correspondent to the *National Leader, Detroit Plaindealer*, and the *Southern Christian Recorder*." She "contributed to the *A.M.E. Church Review*" and *Woman's Era*, "the *Boston Advocate*, Washington *Bee*, Richmond *Planet*, *Catholic Tribune*, Cleveland *Gazette*, New York *Globe*, New York *Age*, and the New York *Enterprise*." She published stories in "*Waverly Magazine*, the New York *Weekly*, the *Family Story Paper*, and *Ringwood Journal of Fashion*."

66. McHenry, *Forgotten Readers*, 192.

67. *Woman's Era,* August 1895, 15; February 1896, 1.

68. Lemke, "Introduction," in Elizabeth Lindsay Davis, *Lifting as They Climb,* xvii.

69. Bruce published as "Bruce Grit" in the *New York Times, Washington Evening Star,* and other mainstream papers, in his columns in the *New York Age* and the *Cleveland Gazette,* and in his contributions to over one hundred Black newspapers. He founded several periodicals, was part of the Niagara Movement and was a founder in 1911, with Arthur Schomburg, of the Negro Society for Historical Research. His mystery novel *The Black Sleuth* was originally serialized. For more on Bruce, see Gruesser, "Introduction," in John Bruce, *The Black Sleuth.* Also see Penelope Bullock, *The Afro-American Periodical Press,* 78.

70. Bruce also wrote that Matthews "was not the type of Negro woman to deify any race at the expense of her own especially when she knew that her own race had more to offer in proof of its primacy of civilization and culture than any of the holy races now claiming to be *superior.*" He is discussing textbooks that Matthews ostensibly authored. No record shows that any were published; if they were they don't seem to be extant. John Bruce Collection, "Noted Race Women I Have Known and Met." Schomburg Library, SC Microfilm, R905, Reel #2, 539/540, 8–11 and unnumbered transcript.

71. As Bruce points out, Emerson is a popular figure in Black women's writing: for example, Anna Julia Cooper closes her 1886 speech "Womanhood: A Vital Element in the Regeneration and Progress of a Race" (which will form a part of a *Voice from the South* in 1892) with an extended citation of Emerson's call for the "defense of our right." (Cooper, "Womanhood," 74.) At first I thought that Bruce must have been referring to the important, highly political Woman's Loyal Union (WLU), which Matthews cofounded a decade later in 1892, because I had seen no references to the Enquiry Club or its chapters. Yet, in the second copy of the speech, when Bruce notes that he saw Matthews on a trip to visit his cousins, he crosses out "in the early 80s" and writes in 1882 over that phrase. (In the first version of the speech, he notes that the Enquiry Club also had multiple chapters "scattered in various parts of the country." John Bruce, "Noted Race Women," 11.) The WLU was a "protest and women's rights society." It ran national campaigns to diffuse "accurate and extensive information relative to the civil and social status of the Afro-American, that they may be directed to an intelligent assertion of their rights, and unite in the employment of all lawful means to secure and retain the undisputed exercise of them" (as reported in the inaugural and subsequent issues of *Woman's Era*). Osofsky, *Harlem,* 56. Also see *Woman's Era* 1, no. 1 (March 1894); repeated in *Woman's Era* 2, no. 5 (August 1895), 5.

72. White Rose Mission Folder, Special Collection, Schomburg Library.

73. Higginbotham, *Righteous Discontent,* 191.

74. Ibid.

75. Hallie Q. Brown, *Homespun Heroines,* 211–12.

76. Thornbrough, *T. Thomas Fortune,* 126.

77. Pamphlet, White Rose Mission Folder, Special Collections, Schomburg Library.

78. The *New York Evening Post,* n.d. The material in the White Rose Mission folder also names the wide array of Anglo American and African American supporters, including Mrs. Collis P. Huntington, Mrs. Wm. Choate, Mrs. Henry Villard, and Rev. Adam Clayton Powell. W. E. B. DuBois and James Weldon Johnson are members. The *Evening Post* account reports that many well-to-do African Americans refused their support because

of dancing and "whist clubs, which are regarded by Mrs. Matthews as one of the most successful ventures ever tried there." "Any respectable colored girl" may become a member for $1 a year. If "any member desires to entertain friends, she may provide refreshments etc. and may arrange to have the use of the parlors for a card party or other form of entertainment. Sometimes dances are given." See Sherrard-Johnson's essay, "Radical Tea," for more on consumption, enjoyment, and the connections between leisure and service. Also see Steve Kramer's recently published article, "Uplifting Our 'Downtrodden Sisterhood.'"

79. To this date, despite years of research, I have been unable to recover any "evidence" that establishes that Kelley-Hawkins knew of the writings of "Victoria Earle" or that they circulated in overlapping circles. The WLU had chapters in New Bedford where Kelley lived for several years as a child. The present lack of historical overlap does not foreclose the cross-pollination clearly evident in the text, as nice as it would be to be able to establish the links more directly.

80. Brooks, *Bodies in Dissent*, 135, 136.

81. Here, I do mean to be in conversation with Barthes, when, in *Camera Lucida*, 12, 13, he states that the scale of photography creates a "disturbance (to civilization)" that "is ultimately one of ownership." "To whom," he goes on, "does the photograph belong?" On another note, I do not mean to overlook the problematics of light-skinned privilege and its relation to white beauty and supremacy in an overromanticized commentary on Blacks who have been socially and familially disowned by whites and claimed by African Americans.

Chapter 5

1. See Mrs. N. F. Mossell, "Introduction" in *The Work of the Afro-American Woman*, 4. The Schomburg uses the second 1908 edition for its reprint.

2. In the Schomburg reprint edition taken from the 1894 original, the novel is titled *The Hazeley Family*. In the advertisement it is followed by "*or, Hard but Wholesome Lessons.*"

3. The first edition includes these advertisements. Mossell, *The Work of the Afro-American Woman* (1894, 1st ed.), 179. The advertisements are not paginated.

4. The introduction is signed "AEJ" which, if we cross-check it with A. Briscoe Koger's treatment of Harvey Johnson, confirms that "the introduction is written by Mrs. Johnson." Koger, *Dr. Harvey Johnson*, 21. As timely and well-written as it still is, Harvey Johnson's *The Nations* itself is rarely consulted; this is the first time in recent scholarship that the introduction is attributed to Amelia Johnson. Her other writing has not been considered in the context of the political and racial ideology she outlines there. Amelia Johnson, "Introduction," in Harvey Johnson, *Nations from a New Point of View*, 18.

5. Barkley Brown, "To Catch the Vision of Freedom," 99 n. 62.

6. Higginbotham, *Righteous Discontent*, 49, points out that Blacks worked together across gender and also illuminates the ways in which this comradeship was an imagined community.

7. See Feimster, "Introduction," in "'Ladies and Lynching,'" where she coins the term "rape/lynch" discourse or narrative to better conceptualize the gendered politics and practices of what is conventionally called, simply, lynching.

8. See Introduction and chapter 2 in this text for a fuller explication of the term "simultextuality." This study illustrates how challenging, sometimes contradictory, multivalent meanings are "simultextually" available at the primary level of narrative interpretation rather than being subtextually buried beneath a reformist message of African American empowerment. Simultextual discussions disrupt narrative transparency, the ideal of a self-effacing narrative simplicity that is one key assumption about domestic fiction.

9. Amelia Johnson, "Introduction," in Harvey Johnson, *Nations from a New Point of View*, 17.

10. See Penn, *Afro-American Press*, 415–16, 418, 422–24, and Scruggs, *Women of Distinction*, 117. The careful Johnson entry included in Scruggs's book notes that "a large number of women wrote for this paper," which is called *Ivy*. It seems that the journal may have changed names, but not mission, as Scruggs refers to "a monthly of eight pages" to "guide and elevate *our own young people*" (emphasis in original). White Baptist journals reprinted its contents. Penn notes that the *National Baptist*, "one of the largest circulated white denominational journals," reproduced poems from *Joy* and also reprinted one of Johnson's stories. The *Baltimore Baptist*, another white denominational paper, reviewed *Joy*. Penn suggests that Mary Britton, of Lexington, Kentucky, who published under "Meb" and "Aunt Peggy," published in *Ivy* (which he places in Baltimore with a young readership but doesn't attribute to Johnson). Penn also refers to the folder of newspaper clippings Johnson had "testifying" to the appreciation the journal elicited. See Majors, *Noted Negro Women*, 216 and Penn, *Afro-American Press*, 415–16, 424.

11. It was not until 1900 when William Dean Howells, the dean of American letters, reviewed Chesnutt's *The Conjure Woman* and *The Wife of His Youth and other Stories of the Color Line* (1899) that Chesnutt's racial identity was revealed to the general readership.

12. See minutes, "Treasurer's Report," and "Personal Contributions," in *History of the Club Movement*, 59; and, for the following year, "Directory," 119. It reads "Maryland, Baltimore, Mrs. A. E. Johnson, delegate; tax, $1."

13. Rev. Walter Brooks joined Frederick Douglass as a featured speaker at the Brotherhood's first national meeting. More than thirty-five years later, following Harvey Johnson's arrangements for his own funeral, Rev. Brooks, still pastor of Washington D.C.'s Nineteenth Street Baptist Church, conducted the short service. See the *Baltimore Sun*'s front page byline on Johnson's death. Also see Koger, *Dr. Harvey Johnson*, 24, who describes Brooks as a "long and tried friend." See *New York Freeman*, October 31, 1885, 4.

14. Minutes from the 1895 and 1896 conventions, *History of the Club Movement*, 35–37.

15. Tillman, "Afro-American Women and Their Work," 495.

16. Penn, *Afro-American Press*, 425–26.

17. Amelia Johnson, "Afro American Literature."

18. Scruggs, *Women of Distinction*, 119.

19. Higginbotham, *Righteous Discontent*, 66.

20. Though the term "New Negro" is often associated with Alain Locke's Harlem Renaissance anthology of that name, it appeared as early as 1895. See Willis, "Sociologist's Eye," 51–53. See also Gates, "Trope of the New Negro," 129.

21. DuBois, "General Summary of the Baptists in the United States," in DuBois, *The Black Church*, 115.

22. Penn, *Afro-American Press*, 372.

23. The report of the Negro Baptists in 1903 to the Eighth Atlanta Conference notes that according to the 1900 census, illiteracy in the South reached over 50 percent. They suggest that this figure may be overdrawn. "It is perfectly safe to say that 40 per cent of the colored people are illiterate and 20 per cent of those who can read and write are not fluent readers. *Sixty per cent of those who can read are youths—children.*" DuBois, "General Summary of the Baptists in the United States," in DuBois, *The Black Church*, 116.

24. Higginbotham calls the church a "multiple site" of public space open to secular and religious groups. One example of this youth emphasis was a full report featuring "the testimony of children themselves" on their feelings about the church as reported in DuBois, *The Black Church*. See Higginbotham, *Righteous Discontent*, 7, 185–90, 2, 10.

25. Though H. Highland Garnet is sometimes reported to have attended the conference, only Douglass, who spoke on "Self-Made Men" (an address in which he featured Garnet) was advertised and reported as the principal speaker. Garnet died in Liberia in 1882, three years before the Brotherhood's inaugural conference. See Suggs, "Romanticism, Law, and the Suppression of African-American Citizenship," 89, reproducing the error in Koger, *Dr. Harvey Johnson*, 12–13. See *New York Freeman*, October 31, 1885, 4, for full coverage of the conference. See *Baltimore Sun*, October 19, 1885, morning edition, 2, for Douglass's announcement.

26. Membership would peak in 1914 at 3,028. Amelia Johnson, "Introduction," in Harvey Johnson, *Nations from a New Point of View*, 21; Koger, *Dr. Harvey Johnson*, 3.

27. Koger, *Dr. Harvey Johnson*, 5. Growing in strength and number and economic self-sufficiency, believing that a self-supporting church was a healthy church, Johnson was poised to challenge the white Baptist establishment. He demanded full church status, recognitions of Black preachers as equals, "eligible to hold office and chairmanship of committees." When this was refused, Johnson withdrew from the larger association. His written challenge to the Baptist conventions and his insistence that either Blacks would have full recognition and equality or they would form their own denomination was reprinted in full in dailies, says Koger. Johnson also organized the Colored Baptist Convention of Maryland in 1898.

Koger was a Howard-trained lawyer and, the Union Baptist Archives chairwoman tells me, a member of Union. Interestingly, Joseph E. Briscoe was the president of the Colored Advisory Council that worked on the same antidiscrimination issues: bastardy laws, teacher representation, appropriations for colored schools, and so forth. See *Baltimore Sun*, January 30, 1886, 4. Two other Briscoes, Arthur E. and John B. (born 1891) became lawyers in the state. See Koger, *Negro Lawyer*, Appendix, "rooster of lawyers," "now deceased." Census records and the Social Security death index do not confirm a relation (on A. Briscoe Koger's mother's side, through her maiden name) between the Briscoe lawyers and activists and the lawyer who would memorialize them, A. Briscoe Koger. Ibid., 22.

28. Higginbotham, *Righteous Discontent*, 147, notes that "black feminist theology won outstanding male converts. It gained the respect of such ardent race leaders as William Simmons, Charles Parrish, Walter H. Brooks and Harvey Johnson." And the Johnsons' son, Harvey Jr., when interviewed in the 1950s, reported "with pride" that "my mother was my father's best friend, and his chief comfort. . . ." Harvey Johnson Jr.'s attention had to be "steered" away from his mother and to Koger's subject, Harvey Sr. Koger, *Dr. Harvey Johnson*, 22.

29. *History of the Club Movement*, 37.

30. *The Hamite* and *Clarence and Corrine* were reviewed in the *Home Protector* and *Sower and Reaper,* both in Baltimore, and in Louisville, Kentucky's *American Baptist.* See Penn, *Afro-American Press,* 424–25; and Amelia Johnson, "Introduction," in Harvey Johnson, *Nations from a New Point of View,* 29–30.

31. See Penn, *Afro-American Press,* 424–25, and Amelia Johnson, "Introduction," in Harvey Johnson, *Nations from a New Point of View,* 28–34. Also included are personal letters of response to Harvey Johnson's published pamphlets such as those by Martin Delany, John E. Bruce (Bruce Grit), and I. Garland Penn.

32. (Mrs.) A. E. Johnson, "Afro-American Literature," *New York Age,* January 30, 1892, 1. A. E. Johnson, "The History of a Story," *Richmond Planet,* February 22 and 29, 1896, 3.

33. Amelia Johnson, "Some Parallels in History."

34. In 1905 Harvey Johnson and the Brotherhood contingent would make up five of the twenty-nine people from fourteen states who met near Buffalo, New York. Bettye Collier-Thomas notes that DuBois was in "close contact with members of the Brotherhood . . . as he frequently traveled there to deliver speeches" from 1895 to 1910. The Brotherhood, she goes on, "willingly shared twenty years of experience, strategy development and know-how with the founders at Niagara." See Collier-Thomas, "Harvey Johnson," 224.

35. According to Alexander, *Our Day In Court,* 8, the office address was 2 East Saratoga St. near Calvert. The Johnsons' house was at 1923 Druid Hill Ave. Koger, *Dr. Harvey Johnson,* 22. See *Baltimore City Directory, 1906,* 948.

36. Harvey Johnson, "The Question of Race," 7. This paper was read before the Monumental Literary and Scientific Association of Baltimore, Maryland, and printed at their request, according to the Daniel A. P. Murray Pamphlet Collection at the American Memory site provided by the Library of Congress.

37. Among the members listed are Harry S. Cummings, the first Black man elected to the city council in 1890; W. Ashbie Hawkins, a Howard law school graduate, civil rights lawyer, and editor of the short-lived *Educational Era;* and Warner T. McGuinn. See Chapelle, *Baltimore,* 167.

38. Visit by author to 1923 Druid Hill Ave. and Union Baptist Church, November 2003. The distance from the stairs to Druid Hill Ave. is not evident from looking at the photograph.

39. DuBois Circle Minutes, November 3, 1908, 10. Also see February 1, 1910.

40. See DuBois Circle Minutes, December 3, 1907, 27; March 26, 1907, 9. DuBois Circle papers viewed at the home of the then-elected executive board member and historian, Mrs. Patelle Harris, Baltimore, August 2004.

41. Several sources suggest that five Brotherhood of Liberty members attended the national Niagara Movement conferences and that Harvey Johnson was among them; I did not find him in any photographs of the meetings, however. The records at Harpers Ferry National Historical Park, site of the 1906 Niagara meeting, show that James Robert Lincoln Diggs and Rev. Garnett Russell Waller attended the 1905 meeting in Fort Erie, Ontario. Rev. G. R. Waller and a larger group traveled to Harpers Ferry for the national gathering the next year. The Baltimore delegation also included Rev. George F. Bragg, Dr. Howard E. Young, Prof. Carrington Davis, Prof. Mason Albert Hawkins, William Ashbie Hawkins, and Prof. C. L. Davis. E-mail from Kim Biggs, Harpers Ferry National Historical Park, to Gabrielle Foreman, September 22, 2005.

42. McHenry, *Forgotten Readers*, 3.

43. I have not yet been able to locate any copies of this paper.

44. Lucy Thurman, who was one of the leading Black temperance activists of the era and was then the head of the Federation of Club Women, along with Frances Harper visited on March 17, 1908; they were invited to join the national association. DuBois Circle Minutes, March 17, 1908, 47.

45. McHenry, *Forgotten Readers*, 10.

46. In the April 7, 1908 meeting, the president stated that she had received a letter from "Mrs. Harvey Johnson stating her inconvenience on account of poor health to attend the meetings of the circle and wishing for that reason to resign. It was agreed by all present that we would like to retain Mrs. Johnson as a member as she has proven herself quite a valuable addition to our circle—one always interested in the work carried on by the Organization. The secretary was asked to write a letter to Mrs. Johnson voicing the sentiments of the Association." DuBois Circle Minutes, 51. On April 21, 1908, the secretary stated that instead of writing to Mrs. Harvey Johnson, as requested, she had seen the latter personally and explained the wishes of the ladies to retain her as a member and that Mrs. Johnson had stated that "as soon as health would permit she would be with us again." By June 2, she is again an active dues-paying member. She hosts another meeting on April 6, 1909, and resigns that fall. On November 16, "the resignation of Mrs. Harvey Johnson was accepted and the corresponding secretary was directed to write a letter to that effect to Mrs. Johnson. Much regret was expressed by all the members upon hearing the resignation of Mrs. Johnson as she had always been a faithful worker and inspiring helper." Johnson evidently remained an "inspiring helper." Ibid., 53.

47. Programs found in the DuBois Circle Papers, Baltimore. The second Mrs. G. R. Waller, Lelia Waller, was as active in activist Black Baltimore as was the first Mrs. G. R. Waller (who was one of the few female members of the Brotherhood). Lelia Waller, who like her husband was from Virginia, was thirty-one years old in 1910. She had been married to Rev. Waller (age fifty-two) for nine years; together they had five natural children, and three older children by his first marriage also lived in their household. 1910 U.S. Census, Baltimore Ward 12, Baltimore (Independent City), Maryland; Roll: T624_556, 4A; Enumeration District: 185; Image: 1299.

48. Barkley Brown, "To Catch the Vision of Freedom," 67–68.

49. Kerr-Ritchie, *Freedpeople*, 75.

50. "'A Long, Full, Big Life': Johnson's Political Activism," Maryland State Archives, available at http://www.msa.md.gov/ (accessed December 11, 2008).

51. Koger, *Dr. Harvey Johnson*, 11. Others suggest that the Brotherhood was functioning informally by this point, and that Johnson and his associates had agreed to absorb the cost of the ongoing litigation necessary to desegregate the Maryland bar. William Alexander suggests that court costs ran as high as $250 even before recruiting Waring. Whatever the case, the Johnson household, and probably others, made significant contributions and learned that no individual, or even church, could finance sustained legal challenges. In the future, they collectively organized and funded such efforts. Alexander, *Our Day In Court*, 6. See also Brackett, *Notes on the Progress*, 75.

52. "For thirty of the fifty years he served Union, his salary averaged about a hundred dollars per month." Koger, *Dr. Harvey Johnson*, 22, 23. In 1890, Black men in the sought-

after occupation of a private coachman, if supplemented with butlering, could make about $400 annually in Philadelphia. Cooks made more, about $750 a year. About 90 percent of Black women worked as domestic servants making about $150 a year, approximately the amount that the Johnsons expended on litigation. See Williams, *The Christian Recorder,* 7–8.

53. Holt, "Empire over the Mind," 299, as quoted in Barkley Brown, "To Catch the Vision of Freedom," 68.

54. This is Kerr-Ritchie's language, *Freedpeople,* 75. Baltimore was the city with the largest number of freed and free Blacks after the war. Its history of Black participation in unions, societies, newspapers, and civic organizations was the backdrop for the Brotherhood's formation and largely successful challenges to Jim Crow incursions that succeeded in so many other places in the South. It is in this context that I make claims that the cross-gendered collaborations historians note in the period of 1865 to 1880, so well documented in Richmond by Barkley Brown, extend well into that decade in Baltimore. Harvey Johnson makes the geographic as well as the activist link. He spent time regularly at his home and farm eight miles outside of Richmond during the 1880s and 1890s. See Simmons, *Men of Mark,* 510, and Koger, *Dr. Harvey Johnson,* 23.

55. Baltimore's Republican-led papers were cool on the idea of Black attorneys, while the Democratic organ, the *Sun,* supported the Brotherhood's efforts. See Collier-Thomas, "Harvey Johnson," 217; Delaney, *From the Darkness Cometh the Light,* 35.

56. Koger, *Dr. Harvey Johnson,* 12. The meeting was held on June 22, 1885, at 362 West Lexington Street. The Johnsons lived both at 775 West Lexington Street and 362 Lexington Street, according to Koger; though he sites the 775 Lexington Street address as the place where the first meeting took place, he suggests that they don't move there until 1890. Yet the Baltimore City Directory for 1886 lists "Johnson, Harvey Rev, pastor Union Baptist Ch, h, 362 Lexington." Others confirm the location but date the meeting as June 2, 1885. See *Baltimore City Directory for 1886,* 777. See Alexander, *Our Day In Court,* 7.

57. Legal cases followed on the heels of a petition drive that didn't effect immediate change. On March 19, 1885, after months of planning and litigation, the Supreme Bench of Baltimore City ruled that the color line would not ban Blacks from the bar. Nonetheless, they denied entrance to Charles Wilson, who had applied for admission, declaring that he was not qualified. Johnson then went to Washington, D.C., to recruit Waring, who was admitted on October 10, 1885. The decision also led to the University of Maryland's law school admitting its first Black students soon after. See Koger, *Negro Lawyer,* 6–7; Collier-Thomas, "Harvey Johnson," 217; and Bogen, "Transformation of the Fourteenth Amendment," 939–1037.

58. *A.M.E. Church Review* 4 (1887): 496–505.

59. Harriet Jacobs, *Incidents,* (Yellin edition), 177.

60. By no means do I mean to imply that the Brotherhood exclusively focused on women's issues. In daily papers it advertised a $500 reward for the arrest and conviction of the lynch mob murderers of a Mr. Biggs of Frederick, Maryland. And Harvey Johnson and the Brotherhood's counsel were very active in the Navassa case, defending men who launched an uprising when they were virtually imprisoned on an island under horrific slavery-like labor conditions. Johnson personally appealed to the Maryland attorney general, governor, and U.S. President Benjamin Harrison. See Alexander, *Our Day In Court,*

20–21, 22–24. See Brackett, *Notes on the Progress,* 81. On the Navassa case, see *New York Age,* April 19 and 26, 1890. On defense against lynching, see *New York Age,* December 13, 1890. On a linked suit against steamers, see *New York Age,* May 10, 1890. The libellant, Rev. Robert A. McGinn, was a clergyman and member of the Brotherhood.

61. See Alexander, *Our Day In Court,* 6; Sumler-Edmond, "Quest for Justice," 109; and Collier-Thomas, "Harvey Johnson," 218. The women were each awarded $100 in damages. It was a limited but important success. In what later would be codified into a national "separate but equal" policy, the decision affirmed both segregation and that businesses could not offer second-class services for customers who purchased first-class tickets. It also bolstered Johnson's faith in legal means of redress and energized his efforts to form the Brotherhood and challenge Black attorneys' ability to argue before the Maryland bar.

62. *New York Freeman,* October 31, 1885, 4.

63. Waring, "Colored Man before the Law," 504.

64. Barkley Brown, "To Catch the Vision of Freedom," 74.

65. They were Irene Davis, Sadie T. Galamison, Mary O. Dickerson, and the first Mrs. G. R. Waller. Born in Virginia, Sadie (Madden) Galamison was twenty-three years old and married for two years to Joseph A. Galamison when she appears as a Brotherhood member; 1900 Federal Census, Baltimore Ward 8, Baltimore City (Independent City), Maryland; Roll: T623 611; 17A; Enumeration District: 99. The absence of a 1890 census makes the other women more difficult to locate.

66. She was married to Rev. Garnett R. Waller of Trinity Baptist Church (one of the eleven ministers ordained out of Johnson's congregation) and was mother of three children, including Mary E. Waller and Garnet R. Waller Jr. Johnson nominates G. R. Waller as the first president of the Baltimore NAACP, the second branch established in the nation. See *Afro-American,* February 25, 1958.

67. These do not count those who use initials but are identifiable as male by the title Reverend or Esquire. Alexander, *Our Day In Court,* 4.

68. Ibid., 43–44. The women include Matilda Crist, Elizabeth Reeves, Martha E. Stewart, Patsey Hubert, Mary Holmes, and Mary M. Johnson. Again there are eight names that use gender-neutral initials that I am not able to identify. Since "A. E. Johnson" appeared in print regularly, though not in these lists, it's reasonable to assume that some of those using their initials could also be women. H. S. Cummings, however, is a man; he was one of the two students to integrate the University of Maryland's law school and would become an official member of the Brotherhood. He is included in the Druid Hill Avenue photograph.

69. Barkley Brown, "To Catch the Vision of Freedom," 74.

70. See *Maryland Code,* 62.

71. *Hawbecker v. Hawbecker,* 2.

72. Brackett, *Notes on the Progress,* 67.

73. Alexander, *Our Day In Court,* 11.

74. Sumler-Edmond, "Quest for Justice," 117.

75. One commentator wrote, "It is important to note that the colored leaders desired a repeal of this law, as of all such laws, not on the grounds of social equality but chiefly because they thought it a race discrimination." Brackett, *Notes on the Progress,* 67.

76. Gertrude Bustill (Mossell), author of *The Work of the Afro-American Woman,* married Dr. Nathan Francis Mossell, who was the first graduate of the University of

Pennsylvania's medical school. Together they spearheaded a campaign to raise money to found and finance the Frederick Douglass (training) Hospital. Dr. Mossell also led a campaign against Thomas Dixon's bestseller *The Clansman*. He was brother to Aaron Mossell, University of Pennsylvania's first Black law school graduate. He left his family, but his daughter Sadie became the first Black woman graduate of Penn's law school and the first Black woman to get a PhD in the United States. Aaron and Nathan's younger brother Charles is the A.M.E. preacher "Rev. C. W. Mossell," a graduate of Lincoln Theological Seminary who appears on the list of Brotherhood "life members." He is the only one of the siblings to return to Baltimore where his parents had been in business before moving to Ontario so as not to have children in the United States during slavery. All three boys attended Lincoln University. For the Brotherhood membership list, see Alexander, *Our Day In Court*, 4.

77. Aaron Mossell, "Unconstitutionality of the Law," 77.

78. Brackett, *Notes on the Progress*, 79. A petition from Frederick County included 76 signatures; one from Alleghany included more than 240.

79. Alexander, "Brotherhood of Liberty," 15–16.

80. Brackett, *Notes on the Progress*, 79.

81. Collier-Thomas reports that John Prentiss Poe is Edgar Allen Poe's father; J. P. Poe did, in fact, have a son named Edgar Allen, but he was not the writer, who was J. P. Poe's cousin. See Collier-Thomas, "Harvey Johnson," 219; see also Bogen, "Transformation of the Fourteenth Amendment," 1043, nn. 363, 364. The 1902 amendment that sought to disenfranchise African Americans, the Poe amendment, carried John Prentiss's name. See Mjagkij, *Organizing Black America*, 89.

82. The Brotherhood's early leadership was made up of Baptists. A.M.E. women also seemed to be prominent in this campaign. See Brackett, *Notes on the Progress*, 79.

83. *Independent* 56 (March 17, 1904): 588. As quoted in Guy-Sheftall, *Daughters of Sorrow*, 59.

84. "More Slavery at the South," *Independent* 72 (January 25, 1912): 176–77. As quoted in Guy-Sheftall, *Daughters of Sorrow*, 58.

85. Higginbotham, *Righteous Discontent*, 41, 42. She points out that in 1890 there were a total of 15,100 Black teachers, with women outnumbering men by fewer than 600. The shift toward women teachers was a national, cross-racial trend; in New England, for example, by 1900, 85 percent of teachers were women.

86. Higginbotham, *Righteous Discontent*, 54–55.

87. Collier-Thomas, "Harvey Johnson," 220.

88. Collier-Thomas, "Public Education and Black Protest," 386.

89. The men and women of Baltimore continued to advocate for better education. Minutes of the January 18, 1910, DuBois Circle note that "the men's branch" of the local Niagara Movement comes to their meetings to discuss partnerships and larger meetings. Ashbie Hawkins decries the "deplorable conditions of the public schools." He urges a member to come speak and organize. The DuBois Circle responds to the appeal on February 1, 1910. They propose taking the case before the "Progressive League or some other such organization, so that the matter could be taken before the Legislature." Amelia Johnson had resigned due to ill health on November 16, 1909, just two months before these meetings.

90. See Collier-Thomas, "Public Education and Black Protest." Also see "Our Public Schools," *Afro-American*, October 19, 1895.

91. Collier-Thomas, "Harvey Johnson," 221–22.

92. Higginbotham, *Righteous Discontent*, 41.

93. Alexander, *Our Day In Court*, 16, 17. The Ford theater wasn't generally this hospitable to Blacks. See "Colorphobia in Baltimore," *New York Age*, November 1, 1890.

94. Calloway and Rollins, *Of Minnie the Moocher*, 11, 12, and 19. Alexander, *Our Day In Court*, front matter, unpaginated, and also "President Reed's Statement of the Navassa Case," 41–42. Calloway notes that his family had status in the Negro community "but that doesn't mean we had money. Negro professionals were paid a hell of a lot less than white professionals with the same jobs." The Calloways lived at 1017 Druid Hill Avenue not far from the Johnsons' home at 1923 Druid Hill Avenue.

95. "Countdown Begins on Douglass High's 100th Anniversary," *Afro-American*, September 10, 1983. Despite its award-winning debate team, music program, and basketball team, in 2007, two-thirds of the school's teachers were noncertified. According to the film, "Hard Times at Douglass High: A No Child Left Behind Report Card," about half of ninth graders will drop out in their first year. The school has been told to raise assessment test scores or face a state takeover.

96. Chapelle, *Baltimore*, 194. Cab Calloway and Thurgood Marshall both attended Frederick Douglass High in 1925, the year in which the Black high school moved into an adequate building on Calhoun and Baker streets. Calloway and Rollins, *Of Minnie the Moocher*, 34.

97. Christian, "Introduction," in Amelia E. Johnson, *The Hazeley Family*, xxviii.

98. Amelia Johnson's *Martina Meriden* has not been republished.

99. Penn, *Afro-American Press*, 424–26.

100. Harper, *Iola Leroy*, 3.

101. duCille, *Coupling Convention*, 63.

102. Suggs, "Romanticism, Law, and the Suppression of African-American Citizenship," 67; Brotherhood of Liberty, *Justice and Jurisprudence*, i.

103. Some historians suggest that the body of *Justice and Jurisprudence* was written by an anonymous white lawyer who perhaps was John Henry Keene. The *New York Age*'s report in 1890 that "Harvey Johnson, D.D. is preparing a manual upon Parliamentary Law" might support others' contention that he had a major hand in its authorship. "Suits Begun in Baltimore," *New York Age*, December 27, 1890, 1. This announcement comes out a full year after *Justice and Jurisprudence* was published in Baltimore, reflecting the general confusion about the book's authorship. The book's style is radically different than Johnson's own. Still, its preface is written in the second person, and it includes an "original letter of Brotherhood to counsel" stating that "we wish your opinion, whether the Fourteenth Amendment is sovereign, of whether citizen-kinds in America have prerogatives superior to those dictates of reason and justice." Brotherhood of Liberty, *Justice and Jurisprudence*, 42. The puzzle as to why the Brotherhood would retain a white author to outline "the portentous struggle of *your* minority with this majority" still has missing pieces; ibid., "Answer of the Counsel to the Brotherhood," emphasis mine. Since 1885, when they successfully integrated the Maryland bar, they had employed Black counsel. Likewise, in his pastorate, and in his relation to the national Baptist leadership, Johnson counseled and asserted independent action in the face of white paternalism and prejudice. Then again, between at least 1881 and 1891, that is, until two years after *Justice and*

Jurisprudence was published with J.B. Lippincott and Co., Johnson was using the printing office of J. F. Weishampel for his pamphlets. By the time he pens "A plea for our work as colored Baptists, apart from the whites" in 1897, he is using the Afro American Company, Printers. See the Daniel A. P. Murray Pamphlet Collection, Library of Congress.

104. I have seen no secondary sources noting that the Baltimore Brotherhood had a branch and no previous mention of *The Power-Holding Class versus the Public*. Yet the *Washington Bee* (October 17, 1885, 3) reports, "The first branch of the United Brotherhood of Liberty was organized by the Rev. Harvey Johnson of Baltimore in the Shiloh Baptist Church, Newport, R.I. Rev. H. N. Jeter, pastor." "Rev. J. N. Jeter [*sic*]" sent one of the letters of regret that was read at the inaugural conference in Baltimore. *New York Freeman*, October 31, 1885, 4. He and Harvey Johnson spent three overlapping years at Wayland Seminary together, from 1869 to 1872. See Simmons, *Men of Mark*, 399, 509. But his own memoir, *Pastor Henry N. Jeter's Twenty-five Years Experience with the Shiloh Baptist Church and Her History. Corner School and Mary Streets, Newport, R. I.* (1901), makes no reference to Rev. Johnson, or the Brotherhood. Both men retained very close relations to Rev. Walter Brooks of the Nineteenth Street Baptist Church.

105. Christian, "Introduction," in Amelia E. Johnson, *The Hazeley Family*, xxvii.

106. The Johnsons' library was well known enough to elicit comments in the press. The national edition of the *Afro-American* announcing Harvey Johnson's burial mentions his "fine library" that included "one of the most valuable set of clippings in Maryland dealing with the race topic" as well as his books on "theology, ethnology, history" and current events. Koger notes that the library was "one of the best within the city" (*Harvey Johnson*, 23). Though the library is generally referred to as belonging to Harvey Johnson, Amelia was a recognized editor and writer whose commitments and work no doubt made her a full partner in the reading interests of the house. Contrast this to the Home Missionary Society's report, circa 1895, affirmed and quoted in the 1903 Negro Baptist Report to the Eighth Atlanta Conference. It states "There are sixty per cent of the ministers whose libraries do not average a dozen volumes." Still, following Eric Gardner's research on the extant nineteenth-century editions of *Our Nig*, it is unlikely that one found its way to the Johnsons' library. DuBois, "Present Condition of Churches—The Baptists," 122. See also Gardner, "Harriet Wilson's *Our Nig*"; *Afro-American*, January 19, 1923, 1.

107. Wilson, *Our Nig*, 8.

108. Amelia E. Johnson, *Clarence and Corrine*, 5 (hereinafter cited in the text as *CC*).

109. Spillers, "Introduction," in Amelia E. Johnson, *Clarence and Corrine*, xxxi.

110. Cooper, *Voice from the South*, 29.

111. Higginbotham, *Righteous Discontent*, 42. She cites Jacqueline Jones, in *Labor of Love, Labor of Sorrow*, 144, who notes that Black women's teaching salaries averaged 45 percent of those of whites. Black women teachers made $25 to $30 a month—less than white men, white women, or Black men in the profession. By 1910, Black female teachers would outnumber men 3:1. There were exceptions to this. Memphis, where Wells had taught, paid teachers the same amount regardless of race, and, after 1878, gender. And they paid well. Wells averaged $60 per month in 1886. See McMurray, *To Keep the Waters Troubled*, 78. In contrast, Blacks in Baltimore at that time were fighting the ban on Black teachers.

112. DuBois, "Present Condition of Churches—The Baptists," 122. The report repro-

duces a portion of a Home Missionary Society study from the late 1890s that "seems a fair presentation."

113. *History of the Club Movement,* 56; Frances Smith Foster, *A Brighter Coming Day,* 218.

114. Frances Smith Foster, *Written by Herself,* 88. Harper commented at the National Woman's Rights Convention in 1866, "I do not believe that white women are dew drops just exhaled from the skies."

115. Tompkins, *Sensational Designs,* 124.

116. Parsons, *Manhood Lost,* 4.

117. *History of the Club Movement,* 47.

118. The temperance symposium is found in the *A.M.E. Church Review* 7, no. 4 (April 1891): 372–81.

119. See, for example, Painter, "Martin R. Delany," 151.

120. Penn, *Afro-American Press,* 408. Fortune was said to have written that Wells handles "a goose-quill, with diamond point, as easily as any man in the newspaper work. If Iola were a man, she would be a humming independent in politics." Wells's short story, "Two Christmas Days: A Holiday Story," appeared in the *A.M.E. Zion Church Quarterly.*

121. Quoted from Yellin, *Harriet Jacobs: A Life,* 208, who cites Stanton, *History of Woman Suffrage,* 2:347, 353, 382–83, 391–92.

122. Quoted from her recollection of the speech in a newspaper article a year later. Felton to the *Atlantic Constitution,* December 19, 1898, Rebecca Latimer Felton Collection, Box 28, Scrapbooks #24–27, pages unnumbered. The scrapbook account I use here differs just a bit from Williamson, *Crucible of Race,* 128. The speech took place on Tybee Island and is sometimes called by that name.

123. Nathaniel Southgate Shaler, Harvard professor and then dean of the Lawrence School of Science, promoted the theory of racial retrogression. Frederick L. Hoffman was a statistician for Prudential Insurance Company who successfully argued that sexual immorality was a race trait that could find no "relief" in "religion, education or economic improvement." Prudential and other insurance companies began to offer benefits to Blacks with payoffs that were one tier less than those to whites. They eventually stopped soliciting Black business. For in-depth discussions of white "radical thinkers," see Williamson, *Crucible of Race,* 119–39 (the Hoffman quote is on page 122).

124. Whites, "Wife's Farm," 271. No date cited. Felton's comments appear in response to her Tybee Island speech.

125. Felton, *Country Life,* 93. Her repetitive use of the phrase "grow and increase" is also found in her *Atlantic Constitution* recollection, Rebecca Latimer Felton Collection, Box 28, Scrapbooks #24–27, pages unnumbered.

126. Whites, "Wife's Farm," 371–72.

127. Parsons, *Manhood Lost,* cited on 119.

128. The narrative energy of the text is devoted to following and then reuniting the lives of the eponymous characters. When they first find each other, Corrine shows Clarence a newspaper that reads,

> A man, while crossing K Street, was knocked down and run over by a runaway horse and wagon. He was fatally injured and was carried to the hospital, where he died after suffering a great deal. Before he died, the man told a sad story of a debauched life. He stated that his name was James Burton, and that he had two children, a boy and

a girl, whom he had deserted at the death of their mother, because he did not wish to be burdened with them. He expressed sorrow for his misspent life, but laid all the blame on whisky.

Amelia Johnson, *Clarence and Corrine*, 177–78.

129. Amelia Johnson, "Introduction," in Harvey Johnson, *Nations from a New Point of View*, 18.

130. Felton, "Problems That Interest Motherhood," in *Country Life*, 281.

131. See McMurray, *To Keep the Waters Troubled*, 245–47.

132. Felton, "Why I am a Suffragist," in *Country Life*, 255.

133. Arguing for separate penal facilities for men and women, she writes that the inspiration for her advocacy is a "poor forsaken colored girl," suffering on a chain gang under a "sentence so disproportioned [*sic*] to the offense that I could not forget it." "Mrs. Felton's Message To the 20th-Century," April 24, 1901, in Felton, *Country Life*, 155–56.

134. Whites, "Rebecca Latimer Felton and 'Protection,'" 52.

135. "Rescue Work," as quoted in ibid., 53.

136. I use Shawn Michelle Smith's language in another context here. *American Archives*, 92.

137. The 1834 New York riots, in which five hundred Blacks were displaced in a bloody five days, had begun with a call to shut down Five Points, the lower East Side neighborhood where Black prostitution and interracial sex abounded. See Robert Fanuzzi's forthcoming work on nineteenth-century masculinity and race riots (from the American Studies Association presentation, "Civic Culture and Public Sex").

138. Whites, "Rebecca Latimer Felton and 'Protection,'" 53.

139. Spillers, "Introduction," in Amelia E. Johnson, *Clarence and Corrine*, xxviii.

140. Her reviewers stress the status of Johnson's novel as the first by an African American or a woman to be published by the American Baptist Publication Society, the first Sunday School novel to be penned by an African American, and so forth. For reviews, see Penn, *Afro-American Press*, 422–24. See Spillers, "Introduction," in Amelia E. Johnson, *Clarence and Corrine*, xxxvii.

141. duCille, *Coupling Convention*, 63.

142. An "inequality" is the mathematical term. "Equations" balance on either side of an "=" (equal) sign. Inequalities use "<" (less than) or ">" (greater than) symbols.

Coda

1. See Alice Walker's "Looking for Zora," in *In Search of Our Mothers' Gardens*, 93–116.

2. *Afro-American*, January 19, 1923, 1.

3. Walker, "Saving the Life That Is Your Own," in *In Search of Our Mothers' Gardens*, 13.

4. Holloway, *Passed-On Stories*, 4.

5. Nichols, *The State of Black Los Angeles*, 50.

6. "Out of Control: AIDS in Black America."

7. Center for Disease Control and Prevention, "HIV/AIDS among African Americans." http://www.cdc.gov/hiv/topics/aa/resources/factsheets/pdf/aa.pdf (accessed Feb. 6, 2009).

8. Holzman, *Public Education and Black Male Students,* ii.

9. "Black Student College Graduation Rates Inch Higher."

10. I had attributed the second epigraph to Saul Williams as part of a poem that begins "cemeteries are our only tended gardens" (from the book *She,* 105) but after an exhaustive search could *only* find it online in a blog posted by a young man in Texas who also, and independently, suggested that Williams was its author. Williams, could not solve the mystery and cannot identify the poem that follows his own. So it appears here without attribution.

11. Photo by Marcus Amick, photojournalist, 1996. As Amick explains, the photograph "was taken from a posting painted and mounted on a memorial site in Detroit in 1992 in memory of Malice Green, a Black man who was beaten to death by two white Detroit police officers. The memorial or 'shrine' as it's been called was erected in front of the building where Green was beaten. The memorial was initiated by Detroit artist Benny White who painted an image of Malice Green on the building. It consisted of actual paintings, postings, and bumper stickers like 'Be All That You Can Be.'" E-mail communication with author, November 27, 2007. The "Be All That You Can Be" sticker appears directly outside of the black frame of the writing but within the photograph's frame itself, adding the colors of black, red, and green to the white print.

12. Holloway, *Passed-On Stories,* 3.

Bibliography

Collections

Dubois Circle Minutes. Private Papers. Baltimore, Md.
Frederick Douglass Papers. Library of Congress. Washington, D.C.
John Bruce Collection. Schomburg Library. New York City, N.Y.
Latimer Case Scrapbook. Massachusetts Historical Society. Boston, Mass.
Latimer Family Papers. Long Island Division of the Queens Borough Public Library. Jamaica, N.Y.
Rebecca Latimer Felton Collection. Scrapbooks #24–27. University of Georgia. Athens, Ga.
Spike Harris Collection. Schomburg Library. New York City, N.Y.
White Rose Mission Folder. Special Collections. Schomburg Library. New York City, N.Y.

Nineteenth-Century Journals

A.M.E. Church Review. January 1885; July 1887; 1888, vol. 5, no. 2; April 1891, vols. 1 and 2; April 1892; October 1894.
Baptist Magazine. July 1899.

Twentieth-Century Journals

Independent. March 1904; January 1912.

Twenty-First Century Journals

Journal of Blacks in Higher Education, January 11, 2008.
Chronicle of Higher Education, March 18, 2005.

Newspapers

Afro-American. January 1923.
Baltimore Sun. October 1885; January 1886.
Christian Recorder. October 1889.
Herald of Freedom. January 1843.
Indianapolis Freeman. February 1889.
Liberator. 1842; January 1843.
New York Age. September 1890; 1891; 1892.
New York Evening Post. n.d. White Rose Mission folder. Special Collections. Schomburg Library. New York City, N.Y.
New York Freeman. September 1885; October 1885; August 1886.
New York Globe. 1885.
North Star. June 1848.
Richmond Planet. February 1896.
Washington Bee. October 1885; December 1889.
Woman's Era. March, November 1894; June 1895.

Books, Articles, and Pamphlets

Abel, Elizabeth. "Black Writing, White Reading: Race and the Politics of Feminist Interpretation." In Abel, Christian, and Moglen, eds., *Female Subjects in Black and White,* 102–33.

Abel, Elizabeth, Barbara Christian, and Helene Moglen, eds. *Female Subjects in Black and White: Race, Psychoanalysis, Feminism.* Berkeley: University of California Press, 1997.

Alexander, William. *Our Day In Court; or the Mutual Brotherhood of Liberty.* Baltimore: W. F. Weishampel, 1891.

Ammons, Elizabeth. *Conflicting Stories: American Women Writers at the Turn and into the Twentieth Century.* New York: Oxford University Press, 1992.

———. "Stowe's Dream of the Mother-Savior: *Uncle Tom's Cabin* and American Women Writers before the 1920s." In *New Essays on Uncle Tom's Cabin.* Edited by Eric Sundquist, 155–95. Cambridge: Cambridge University Press, 1986.

Andrews, William L. "Introduction." In *Two Biographies by African-American Women.* Schomburg Library of Nineteenth-Century Black Women Writers. New York: Oxford University Press, 1991.

———. "The Novelization of Voice in Early American Narrative." *PMLA* 105 (January 1990): 23–35.

———. "A Poetics of Afro-American Autobiography." In *Afro-American Literary Study in the 1990s.* Edited by Houston A. Baker Jr., and Patricia Redmond, 78–90. Chicago: University of Chicago Press, 1989.

———. *To Tell A Free Story: The First Century of Afro-American Autobiography, 1760–1865.* Urbana: University of Illinois Press, 1986.

Andrews, William and Mitch Kachun, eds. *Curse of Caste; or The Slave Bride: A Rediscovered African American Novel by Julia C. Collins.* New York: Oxford University Press, 2006.

———. "Editors' Introduction: The Emergence of Julia C. Collins." In Andrews and Ka-chun, eds., *Curse of Caste,* xi–lxvi.

Auerbach, Nina. *Communities of Women: An Idea in Fiction.* Cambridge: Harvard University Press, 1978.

Auser, Cortland. *Nathaniel P. Willis.* New York: Twayne, 1969.

Baker, Houston A. Jr. *Blues, Ideology, and Afro-American Literature: A Vernacular Theory.* Chicago: University of Chicago Press, 1984.

———. "Caliban's Triple Play." In *"Race," Writing, and Difference.* Edited by Henry Louis Gates Jr., 381–95. Chicago: University of Chicago Press, 1986.

———. *Workings of the Spirit: Poetics of Afro-American Women's Writing.* Chicago: University of Chicago Press, 1991.

Bakhtin, Mikhail. *The Dialogic Imagination: Four Essays.* Austin: University of Texas Press, 1982.

Baltimore City Directory for 1886. Baltimore: Baltimore Directory Co., 1886.

Baltimore City Directory, 1906. Baltimore: R. L. Polk, 1906.

Banks, Charles Edward. "The History of Martha's Vineyard, Duke's County, Massachu-setts," Vol. 2, 1911. Reprint. Edgartown: Dukes County Historical Society, 1966.

Bardaglio, Peter W. *Reconstructing the Household: Families, Sex and the Law in the Nineteenth-Century South.* Chapel Hill: University of North Carolina Press, 1995.

Barkley Brown, Elsa. "To Catch the Vision of Freedom: Reconstructing Southern Black Women's Political History, 1865–1880." In Gordon, ed., *African American Women and the Vote,* 68–87.

Barthes, Roland. *Camera Lucida: Reflections on Photography.* New York: Hill and Wang, 1981.

———. *Mythologies.* New York: Hill and Wang, 1972.

Barthelemy, Anthony G. "Introduction" to *Collected Black Women's Narratives.* Schomburg Library of Nineteenth-Century Black Women Writers. New York: Oxford University Press, 1988.

Bassard, Katherine Clay. *Spiritual Interrogations: Culture, Gender, and Community in Early African American Women's Writing.* Princeton: Princeton University Press, 1999.

Bay, Mia. *The White Image in the Black Mind: African American Ideas about White People, 1830–1925.* New York: Oxford University Press, 2000.

Beers, Henry. *American Men of Letters: N. P. Willis.* New York: Houghton Mifflin, 1885.

Bhabha, Homi. "Representation and the Colonial Text: Critical Exploration of Some Forms of Mimeticism." In *The Theory of Reading.* Edited by Frank Gloversmith, 93–122. Latham, Md.: Rowman & Littlefield Publishers, Inc., 1984.

"Black Student College Graduation Rates Inch Higher But a Large Racial Gap Persists," *Journal of Blacks in Higher Education,* January 11, 2008. Available at http://www.jbhe .com/preview/winter07preview.html (accessed December 16, 2008).

Blair, Karen. *The Clubwoman as Feminist: True Womanhood Redefined, 1868–1914.* New York: Holmes and Meier, 1980.

Blassingame, John. *The Slave Community: Plantation Life in the Antebellum South.* New York: Oxford University Press, 1979.

Bogen, David S. "The Transformation of the Fourteenth Amendment: Reflections from the Admission of Maryland's First Black Lawyers." *Maryland Law Review* (Summer 1985): 939–1037.

Boyd, Melba Joyce. *Discarded Legacy: Politics and Poetics in the Life of Frances E. W. Harper, 1825–1911*. Detroit: Wayne State University Press, 1994.

Brackett, Jeffrey R. *Notes on the Progress of the Colored People of Maryland since the War*. Baltimore: John Murphy and Co. Printers, 1890.

Braxton, Joanne. "Introduction." In Mrs. N. F. Mossell, *The Work of the Afro-American Woman*. 1894. Schomburg Library of Nineteenth-Century Black Women Writers. Reprint, New York: Oxford University Press, 1988.

Brink, Carol. *Harps in the Wind: The Story of the Singing Hutchinsons*. New York: MacMillan, 1947.

Brodhead, Richard H. *Cultures of Letters: Scenes of Reading and Writing in Nineteenth-Century America*. Chicago: University of Chicago Press, 1993.

———. "Sparing the Rod: Discipline and Fiction in Antebellum America." In Philip Fisher, ed. *The New American Studies*, 41–70. Berkeley: University of California Press, 1991.

Brody, Jennifer. *Impossible Purities: Blackness, Femininity, and Victorian Culture*. Durham, N.C.: Duke University Press, 1998.

Brooks, Daphne A. "'All the News That's Fit to Print': Nineteenth-Century Black Women Journalists and Sentimental Novelists." Undergraduate thesis. University of California, Berkeley, 1990.

———. *Bodies in Dissent: Spectacular Performances of Race and Freedom, 1850–1910*. Durham, N.C.: Duke University Press, 2006.

———. "Fraudulent Bodies: Black Imposture, Brechtian Theory, and the Case of Millie-Christine." Conference paper, CAAR, Sardinia, 2000.

———. "Fraudulent Bodies/Fraudulent Methodologies." *Legacy* 24, no. 2 (2007): 306–14.

Brotherhood of Liberty. *Justice and Jurisprudence: An Inquiry Concerning the Constitutional Limitations of the Thirteenth, Fourteenth, and Fifteenth Amendments*. 1889. Reprint. New York: Negro Universities Press, 1969.

———. *The Power-Holding Class versus the Public. Imaginary Dialogue of McKinley and Hanna. Prosperity, Trust and Imperialism*. Newport, R.I, 1900.

Brown, Hallie Q. *Homespun Heroines and Other Women of Distinction*. 1926. Schomburg Library of Nineteenth-Century Black Women Writers. Reprint, New York: Oxford University Press, 1988.

Brown, Lois Lampere. "To Allow No Tragic End: Defensive Postures in Pauline Hopkins's *Contending Forces*." In Gruesser, ed., *The Unruly Voice*, 50–70.

Brown, William Wells. "Memoirs of the Author." In *Clotel: or the President's Daughter, A Narrative of Slave Life in the Southern States*. 1853. Reprint, New York: Collier Books, 1970.

Bruce, Dickson D. Jr. *Archibald Grimké: Portrait of a Black Independent*. Baton Rouge: Louisiana State University Press, 1993.

Bruce, John. "Noted Race Women I Have Known and Met." John Bruce Collection, Schomburg Library, SC Microfilm, R905, Reel #2, 539/540, 8–11 and unnumbered transcript.

Bullock, Penelope. *The Afro-American Periodical Press, 1838–1909*. Baton Rouge: Louisiana State University Press, 1981.

Burkett, Randall. "Introduction." In Hallie Q. Brown, *Homespun Heroines and Other*

Women of Distinction. 1926. Schomburg Library of Nineteenth-Century Black Women Writers. Reprint, New York: Oxford University Press, 1988.

Burton, Annie L. *Memories of Childhood's Slavery Days.* In *Six Women's Slave Narratives.* 1891. Schomburg Library of Nineteenth-Century Black Women Writers. Reprint, New York: Oxford University Press, 1988.

Butler, Judith P. *Bodies That Matter: On the Discursive Limits of "Sex."* New York: Routledge, 1993.

———. "Discussion." *October* 61 (Summer 1992): 108–20.

———. "Passing, Queering: Nella Larsen's Psychoanalytic Challenge." In Abel, Christian, and Moglen, eds., *Female Subjects in Black and White,* 266–84.

Calloway, Cab, and Bryant Rollins. *Of Minnie the Moocher and Me.* New York: Thomas Y. Crowell, 1976.

Carby, Hazel V. "Introduction." In Harper, *Iola Leroy.*

———. *Reconstructing Womanhood: The Emergence of the Afro-American Woman Novelist.* New York: Oxford University Press, 1987.

Casmier-Paz, Lynn A. "Slave Narratives and the Rhetoric of Author Portraiture." *New Literary History* 34, no. 1 (2003): 91–116.

Chapelle, Suzanne Ellery Greene. *Baltimore: An Illustrated History.* Sun Valley, Calif.: American Historical Press, 2000.

Cheek, William, and Aimee Lee Cheek. "John Mercer Langston: Principle and Politics." In *Black Leaders of the Nineteenth-Century.* Edited by Leon F. Litwack and August Meier, 103–26. Urbana: University of Illinois, 1988.

Chideya, Farai. "The Truth about Emma Dunham Kelly-Hawkins." *News and Notes with Ed Gordon.* National Public Radio. March 21, 2005.

Chinn, Sarah E. *Technology and the Logic of American Racism: A Cultural History of the Body as Evidence.* London: Continuum, 2000.

Christian, Barbara. *Black Women Novelists: The Development of a Tradition, 1892–1976.* Westport, Conn.: Greenwood Press, 1980.

———. "Introduction." In Amelia E. Johnson, *The Hazeley Family.* 1894. Schomburg Library of Nineteenth-Century Black Women Writers. Reprint, New York: Oxford University Press, 1988.

———. "Uses of History: Frances Harper's *Iola Leroy; or, Shadows Uplifted.*" In *Black Feminist Criticism: Perspectives on Black Women Writers.* New York: Pergamon, 1985.

Collier-Thomas, Bettye. "Harvey Johnson and the Baltimore Mutual United Brotherhood of Liberty, 1885–1910." In Kenneth L. Kusmer, ed. *Black Communities and Urban Development in America, 1720–1990,* vol. 4, *From Reconstruction to the Great Migration,* bk. 1. New York: Garland, 1991.

———. "Public Education and Black Protest in Baltimore, 1865–1900." *Maryland Historical Magazine* 71, no. 3 (1976): 381–91.

Collins, Julia C. "A Letter from Oswego: Originality of Ideas." *Christian Recorder* 10 (December 1864). In Andrews and Kachun, eds., *Curse of Caste,* 127–28.

Cooper, Anna Julia. *A Voice from the South.* 1892. Schomburg Library of Nineteenth-Century Black Women Writers. Reprint, New York: Oxford University Press, 1988.

———. "Womanhood, A Vital Element in the Regeneration and Progress of a Race." In Logan, ed., *With Pen and Voice,* 53–74.

Cortázar, Julio. *Hopscotch*. New York: Pantheon Books, 1966.

Craft, Hannah. *The Bondswoman Narrative*. Edited by Henry Louis Gates Jr. New York: Warner Brothers, 2002.

Cromwell, Adelaide D. "The History of Oak Bluffs as a Popular Resort for Blacks." *The Dukes County Intelligencer* 26, no.1 (1984): 2–35.

Davidson, Cathy, ed. *Charlotte Temple*. 1794. Reprint, New York: Oxford University Press, 1986.

———, ed. *The Coquette*. 1797. Reprint, New York: Oxford University Press, 1987.

———. *Revolution and the Word: The Rise of the Novel in America*. New York: Oxford University Press, 1988.

———, ed. *Reading in America: Literature and Social History*. Baltimore: Johns Hopkins Press, 1989.

Davis, Angela. "The Legacy of Slavery: Standards for a New Womanhood." In Angela Davis, *Women, Race, and Class*, 3–29.

———. "Rape, Racism and the Myth of the Black Rapist." In Angela Davis, *Women, Race, and Class*, 172–201.

———. *Women, Race, and Class*. New York: Vintage Books, 1981.

Davis, Asa J. "The Two Autobiographical Fragments of George W. Latimer (1820–1896)." *Journal of the Afro-American Historical and Genealogical Society*, 1, no.1 (1980): 3–18.

Davis, Elizabeth Lindsay. *Lifting as They Climb*. 1933. New York: G. K. Hall, 1996.

Dawkins, Wayne. "Lost in Time." *Black Issues Book Review* 7, no.5 (2005): 36–37.

Delaney, Lucy A. *From the Darkness Cometh the Light, or Struggles for Freedom*. In *Six Women's Slave Narratives*. Schomburg Library of Nineteenth-Century Black Women Writers. Reprint, New York: Oxford University Press, 1988.

Diamond, Elin. *Unmaking Mimesis: Essays on Feminism and Theater*. London: Routledge, 1997.

Dittmer, John. "The Education of Henry McNeal Turner." In *Black Leaders of the Nineteenth Century*. Edited by Leon Litwack and August Meier, 253–72. Urbana: University of Illinois Press, 1991.

Doody, Margaret A. "Introduction." In Samuel Richardson, *Pamela*. Edited by Peter Sabor. London: Penguin Classics, 1980.

Douglass, Frederick. *Narrative of the Life of Frederick Douglass, An American Slave, Written by Himself*. Edited by Houston. A. Baker Jr. New York: Penguin Books, 1982.

DuBois, Carol Ellen, and Linda Gordon. "Seeking Ecstasy on the Battlefield: Danger and Pleasure in Nineteenth-Century Feminist Sexual Thought." In *Pleasure and Danger*. Edited by Carole Vance. 31–49. London: Routledge & Kegan Paul, 1984.

DuBois, W. E. B. "General Summary of the Baptists in the United States." In DuBois, ed., *The Black Church*.

———. "Present Condition of Churches—The Baptists." In DuBois, ed., *The Black Church*.

———. *The Souls of Black Folk*. 1903. Mineola, N.Y.: Dover, 1994.

———, ed. *The Black Church: Report of a Social Study made under the direction of Atlanta University; together with the Proceedings of the Eighth Conference for the Study of the Negro Problems held at Atlanta University, May 26th, 1903*. Atlanta: Atlanta University Press, 1903.

duCille, Ann. *The Coupling Convention: Sex, Text, and Tradition in Black Women's Fiction.* New York: Oxford University Press, 1993.

Elder, Arlene. *The Hindered Hand: Cultural Implications in Early African American Fiction.* Westport, Conn.: Greenwood Press, 1978.

Ellison, Ralph. "Change the Joke and Slip the Yoke." In Ralph Ellison, *Shadow and Act,* 45–59. New York: New American Library, 1967.

———. *The Invisible Man.* New York: Vintage Books, 1972.

Ernest, John. *Resistance and Reformation in Nineteenth-Century African-American Literature.* Jackson: University of Mississippi Press, 1995.

Fanuzzi, Robert. "Civic Culture and Public Sex: Race Riots in *Marie.*" Presentation, annual meeting of the American Studies Association. Hartford, Conn. October 19, 2003.

Feimster, Crystal Nicole. "'Ladies and Lynching': The Gendered Discourse of Mob Violence in the New South, 1880–1930." Ph.D. diss., Princeton University, 2000.

Felton, Rebecca Latimer. *Country Life in Georgia in the Days of My Youth and Addresses.* Atlanta: Index Printing Co., 1919.

Filler, Louis. *Crusade against Slavery: Friends, Foes and Reforms, 1820–1860.* Algonac, Mich.: Reference Publications, 1986.

Fisher, Philip. *Hard Facts: Setting and Form in the American Novel.* New York: Oxford University Press, 1985.

Flynn, Katherine E. "A Case of Mistaken Racial Identity: Finding Emma Dunham (nee Kelley) Hawkins." *National Genealogical Society Quarterly* 94, no.1 (2006): 5–22.

———. "Profile: Emma-Dunham Kelley-Hawkins (1863–1938)." *Legacy* 24, no.2 (2007): 278–93.

———. "Uncovering the Facts." *Black Issues Book Review* 8, no.1 (2006).

Foner, Eric. *A Short History of Reconstruction.* New York: Harper Perennial, 1990.

Foner, Philip S. "Introduction." In *The Life and Writings of Frederick Douglass.* Vol. 1. New York: International Publishers Co., 1950.

Foreman, P. Gabrielle. "*The Christian Recorder,* Broken Families and Educated Nations in Julia Collins's Civil War Novel *The Curse of Caste.*" *African American Review* 40 (2006): 705–16.

———. "Looking Back from Zora, or Talking Out Both Sides My Mouth for Those Who Have Two Ears." *Black American Literature Forum* 4 (1990): 649–66.

———. "Passing and its Prepositions." *Legacy* 24, no. 2 (2007): 158–62.

———. "'Reading Aright': White Slavery, Black Referents and the Strategy of Histotextuality in *Iola Leroy.*" *Yale Journal of Criticism* 10, no.2 (1997): 327–54.

———. "Recovered Autobiographies and the Marketplace: *Our Nig's* Generic Genealogies and Harriet Wilson's Entrepreneurial Enterprise." *Harriet Wilson's New England: Race, Writing, and Region.* Edited by JerriAnne Boggis, Eva Raimon, and Barbara White. Lebanon, N.H.: University Press of New England, 2007.

———. "Sentimental Abolition in Douglass's Decade: Revision, Erotic Conversion, and Politics of Witnessing in *Heroic Slave* and *My Bondage and My Freedom.*" In Henry B. Wonham, ed., *Criticism and the Color Line: Desegregating American Literary Studies,* 191–204. New Brunswick: Rutgers University Press, 1996.

———. "Sentimental Subversions: Reading Race and Sexuality in the Nineteenth Century." Dissertation, University of California–Berkeley. Ann Arbor: Proquest/UMI, 1992.

———. "The Spoken and the Silenced in *Incidents in the Life of a Slave Girl* and *Our Nig*." *Callaloo* 13, no. 2 (Spring 1990): 313–24.

———. "Who's Your Mama? 'White' Mulatta Genealogies, Early Photography and Anti-Passing Narratives of Slavery and Freedom." *American Literary History*, 14, no. 3 (Fall 2002): 505–39.

Foreman, P. Gabrielle, and Cherene Sherrard-Johnson. "Racial Recovery, Racial Death: An Introduction in Four Parts," *Legacy* 24, no. 2 (2007): 157–70.

Foreman, P. Gabrielle, and Reginald Pitts, eds. *Our Nig or, Sketches from the Life of a Free Black*. New York: Penguin Books, 2005.

Foster, Frances Smith. "'Hurry Up, Please. It's Time,' Said the White Rabbit as S/he Followed B'rer Rabbit into the Briar Patch." *Legacy* 24, no.2 (2007): 322–30.

———. "'In Respect to Females . . .': Differences in the Portrayals of Women by Male and Female Narrators." *Black American Literature Forum* 15 (Summer 1981): 66–70.

———. "Resisting Incidents." In Garfield and Zafar, eds., *Harriet Jacobs and "Incidents in the Life of a Slave Girl,"* 57–75.

———. *Written by Herself: Literary Production by African American Women, 1746–1892*. Bloomington: Indiana University Press, 1993.

———, ed. *A Brighter Coming Day: A Frances Ellen Watkins Harper Reader*. New York: Feminist Press at the City University of New York, 1990.

———, ed. *Minnie's Sacrifice, Sowing and Reaping, Trial and Triumph: Three Rediscovered Novels*, by Frances E. W. Harper. Boston: Beacon Press, 1994.

Foucault, Michel. *The History of Sexuality, Vol. 1*. New York: Vintage, 1980.

Fox-Genovese, Elizabeth. *Within the Plantation Household: Black and White Women of the Old South*. Chapel Hill: University of North Carolina Press, 1988.

Fredrickson, George. *The Black Image in the White Mind: The Debate on Afro-American Character and Destiny, 1817–1914*. Middletown, Conn.: Wesleyan University Press, 1971.

Freud, Sigmund. *The Uncanny*. Translated by David McLintock. New York: Penguin Books, 2003.

Frey, Cecile P. "The House of Refuge for Colored Children." *Journal of Negro History* 65, no.1 (Spring 1981): 10–26.

Fulton, DoVeanna. "Sowing Seeds in an Untilled Field: Temperance and Race, Indeterminancy and Recover in Frances E. W. Harper's *Sowing and Reaping*." *Legacy* 24, no.2 (2007): 207–24.

———. "Speak Sister, Speak: Oral Empowerment in *Louisa Piquet, The Octoroon*." *Legacy* 15 (1998): 98–103.

Gaines, Kevin K. *Uplifting the Race: Black Leadership, Politics, and Culture in the Twentieth Century*. Chapel Hill: University of North Carolina Press, 1996.

Gardner, Eric. "African American Women's Poetry in the *Christian Recorder*, 1855–1865: A Bio-Bibliography with Sample Poems." *African American Review* 40, no.4 (Winter 2006): 813–31.

———. "Coloring History and Mixing Race in Levina Urbino's *Sunshine in the Palace and Cottage* and Louise Heaven's *In Bonds*." *Legacy* 24, no.2 (2007): 187–206.

———. "'Face to Face': Localizing Lucy Delaney's *From the Darkness Cometh the Light*." *Legacy* 24, no.1 (2007): 50–71.

———. "Harriet Wilson's *Our Nig*: From Printer to Reader." *New England Quarterly* (June 1993): 226–46.
———. "'You have no business to whip me': The Freedom Suits of Polly Wash and Lucy Ann Delaney." *African American Review* (Spring, 2007): 33–50.
———, ed. "'The Complete Fortune Teller and Dream Book: An Antebellum Text' by Chloe Russel, a Woman of Colour." *New England Quarterly* (June, 2005): 259–88.
Garfield, Deborah M. "Earwitness: Female Abolitionism, Sexuality, and *Incidents in the Life of a Slave Girl*." In Garfield and Zafar, eds., *Harriet Jacobs and "Incidents in the Life of a Slave Girl,"* 100–130.
Garfield, Deborah M., and Rafia Zafar, eds. *Harriet Jacobs and "Incidents in the Life of a Slave Girl": New Critical Essays*. New York: Cambridge, University Press, 1996.
Gates, Henry Louis Jr. "Foreword." In *Schomburg Library of Nineteenth Century Black Women Writers*. Oxford: Oxford University Press, 1988.
———. "Introduction." In Harriet Wilson, *Our Nig*. New York: Vintage Books, 1983.
———. "The Trope of the New Negro and the Reconstruction of the Image of the Black." *Representations* 24 (Autumn 1988): 129–55.
———, ed. *Reading Black, Reading Feminist*. New York: Meridian Books, 1990.
Gere, Anne Ruggles. *Intimate Practices: Literacy and Cultural Work in U.S. Women's Clubs, 1890–1920*. Chicago: University of Illinois Press, 1997.
Gilman, Sander L. "Black Bodies, White Bodies: Toward an Iconography of Female Sexuality in Late Nineteenth Century Art, Medicine, and Literature." *Critical Inquiry* 12 (Autumn 1985): 204–42.
Goldsby, Jacqueline. "'I Disguised My Hand': Writing Versions of the Truth in Harriet Jacobs' *Incidents in the Life of a Slave Girl* and John Jacobs' 'A True Tale of Slavery.'" In Garfield and Zafar, eds., *Harriet Jacobs and "Incidents in the Life of a Slave Girl,"* 11–43.
———. *A Spectacular Secret: Lynching in American Life and Literature*. Chicago: University of Chicago Press, 2005.
Gordon, Ann D., ed. *African American Women and the Vote, 1837–1965*. Amherst: University of Massachusetts Press, 1997.
Gould, Medora. "Literature." *Woman's Era* (March 24, 1894): 10.
Graff, Gerald. "Literature as Assertions." In Ira Konigsberg, ed. *American Criticism in the Post-Structuralist Age*, 135–61. Ann Arbor: University of Michigan Press, 1981.
Griffith, Mattie. *Autobiography of a Female Slave*. Edited by Joe Lockard. Jackson: University of Mississippi, Banner Books, 1998.
Gross, Ariela. "Litigating Whiteness: Trials of Racial Determination in the Nineteenth-Century South." *Yale Law Journal* (October 1998): 109–88.
Gruesser, John Cullen. "Introduction." In John Bruce, *The Black Sleuth*. Edited by John Cullen Gruesser. Boston: Northeastern University Press, 2002.
———, ed. *The Unruly Voice: Rediscovering Pauline Elizabeth Hopkins*. Urbana: University of Illinois Press, 1996.
Gubar, Susan. *Race Changes: White Skin, Black Face in American Culture*. New York: Oxford University Press, 1997.
Gunning, Sandra. "Nancy Prince and the Politics of Mobility, Home and Diasporic (Mis) Identification." *American Quarterly* 53, no.1 (2001): 32–69.

————. *Race, Rape, and Lynching: The Red Record of American Literature, 1890–191*. New York: Oxford University Press, 1996.

————. "Reading and Redemption in *Incidents in the Life of a Slave Girl*." In Garfield and Zafar, eds., *Harriet Jacobs and "Incidents in the Life of a Slave Girl*." 131–55.

Guy-Sheftall, Beverly. *Daughters of Sorrow: Attitudes toward Black Women, 1880–1920*. New York: Carlson, 1990.

Halttunen, Karen. *Confidence Men and Painted Women: A Study of Middle-Class Culture in America, 1830–1870*. New Haven, Conn.: Yale University Press, 1982.

"Hard Times at Douglass High: A No Child Left Behind Report Card." HBO Documentary Films Series, 2008. Directed by Alan and Susan Raymond. Available at http://www.hbo.com/docs/docuseries/hardtimes (accessed December 11, 2008).

Harper, Frances E. W. "The Democratic Return to Power—Its Effects." *A.M.E. Church Review* (1884). Quoted in Logan, ed., *With Pen and Voice*.

————. *Iola Leroy: or Shadows Uplifted*. New York: Beacon Press, 1987.

Harris, Jennifer. "Black Like?: The Strange Case of Emma Dunham Kelley-Hawkins." *African American Review* 40 (2006): 401–19.

Harris, Susan. *19th-Century American Women's Novels: Interpretive Strategies*. New York: Cambridge University Press, 1992.

Hartman, Saidiya V. *Scenes of Subjection: Terror, Slavery and Self-Making in Nineteenth-Century America*. New York: Oxford University Press, 1997.

Hawbecker v. Hawbecker, 1876 WL 5400 (Md.), Maryland Court of Appeals, Feb. 8, 1876.

Henderson, Mae. "Speaking in Tongues: Dialogics, Dialectics and the Black Women's Literary Tradition." In Cheryl Wall, ed. *Changing Our Own Words: Essays on Criticism, Theory, and Writing by Black Women*, 16–37. New Brunswick: Rutgers University Press, 1991.

Higginbotham, Evelyn Brooks. *Righteous Discontent: The Women's Movement in the Black Baptist Church, 1880–1920*. Cambridge: Harvard University Press, 1993.

Hine, Darlene Clark, Elsa Barkley Brown, and Rosalyn Terborg, et al., eds. *Black Women in America: A Historical Encyclopedia*. Vol. 1–4. Bloomington: Indiana University Press, 1993.

————. *Hine Sight: Black Women and the Re-Construction of American History*. Bloomington: Indiana University Press, 1997.

————. "Lifting the Veil, Shattering the Silence: Black Women's History in Slavery and Freedom." In Darlene Clark Hine, ed. *The State of Afro-American History*, 223–49. Baton Rouge: Louisiana State University Press, 1986.

————. "Rape and the Inner Lives of Black Women in the Middle West: Preliminary Thoughts on the Culture of Dissemblance." *Signs: Journal of Women in Culture and Society* 14, no. 4 (1988): 912–20.

A History of the Club Movement among the Colored Women of the United States of America: Minutes of the Conventions. Washington, D.C.: National Association of Women's Clubs, 1902.

Hite, Holly. "Introduction." In Emma Dunham Kelley, *Megda*. 1891. Schomburg Library of Nineteenth-Century Black Women Writers. New York: Oxford University Press, 1988.

Hobson, Barbara Neil. *Uneasy Virtue: The Politics of Prostitution and the American Reform Tradition.* 1987. Reprint. Chicago: University of Chicago Press, 1990.

Holland, Jacqueline L. "The African American Presence on Martha's Vineyard." *The Dukes County Intelligencer* 33, no.1 (1991): 3–26.

Holloway, Karla. *Passed-On Stories: African American Mourning Stories.* Durham, N.C.: Duke University Press, 2002.

Holt, Thomas C. "An Empire over the Mind: Emancipation, Race, and Ideology in the British West Indies and the American South." In J. Morgan Kousser and James McPherson, eds., *Region, Race, and Reconstruction: Essays in Honor of C. Vann Woodward,* 283–314. New York: Oxford University Press, 1982.

Holzman, Michael. *Public Education and Black Male Students: The 2006 State Report Card: Schott Educational Inequity Index* (Cambridge, Mass.: The Schott Foundation for Public Education, 2006). Available at http://www.schottfoundation.org/publications/ Schott%202006%20Report.pdf (accessed December 16, 2008).

Hopkins, Pauline E. *Contending Forces: A Romance Illustrative of Negro Life North and South.* 1900. Schomburg Library of Nineteenth-Century Black Women Writers. Reprint, New York: Oxford University Press, 1988.

Horton, Lois E. "Community Organization and Social Activism: Black Boston and the Anti-Slavery Movement." *Sociological Inquiry* 55 (Spring 1985): 182–99.

Howard University School of Medicine. *University Medical Department, Washington, D.C.* 1900. Edited by Daniel Smith Lamb. Reprint, Manchester, N.H.: Ayer Publishing, 1971.

Hutchinson, John Wallace. *The Story of the Hutchinsons.* 2 vols. Compiled and edited by Charles E. Mann. New York: Da Capo Press, 1977.

Jackson, Blyden. *A History of Afro-American Literature.* Vol. 1, *The Long Beginning.* Baton Rouge: Louisiana State University Press, 1989.

Jackson, Holly. "Identifying Emma Dunham Kelley: Rethinking Race and Authorship" *PMLA* 122, no.3 (May 2007): 721–48.

———. "Mistaken Identity: What if a Novelist Celebrated as a Pioneer of African-American Women's Literature Turned Out Not to Be Black at All?" *Boston Globe* 20 (February 2005).

Jacobs, Harriet. *Incidents in the Life of a Slave Girl.* 1861. Reprint, edited by Jean Fagan Yellin. Cambridge: Harvard University Press, 1987, 2000.

———. *Incidents in the Life of a Slave Girl.* 1861. Reprint, edited by Nell Irvin Painter. New York: Penguin, 2000.

Jacobs, John. "A True Tale of Slavery." In *The Leisure Hour.* London: February 1861.

Jarrett, Gene A. "Addition by Subtraction: Toward a Literary History of Racial Representation." *Legacy* 24, no.2 (2007): 315–21.

Jaschik, Scott. "Loose Canon." Insidehighered.com. February 24, 2005. Available at http:// insidehighered.com/news/2005/02/24/author2_24 (accessed November 17, 2008).

Jaus, Hans Robert. "Literary History as a Challenge to Literary Theory." In *New Literary History* 2 (1970–71): 7–37.

"Jean Hutson, Schomburg Chief, Dies at 83." *New York Times.* February 7, 1998: B18.

Jefferson, Thomas. *Notes on the State of Virginia.* Edited by William Peden. Chapel Hill: University of North Carolina Press, 1954.

Johnson, Amelia E. "Afro American Literature." *New York Age,* January 30, 1892, 1.

———. *Clarence and Corrine.* 1890. Schomburg Library of Nineteenth-Century Black Women Writers. Reprint, New York: Oxford University Press, 1988.

———. *The Hazeley Family.* 1894. Schomburg Library of Nineteenth-Century Black Women Writers. Reprint, New York: Oxford University Press, 1988.

———. "Introduction." In Harvey Johnson, *Nations from a New Point of View.*

———. *Martina Meriden; or What is my Motive?* Philadelphia: American Baptist Publishing Society, 1901.

———. "Some Parallels in History." *Baptist Magazine* 7, no. 1 (July 1899), 1–5.

Johnson, Harvey. *The Nations from a New Point of View.* Nashville, Tenn: National Baptist Publishing Board, 1903.

———. "The Question of Race : A Reply to W. Cabell Bruce, Esq." Baltimore: Printing Office of J. F. Weishampel, 1891. Also in *The Nations from a New Point of View.*

———. "The White Man's Failure in Government." Baltimore: Press of Afro-American Co., 1900. Also in *The Nations from a New Point of View.*

Jones, Jacqueline. *Labor of Love, Labor of Sorrow: Black Women, Work and the Family, from Slavery to the Present.* New York: Vintage Books, 1985.

Kelley, Emma Dunham. *Megda.* 1891. Schomburg Library of Nineteenth-Century Black Women Writers. Reprint, New York: Oxford University Press, 1988.

Kelley-Hawkins, Emma Dunham. *Four Girls at Cottage City.* 1895, 1898. Schomburg Library of Nineteenth-Century Black Women Writers. Reprint from second edition, New York: Oxford University Press, 1988.

Kelley, Mary. *Learning to Stand and Speak: Women, Education, and Public Life in America's Republic.* Chapel Hill: University of North Carolina Press, 2006.

Kelley, Robin D. G. "Foreword." in Willis, *Reflections in Black,* ix–xi.

Kerr-Ritchie, Jeffrey. *Freedpeople in the Tobacco South: Virginia, 1860–1900.* Chapel Hill: University of North Carolina Press, 1999.

Klein, Aaron E. *The Hidden Contributors: Black Scientists and Inventors in America.* Garden City, N.Y.: Doubleday, 1971.

Koger, A. Briscoe. *Dr. Harvey Johnson, Pioneer Civic Leader.* Baltimore: [s.n.], 1957.

———. *The Negro Lawyer in Maryland.* Baltimore: Clark Press, 1848.

Kramer, Steve. "Uplifting Our 'Downtrodden Sisterhood': Victoria Earle Matthews and New York City's White Rose Mission, 1897–1907." *Journal of African American History* 91, no. 3 (2006): 243–67.

Lane, Lunsford. *The Narrative of Lunsford Lane.* Boston: J.G. Torrey, Printer, 1842. Documenting the American South, available at http://docsouth.unc.edu/neh/lanelunsford/menu.html (accessed November 17, 2008).

Lang, Amy S. "Class and the Strategies of Sympathy." In Samuels, ed., *The Culture of Sentiment,* 128–42.

Lasser, Carol. "A Pleasingly Oppressive Burden: The Transformation of Domestic Service and Female Charity in Salem, 1800–1840." *Essex Institute of Historical Collections* 116, no.3 (1980): 156–75.

Latimer, Lewis H. *Incandescent Electric Lighting.* New York: D. Van Nostrand, 1890.

Lefevere, André. "On the Refraction of Texts." In Spariosu, ed., *Mimesis in Contemporary Theory,* 217–37.

Lemke, Sieglinde. "Introduction." In Elizabeth Lindsay Davis, *Lifting as They Climb*.

Lipsitz, George. *Time Passages: Collective Memory and American Popular Culture*. Minneapolis: University of Minnesota Press, 2000.

Litwack, Leon, and August Meier, eds. *Black Leaders in the Nineteenth Century*. Urbana: University of Illinois Press, 1991.

Logan, Shirley Wilson. *"We Are Coming": The Persuasive Discourse of Nineteenth-Century Black Women*. Carbondale: Southern Illinois University Press, 1999.

———, ed. *With Pen and Voice: A Critical Anthology of Nineteenth-Century African-American Women*. Carbondale: Southern Illinois University Press, 1995.

Lowenberg, Bert and Ruth Bogin, ed. "Frances E. W. Harper, 'Women's Political Future,'" in *Black Women in Nineteenth-Century America*. University Park: Penn State University Press, 1976.

Lukács, Georg. *The Historical Novel*. London: Oxford University Press, 1962.

Mabee, Carleton. "Charity in Travail: Two Orphan Asylums for Blacks." *New York History* 55 (1974): 55–77.

Majors, A. Monroe. *Noted Negro Women: Their Triumphs and Activities*. 1893. Reprint. Salem, N.H.: Ayer, 1986.

Martin, Theodora Penny. *The Sound of Our Own Voices: Women's Study Clubs, 1860–1910*. Boston: Beacon Press, 1987.

Maryland Code: Public General Codes. Compiled by Otho Scott and Hiram M'Cullough. Baltimore: John Murphy and Co. Printers, 1860.

Matthews, Victoria Earle. "The Value of Race Literature: An Address Delivered at the First Congress of Colored Women of the United States." In Logan, ed., *With Pen and Voice*, 126–48.

Mattison, Hiram, ed. *Louisa Piquet, the Octoroon*. 1861. In *Collected Black Women's Narratives*. Schomburg Library of Nineteenth-Century Black Women Writers. New York: Oxford University Press, 1988.

McBride, Dwight. *Impossible Witness: Truth, Abolitionism, and Slave Testimony*. New York: New York University Press, 2001.

McDaniel, Caleb. *Mode for Caleb*. June 7, 2006. Available at http://modeforcaleb.blogspot .com/2006/06/latest-on-emma-dunham-kelley-hawkins.html (accessed November 17, 2008).

McDowell, Deborah E. "'The Changing Same': Generational Connections and Black Women Novelists." In Gates, ed., *Reading Black, Reading Feminist*, 91–115.

———. "In the First Place: Making Frederick Douglass and the Afro-American Narrative Tradition." In William L. Andrews, ed. *Critical Essays on Frederick Douglass*, 192–214. Boston: G. K. Hall, 1991.

———. "Introduction." In Kelley-Hawkins, *Four Girls at Cottage City*. 1895, 1898. Schomburg Library of Nineteenth-Century Black Women Writers. Reprint from second edition, New York: Oxford University Press, 1988.

McFeely, William S. *Frederick Douglass*. New York: W. W. Norton, 1991.

McHenry, Elizabeth. *Forgotten Readers: Recovering the Lost History of African-American Literary Societies*. Durham, N.C.: Duke University Press, 2002.

McKay, Nellie. "Introduction." In Gruesser, *The Unruly Voice*.

McLaurin, Melton A. *Celia, A Slave*. Athens: University of Georgia Press, 1991.

McLemee, Scott. "In Black and White." *Inside Higher Ed.* March 1, 2005.

Mcmurray, Linda O. *To Keep the Waters Troubled: The Life of Ida. B. Wells.* New York: Oxford University Press, 1998.

Mehegan, David. "Based on Work of Brandeis Doctoral Student, Author's Work to Be Removed from Prestigious Collection." *Boston Globe.* March 7, 2005.

Milton, John. *Paradise Lost.* Edited by Merritt Hughes. New York: Odyssey Press, 1962.

"Misidentification. 'In Brief,'" *Chronicle of Higher Education,* March 18, 2005.

Mjagkij, Nina, ed. *Organizing Black America: An Encyclopedia of African American Associations.* New York: Garland, 2001.

Moses, Wilson Jeremiah. "Domestic Feminism Conservatism, Sex Roles and Black Women's Clubs 1893–1896." In Hine et al., eds., *Black Women in United States History,* vol. 3. New York: Carlson Publishing, Inc., 1990.

Mossell, Aaron A. "The Unconstitutionality of the Law against Miscegenation." *A.M.E. Church Review* 5, no. 2 (1888): 73–79.

Mossell, Mrs. N. F. (Gertrude). *The Work of the Afro-American Woman.* 1894. Schomburg Library of Nineteenth-Century Black Women Writers. Reprint, New York: Oxford University Press, 1988.

Mullen, Harryette. "Introduction." In Fran Ross, *Oreo.* 1974. Reprint. Boston: Northeastern University Press, 2000.

———. "Optic White: Blackness and the Production of Whiteness." *Diacritics* 24 (1994): 71–89.

———. "Runaway Tongue: Resistant Orality in *Uncle Tom's Cabin, Our Nig, Incidents in the Life of a Slave Girl,* and *Beloved.*" In Samuels, ed., *The Culture of Sentiment,* 244–64.

Mutual United Brotherhood of Liberty (MUBL). *Justice and Jurisprudence.* Baltimore: J. B. Lippincott, 1889; New York: Negro Universities Press, 1969.

Nathan, David. "Doctoral Student Makes Startling Discovery." my.brandeis.edu. Brandeis University. March 16, 2005. Available at http://my.brandeis.edu/profiles/one-profile?profile_id=517 (accessed November 17, 2008).

"New Bedford Gaiety." *New York Age.* September 13, 1890.

Nichols, Marge. *The State of Black Los Angeles* (2005), Full Report. Los Angeles: The Los Angeles Urban League and the United Way of Greater Los Angeles, 2005.

Noble, Marianne. *The Masochistic Pleasure of Sentimental Literature New York Age.* Princeton: Princeton University Press, 2000.

Norman, Winifred Latimer, and Lily Patterson. *Lewis Latimer: Scientist.* New York: Chelsea House, 1994.

Northrup, Solomon. *Solomon Northrup, Twelve Years a Slave.* Baton Rouge: Louisiana State University Press, 1968.

Olney, James. *Autobiography: Essays Theoretical and Critical.* Princeton: Princeton University Press, 1980.

Osofsky, Gilbert. *Harlem; The Making of a Ghetto; Negro New York, 1890–1930.* New York: Harper and Row, 1966.

"Out of Control: AIDS in Black America," ABC News Primetime, August 23, 2006; available at http://abcnews.go.com/Primetime/story?id=2346857 (accessed December 16, 2008).

Painter, Nell Irvin. *Exodusters: Black Migration to Kansas after Reconstruction.* Chapel Hill: University of North Carolina Press, 1977.

———. "Martin R. Delany: Elitism and Black Nationalism." In Litwack and Meier, eds., *Black Leaders in the Nineteenth Century,* 149–72.

Pamphlet. 1918. White Rose Mission folder. Special Collections. Schomburg Library. New York City, New York.

Parsons, Elaine F. *Manhood Lost: Fallen Drunkards and Redeeming Women in the Nineteenth-Century United States.* Baltimore: Johns Hopkins University Press, 2003.

Penn, I. Garland. *The Afro-American Press and Its Editors.* 1891. Reprint. New York: Arno Press, 1969.

Peterson, Carla L. "Capitalism, Black (under)Development, and the Production of the African American Novel in the 1850s." *American Literary History* 4 (1992): 559–83.

———. *Doers of the Word: African-American Women Speakers and Writers in the North (1830–1880).* New Brunswick, N.J.: Rutgers University Press, 1998.

———. "Frances Harper, Charlotte Forten, and African American Literary Reconstruction." In Joyce W. Warren and Margaret Dickie, eds., *Challenging Boundaries: Gender and Periodization,* 39–61. Athens: University of Georgia Press, 2000.

———. "New Negro Modernity: Worldliness and Interiority in the Novels of Emma Dunham Kelley-Hawkins." In Ann L. Ardis and Leslie W. Lewis, eds., *Women's Experience in Modernity, 1875–1945.* Baltimore: Johns Hopkins University Press, 2003.

———. "Subject to Speculation: Assessing the Lives of African American Women in the Nineteenth Century." In Kate Conway Turner, Suzanne Cherrin, Jessie Schiffman, and Kathleen Doherty Turkel, eds., *Women's Studies in Transition: The Pursuit of Interdisciplinarity,* 109–17. Newark: University of Delaware Press, 1998.

The Photography of Hamilton Sutton Smith. The Museum of Afro-American History. 1996.

Pillsbury, Parker. *Acts of the Anti-Slavery Apostles.* Rochester: Clague, Wedman, Schlicht, 1883.

Piper, Adrian. "Passing for White, Passing for Black." *Transition* 58 (1992): 4–52.

Potter, Eliza. *A Hairdresser's Experience in High Life.* 1859. Edited by Sharon Dean. Reprint, New York: Oxford University Press, 1991.

Pratofiorito, Ellen. "'To Demand Your Sympathy and Aid': *Our Nig* and the Problem of No Audience." *Journal of American and Comparative Cultures* 24, no.1 (2001): 31–48.

Preston, Laura (Louise Palmer Heaven). *In Bonds.* New York and San Francisco: A. Roman and Company, 1867.

Ramsdell, George A. *The History of Milford.* Concord, N.H.: Rumford, 1901.

Reid-Pharr, Robert F. *Conjugal Union: The Body, the House and the Black American.* New York: Oxford University Press, 1999.

"Report of the Frances E. W. Harper League of Pittsburgh and Allegheny, July 15, 1896." In *A History of the Club Movement among the Colored Women of the United States of America: Minutes of the Conventions.* Washington, D. C.: National Association of Women's Clubs, 1902.

Richardson, Samuel. *Pamela.* Edited by Peter Sabor. London: Penguin Classics, 1980.

Ripley, C. Peter, ed. *The Black Abolitionist Papers.* Vol. 3. Chapel Hill: University of North Carolina Press, 1991.

Robinson, Amy. "It Takes One To Know One: Passing and Communities of Common Interest." *Critical Inquiry* 20 (Summer 1994): 715–36.

Rollin, Frank (Frances) A. *Life and Public Services of Martin R. Delany.* 1868, 1883. Schomburg Library of Nineteenth-Century Black Women Writers. Reprint from second edition, New York: Oxford University Press, 1988.

Rosen, Ruth. *The Lost Sisterhood: Prostitution in America.* Baltimore: Johns Hopkins University Press, 1982.

Ruffin, Josephine St. P. Presidential Address. First National Conference of the Colored Women of America. Boston, July 29–31, 1895. In Elizabeth Lindsay Davis, *Lifting as They Climb,* 17–19.

Russell, Dick. *Black Genius and the American Experience.* New York: Carroll & Graf, 1998.

Said, Edward W. *Beginnings: Intention and Method.* New York: Basic Books, 1975.

Saks, Eva. "Representing Miscegenation Law." *Raritan* 8 (Fall 1988): 39–69.

Samuels, Shirley, ed. *The Culture of Sentiment: Race, Gender and Sentimentality in Nineteenth-Century America.* New York: Oxford University Press, 1992.

Sánchez-Eppler, Karen. "Harriet Jacobs: Righting Slavery and Writing Sex." In Sánchez-Eppler, *Touching Liberty.*

———. *Touching Liberty: Abolition, Feminism, and the Politics of the Body.* Berkeley: University of California Press, 1993.

Santamarina, Xiomara. *Belabored Professions: Narratives of African American Working Womanhood.* Chapel Hill: University of North Carolina Press, 2005.

Schechter, Patricia A. *Ida B. Wells-Barnett and American Reform, 1880–1930.* Chapel Hill: University of North Carolina Press, 2001.

Scott, Anne Firor. *Natural Allies: Women's Associations in American History.* Chicago: University of Illinois Press, 1992.

Scott v. Sandford, 60 U.S. 393 (1857).

Scott-Childress, Reynolds J., ed. *Race, and the Production of Modern American Nationalism.* New York: Garland, 1999.

Scruggs, Lawson A. *Women of Distinction: Remarkable in Works and Invincible in Character.* Raleigh, N.C., 1893.

Scruggs, Otey. *Encyclopedia of African-American Culture and History.* Vol. 2. Edited by Jack Salzman, et al. New York: MacMillan Press, 1991.

Sekora, John. "Black Message/White Envelope: Genre, Authenticity, and Authority in Antebellum Slave Narrative." *Callaloo* 10 (Summer 1987): 482–515.

Sekula, Allan. "The Body and the Archive." *October* 39 (1986): 3–64.

Shaw, Stephanie. *What a Woman Ought to Be and to Do: Black Professional Women Workers During the Jim Crow Era* Chicago: University of Chicago Press, 1996.

Sherrard-Johnson, Cherene. *Portraits of the New Negro Woman: Visual And Literary Culture in the Harlem Renaissance.* New Brunswick, N.J.: Rutgers University Press, 2007.

———. "Radical Tea: Racial Misrecognition and the Politics of Consumption in Emma Dunham Kelley-Hawkin's *Four Girls at Cottage City. Legacy* 24, no.2 (2007): 225–47.

———. "Why Emma? Or, Responsible Speculation" in "Racial Recovery, Racial Death: An Introduction in Four Parts." *Legacy* 24, no.2 (2007): 162–64.

Simmons, William J. *Men of Mark; Eminent, Progressive and Rising.* 1887. Reprint. New York: Ayer, 1968; Chicago: Johnson, 1970.

Six Women's Slave Narratives. 1891. Schomburg Library of Nineteenth-Century Black Women Writers. Reprint, New York: Oxford University Press, 1988.

Smith, Shawn Michelle. *American Archives: Gender, Race, and Class in Visual Culture.* Princeton: Princeton University Press, 1999.

———. *Photography on the Color Line: W. E. B. Du Bois, Race, and Visual Culture.* Durham, N.C.: Duke University Press, 2004.

Smith, Sidonie. *The Poetics of Women's Autobiography: Marginality and the Fiction of Self-Representation.* Bloomington: Indiana University Press, 1987.

Smith, Valerie. "'Loopholes of Retreat': Architecture and Ideology in Harriet Jacobs' *Incidents in the Life of a Slave Girl.*" In Gates, ed., *Reading Black, Reading Feminist,* 212–26.

———. *Self-Discovery and Authority in Afro-American Narrative.* Cambridge: Harvard University Press, 1987.

Smith-Rosenberg, Carroll. *Disorderly Conduct: Visions of Gender in Victorian America.* New York: Oxford University Press, 1985.

Sollors, Werner, ed. *Frank J. Webb: Fiction, Essays, Poetry.* London: Toby, 2004.

Spariosu, Mihai, ed. *Mimesis in Contemporary Theory: An Interdisciplinary Approach.* Philadelphia: John Benjamins, 1984.

Spillers, Hortense. "Introduction." In Amelia E. Johnson, *Clarence and Corrine.* 1890. Schomburg Library of Nineteenth-Century Black Women Writers. Reprint, New York: Oxford University Press, 1988.

———. "Mama's Baby, Papa's Maybe: An American Grammar Book." *Diacritics* 17, no. 2 (Summer 1987): 65–81.

The State of Black Los Angeles. United Way of Greater Los Angeles. Los Angeles Urban League, 2005.

Stephens, Walter E. "Mimesis, Mediation and Counterfeit." In Spariosu, ed., *Mimesis in Contemporary Theory,* 238–75.

Stepto, Robert B. "Distrust of the Reader in Afro-American Narratives." In Sacvan Bercovitch, ed. *Reconstructing American Literary History,* 300–322. Cambridge: Harvard University Press, 1986.

———. *From Behind the Veil: A Study of Afro-American Narrative.* Urbana: University of Illinois Press, 1979.

Sterling, Dorothy. *The Making of an Afro-American: Martin Robison Delany: African Explorer, Civil War Major and Father of Black Nationalism.* New York: Da Capo Press, 1971.

———. *We Are Your Sisters: Black Women in the Nineteenth Century.* New York: W. W. Norton, 1997.

Stern, Julia. "Excavating Genre in *Our Nig.*" *American Literature* 67, no. 3 (September 1995): 439–46.

Stoddard, Chris. *A Centennial History of Cottage City.* Oak Bluffs, Mass.: Oak Bluffs Historical Commission.

Stuckey, Sterling. "A Last Stern Struggle: Henry Highland Garnet and Liberation Theology." In Litwack and Meier, eds., *Black Leaders in the Nineteenth Century,* 129–48.

Suggs, Jon-Christian. "Romanticism, Law, and the Suppression of African-American Citizenship." In Scott-Childress, ed., *Race, and the Production of Modern American Nationalism,* 67–95.

Sumler-Edmond, Janice. "The Quest for Justice: African American Women Litigants, 1867–1890." In Gordon, ed., *African American Women and the Vote,* 100–119.

Tanner, Sarah T. "Reading," *Woman's Era* (June 1895): 13.

Tarbox, Gwen. *The Clubwomen's Daughters: Collectivist Impulses in Progressive-Era Girl's Fiction.* New York: London: Garland, 2000.

Tate, Claudia. *Domestic Allegories of Political Desire: The Black Heroine's Text at the Turn of the Century.* New York: Oxford University Press, 1996.

———. "Introduction" to *The Works of Katherine Davis Chapman Tillman.* Schomburg Library of Nineteenth-Century Black Women Writers. New York: Oxford University Press, 1988.

———. *Psychoanalysis and Black Novels: Desire and the Protocols of Race.* New York: Oxford University Press, 1998.

Terborg-Penn, Rosalyn. *African American Women in the Struggle for the Vote, 1850–1920.* Bloomington: Indiana University Press, 1998.

"The Terrell Cottage, Martha's Vineyard, Cottage City." *New York Freeman.* August 7, 1886.

Thompson, Mildred I. *Ida B. Wells-Barnett: An Exploratory Study of an American Black Woman.* New York: Carlson Publications, 1990.

Thornbrough, Emma Lou. *T. Thomas Fortune, Militant Journalist.* Chicago: University of Chicago Press, 1972.

Tillman, Katherine Davis Chapman. "Afro-American Women and Their Work." *A.M.E. Church Review* (October 1, 1894): 477–99.

———. *Beryl Weston's Ambition.* In *The Works of Katherine Davis Chapman Tillman.* Schomburg Library of Nineteenth-Century Black Women Writers. New York: Oxford University Press, 1988. First published in July and October, 1893 in the *A.M.E. Church Review.*

Tillman, Katherine D. *The Works of Katherine Davis Chapman Tillman.* 1888–1902. Schomburg Library of Nineteenth-Century Black Women Writers. New York: Oxford University Press, 1988.

Tompkins, Jane. *Sensational Designs: The Cultural Work of American Fiction, 1790–1860.* New York: Oxford University Press, 1985.

Tushnet, Mark. *The American Law of Slavery, 1810–1860: Considerations of Humanity and Interest.* Princeton: Princeton University Press, 1981.

Urbino, L.[evina] B. *Sunshine in the Palace and the Cottage.* Boston: Heath and Graves, 1854.

Wald, Priscilla. *Constituting Americans: Cultural Anxiety and Narrative Form.* Durham, N.C.: Duke University Press, 1995.

Walker, Alice. "If the Present Looks Like the Past . . ." In Walker, *In Search of Our Mothers' Gardens,* 296–99.

———. "Looking for Zora." In Walker, *In Search of Our Mothers' Gardens,* 93–116.

———. *In Search of Our Mothers' Gardens.* New York: Harcourt, 1983.

———. "Saving the Life That Is Your Own." In Walker, *In Search of Our Mothers' Gardens,* 3–14.

Waring, E[verett] J. "The Colored Man before the Law." *A.M.E. Church Review* 3 (July 1887): 496–505.

Washington, Mary Helen. "Introduction" to *A Voice from the South,* by Anna Julia Cooper. 1892. Schomburg Library of Nineteenth-Century Black Women Writers. Reprint, New York: Oxford University Press, 1988.

————, ed. *Invented Lives: Narratives of Black Women.* New York: Doubleday, 1987.

Webb, Frank J. *The Garies and Their Friends.* 1853. Reprint. New York: Arno Press, 1969.

Weintraub, Elaine, and Carrie Camillo Tankard. *African American Heritage Trail of Martha's Vineyard.* Martha's Vineyard, Mass.: Martha's Vineyard Chapter of the N.A.A.C.P., 1997.

Wells, Ida B. *Crusade for Justice: The Autobiography of Ida B. Wells.* Edited by Alfreda M. Duster. Chicago: University of Chicago, 1970.

————. *The Memphis Diary of Ida B. Wells.* Edited by Miriam Decosta-Willis. Boston: Beacon Press, 1995.

————. "The Model Woman: A Pen Picture of the Typical Southern Girl." In *The Memphis Diary of Ida B. Wells.* Edited by Miriam Decosta-Willis. Boston: Beacon Press, 1995.

————. "Preface" to *Southern Horrors: Lynch Law in All Its Phases.* 1892. Reprinted in *Southern Horrors and Other Writings: The Anti-Lynching Campaign of Ida B. Wells, 1892–1900.* Edited by Jacqueline Jones Royster. Boston: Bedford Books, 1997.

————. *Southern Horrors: Lynch Law in All Its Phases.* New York Age, 1892.

————. "Two Christmas Days. A Holiday Story." *A.M.E. Zion Church Quarterly* 4 (January 1894): 129–40.

————. "Woman's Mission." In *The Memphis Diary of Ida B. Wells.* Edited by Miriam Decosta-Willis. Boston: Beacon Press, 1995.

Wexler, Laura. "Techniques of the Imaginary Nation: Engendering Family Photography." In Scott-Childress, ed., *Race and the Production of Modern American Nationalism,* 359–82.

White, Barbara A. "'Our Nig' and the She-Devil: New Information about Harriet Wilson and the 'Bellmont' Family." *American Literature* 65, no. 1 (March 1993): 19–52.

Whites, Leann. "Rebecca Latimer Felton and 'Protection.'" In Nancy A. Hewitt and Suzanne Lebsock, eds., *Visible Women: New Essays on American Activism,* 41–61. Chicago: University of Illinois Press, 1993.

————. "Rebecca Latimer Felton and 'The Wife's Farm': The Class and Racial Politics of Gender Reform." *Georgia Historical Review* 75, no. 2 (Summer 1992): 354–72.

Wiecek, William M. "Latimer: Lawyers, Abolitionists, and the Problem of Unjust Laws." In Lewis Perry and Michael Fellman, eds., *Antislavery Reconsidered: New Perspectives on the Abolitionists,* 219–37. Baton Rouge: Louisiana State University Press, 1979.

Williams, Gilbert Anthony. *The Christian Recorder, A.M.E. Church, 1854–1902.* Jefferson, N.C.: McFarland & Company, 1996.

Williams, Patricia. *The Alchemy of Race and Rights.* Cambridge: Harvard University Press, 1991.

Williams, Saul. *She.* New York: Pocket Books, 1999.

Williamson, Joel. *The Crucible of Race: Black/White Relations in the American South since Emancipation.* New York: Oxford University Press, 1984.

Willis, Deborah. *Reflections in Black: A History of Black Photographers, 1940 to the Present.* Washington, D.C.: Smithsonian Press, 2000.

————. "The Sociologist's Eye: W. E. B. Du Bois and the Paris Exposition." In *A Small Nation of People: W. E. B Du Bois and African American Portraits of Progress.* New York: Amistad Books, 2003.

Wilson, Harriet. *Our Nig.* New York: Penguin Books, 2005.

Wilson, Kimberly A. C. "The Function of the 'Fair' Mulatto: Complexion, Audience, and Mediation in Frances Harper's *Iola Leroy.*" *Cimarron Review,* no. 106 (January 1994): 104–15.

Wood, Marcus. *Blind Memory: Visual Representations of Slavery in England and America, 1780–1865.* New York: Routledge Press, 2000.

Woodson, Carter G., ed. *The Works of Francis J. Grimké.* Vol. 1. Washington, D.C.: Associated Publishers, 1942.

Yarborough, Richard. "The First Person in Afro-American Fiction." In *Afro-American Literary Studies in the 1990s.* Edited by Houston A. Baker Jr. and Patricia Redmond. 105–21. Chicago: University of Chicago Press, 1989.

———. "Introduction" to *Contending Forces.* Schomburg Library of Nineteenth-Century Black Women Writers. New York: Oxford University Press, 1988.

———. "Race, Violence and Manhood: The Masculine Ideal in Frederick Douglass' 'Heroic Slave.'" In Eric Sundquist, ed., *Frederick Douglass: New Historical and Literary Essays,* 166–88. Cambridge: Cambridge University Press, 1991.

Yellin, Jean Fagan. *Harriet Jacobs: A Life.* New York: Civitas Books, 2004.

———. "Introduction." In Harriet Jacobs, *Incidents in the Life of a Slave Girl.* Cambridge: Harvard University Press, 2000.

———. "Text and Contexts of Harriet Jacobs' *Incidents in the Life of a Slave Girl: Written by Herself.*" In Charles T. Davis and Henry Louis Gates Jr., ed., *The Slave's Narrative,* 262–82. New York: Oxford University Press, 1985.

———. *Women and Sisters: The Antislavery Feminists in American Culture.* New Haven, Conn.: Yale University Press, 1989.

Zafar, Rafia. *We Wear the Mask: African Americans Write American Literature, 1760–1870.* New York: Columbia University Press, 1997.

Index

PIER GABRIELLE FOREMAN is professor of English and American Studies at Occidental College. She is author of numerous articles on nineteenth-century race, sexuality, culture, and reform as well as the editor or coeditor of special issues and two books, including a groundbreaking edition of Harriet Wilson's *Our Nig; or Sketches from the Life of a Free Black*. She lives in Los Angeles where her collaborations on social justice issues have been recognized by foundations and community groups.

The New Black Studies Series

The University of Illinois Press
is a founding member of the
Association of American University Presses.

Composed in 10.5/13 Adobe Minion Pro
by Jim Proefrock
at the University of Illinois Press
Manufactured by Cushing-Malloy, Inc.

University of Illinois Press
1325 South Oak Street
Champaign, IL 61820-6903
www.press.uillinois.edu